THE POLITICS
OF SURVIVAL

Artisans in Twentieth-Century France

STEVEN M. ZDATNY

New York   Oxford
OXFORD UNIVERSITY PRESS
1990

Oxford University Press

Oxford   New York   Toronto
Delhi   Bombay   Calcutta   Madras   Karachi
Petaling Jaya   Singapore   Hong Kong   Tokyo
Nairobi   Dar es Salaam   Cape Town
Melbourne   Auckland

and associated companies in
Berlin   Ibadan

Grateful acknowledgment
is made to *French Historical Studies*
and *European History* for permission to reprint
previously published material.

Published by Oxford University Press, Inc.,
200 Madison Avenue, New York, New York 10016

Oxford is a registered trademark of Oxford University Press

Library of Congress Cataloging-in-Publication Data
Zdatny, Steven M.
The Politics of Survival:
artisans in twentieth-century France
Steven M. Zdatny.
p.   cm.   Includes bibliographical references.
ISBN 0-19-505940-9
1. Artisans—France—Political activity—History—20th century.
2. Middle classes—France—Political activity—History—20th century.
3. Fascism—France—History—20th century.
4. France--Politics and government—20th century.
I. Title.   HD2346.F8Z38   1990
322'2'09440904—dc20   89-36983   CIP

2 4 6 8 9 7 5 3 1

Printed in the United States of America
on acid-free paper

To My Mother and Father

Preface

I walked out of the *boulangerie* on the rue de Flandre, unwrapped my warm croissant, and happened upon a small surprise. "For the health of your child," was written on the waxy paper, "Le Pain Artisanal!" Intrigued, I read on:

> Bread is a fundamental part of the child's dietary equilibrium;
>
> There exists, from a caloric point of view, a natural regulation in the child's diet. If the place of bread, beyond consideration of its simple nutritional qualities, is increased in the child's dietary allowance, he will consume fewer foods less favorable to his health.
>
> [Therefore] the child must eat bread at every meal from the time that he gets his first teeth.
>
> *From the report of the Commission Pain et Santé,*
> *Etats-Généraux de la Boulangerie Artisanal*

It was an advertisement, of course; one more exhortation to buy and, as such, unremarkable. There was a substance to the message, however, that made this something more: an artifact, a document, a testimony about the social and political aims of master bakers in the twentieth century. The "simple nutritional value," the "natural regulation of the child's diet"—the excellence of artisanal bread, so the wrapper implied, resides in the special ingredients from which it is baked. Along with the flour and the yeast the good *boulanger* pours a measure of virtue into his baguettes and *brioches*. Low prices can be deceiving. Our children's future is at stake. The responsible citizen will therefore buy his bread at the corner *boulangerie*, not at the bakery counter of the *hypermarché*. It is good for society. It is good for the Nation. So declares the Estates-General.

The sentiment is significant because the cities, towns, and villages of contemporary France are full of just such small shops and master artisans, spread along the streets or tucked back in the *cours*. Yet the bakers and grocers, the shoemakers and the blacksmiths—that vast territory known as the *classes moyennes*—remain largely unexplored by historians of the present century. It is among these middle classes, in particular independent master artisans, that this work finds its subject.

The absence of artisans from French history after 1914 seems all the more surprising in view of their high profile in other times and places. As the most visible and retrievable of popular elements, for example, skilled workers dominate the historiography of the laboring classes from the French Revolution to World War I. Here the men and women of trades parade across history as the victims of industrialization and the leaders of working-class politics—as sans-culottes, republicans, Communards, or as the avante-garde of *fin-de-siècle* syndicalism. After this, artisans all but vanish from the literature.

There is one reason why this makes sense. From the *compagnons* of the Reveillon riots to the glassworkers of Carmaux, new techniques and new forms of manufacture kept the world of petty production in constant flux. This provoked a natural response from tradesmen, who fought a continuing rear-guard action in defense of their independence and their incomes. That was the great social battle of the nineteenth century and, for the most part, it was a lost battle. The present century has witnessed the triumph of the machine over the *métier*, with the consequent diminution of handicrafts and the absorption of the industrial workers' "aristocracy" into a more self-consciously proletarian labor movement. As the artisans of the last century have become the *ouvriers qualifiés* of this one, labor historians have turned logically from the workshop to the factory.

In another way, the disappearance of artisans is as much a matter of words as of things. That is to say, as we move through the Belle Epoque and World War I, the term *artisan* undergoes a subtle shift in meaning. Traditionally ambiguous, "artisan" had loosely designated any worker with a certain degree of professional know-how and autonomy. With the progress of industrial methods and the assimilation of skilled industrial workers into the mass of factory hands, however, *handicrafts* came to denote specifically a class of craftsmen who were also small proprietors: members, that is, of the so-called lower middle classes. And it is as a part of the petty bourgeoisie that artisans have been implicated in a second historiographical problem: that of the social bases of fascism.

The inspiration for the social interpretation of fascism derives from Marx's remarks in the *Eighteenth Brumaire of Louis Bonaparte* about the reactionary instincts of the petty bourgeoisie. The strictly Marxist analysis has since been elaborated into more Weberian theories of the "losers of industrialization" and of the "extremism of the center." For obvious reasons, Germany has served as the primary object of attention. Here, in work ranging from the examination of popular antimodernism among Wilhelmine master artisans to studies of the politics of small businessmen to considerations of the social profile of National Socialist voters, independent craftsmen have been labeled as natural and actual supporters of fascism.

The troubling history of the German *Mittelstand* raises parallel questions about the politics of the lower middle classes in France: Did the defense of these *français moyens* spill over into fascism? Students of both the "proto-fascism" of the 1880s and 1890s and of the "mature" fascism of the inter-war era usually hint at the complicity of the petty bourgeoisie, as infantry to the generalship of Déroulède, Maurras, Valois, Doriot, and the others. The image of angry shopkeepers and tradesmen acclaiming Boulanger, denouncing Dreyfus, and charging the police on the Pont de la Concorde is a compelling but problematical one, however, for there exists no genuine social history of French fascism. The history of the radical right in France has remained the province of intellectual and organizational history and of biography, the political role of the lower middle classes a presumption rather than an established fact.

Passed by in both political and social history but so central to the events of this turbulent century, artisans deserve to have their story told: a history "from the middle up." My analysis will be guided by three main questions. The first is empirical: Who were these independent craftsmen and what, politically speaking, did they do? The second is more theoretical: What does the example of master artisans say about social class as a political and historical organizing principle? The third is broadly historiographical: How do the experiences of artisans reflect the evolution of French society and the functioning of the Third and Fourth Republics?

My main concern is with artisans' politics and my primary task to assemble the facts of their political behavior, paying special attention to their presumed attraction to fascism. Suspicions about the character of politics, however, have forced me to broaden my perspective. I assume, first of all, that the politics of this social group are intimately connected to its economic fortunes, which has led me to trace the fate of handicraft production in a developing capitalist economy. While I find, in this regard, the concept of the "losers of industrialization" too pat, I have retained the basic sociological perspective: Continuing industrialization had a profound, if complex, impact on those whose methods of production were intrinsically nonindustrial, and this necessarily rebounded on their political activities.

Yet the road from interests to politics is not a straight one. To follow it requires addressing questions of perception and ideology. Why did artisans interpret their troubles in this particular way and not another? Why did they prescribe some kinds of remedies and not others? Why, to take only the most trenchant example, did French artisans prove to be relatively immune to the fascist contagion? Indeed, I will argue that ideology is central not just to the tactics but to the very existence of the artisanal movement, which began to clear a place in French politics only when it recognized itself as a distinct social entity.

Finally, the tale of the artisanal movement is inseparable from the larger history of France in the twentieth century. As I pursue the "defense of the little guy," therefore, I will necessarily reconsider the themes that have dominated that history: the shape of French economic development and the question of "backwardness"; the social contract of the so-called *stalemate society*, and the ways in which it was preserved and eventually rewritten; the nature of political populism and the ultimate commitment of *les petits* to a democratic republic.

In the course of preparing this book I have inevitably run up a considerable number of debts. The University of Pennsylvania, the French Foreign Ministry, the American Philosophical Society, and Rice University provided the funds without which research would have been impossible. In Europe my efforts benefited from the guidance of the staffs of a number of institutions, especially the Bibliothèque Nationale and the Archives Nationales. Monsieur Glénisson welcomed me to the archives of the Chambre de Commerce et d'Industrie de Paris. The librarians at the Assemblée Permanente des Chambres de Métiers merit an extra measure of thanks. Mesdames Boulanger, Cressent, Roussier, Stouls, and Vasseur always received me with kindness. They helped me find my way around their own impressive collection and pointed me to other sources in Paris. Georges Chaudieu, Jean Malassigne, François Magnien, Pierre Simon, and Jean Verrier graciously shared with me their experiences of the artisanat. At various stages of conception, the manuscript profited from my conversations with Geoffrey Crossick, François Gresle, Bernard Zarca, Philippe Vigier, and the late Jeanne Gaillard. Juliette Chapman made possible my stay during the summer of 1983. On the American side, Alfred J. Rieber, Martin Wolfe, and Richard F. Kuisel read parts of the manuscript and were generous with their advice. At the earliest moments of this enterprise my dissertation director, Jack E. Reece, mixed encouragement and criticism in just the right portions. Dana Kirk helped draw the maps. Nancy Hewitt, Susan Pennybacker, Roma Heaney, and particularly Marcus Rediker, my colleagues and friends, helped me to think about master artisans and about history in general. Finally, I owe a very special thanks to Edward McNally and Isabelle Tolila, for their friendship and unflagging hospitality and to Sophie Huntington-Whiteley, for her editing and loving support.

Houston   S.M.Z.
March 1989

Contents

The Politics of Survival

Chacun son métier, et les vaches seront bien gardées.
French proverb

1

Inventing the Artisanat, 1900–1925

By reputation and fact, France has been the pre-eminent nation of small manufacture and skilled craftsmen. "There is no doubt," wrote André Siegfried, "that the type most representative of French qualities is that of the artisan; thus it is necessary to defend him, to encourage him, to permit him to survive."[1] It may therefore seem paradoxical to say that France had no "artisanat" before the World War I, at least none aware of its own existence and organized accordingly. Yet it was not until October 1920, in an article in the Alsatian weekly, the *Gazette des Métiers*, that Julien Fontègne introduced the word into the vocabulary of French politics.[2] The first question about the artisanat then is one of genesis, of the awakening of a social class. At the end of World War I France's master craftsmen possessed no national organizations, no representation in the state administration, no special notice in the census reports. Indeed, the *artisanat*, as Fontègne called it, had no formal existence at all.

By 1925, however, all this had changed. Several hundred thousand master tradesmen belonged to the national confederation of artisans, and these had received representation on many of the *conseils* and *commissions* of an expanding state bureaucracy. The Chamber of Deputies and the Senate had rallied to the cause, each producing its own Groupe de defense artisanale and providing small masters with preferential tax treatment, easy credit, and their own corporate institutions. It marked, in effect, a kind of official recognition of artisans' collective reality. In short, a self-conscious and politically active artisanal movement had appeared.

To maintain that France had no artisanat is not to deny that it possessed a plenitude of artisans. In this sense Siegfried was right. But how many? In which trades? And where did these petty producers fit into what was, after all, the world's fourth largest industrial economy? An individual "typical" artisan would seem easy enough to identify: a big man, slightly tousled hair, bushy moustache, apron, sleeves rolled up to reveal powerful forearms above strong, dirty hands—a working man, clearly, but with a proud, almost defiant bearing. He might be a cobbler, or a carpenter, or a member of any of a hundred trades. He stands before his tools, in his workshop, practicing his profession with intelligence and skill. Perhaps he works in a neighborhood like the faubourg Saint-Antoine described by the furniture maker, Laurent Azzano, in his autobiography, *Mes joyeuses années au faubourg*.[3] The Saint-Antoine is a bazaar of workers rushing about with the materials of their trades, of *concierges*, pedestrians, and carriages; a quarter of small, working class apartments, with dark, almost suffocating *rez de chaussée* workshops, and cafés—everywhere and always open. "A person is not likely to die of thirst in this quarter," Azzano quipped.[4] While we might know an artisan when we see one, identifying the artisanat—the class of artisans—presents more daunting problems of definition.[5]

For the purposes of this study the artisanat will be defined as that class of skilled laborers, working for themselves, owning their own tools, disposing freely of their products and services, and participating personally and directly in production.[6] At least in post-1919 France an artisan is not what he appears to be in an earlier era: a skilled industrial worker, a labor "aristocrat" at one stage or another of dependence on the factory.[7] Nor is an artisan a small capitalist, who never himself touched a forge, or a lathe, or a sewing machine. Every definition between the world wars specified that a master artisan must himself be a laborer. Finally, an artisan is not a *compagnon* or "journey-man"—a member, to be sure, of the artisanal corporation, but a wage earner, nonetheless. The lines between master and journeyman were clearly drawn in both practice and law even by those who thought them permeable. As a definition of a social class this one may seem inexact and unsatisfying; but it is necessarily so, for the boundaries of the artisanat in the twentieth century are both indeterminate and in constant flux. As a working definition, however, it is faithful to the manner in which artisans conceived themselves and to the multifarious official definitions of the period.

Three aspects further confuse the issue. First, the question of who is an artisan lay very much at the center of political and ideological battles between the state, contiguous social groups, and artisans themselves: *Artisanat*, as we will see time and again, was not a description but an Idea. Any particular artisanat was therefore the product of self-interest, wishful thinking, and the group's intended social function rather than the faithful rendering of an eco-nomic fact. As jurisprudence met politics, defining the artisanat became a matter of deciding what role these independent craftsmen would play in a contested French development. Second, the outline of the artisanat was blurred by its rapid evolution. A definition that fit well one day might be short at the ankles and long at the sleeves the next. Under the circumstances too much precision would be only a pretention to rigor. Third, so much of the information gathered in this period is at present either missing or incomplete: a casualty of time, war, and neglect. Surviving statistics do not provide consistent and precise data about the artisanat.[8]

Despite all this, we can begin to reconstruct a reliable if impressionistic portrait of the artisanat in the first years of the twentieth century. France in the Belle Epoque, writes Charles Kindleberger, was a nation of *petites situations*,[9] perhaps more so in 1900 than in 1880, for the depression of those years produced what Geoffrey Crossick and Heinz-Gerhard Haupt call the classic effect of crisis on small enterprise: "concentration alongside the proliferation of marginal independents." Indeed, in the first decade of the new century some economists were talking about a "morcellisme industriel," a reversal of the nineteenth-century trend toward the concentration of production. "We are going to see," one economist prophesied, "a counterrevolution, a comeback of the small workshop,"[11] abetted by the new technologies of the electric motor and the internal combustion engine[12] and by the eternal desire of the French to *s'établir*, to set themselves up in a small business—"l'évasion par la boutique," as Michelle Perrot calls it.[13]

The figures bear this out. In her article on the changing structure of French business, Lucienne Cahen remarks that, although the details remain "necessarily obscure," the number of enterprises in France peaked in the 1906 census: 7,475,000 establishments. Some 4.5 million of these were *isolés*—workers working alone, not declaring themselves *établissements*—and another 588,000 were "establishments employing no workers."[14] In 1906 fully 32 percent of all employees worked in firms employing fewer than ten workers.[15] The dominance of smaller firms was especially marked in those sectors where artisanal production was prominent: textiles, leather and skins, woodworking, quarrying, stonecutting, the food and construction trades.[16] As these figures make clear, a major portion of French production remained in the hands of *petits*, and a good part of these would fit our definition of *artisan*.[17]

The substance of a small business, rather than just its form, depended on its stability and its degree of independence. The continued strong presence of petty producers in the economy does not, therefore, imply the solidity of individual *petites entreprises*. Instead, such sketchy evidence as exists suggests the insecurity of life in the *petit patronat*.[18] Turnover was incessant. New businesses sprang up, while old ones fell into bankruptcy or simply closed their doors. Social instability was endemic, and more often than not this meant returning to the working class rather than moving up into the secure middle classes.[19]

Among the most vulnerable were those rural artisans so central to the agricultural economy. Such tradesmen were legion, but the structure of the *artisanat rural* was complex and its evolution a mosaic of fortunes. In the town of Vron, an agricultural parish in the department of the Somme, for instance, 15 percent of the working population in 1911 were craftsmen either in the building trades or as blacksmiths, wheelwrights, and saddlers working for the farming community.[20] In the commune of d'Aulhat, not far from Clermont-Ferrand, Paul Roux found 15 artisans out of a total population of 364; however, most of these, Roux noted, were also farmers, their trades an *activité adjointe.*[21] "Almost all [rural artisans]," wrote Augé-Laribé, "have a little bit of land that they cultivate in their leisure time with the help of their clients."[22]

The economic developments of the Belle Epoque brought hard times to many of these people. Industrial growth and urbanization may have been the foundations of a new France, but they were set at a heavy cost to the old. Some artisans, such as nailmakers and lacemakers, were devastated by increasing factory competition. Others suffered more simply from the disappearance of their customers. Between 1861 and 1911 almost 4 million persons left the countryside for the cities—most dramatically during the industrial boom periods of 1896–1901 and 1906–1911.[23] Many livelihoods went with them.

The number of blacksmiths, for example, decreased significantly between 1911 and 1921.[24] A Monsieur Mermoz, in a report to the Fédération des artisans du Sud-Est (FASE) in 1921, attributed this decrease to both a surfeit of smiths and a lack of good business habits. Mermoz added a personal observation to his analysis: "We drink too much; we have the nasty habit of going to have a few drinks with our clients several times a day."[25] Georges Chaudieu, in his sentimental tribute to his childhood village of Blunay (Seine-et-Marne), substantiates Mermoz' picture. Chaudieu remembers being charmed by the lusty socializing and casual work habits of the village smithy, who kept beside his anvil a bottle of red wine and a couple of (unwashed) glasses for himself and his clients.[26] The real problem was undoubtedly less colorful. The blacksmith might ruin his liver with too much wine, but he would more likely ruin his business with bad accounting and inappropriate pricing.

G. Olphe-Galliard discovered the germ of this process on his travels through the village of La Vallée. There he found a Monsieur G., who had been a *tisserand* ("weaver") all his life. Only rarely, during very slow periods and under the shadow of virtual starvation, would Monsieur G. consent to go to work for a small manufacturer in Louviers. Otherwise he worked *à façon*, facing up philosophically to his diminishing opportunities. Yet he recognized that for the young city life and factory work were preferable to the hard, uncertain existence of his *métier*. His son became a farm laborer near La Vallée, but Monsieur G.'s four daughters went off to the city to find jobs as domestics and factory hands.[27]

If sheer endurance was the first priority for an artisan, independence was the second. Alain Cottereau estimates that in 1901, despite the preponderance of small businesses described by Cahen, only 1.9 percent of the working population was truly independent.

> [Craft production] is no longer based on the knowledge passed on from the family to the child, from the master to his apprentice. The centers of capitalist organization, of international finance, of department stores, and of industry are constantly redistributing the work, rearranging their operations in order to give the greatest possible part to unskilled workers: manual laborers, women, the very young, and the very old.[28]

Lee Shai Weissbach found this to be true in the furniture-making industry, (*ébénisterie*). At the end of the nineteenth century the industry began to fracture. Furniture for the mass market was increasingly fabricated in factories where the division of labor and the parcelization of tasks reduced the artisan-*ébéniste* to a semi-skilled worker. By 1900, according to Weissbach, approximately half the capital's 17,000 *ébénistes* worked in these large shops, although these comprised but 3 percent of all furniture-making enterprises. Only in the limited luxury furniture market did the true artisan-*ébéniste* survive.[29]

Haupt, too, points to the widespread dependence of craftsmen on their suppliers. A small producer might still own his tools and workshop but might lose control over a large part of production and distribution, reduced, in effect, to *travail à façon*. Many artisans depended on such putting-out work from capitalists, which sometimes led to the paradox of craftsmen defending the virtue of "littleness" in theory and the department stores in practice. Monsieur Tréfousse, for example, was a glove merchant from Troyes. Of 100,000 pairs of gloves made annually for the Tréfousse house, some 40,000 were sold to Au Bon Marché, the Paris department store. "All limits set to the expansion of department stores," wrote Tréfousse, "would spell ruin for working glove makers."[30]

Travail à façon was especially pronounced among female artisans concentrated in textiles and in domestic production for the clothing industry. Thirty-six percent of women in the working population were *travailleuses à domicile*, with 73 percent of them in these trades.[31] Marilyn Boxer found, for example, that among the 24,000 flowermakers of Paris from 1896 to 1906, 80 to 85 percent were women, of whom an increasing number were working at home.[32] The end of the nineteenth century brought particular hardship to these workers, as the mechanization and concentration of production in factories limited the need for domestic production and depressed the wages of domestic workers.[33]

Cotton was the most highly mechanized of the textile industries. Olphe-Galliard traced the disappearance of domestic cotton manufacture in the region around Rouen, where 103,000 *tisserands à bras* in 1810 became a mere 5,000 by 1905. In the arrondissement of Yvetot, the number of hand weavers fell from 15,000 in 1810 to 400 in 1905. Wool manufacture was also becoming mechanized although at a slightly slower pace. In the woolmaking center of Elbeuf, for example, the 250 manufacturers of 1870 decreased to 35 in 1906. The same pattern fit the Lyon silk industry. Between 1875 and 1914 the number of mechanical looms multiplied from 7,000 to more than 42,000, while the number of hand looms dwindled from 80,000 to approximately 17,000.[34]

Likewise, in his study of industrial development in the Alpes department, Jacques Lefebvre found that at the end of the nineteenth century, due primarily to the primitive structure of transportation and energy in the Alpes, small, largely familial production of textiles still predominated. With the twentieth century, however, the arrival of the railroads and the improvements of the roads broke up the system of local markets, while the spread of hydroelectric energy made factory production more practical. As a result, the manufacture of wool and hemp was gradually industrialized, a transition especially pronounced in a region that had slipped the first industrial revolution only to be caught flush by the second. On the other hand, some industries, notably silk- and glovemaking, did not become thus concentrated. Rather merchants profited from the availability of skilled labor to expand the putting-out system, whose products could now be sold to a national market.[35]

Caron took a similar look at the evolution of glovemaking in Grenoble. To the last quarter of the nineteenth century, this industry had enjoyed a singular prosperity, based primarily on the reputation of France's *gantiers*. The value of French production had soared, from 36 million francs in 1847 to some 80 million in 1878. But then the industry found itself threatened by the development of glove factories in the United States and a consequent drop in prices. Whereas Grenoble glovemakers had produced 900,000 dozen pairs in 1867, increasing to 1.5 million dozen pairs in 1893, by 1902 production had fallen back to only 800,000. The Grenoblois, however, managed to stabilize their situation through the rationalization of production, though not through the complete elimination of *travail à domicile*. Thus, instead of the 180 master *gantiers* in 1867, one finds 66 *fabricants* in 1902. At the same time, the increased use of sewing machines halved the number of workers, from 30,000 to 15,000.[36]

It is not true then, as William Sewell noted, even for 1848, that artisans were simply "ground down from respectable craftsmen to an oppressed proletariat."[37] Sometimes tradesmen managed to hold on to their independence at the cost of an eroded standard of living. At other times, they found ways to profit from changing economic circumstances. Paul Marcelin, in his *Souvenirs d'un passé artisanal*, presented a personal and anecdotal picture of this process. Marcelin's father had spent his life as an artisan-tinsmith (*ferblantier*). When it came time for young Paul to begin his apprenticeship, he too was taught to work with tin. This was at the end of the nineteenth century, before the era of the indoor bathroom, when tin often served for the necessary amenities. With the coming of indoor plumbing, other metals, notably brass, began to replace tin. Marcelin quickly realized that he would either have to expand his repertoire of skills or suffer a chronic lack of employment. He therefore learned how to work with lead and zinc (*plombier-zingeur*) and opened a small shop where, in addition to his manual expertise, Paul sold items connected with his trade.[38] Multiply Marcelin's experience several thousandfold; take into account those tinsmiths possessed of less foresight or fortune than he, and one has the evolution of a trade.

This continual ebb and flow within small business, and by extension within the artisanat, bears out the perceptive remark of Peter Merkl that the lower middle class was not a homogeneous group universally characterized either by prosperity or disaster. It was rather a diverse collection of individuals: some on the social rise, some in decline, and some treading water.[39] Crossick, in his survey of small business in nineteenth-century England, painted a complex picture. He distinguished three types of small enterprise. The first was

TABLE 1.1.   Distribution of labor force by size of establishment

	% of workforce	
Number of paid employees by firm	*1906*	*1926*
0	27	14
1–4	26	21
5–9	5	6
10 and more	42	59

Source: J.-J. Carré, P. Dubois, and E. Malinvaud, *French Economic Growth*, trans. John P. Hatfield (Stanford: Stanford University Press, 1975), p. 162.

"archaic," that is to say changing little in either organization or technique. The second was complementary to and thus benefited from industrial development. The third was a sector within which, even in a highly industrialized economy, small scale production remained the most "rational" sort.[40] Caron adapted this model to twentieth-century France, explaining the tenacity and diversity of small establishments by their adaptability to an evolving economy: (1) in the "natural and traditional domain" of *petite production*, such as the food trades, woodworking, and laundry; (2) within highly industrialized sectors, producing at competitive costs goods of either very high or very low quality; (3) auxiliary to industrial production, as subcontractors or repairmen.[41] Some small producers were able to find a niche or to adjust and survive. Others—for lack of ambition, training, liquidity, or just circumstance—faltered and were gradually squeezed out. An "elite" among urban craftsmen—butchers, bakers, and "to some extent craftsmen and members of the building trades"—became solid members of the petty bourgeoisie. Tailors and shoemakers were more likely to find themselves back in the working class from which they had probably come.[42]

A more detailed picture of the evolving structure of artisanal production after World War I will be drawn later, but a few general points will be made here. The imperatives of a war economy of course accelerated the development of French capitalism and led to an overall concentration of French production that continued through the 1920s.[43] As measured by Carré, Dubois, and Malinvaud, the number of *établissements* employing fewer than ten workers fell from 58 percent of the total in 1906 to 41 percent in 1926 (see Table 1.1).

As Cahen's investigations make clear, however, the speed and degree of capital concentration varied tremendously from sector to sector, bringing striking changes in scale to the chemical, metallurgical, and rubber industries, for example, while hardly affecting woodworking, leather and skins, or clothing manufacture, sectors in which artisanal production was especially strong (see Table 1.2). It is important to note, in addition, that this table omits *isolés*, which clustered in those same sectors, and thus understates the dispersion within the artisanat.

Thus economic and social observers who began after 1919 to search for

TABLE 1.2. Industrial concentration: 1906–1921

Sector	Mean number of employees	
	1906	1921
Mining	499	561
Quarrying	8.8	11.8
Food industries	3.3	4
Chemicals	22.4	31
Rubber, paper, cardboard	33.1	38.5
Book manufacture	13.5	13.6
Textiles	18.3	24.8
Clothing	3.2	3.9
Leather and skins	4.1	5.2
Woodworking	3.3	4.4
Metallurgy	428	458
Metalworking	6.8	11.7
Stonecutting	4.4	4.9
Landscaping and construction	4.9	7.3
Ceramics	17	25
Total	6	8.7

Source: Lucienne Cahen, "La concentration des établissements en France de 1896 à 1936," Etudes et Conjoncture 9 (September 1954): 874.

the artisanat discovered that it was surviving, even in some cases prospering. Estimates of the absolute size of the artisanat might vary, but it seems certain that the number of artisanal businesses hovered around 1 million and that these involved more or less 10 percent of the working population. Therefore it is important to note that the first part of the twentieth century was a time of economic turmoil for many, but the appearance of the artisanal movement in France did not correspond to any massive "proletarianization" of small tradesmen.

Such was the protean shape of petty production in France when the National Assembly first breathed life into the artisanal movement. The Chamber of Deputies and the Senate began in the immediate postwar years by providing the smallest and most vulnerable petty producers with tax preferences and special access to business credits. The ongoing reform of the recent income tax laws after the war provided the opportunity for the invention of the *artisan fiscal*. There had been calls for such a direct levy on property for some time, championed by Joseph Caillaux, among others; but opposition to what the propertied classes perceived as socialistic redistribution, not to say theft, broke only under the unprecedented strain of war finance.[44] The income tax of 1917 aimed primarily to raise revenue. After 1918, however, as the parliament reconsidered the details of the income tax, other considerations came to weigh in the balance, and the tax law became something else: a way to make social policy.[45]

Traditionally, petty producers had paid a number of direct taxes: a *patente*, on the exercise of a profession, a small fee to the local chamber of commerce, and perhaps an additional contribution to a local fund for the regulation of apprenticeship.[46] These obligations expanded substantially under the new tax regime. The tax laws of 1917 and 1920 grouped small masters with merchants and industrialists, fellow businessmen, and placed petty craftsmen under the schedule for commercial profits (*bénéfices industriels et commerciaux*). The state levied this tax on profits at a flat rate of 8 percent, applied to all profits of more than 1,500 francs; it allowed no exemptions over this nominal figure, even for the most modest incomes. In contrast, the tax laws treated wage earners much more favorably. Those who qualified as *workers* paid income taxes according to a schedule applied to salaries and wages (*traitments et salaires*), assessed at only 6 percent, and paid nothing on the first 10,000 francs of income. As *businessmen*, moreover, artisans also owed a turnover tax (*taxe sur le chiffre d'affaires*) on the value of their commercial activity. Artisans found this tax particularly onerous because it had to be paid each month and therefore required them to keep careful accounts, a responsibility that many small tradesmen were unprepared to support and that they considered an unprecedented intrusion by the state into their private affairs.[47] The taxable difference between a *businessman* and a *wage earner* could therefore be substantial. For example, a master-cooper earning the barely adequate sum of 15,000 francs annually and subject to the schedule for commercial profits would owe 1,200 francs in income tax. A similarly skilled workman, perhaps working for the same master cooper, paid a wage of 15,000 francs per year, would owe but 300 francs in tax. And the master would still be responsible for the turnover tax, the *patente*, and the various other levies.

This unfavorable fiscal posture presented the burgeoning artisanal movement with a compelling issue and an immediate source of unity. The first sounds of a nascent artisanat were complaints about the injustice of the tax system and demands for a better deal for petty producers.[48] Artisans argued the moral and political case, rather than the strictly economic one. An artisan, they asserted, was a worker not an entrepreneur. He lived by his skill and his sweat, by working with his own hands, and not by exploiting the labor of others or by speculating on the added value of consumer goods. The master tradesman therefore deserved to keep more of his money because "work" was a more honest form of income than "commerce". Besides, under the existing system of taxation, as in the case of the coopers, an employee could easily earn more than his employer and a journeyman more than his master, a situation that artisans saw as an affront to common sense. They went further, however, by tying the social imperative to protect petty producers, "whose history for centuries is identical with that of the nation,"[49] to the political imperative to defend that nation. As Marius Coulon put it:

> To favor the prosperity of these small businesses is to contribute thereby to the maintenance of family life and social peace; it is to conserve, in the economic realm, those good workers practicing their crafts to perfection.[50]

By taxing artisans so heavily, by confounding them with more prosperous elements of the middle classes, so the argument went, the state threatened to destroy family production. The family would soon follow and the nation in its wake.[51]

Before long parliamentary politicians began to echo these sentiments. It is important to remember that the artisanal movement emerged at a moment of instability and was at first patronized by politicians searching for ways to preserve a teetering status quo. The legislators did not, in granting favors to *petits artisans*, seek to promote the growth and the transformation of the French economy. They merely sought to help those at the edge of the middle class avoid falling into the "ranks of the discontented," with all the anticipated "unhappy consequences" for France.[52] Considering the "disastrous consequences that would follow upon the artisanat's fall into the working class," explained Jean Caro, "the regime of the *artisan fiscal* is not a favor to the artisans but a favor to France."[53] Senator Louis Serre put the matter more starkly:

> The artisanat has become a force; what will this force become? In this period of discontent will [artisans] remain patient, peaceful citizens, or will they swell the ranks of the discontented? It has often been said [in this Senate], and for my part I have repeated it often elsewhere: We must take care of the small proprietors, for they are the soul of the resistance of our nation.[54]

The first concrete gesture came from the Chamber of Deputies in June 1921 when, during a debate on tax reform, Robert Thoumyre introduced an amendment to shift *petits artisans-façonniers* from the schedule for business profits to that for wages. It would also exempt them from the turnover tax.[55] The specific logic of Thoumyre's proposal was that *façonniers* were not businessmen but domestic workers, a station in between wage employees and master craftsmen. The *façonnier* owned the tools of his profession and worked at home rather than in a factory; yet he fashioned the materials provided him by a merchant. A *façonnier* was not a true independent, Thoumyre reasoned, and, like the skilled factory hand, should be taxed at the lower rate. Alexander Israel, speaking for the amendment in the Chamber of Deputies, stressed the social utility of domestic production, avoiding the slippery ideal of fiscal justice. "The domestic workshop," Israel said, "is an essential moralizing force; we have every interest in protecting it."[56]

The legislators soon discovered that it was far easier to canonize the family workshop than to identify it. Few in the Senate or the Chamber of Deputies disputed the right of "true" artisans (as distinguished from small businessmen) to a measure of fiscal relief. But what was a "true" artisan? How *petit* was the genuine "little guy"? How independent the "independent" producer? Thoumyre's original concern had been for the large number of domestic workers in the various textile trades. The borders of work *à façon*, however, were unclear at best, and this translated into the practical problem of fixing a definition. Would *artisan fiscal* designate only those engaged in work *à domicile*; that is, for those producing for a merchant? And would they even then be allowed to employ an assistant from outside their family, as was so often the case among domestic workers? Israel lobbied for the broad construction. His principle opposition came from Doumer, the minister of finance, and Bokanowski, the chairman of the Chamber Finance Committee, who felt that in employing someone from outside the family, the artisan-façonnier became an entrepreneur. On June 14 the Chamber of Deputies overwhelmingly accepted Israel's interpretation with a vote of 562–7. Two days later the deputies extended these privileges to those who bought and sold their own materials—to artisans proper.

In the creaking fashion of French legislation, the bill on tax relief for artisans and *façonniers* reached the floor of the Senate a year later, in July 1922, where it met with a cold reception. The senators recognized the principle of lightening the tax load for the nation's *petits*, and agreed that a failure to incubate the family workshop would bring on the "worst calamities."[57] They disagreed, however, with the scope of the Chamber bill in two respects: the Senate version of the bill included only dependent *façonniers*, and it excluded all those who employed any outside labor.

Eighteen months later, as the National Assembly debated the 1923 budget, the issue of the *artisan fiscal* resurfaced. In the Chamber of Deputies a new offensive, led by the recently formed Groupe de défense artisanale, sought to reverse the Senate's decision and to broaden the scope of tax relief. The Groupe de défense artisanale in the Chamber of Deputies had been put together simultaneously with the formation of the Confédération générale de l'artisanat français (CGAF) in March 1922. The defense group's chief organizer and chairman was Joseph Courtier, deputy from the Haute-Marne and member of the center-right Républicains de Gauche. The group expanded rapidly. The *Gazette des Métiers*, the journal of the Alsace Chamber of Trades, reported in November 1922 that it had already attracted 60 deputies, and one month later there were 104. By the summer of 1923 the group counted some 244 adherents, drawing its membership in the main from the right side of the Chamber of Deputies.[58] It would be a mistake, however, to insist too much on the conservative hue of this parliamentary support. Although the victory of the *Bloc National* in 1919 had left the Chamber of Deputies heavily weighted to the right, votes on benefits for petits artisans generally rolled up massive majorities. In addition, the group expanded steadily, attracting deputies from the left and even increasing its strength after the 1924 election, which returned the *Cartel des Gauches*.[59]

Edouard Néron (Haute-Loire) led the assault in January 1923 with an amendment that would allow *façonniers* to hire assistants from outside their families.[60] Courtier then introduced a motion that would once again extend tax preferences to independent artisans. This revived the debate of 1922, and as before, the champions of the artisanat clashed with Bokanowski and with the new finance minister, de Lasteyrie, who objected that "it is not feasible to complicate the laws to infinity."[61] But in the Chamber of Deputies the chairman and the minister were outgunned.

The reverse was true in the Senate and, in their debates of January 1923, the senators held their ground against extending fiscal exemptions. This time

Louis Serre took up the cudgel for artisans, "who have been the glory of old France and who remain today a source of production and renown."[62] His colleagues were not persuaded. In particular, the Senate's reporter for the budget bill set himself against this "leak in the fiscal vessel" that he estimated, with exaggeration, would cost the Treasury 100 million francs.[63] The reporter contended as well that artisans who not only manufacture but sell their goods to the public, thereby commit a commercial act. This makes them not workers but small businessmen, and they should be taxed accordingly. The Senate voted down Serre's amendment 210–91.

This deadlock continued into the summer. Finally, at the end of June, the Chamber of Deputies got its way. Again led by Israel and Courtier the deputies unanimously passed the following amendment:

> Will be subject to the schedule for "wages and salaries," artisans working at home or outside it, supporting themselves *principally* through the sale of *products of their own labor*, with the assistance only of their mother and father, their wife, their children and grandchildren living with them, an apprentice under 16 years of age, and *one* assistant—so long as the total number of workers is *no more than five*. [emphasis added][64]

The Chamber of Deputies also exempted the petty producer from the turnover tax. The next day the Senate capitulated and passed the bill. The *artisan fiscal* was born.

The leaders of the new artisanal movement naturally applauded the artisans' revised tax status. Eyraud, speaking for the blacksmiths, wheelwrights, and farriers of the Southeast, cheered, "This will mean a total exemption for almost all of us!"[65] These new fiscal preferences, however, meant more than just an exemption for *petits* artisans and a subsidy for the family workshop. They became the cornerstone of artisanal legislation and the single most important issue for the growing movement. The law of June 30, 1923 was the most tangible and, to that moment, the only product of the artisanal renaissance; the promise that it would extend these benefits the movement's chief attraction for new members.

It was one thing for the Parliament to pass a new tax law, another to have it put into effect. And here artisans experienced what was to become one of their enduring frustrations: the gap between the legislature's solicitude and the administration's neglect. The *Artisan*, voice of the Lyonnais artisanat, remarked bitterly on the confusion in the manner in which the new code was being applied. It reported that tax officials (*contrôleurs*) on the ground, in the absence of clear administrative guidelines, applied the law willy-nilly, including in one place those who were excluded in another and vice versa. The government recognized the problem and issued a circular in June 1924 to clarify administrative policy with regard to the *artisan fiscal*. Yet artisans continued to chafe at the bureaucracy's lack of sympathy for their needs.[66]

The parliamentary sponsors of the artisanat gained a second legislative victory soon after the first. On December 27, 1923, the National Assembly passed without debate a bill to provide *petits* artisans with easier access to credit at reduced interest rates.[67] The original intent of the legislation had been to encourage the revitalization of the countryside by supporting rural artisans. Under the influence of the Chamber's Groupe de défense artisanale, however, the scope of the bill was broadened to include all *petits* artisans, rural or not.

The extent to which credit was genuinely available to *petits* artisans and to which they profited from it remains in doubt;[68] however, the law did have substantial indirect effects. It added weight to the category of *petit* artisan, which had become in a sense the calling card of the artisanal movement. The definition of *artisan* for credit differed slightly from that for taxes, allowing the employment of two *compagnons* instead of one. Yet it once more excluded those *moyens* artisans who had associated themselves with the movement. The credit legislation therefore reinforced the impact of the tax code. It funneled a good part of the artisanal movement's energies into lobbying the government to broaden the definition of *artisan* and thereby to enlarge the benefits it had granted *petits*.

In addition, as the definition of *petits* helped to set the movement's boundaries and agenda, the specific means by which credit was made available also helped to shape the internal organization of the artisanal movement. The law of December 27 provided credit to master tradesmen only at one removed. The government would loan the money to syndical cooperatives, such as those previously organized for agriculture, which could in turn distribute it among their members. Nonsyndical organizations—that is, associations established according to the law of 1901—enjoyed no similar access to funds. The credit law thus privileged those elements of the artisanal movement organized according to the syndical laws of 1884 and 1920[69] and gave significant leverage to the large trade federations and to the young CGAF. This was hardly a coincidence. The Confederation had from the start made credit for artisans one of its top priorities and had worked closely with its friends in the Chamber defense group to insure that the CGAF would gain an institutional advantage from the new law.

The apparent slowness with which funds actually became available to artisanal syndicates, however, raised once more the question of administrative cooperation, which moved artisans and their friends in the Chamber of Deputies to try to close the breach between the intent of the Parliament and the inaction of the state's agents. Artisanal groups were given representation on the Conseil supérieur du travail and similar administrative corporate bodies. The legislators even invented a bureaucracy specifically devoted to the problems of petty producers. In December 1922, the labor minister issued a decree creating an interministerial commission to study measures to encourage artisanal production. Its composition became a model: two senators, four deputies, six representatives of the CGAF, two each from the Ministries of Labor, Finance, and Commerce.[70] This commission rarely met and had no detectable influence. Yet the decree set an important precedent in recognizing the CGAF as *the* national representative for the artisanat. This would prove to be of enormous significance in later years, for, as the movement began to splinter, official sanction gave the CGAF decisive leverage in its struggle for primacy in artisanal politics. Similarly, the law of December 27, 1923, established a special commission to oversee the operation of artisanal credit, which soon evolved into the Commission supérieure de l'artisanat,[71] whose competence gradually expanded to all questions relevant to the artisanat. In particular, the labor minister was obliged to consult the commission whenever he delved into artisanal affairs. The commission rounded up the usual suspects from the Senate, the Chamber of Deputies, the various ministries, the Bank of France, the *banques populaires*, and the artisanal trade federations and cooperatives. Edgar Hector, in his survey of interwar artisanal legislation, sponsored incidentally by the CGAF, wrote that the commission, through its advisory function on laws and decrees, attained an influence in artisanal matters comparable to that of the National Economic Council (CNE) or the Council of State (*Conseil d'Etat*). Hector again mistook the word for the act, however.[72] Like the earlier interministerial commission, the Commission supérieure de l'artisanat played no discernible role in the evolution of artisanal affairs and, in fact, given its spectral membership, probably never could. The insignificance of the commission became evident in 1938 when a new government pledge to address the misfortunes of petty producers led to the creation of a new special artisanal commission.[73] The appearance and irrelevance of the two artisanal commissions of 1922 and 1923 hinted at what later became obvious: policy provoked disagreement, but everyone was amenable to gestures. While the presence of the artisanat in the bureaucracy multiplied, its influence remained tiny.

The state's discovery of the artisanat coincided with the stirring of consciousness and organization within the artisanat itself. Twentieth-century artisans, to be sure, inherited a long tradition of unity and political action. From the cat-massacring journeymen printers in Old Regime Paris, to the *sans-culottes* of Year II, the Lyon silkweavers in 1830, and the defeated revolutionaries of 1848 and 1871, petty tradesmen had swept dramatically across the French political stage.[74] Moreover, as the nineteenth century faded into the twentieth, skilled workers moved front and center of the new labor movement.[75]

Throughout this history, the centerpiece of artisans' collective self-image and, hence, the basis of their common action, had always been the *métier*— the Trade, the Profession—and the natural unity of those who shared "the same ethic of professional excellence and social success."[76] The trade had set the boundaries of artisans' organization, and this continued to be true in the contemporary era. It is interesting to note more precisely how this worked in practice. Early in the twentieth century France's blacksmiths found their old turf invaded by veterinarians, who launched a campaign (focused on the so-called Darlot law) to monopolize the care of livestock. It was this challenge to the blacksmiths' traditional jurisdiction, rather than any vague apprehensions about the modernization of the countryside, that politicized what had until then been a cooperative movement among rural artisans. It led directly to the formation of the National Federation of Blacksmiths, Wheelwrights, and Farriers in 1907.[77]

If his trade allowed the craftsman to recognize himself and his artisan colleagues, the skilled, independent master nevertheless occupied a kind of social frontier. According to Bernard Zarca, who has studied contemporary artisans, small tradesmen have always defined themselves by a kind of double negative. Artisans are neither boss nor bossed, neither those who exploit nor those who are exploited; that is to say, neither capitalists nor proletarians.[78] Thus the sharp trade consciousness of the petty *patronat* was always combined with a somewhat blurred social identity. Masters saw themselves as a sort of conduit between the working and the lower middle classes.[79] While their professional consciousness could produce an alliance among related trades, their elastic social identity could link artisans to other elements of the laboring classes and the petty bourgeoisie, as in the so-called *syndicats mixtes*, which united journeymen, masters, and even small *industriels* from the same trade in a given locale. For example, the Syndicat mixte de patrons et d'ouvriers en bâtiment of the department of the Aude, founded in 1884 had for its goal,

> to base the relations among its adherents on the laws of justice and Christian charity, and thus to re-establish among its members a harmony and understanding of their common interests; to develop professional know-how, first of all through the reestablishment of laws on apprenticeship and by the creation of technical schools, and by the study of all those questions relevant to the trade; to defend the industrial and commercial interests of members of the syndicate, and to profit them by means of provident and fraternal institutions.[80]

This tendency began to acquire a more explicitly political form during the Belle Epoque. It seems likely that petty producers, for example, became involved with the activities of Déroulède's Ligue des Patriotes and the anti-Dreyfusard Ligue de la Patrie Française, the foot soldiers of the "new right."[81] At the same time there appeared a French version of what Crossick has labeled a "petty bourgeois International"; that is, organizations for the protection of the middle classes. These rallied around a broad strategy of social harmony, and were dedicated to the proposition that the *classes moyennes* were not so much "the conciliator of class conflict [as] its living denial."[82] The Association de défense des classes moyennes (1907), the Confédération des groupes commerciaux et industriels de France (1913), and the Parti commercial et industriel de France were all short-lived attempts to unite small and middle-sized producers against the forces of concentration and socialism.[83] It is unclear to what extent the membership of the militant trade syndicates, and the *syndicats mixtes* or the political organization of the middle classes overlapped. Logic and some evidence suggest that the latter depended on the disproportionate activity of the more prosperous small businesses, while the so-called contemptible trades, such as shoemakers or tailors, maintained a more rigorous syndicalism.[84]

The spreading organization of artisans in France after World War I was not therefore unprecedented. To be sure, the new borrowed heavily from the old: a corporatist vocabulary and imagery; a pantheon of heroes, such as Proudhon and the legendary *compagnon*, Agricole Perdiguier; and villains, like the Allarde law of 1791 that had destroyed the corporations. Trade syndicates, federations, and confederations remained the organizational base of the new movement, but these never cut themselves off completely from the other elements of the *classes moyennes*. Yet the artisanal movement became something more.

Essential to the new conception of the *artisanat* was an extension, or rather a transformation, of consciousness from Trade to Class. This implied that master craftsmen from different professions had begun to recognize that a shoemaker in Paris, a master mason in Strasbourg, and a cooper in the back country of the Lyonnais shared a common interest. In addition, it meant separating the idea of the *artisanat* from that of the trade, per se, while closing it off from the classes immediately above and below it. The new artisanal movement cut artisans loose from the tutelage of commercial and industrial interests. At the same time, the movement did not look for members among the skilled industrial workers who had been the backbone of early syndicalism. These, as the work of Scott and Hanagan suggests, had largely lost their battles for control of production and against the effects of mechanization. The Confédération générale du travail (CGT) was their natural home in the twentieth century.

Perhaps more surprisingly, the new movement had no intimate ties to the old societies of *compagnonnage* that had been such a central part of artisanal politics in the nineteenth century. In truth, the structure of *compagnonnage*, facing "an industrial world deaf to the anxiety and disarray of the worker's soul,"[85] had been crumbling for some time.[86] Except in a few strongholds and in a handful of trades, the Tour de France had ceased to operate. The societies, hard pressed to maintain their membership, stretched some of their old rules, retaining married journeymen and, even on occasion, those who had set up in business. Emile Coornaert believes that *compagnonnage* suffered above all from a change in mentalities. "Faith in progress, the ideas of liberty and equality, and especially a fear of seeming 'backward'," all weakened the tradition.[87] Coincidentally, the societies found themselves under attack from the workers' syndicates, legalized in 1884, for the *compagnons'* lack of class consciousness and combativeness. Revealingly, the societies of *compagnonnage* showed a reluctance to strike themselves, although they sometimes followed the lead of the trade unions (as was the case in a carpenters' strike in Paris in 1897, or in strikes by farriers in 1899, 1909, and 1910–1911).[88] Overall, secret handshakes, mysterious titles, and fancy funerals proved a poor match for the syndicates' promise of shorter hours and higher pay.

By 1914, therefore, *compagnons* had become more a curiosity than a vital element of the labor movement. At their acme in the nineteenth century, estimated Marcel Bris, the societies of *compagnonnage* had included some 250,000 "fidèles du Devoir," "Coeurs loyaux," and others,[89] whereas in the early twentieth century maybe 20,000 or 25,000 remained.[90] The decline, while universal, was not uniform. Some trades and rites held on more tenaciously than others; *compagnonnage* proved relatively durable in the building trades and among the rural artisans. Surveying *compagnonnage* in 1914, Bris reports approximately 1,000 blacksmiths, 800 or 900 wheelwrights, and 500 saddle- and harnessmakers still in the societies. To further complicate matters, even within a particular trade some rites resisted erosion better than others. The carpenters of the "rite Soubise," for example, prospered in the Belle Epoque, while the carpenters "du Devoir de Liberté" all but disappeared.[91]

A disintegrating *compagnonnage* naturally produced leaders who tried to turn this decline around. In 1889 Abel Boyer, "Périgord Coeur Loyal, Compagnon Maréchal du Devoir," recognizing that some homogenization of rites was essential to any collective action helped to set up the Union Compagnonnique in an attempt to convince the various rites to sacrifice some of their idiosyncrasies and autonomy in the name of unity and strength: "All united for the same ideal, let us rally to our colors; let our hearts beat in unison, and, in the Temple of Wisdom, let us form the fasces of true Brotherhood," wrote Bablot, the editor of the union's new journal.[92] But Boyer and Bablot came up against the obduracy of the *compagnons* of "Soubise," "Maître Jacques," and "Salomon," which frustrated the Union Compagnonnique's intended mission. Likewise, Auguste Bonvous, "Angevin la Fidelité, le Soutien du Devoir, Compagnon Passant Couvreur du Rite Soubise," published a manifesto in 1901, "Etude sociale sur les corporations compagnonniques." Like Boyer, Bonvous wanted to reinforce *compagnonnage* through cooperation among the various rites and to establish a *compagnonnage mixte*, where "employers and workers, fused by the 'esprit compagnon,' would be able to resist . . . syndical, industrial, and political development." To this end, Bonvous elaborated a grand regionalist scheme based on the alliance rather than the fusion of "Soubise," "Jacques," and "Salomon." Bonvous, however, found himself equally unable to reverse the entropy.[93]

Compagnonnage had a brief resurgence after the war. In 1919 the Fédération intercompagnonnique de la Seine launched its journal, *Le Compagnonnage du Tour de France*, open to all rites. It immediately became a forum for debates on the unity, dispersion, and future of *compagnonnage*. Then in 1922 it expanded into the Fédération générale du compagnonnage. At the same time, the warfare between the trade unions and the societies of *compagnonnage* began to abate. Some *compagnons* even began to join the CGT, perceiving that there was no longer any contradiction between the nonpolitical aspects of *compagnonnage* and the demands of the contemporary labor movement. This was a new beginning for *compagnonnage* in a more limited and survivable form, as a quaint cultural appendage of the labor movement. Yet it was the opposite of what Boyer, Bonvous, and the other contributors to *Le Compagnonnage* had in mind, which was to reinfuse the life of the working class with the *esprit compagnon*. Moreover, if the possibilities for the spread of the *compagnon* spirit were limited, the continuing discord among *compagnons* assured their marginality. The rites continued to argue among themselves and recruitment to fall off. The economic crises of the interwar years favored the more politicized approach of the syndicates. Thus the tempest of *compagnonnage* was confined, at least until the Vichy regime (without much success) attempted to resurrect it. These points should be noted: First, the dwindling ranks of *compagnonnage* did not serve as a recruiting ground for the new artisanal movement; second, and rather more curiously, the leadership and the organizations of *compagnonnage* and of the artisanat appear to have had almost no contact with one another. Indeed, one of the artisanal movement's innovations was to reinforce the distinction between masters and journeymen.

In his "New Year's Thoughts" of December 1921, Hubert Ley, general secretary and house philosopher of the Alsace Chamber of Trades, wondered: Is the French artisanat doomed? Its corporate organization destroyed? Its self-consciousness at low ebb, and its welfare ignored by the government? He concluded that all this was true, but continued optimistically that the artisanat was on the rebound.[94] This optimism turned on the progress being made toward the formation of a national artisanal organization, progress due largely to Ley's own efforts.

The earliest calls for artisanal unity and demands for state action immediately after the war came from the artisans in the recovered provinces of Alsace and Lorraine, in particular from the leadership of the chamber of trades in Strasbourg. Amid worry that the economic and social trends of the new century were leading Europe to "un abîme inscrutable,"[95] Ley and his collaborator, president of the Alsace chamber, Frederick Schlieffer, presented the artisanat's historic mission as the guarantor of "social peace" through a "solid union of capital and labor"—a theme much reprised over the next twenty years.

In the basic matters of consciousness and organization, the approximately 37,000 artisanal businesses of Alsace-Lorraine enjoyed a clear headstart on their French counterparts. The Imperial German law of July 26, 1897 had established chambers of trades across the Reich. The ostensible purpose of these chambers was to provide handicraft production (*Handwerk*) in Germany with the means to regulate its internal affairs and to represent its interests to the public authorities.[96] By far the chambers' most important mandate was for apprenticeship and professional training—the future of artisanal production — and it was to these that the Alsace chamber devoted the largest part of its efforts. In 1908, for example, it introduced a compulsory master's examination (*examen de maîtrise obligatoire*) for all who would independently practice an artisanal trade.[97]

The chamber functioned as follows: A young man who wanted to become an artisan and was about fourteen years of age, would go to the chamber's *service d'orientation professionnelle*, which would direct him to the trade most consonant with his tastes and abilities. At the end of two or three years' apprenticeship the young worker would present himself to the chamber to be examined on his professional skills. Alphonse Daniel recorded the following examination for apprentice butchers and bakers:

Butchers

Practical exam—slaughter a large animal; split it and cut it up; clean the intestines.

Theoretical exam—write a business letter; keep accounts; read a business lease; perform professional and mental calculations.

Bakers

Practical exam—prepare the yeast, with butter; prepare the varieties of dough.

Theoretical exam—prepare the leaven, taking care for its appearance; treat the yeast and leavened dough; discuss the influence of temperature on fermentation; perform professional calculations.[98]

It is difficult to gauge the effectiveness of the chamber's efforts at professional education or to assess the quality of German pastry in the hypothetical absence of the chambers of trades; although, to judge by reputation, German bakers were no better trained than their French counterparts. Insofar as the German chambers of trades aimed to secure the economic independence of the "little guy" and to protect him from competition from larger businesses, they were at best a qualified failure, for, as David Blackbourne notes, the period preceding World War I witnessed a decline in the independence of these members of the *Mittelstand*.[99]

The German government also had in mind a more explicitly political mission for the chambers of trades. Their creation was an element of the regime's *Mittelstandpolitik*, an attempt to harness the conservative instincts of the middle classes to the struggle against social democracy.[100] The chambers' role in this was twofold: to encourage conservatism (or perhaps more accurately to discourage discontent) both by safeguarding the prosperity of handicraft production and by being seen to do so.[101] The government built this political function into the chambers' structure. At the foundation it placed the trade corporations of masons, bakers, shoemakers, and others. A quasi-public body, the corporation included all the social elements of a trade: masters, journeymen, and apprentices. In fact, it rested on the principle of social harmony and class collaboration in the interest of the profession that had supposedly suffused the traditional gilds, and which the Wilhelmine state was trying to resurrect.[102] The chambers of trades even had the power, in some cases, to establish compulsory corporations for a given trade in a specific locality—to compel, as it were, collaboration—although these remained a minority. Naturally, the masters dominated the corporations. Compare this professional organization to that extant in France, where the basis of unity among craftsmen were the trade syndicates: socially homogeneous, voluntary, regulated by law but not connected organically to the state. In France, as we have seen, some trades and localities had *syndicats mixtes* to defend broadly professional interests. For the most part, masters and journeymen, employers and workers belonged to different groups.

The definition of *artisan* in German law further augmented the power of the masters within the chambers. Unlike French jurisprudence, which limited the artisanat to only the smallest businesses where the patron took a personal hand in production, that in Alsace and Lorraine defined it by the trade rather than than the size of the workshop. "If an enterprise fits this definition," wrote Hubert Ley, the Strasbourg chamber's general secretary, "it matters little whether it employs five workers or twenty, and it would be wrong to deny its 'artisanal' character because of the importance of its production, when the *form* of production alone should furnish the true criterion of the Artisanat."[103] The Alsatians argued that this wide field profited the artisanat by enabling it to prosper and to spread beyond the economically marginal elements. In practice this meant that a mason in Strasbourg could remain in the chamber of trades even if he employed thirty workers and a foreman. It meant that Fernand Peter, future president of the Strasbourg chamber, could simultaneously serve as president of the local syndicate of building trades employers.[104] Characteristically, the Alsatian artisans concerned themselves less than their French counterparts with the problems of *petits*, and consequently with tax exemptions and credit. They identified the interests of the artisanat with those of employers, opposed the eight-hour day for workers, and even encouraged the practice of scabbing.[105]

Within the chambers of trades, representation was apportioned to the various trades according to their population, with masters overall receiving thirty-six places, technical advisors seven, and *compagnons* twelve.[106] Masters, moreover, enjoyed a monopoly of the leadership positions; workers could sit only on the *comités des compagnons*, which had mostly parochial responsibilities.[107] Only those artisans who belonged to the corporations could vote in the chamber elections, although the chambers exercised their authority across the artisanat. It makes sense to assume that the more prosperous artisans subscribed in greater proportion to the corporations than did *petits* and journeymen. Ley's estimate that only about one quarter of those entitled actually joined the corporations, therefore, suggests an even further skewing of the chambers toward the interests of the masters.[108]

With the Treaty of Versailles and the return of Alsace and Lorraine to France, the Strasbourg Chamber of Trades adapted quickly to its new environment and threw itself enthusiastically into the task of reanimating the French artisanat. The Alsatians built their campaign around the issues of technical education, social peace, and the defeat of the eight-hour law. Ley and the president of the chamber, Frederick Schlieffer, who had spent his years as an apprentice *ébéniste* in the Faubourg Saint-Antoine, traveled the French countryside in 1919 and 1920, speaking at conferences on the problem of apprenticeship, calling on artisans to join their forces and on the government to underwrite this unity. The *Gazette des Métiers* (sixteen pages every

Friday) expanded publication from 3,800 copies a week in 1920, to 8,000 in 1921, to 12,000 in 1922 to meet its new obligation as the clarion of the artisanat.[109]

The propaganda stirred up by Schlieffer and Ley sparked considerable interest, but not strictly or even mostly among artisans. Predictably, the Alsatians' corporatist and statist orientation had a limited appeal to the small, syndicated masters who comprised the mass of organized artisans in France. The Alsace Chamber of Trades' social profile and conservative bent, moreover, often caused it to drift away from the artisanat, strictly speaking, and into alliances with the *classes moyennes*; that is, with smaller industrialists, merchants, shopkeepers, and regionalist groups. In 1920, for example, Schlieffer and Ley lent their efforts to the formation of the abortive Fédération des métiers de France. The federation was headed by Maurice Colrat, who was also president of the Fédération des classes moyennes. Schlieffer and Charles Lamy, president of the Limoges Chamber of Commerce, served as vice-presidents. The misbegotten Fédération des métiers did not survive its first congress.[110]

The Alsatians never surrendered their fundamentally middle class perspective, as their reaction to the Popular Front was to demonstrate so forcefully. But the unraveling of the Fédération des métiers de France taught Schlieffer and Ley an important tactical lesson. They readapted their politics and their rhetoric to be more specifically artisanal and gave their unqualified support to those who were organizing a new artisanal confederation in Paris.

In October 1921 a large conference convened in Lyon to discuss the pressing national problem of technical education. Schlieffer and Ley attended, taking the opportunity to plead the cause of the artisanat. More significantly, it was in Lyon that they made the acquaintance of Georges Grandadam and Robert Tailledet, two artisanal leaders from Paris, who were also trying to put together a national confederation of artisans.[111] The former was a veteran organizer for the Parisian Shoemakers' syndicate, the latter a somewhat elusive figure. Bernard Zarca writes that Tailledet was not truly a *cordonnier* but a merchant, with a business in which shoes were sold and repaired. He adds that Tailledet's attraction to artisanal politics was more political than professional. A freemason, enjoying connections in high places, especially but not exclusively with the Radical party, Tailledet became a kind of career administrator of and spokesman for the CGAF.[112] In 1919 the two men had brought together two shoemakers' groups from the popular quarters of Paris— shoemaking was a notoriously impoverished trade—and founded the Fédération de la petite industrie de la chaussure (FPIC).[113]

Casting about for patronage, Tailledet and Grandadam had also approached Etienne Clémentel, the senator and ex-commerce minister, for his support in obtaining legislative protection for artisan-shoemakers. Clémentel not only agreed to help but went on to encourage them in the FPIC's attempts to expand its efforts to include all petty producers; that is, to the artisanat, as it was coming to be understood.[114] In fact, Clémentel, more than any other single government figure, was responsible for the organization of the artisanal movement, and the movement later recognized this by bestowing on him the honorary title of "Father of the Artisanal Movement."

Clémentel's motives in befriending the artisans are instructive. Both during the war and afterwards Clémentel distinguished himself by his insistence on the need to modernize French capitalism. His principle concern in this was to shore up the economic and, by implication, the social structure so severely damaged by the war. To this end, Clémentel tirelessly lobbied French business leaders to update their obsolete methods and techniques of production, and above all to rationalize their political organization.[115] He also prescribed a healthy dose of government intervention in the economy. As commerce minister, Clémentel reorganized the chambers of commerce, created the first system of economic regions in France, and presided over the formation of the first national syndicate of employers, the Confédération générale de la production française (CGPF) in 1919. He also served as president of the international organization of chambers of commerce. Henry Ehrmann has described Clémentel as the "prototype of the politician who first as deputy and then as senator represented all but openly the interests of organized business in France."[116] Despite his seemingly impeccable credentials, however, Clémentel received largely unfavorable reviews for his neoliberalism within the business community.[117]

It was precisely Clémentel's design to let the state help shape the economy which had alienated so many in the business world, that attracted the shoemakers. Conversely, and not with perfect consistency, it was Clémentel's instinct for rationalization, rather than any nostalgia for the "good old days" that brought him to them. Just as he saw the CGPF as a weapon for effectively tackling the CGT, and economic growth as a palliative against social disorder, Clémentel envisioned a thriving sector of small, independent producers as a pillar of the status quo, "a buffer between those two social forces . . . bourgeoisie and proletariat."[118] The shoemakers were more preoccupied with staying in business than with becoming a "social buffer"; but, with an eye to the main chance, they accepted their patrons without quibbling too much about motivations.

The FPIC had launched its drive for a general confederation of artisans at its congress of March 1921,

> to contribute to the development of artisanal production, to coordinate the efforts of member federations and syndical unions, to group all artisans by trade to support all those professional demands presented by its affiliates.[119]

The shoemakers also appointed two committees, one charged with contacting other artisanal groups and the other with working on a series of reports on artisanal credit, accounting problems, and taxes. They sent a copy of these reports, along with a ballot, to some 30,000 members of the FPIC and to presidents of the assorted artisanal syndicates in other trades.[120] It was armed with this commission that Tailledet and Grandadam came to the Lyon apprenticeship conference the following October, where they apprised both Schlieffer and Clémentel of their intentions.

The shoemakers decided to use their March 1922 congress as a constituent meeting for the new CGAF. Grandadam inaugurated the congress with a report that touched on the need for artisanal credit, and he stressed the artisan's responsibility to adapt to technical innovation so as to remain economically viable. Tailledet added calls for artisan cooperatives and modern tooling. He asked that the parliament grant tax breaks to *petits* artisans, anticipating the victories of 1923.[121] After the artisanal congress had adopted all the resolutions laid out by the FPIC, the Alsatian representatives addressed the body. Schlieffer warned of the perils of the free market both for the artisanat and for society as a whole. He reminded his listeners of the benefits of "quality" production, so deeply rooted in France, in contrast to the perils of mass production.[122] As Ley wrote in his report on the congress:

> Mass production, toward which big industry naturally tends, will never be the form proper to our national economy. The products of the factory illustrate only too well the mechanical process that obscures the personality, and which we accuse of all the social ills. The French character, imbued with initiative and individualism, has nothing to do with this impersonality. It always searches for that form of production which creates in the worker a personal satisfaction because it contains something of himself.[123]

In attendance at this constituent congress, and therefore original affiliates of the CGAF, were several of the national trade federations: tailors, hairdressers, carpenters, wheelwrights, and others.[124] The Alsace Chamber of Trades also gave its enthusiastic endorsement to "the battle for the emancipation of the Trades."[125] Because it was a quasi-public body and not a professional organization, however, the Alsace chamber could not formally enlist in the new confederation. Yet the *Gazette des Métiers* recommended to all its member organizations in the Bas-Rhin, Haut-Rhin, and Moselle that they associate themselves. The CGAF recognized this support by naming Frederick Schlieffer its honorary president. "En avant," cheered the *Artisan* of Lyon. "Let us unite! We have the numbers, we have the strength."[126] The artisans celebrated the birth of their movement and the return of Alsace and Lorraine to the "grande famille artisanale de France" with a Fête de Fraternisation in Strasbourg.[127]

Discussions about organizational structures and membership qualifications had naturally dominated the first congress of the artisanal confederation. It was relatively easy to lay down the basic organization and to name officers. Predictably, Tailledet and Grandadam won election as president and vice-president without opposition. The most volatile question for the young confederation concerned the issue of who, exactly, was an artisan and who would be eligible to affiliate with the CGAF. The deceptive ease with which this was answered in the spring of 1922 merely postponed the reckoning of these disagreements. Because the organizational base of the artisanat in France was the trade syndicate, because the prime movers in the CGAF—not just the shoemakers, but also Bardet, of the tailors' federation, and Ledoux and Forestier of the hairdressers'—were dedicated syndicalists, and because syndical federations were the dominant form of organization at the class level (the most obvious examples being the CGT and the CGPF), the CGAF adopted the logical motif. It encouraged local trade syndicates to join even if their parent federations held out. However, the CGAF would not enroll individuals as such or the more socially homogeneous associations, established under the law of 1901. This meant that while the numerous trade corporations of Alsace could enroll in the artisanal confederation, the Alsace Chamber of Trades could hope, at best, for an indirect influence.[128]

The issue of membership in the CGAF was fundamental, for the shape of the artisanat would largely determine the politics of the movement. A CGAF dominated by the larger and more prosperous artisans, blending at the top into *petits industriels*, would have a perspective and a set of policies very different from a CGAF that remained the province of small, syndically organized masters. The leadership of the Alsace chamber resigned themselves to the structure of the CGAF because a certain syndicalism was the price of doing business in France. Schlieffer and Ley hoped that their organization and experience would allow them nevertheless to have their way in the CGAF and that, in time, the Alsatian system could be reproduced in the metropole. In the first heady days of the artisanal movement, however, these conflicts seemed neither important nor insoluble enough to stand in the way of unity. With a flood of fraternal words and symbolic gestures, the artisans in 1922 tossed some loose dirt over their differences. That they would remain buried was unlikely.

The formation of the artisanal movement, in particular of the CGAF, met with less than universal approval. The CGT, for example, did not share the artisans' view of themselves as a great social buffer. Instead it saw the artisanat as a sector of petty production divided, like industry, into patrons and workers. The CGT journal, *Le Peuple*, wrote:

> What we know certainly is that a return to the superannuated methods of production envisioned by the CGAF constitutes a real danger for all the social advantages that the worker has just succeeded in winning.[129]

It concluded that the factory was preferable to the artisanal workshop from every point of view. The chambers of commerce also opposed the autonomous organization of artisans, which they feared would diminish their own membership.[130]

Yet the appearance of the artisanat in French society and politics received the enthusiastic support of others. An article by Senator J. Philip (Gers) in the Paris daily newspaper, *Le Matin*, noted that the "awakening of the Artisanat is a social event of the first order. The artisan in France can scarcely any longer be considered a figure of the past, the relic of an extinct species."[131] The state, again if gestures are supposed to have substance, responded quickly and favorably. Representatives from the Chamber of Deputies and the Senate received delegations from the CGAF on the very day of its creation. Deputies rallied to the new group for the defense of the artisanat then forming under Courtier. The ministries also cooperated with the CGAF. In early November 1922, Premier Poincaré met with Tailledet, Schlieffer, Grandadam, Ley and a group of their supporters, declaring his sympathy for their goals.[132] Later that month, Albert Peyronnet presided over the Fête de Fraternisation in Strasbourg. And Justin Godart, the labor minister, who had given the CGAF his personal endorsement, once more demonstrated the government's good will in December 1922, with his decree creating the interministerial commission on the artisanat.[133]

Meanwhile, the CGAF faced the delicate task of elaborating a program that would draw support to the artisanal movement but not provoke dissent within it. To stir up interest among the rank and file and to bring pressure to bear on the government, the confederation circulated a "National Petition" in the summer of 1922. Presented to the president of the Council of Ministers on October 26 with, the *Gazette des Métiers* reported, 100,000 signatures, the national petition asked the government for: (1) income tax preferences for *petits* artisans, which the CGAF defined as those employing fewer than five journeymen; (2) a law protecting artisanal commercial property; (3) creation of artisanal chambers of trades in France; and (4) a law, like that for farmers, favoring credit for artisans.[134] The government, as we have seen, proved accommodating.

Even such a limited and general set of demands, however, contained the seeds of discord, for the artisanat was a diverse group. It ranged from *isolés* and *petits*, working alone or with only members of their families and one or two *compagnons*, to the *moyens* and *gros* artisans, who might employ a dozen or more workers and even a foreman. Any program that concentrated on the needs of *petits* to the exclusion of the better-off artisans thus threatened to divide the movement.

A second and overlapping conflict concerned the structure and ultimately the locus of power within the confederation. Should the CGAF operate as an association of more or less autonomous regional and professional groups? Or should it aim to become a homogeneous and tightly disciplined organization, like the CGT? The Alsatian artisans and the Parisian shoemakers found themselves in sharp and often heated disagreement on these issues. The others chose sides.

The first two years of the CGAF's existence witnessed the jockeying for advantage among syndicalists, corporatists, centralizers, and regionalists. Yet for the time being the opposing forces avoided any provocative statements or actions. Tailledet, stifling his strong syndicalist sentiments, played down his notions of class and political conflict:

> What is the artisanat? It is the social class intermediate between capital and labor; it is the link, the treaty of union between the worker and the capitalist. It is not a class that organizes in order to engage in battle, it is rather a

moderating element that must facilitate collaboration among all producers, large or small, employers or employees.[135]

Such odes to social harmony naturally pleased the more conservative artisans in Alsace, and they responded in kind, deemphasizing their corporatist and regionalist plans for the artisanal movement.[136]

The compromising and ambiguous language of the Charter of the Artisanat composed by the second congress of the confederation, held in Bordeaux in the spring of 1923, bore witness to the determination of the CGAF leadership to preserve this precarious concord (see Appendix A). The charter displayed that mixture of political interest, economic theory, and morality that was to characterize the movement throughout its existence. It defended the artisanat as a social buffer and described the social mobility that allowed artisans to transcend class conflict, indeed to be its antidote. It insisted on the need for artisanal chambers of trades and on cooperative answers to economic problems. Finally, the charter skirted the vexing issue of definition and announced the regionalist nature of the movement.[137]

In all these ways, the Charter of the Artisanat cut the paths along which the movement was to develop over the next twenty years: stressing the artisanat's uniqueness and the nonindustrial, unstratified, unalienating nature of its productive methods and rejecting both the liberal and the Marxist ways. Its endorsement of regionalism, which soon became a major source of contention, was deceptive. Article seven of the Charter of the Artisanat represented above all the desire of the confederation's member federations to avoid the domination of either Strasbourg or Paris and not a choice for Schlieffer over Tailledet. Local and professional groups of artisans had shown themselves willing after 1919 to join forces in order to achieve common goals. This was in itself a significant step. It did not, however, imply a desire to sacrifice local autonomy. As the charter expressed it, the artisanal work experience was individual not collective, provincial not cosmopolitan; individualism and provincialism lay at the heart of artisanal consciousness. "Truly," observed Henri Mourier, "artisans have never been impassioned by the internal battles and quarrels over [organizational] interests that divided their leaders."[138] The CGAF was able to forge a measure of solidarity and even on occasion to enforce a light discipline on its members, but French artisans remained always remarkably resistant to centralized authority and collective action.

On July 26, 1925 the legislature approved the so-called Courtier law, which made possible the creation of artisanal chambers of trades throughout France, thereby setting the final stone in the foundation of the artisanal movement. Fiscal relief and credit preferences for *petits* artisans had encountered relatively little opposition from other interests, just the hesitations of the Senate and the Ministry of Finance. Quite the opposite was true of the Courtier law, where the attempt to give the artisanat a base of operations independent of industry and commerce, yet squarely in the control of petty patrons, threatened to roll over some sensitive and powerful toes.

In fact, Courtier's proposition was a late addition to a debate that focused not on artisans, per se, but on the technical training of French workers, the poor quality of which, many felt, had burdened the war effort and left the country critically behind its neighbors in the race to economic rehabilitation. More than this, the ignorance of French workers was a potential embarrassment. "It is unfortunate," read one report on apprenticeship, "to think that the Germans noted with malice that of half a million French prisoners of war scattered among the various camps, at least four hundred thousand had never learned a trade."[139] Maurice Bouilloux-Lafont, deputy from the Finistère, blamed the apprenticeship crisis on the disappearance of the trade gilds and on the machinery and specialization that had "removed all the intelligence" from labor.[140] Georges Dufour, *compagnon* from Burgundy, offered a simpler diagnosis. In the postwar economic slump working class families needed income immediately. Rather than apprentice their sons and sacrifice a small immediate gain for a larger and more secure future, these families sent their children off at fourteen or fifteen years of age to work in a factory so as to enjoy the small but necessary wages.[141]

After the war, through legislation and the efforts of the Office national de l'enseignement technique ("Technical Education"), the state recognized these problems and began to address them. This produced, in July 1919, the Astier law. The new law made technical training mandatory for all school children, to be coordinated in local courses and schools set up by the departmental councils and overseen by the Enseignement technique. Three difficulties soon arose. First, while the Astier law provided for the creation of *cours professionnels* in the communes, it did not organize professional counseling or recruitment of apprentices; nor did it regulate apprentice contracts or directly control the quality of training.[142] Second, and more critically, although the law established the admirable goal of universal technical competence, it did not provide the means to attain it. Left largely to their own devices, local authorities attacked the problem with varying vigor and resources. Third, the Astier law did not settle, or at least not to everyone's satisfaction, the issue of jurisdiction, of who exactly would have the power to "form" the nation's young workers. Was professional training to become the province of business, labor, or a state technocracy?[143]

Dissatisfaction with the Astier law bred continuing attempts to amend it and spawned a number of projects for the creation of chambers of apprenticeship or, as they came to be called, chambers of trades. The variety of proposals reflected continuing differences of opinion over the character of the chambers. The most popular idea, endorsed by the Lyon conference on apprenticeship, was contained in the so-called Verlot bill, which provided for chambers of trades that would operate under state guidance, independent of the chambers of commerce and composed of equal numbers of employees and employers.[144]

To the moment of the deposition of the Verlot bill, in June 1921, the debate over technical training had ignored the artisanat, which had yet to enter French political consciousness. This changed in 1922. With the formation of the CGAF and the Chamber of Deputies' groupe de défense artisanale,

artisans and their parliamentary sponsors seized on the issues of apprenticeship and chambers of trades. In December 1922, Joseph Courtier, president
of the chamber group, put forward a project, co-sponsored by 289 deputies,
belonging to parties "les plus opposés," that would set up independent artisanal chambers of trades in France. Courtier defended his proposal in familiar fashion:

> Artisans offer, from the social aspect, the advantage of being at the same
> time workers and patrons . . . Emancipated from the proletariat, raised to
> petty proprietors, artisans nonetheless remain laborers . . . . They provide
> the nation with a happy element of equilibrium . . . . To defend our artisans
> is from a social point of view . . . to favor the rise of the middle classes who
> are able to contribute so much to the maintenance of order and to the
> prosperity of the country . . . . It is from the economic point of view to revivify
> a production that is quintessentially French . . . . It is to react against the
> rural exodus . . . . [145]

"We need shoemakers," Courtier concluded, "and it is to the cobblers and
not to the industrial shoe manufacturers that we must confide their professional formation."

The artisanal movement's thinking on the matter was necessarily conditioned by the various models of chambers of trades that already existed in
France. The Alsace Chamber of Trades, of course, was one such model.
There were, in addition, a number of smaller chambers of trades scattered
across the country.[146] These were tiny, local bodies with little or no contact
among themselves, preoccupied almost exclusively with apprenticeship, and
invariably tied to the chambers of commerce. They did not in any sense
represent the artisanat in the way that the chambers of commerce and agriculture represented those sectors. It is nevertheless true that the most active
and class conscious artisans inevitably became involved in them, and these,
in turn, became the future leaders in the artisanat's drive for autonomy.

The one partial exception to this rule was the Bordeaux Chamber of
Trades. Set up in December 1919, the Bordeaux chamber was more or less
independent of the local chamber of commerce[147] and was small by comparison, with only 2,300 members in 1923. Compared to the other chambers of
trades, however, it was huge, with a budget of 64,000 francs in 1923, as against
the 20,000 francs of the Tours Chamber of Trades or the 6,000 francs of the
chamber of trades in Poitiers.[148] Like other French chambers of trades, the
one in Bordeaux did not serve as an organ for the defense of *petits métiers*.
It dealt exclusively with "orientation et formation professionnelle," and one
of its most important functions was to carry out rigorous psychological examinations. This enabled the chamber to direct young people to the most
suitable trades and to help them find their way. Apparently, this advice could
run to the elaborate, such as this counsel to a young man seeking a career in
the food trades:

Begin to work as soon as school is over;

Start with a responsible pastry maker for two years;

Follow this with two years' work as an apprentice kitchen boy in a good hotel, either in Bordeaux or at a spa or a seaside resort;

This program will bring you to your seventeenth year;

Travel for a year in England or the United States, a year in South America, in first class hotels.

At the moment you leave for your national service you will already be a man, and the most brilliant future will open up for you if you are serious and frugal;

Come and see us [afterwards], and we will help you find a place in a respectable business.[149]

The chamber in Bordeaux failed, however, in its cross-class approach to the problem of apprenticeship. It was unable to draw employees to its mission. Instead, as the chamber grew it became increasingly patronal in nature. Workers simply were not interested; in fact, they were hostile. The chamber's leadership had tried in 1920 to attract the collaboration of the Union des syndicats des ouvriers fédérés de la Gironde, but these efforts collapsed over the union's insistence that the chamber accept only workers *syndiqués*. When the chamber approached the prefect with a request to establish its own mandatory professional training courses (*cours professionnels obligatoires*), it again ran into the union's successful opposition.[150]

Meanwhile, in the Chamber of Deputies the debate had resolved itself to a contest between the Verlot and Courtier propositions; that is, between chambers of trades generally aimed at professional formation and chambers by and for the artisanat. Outside the Palais Bourbon, artisans' ambitions led them into another of a long series of skirmishes with the chambers of commerce, which objected to losing their hegemony over appreticeship.[151] In early 1923, for example, the Assembly of Presidents of Chambers of Commerce, that of Alsace excepted, issued a resolution condemning Courtier's bill and praising Verlot's. This provoked a sharp response from the CGAF, which minced no words in denouncing those "whose interests are scarcely those of the nation," who support "neither social continuity nor economic stability," who serve as "a perfect example of parasitical and destructive capitalist egotism."[152]

The Courtier bill also ran up against the familiar resistance of the state administration. In particular, artisans failed to win over the Office national de l'enseignement technique, which also endorsed the Verlot project. Typically, Gaston Vidal, director of the Office national, saw the problem of professional training in strictly technical and economic terms. He rejected Courtier's arguments about the survival of a perhaps economically undynamic but socially valuable artisanat.[153] The rationalizing instincts of the administration as usual made it unsympathetic to the interests of petty producers.

For all this, the Courtier proposal made it through the Chamber of Deputies on March 26, 1925 and with Senate approval passed into law at the end of July. This became possible when the Labor Committee of the Chamber

of Deputies arranged a simple but ingenious compromise based on the recognition that while no one vehemently opposed some ill-defined corporate
organ for master tradesmen, everyone objected to giving them jurisdiction
over the technical training of young Frenchmen. The committee merely split
the difference between the Courtier and Verlot bills. "Other nations," the
report read, "have been able to run the risk of developing industry *á outrance*.
Let us conserve our factories in order to establish in our country a happy
harmony of forces and to satisfy our needs; but let us develop our workshops,
because in international competition they will always triumph through their
initiative and their good taste."[154] Thus, while the Courtier law created artisanal chambers of trades and protected "good taste," it left the question of
control over apprenticeship untouched.[155]

While it by no means settled the conflicts between artisans and chambers
of commerce, the Courtier law did allow for the formation of "organs of
professional and economic interest of artisans, masters and *compagnons*."
The chambers of trades received a mandate to organize apprenticeship within
the artisanat (to be fixed by a future law), to participate in the departmental
committees of technical education, to submit resolutions on matters artisanal
to the public authorities, and in general to safeguard the professional and
economic interests of small tradesmen. They were organized around two
bodies, a general assembly and a bureau of officers: president, vice-presidents,
and an administrative general secretary. The assembly, elected by those working in the artisanal trades, comprised one-third journeymen and two-thirds
masters. Members served for six years, and half the assembly was replaced
every three years. The law also envisioned the constitution of an Assembly
of Presidents of Chambers of Trades (APCMF), to meet in Paris and to
coordinate the activities of the local chambers. The chambers received their
funding from a special tax appended to the *patente* for artisans, a small levy
on apprenticeship, and whatever donations and subsidies they might solicit
either from the state or private sources.[156]

All this marked a great victory for the young artisanal movement and was
duly celebrated in the artisanal press. Yet the Courtier law had its shortcomings. The majority of artisans welcomed it with indifference.[156] The law also
failed to answer several fundamental questions. What were to be the social
and economic outlines of the artisanat, and who would qualify to belong to
the chambers of trades? The legislation on taxation and credit for *petits* artisans had carefully defined their constituencies. The Courtier law, on the
contrary, offered only a vague definition: an artisan should work in an "artisanal" trade and participate personally in production. It did not specify the
artisanal trades, which it left for administrative action, and it said nothing
about the size of an artisanal enterprise—an item of some dispute within the
artisanal movement. The law was also silent about the powers that artisans
would eventually yield over apprenticeship. How much jurisdiction would
this cost the chambers of commerce? And would the chambers of trades, for
example, be able to regulate access to certain trades, thereby curtailing freedom of economic choice? Finally, while the Courtier law provided for the

possibility of chambers of trades, it did not give birth to functioning institutions. These remained to be built through the initiative of artisans at the local level, and always in the face of hostility from trade unions and business interests, administrative neglect, disputes and inertia within the artisanat itself.

Thus, in the years following World War I France witnessed the arrival of a new political force: the artisanal movement. In 1919 the word *artisanat* had still to enter the French social lexicon, whereas by 1925 the movement had obtained for master craftsmen an official status and a set of fiscal and legal privileges to go with it. In these six years, moreover, the movement first confronted the parliamentary solicitude, administrative apathy, and class hostility that were to define its social and political relations for the next thirty years.

The formation of the artisanal movement casts an interesting light on the process of the development of the consciousness and organization of a social group—in part spontaneous, in part orchestrated. As artisans began to recognize themselves after 1919, this *prise de conscience* received a critical boost from their recognition by the government. Perhaps the consciousness beginning to percolate through the master craftsmen would sooner or later have achieved organizational form even without state intervention. And certainly the state was never able completely to harness artisans to its own needs. Nonetheless, through its selective patronage the state became both midwife and tutor to the new artisanal movement.

2

A Fractious Movement, 1925–1932

If evening clothes and important speakers are any measure of political success, the CGAF had arrived by 1924. In that January, as it prepared to fight its first national election campaign, the Confédération indulged itself in an amiable French custom: the political banquet. The grand occasion brought out some of the capital's leading political figures. Poincaré, the premier, had been scheduled to preside but was forced to cancel his appearance. He was replaced in the chair by the minister of labor, Albert Peyronnet, who shared the table of honor with the artisanal movement's "guardian angels": Louis Serre, Etienne Clémentel, and Joseph Courtier. At the other tables sat twenty-one of their colleagues from the Senate and sixty from the Chamber of Deputies. Other luminaries included Gaston Doumergue, president of the upper house, Charles Piquenard, the official at the Labor Ministry most directly responsible for artisanal affairs, and the ministers of Finance, Commerce, and Public Works.

The company enjoyed a hearty meal, prepared by the artisans themselves. After the apéritif Tailledet rose to welcome his eminent guests and laid out the CGAF's agenda for the next legislature. The president cautioned his fellow artisans to "judge men by their acts, not by their words." But words were what the evening was about.

Peyronnet sounded the keynote. "From the social point of view"—he told his hosts what they had come to hear—"the artisanat assures the country an excellent school for the renewal of political elites by permitting honesty, perseverance, and hard work to rise, little by little, and true merit to triumph." Artisans, said Peyronnet, could be certain of the government's continuing solicitude. The evening climaxed with the presentation of "Premier Artisan de France" gold medals to Clémentel, Peyronnet, Serre, Courtier, Schlieffer, and Monsieur Cuvillier, director of the Banque Populaire de Paris.[1]

Within two years the CGAF had become a part of the French political establishment. Certainly, it did not enjoy the mass support of the CGT or the *entrée* of the CGPF. Yet it had proved itself able to operate effectively in the limited sphere of artisanal interests. By the beginning of 1925 the CGAF claimed to have 100,000 members.[2] These belonged to 27 national trade federations, a national union of artisanal cooperative societies, and a CGAF-run credit union. In addition to the affiliated national federations, the CGAF had established more than 90 general trades unions for those artisans, mostly rural and *isolé*, who belonged to no national group, and 127 local and departmental organizations for syndicates whose parent federations did not adhere to the CGAF.

Much remained for the CGAF to do, and not only at the national level. Of the country's approximately 1 million master artisans, probably no more than 12 to 17 percent belonged to artisanal unions in the mid-1920s. The numbers were unquestionably higher in the towns than in the countryside.[3] Even in Alsace and Lorraine, with their powerful chambers of trades and quasi-public corporations, fewer than 15,000 of the 39,000 artisans actually belonged to the trade organizations in 1925.[4] The movement was young, however, and perhaps its vitality was better measured by its growth than by its absolute size. By 1929 the population of artisanal syndicates and cooperatives had more than doubled, and this steady expansion continued well into the next decade.

The movement's organizational and political successes could not, however, bridge the wide differences that divided artisans. The Parisian shoemaker syndicalists, Tailledet and Grandadam, had captured the leadership of the CGAF and were in the process of adapting it to their own view that the artisanal movement should be the vehicle to defend the "class" interests of independent, petty craftsmen. They meant to make the CGAF the CGT of the artisanat, whose main purpose was to lobby Parliament and the bureaucracy for policies favorable to petty producers. This implied a confederation with a strong policy making center and with a concentration on Paris, where the effective organs of national power were to be found. Their formal adherence to the regionalist doctrines of the Bordeaux Charter of the Artisanat, notwithstanding, Tailledet and Grandadam did their best to centralize the CGAF's operations, and they stacked the editorial board of their new journal, the *Artisan Français* with Parisian syndicalists.

The structure of the CGAF mediated against such a decisive orientation. This collection of local and professional groups had coalesced in order to fight for some amorphous common interests. Yet the leadership possessed no effective means of discipline, nor were most of these groups inclined to grant it any. Between the center and the regions, each side believed that it held the recipe for artisans' prosperity and that the other was a kind of false prophet. The Parisian leadership found its regional collaborators naïve and inexperienced, unprepared for the tough business of politics. The regions interpreted this as a kind of snobbery and countered with their own claims to authority: a deeper understanding of the master craftsman "comme il est," or simple seniority. "We were involved with the Artisanat while our opponents were still sucking their thumbs," wrote Eyraud, president of the FASE. Matters were further complicated by the participation of the Alsatian artisans, whose unique institutional existence and broad social base gave them an agenda often at odds with those of their French cousins. Even more than the other regional groups those of Alsace-Lorraine were disinclined to delegate responsibility to the CGAF leadership.

The first break within the movement came quickly enough. Surprisingly, it originated not with the Alsatians but with the Lyon-based FASE, largest of the regional groups, over the issue of credit. The trouble derived from ambiguities in the law of December 1923, which had provided that credit flowing to the artisanat had to pass through the agencies of syndical credit cooperatives. It did not specify, however, whether there should be one central credit cooperative or several regional ones. Eager to profit from the new legislation, the FASE began to set up its own Union des coopératives du Sud-Est, under the direction of its president, Eyraud. Eyraud argued that given the diversity of the country and of professional habits a regional credit cooperative would be more effective. "In order to lend you must know your borrower," he counseled.[5] The FASE's initiative, however, brought it directly into conflict with its parent confederation.

Believing, as always, in the superiority of centralized action, the CGAF had established a Union nationale des sociétés coopératives d'artisans de France, controlled by the national committee in Paris and responsible for disbursing credit throughout the artisanat. The leadership were unwilling to brook autonomy on such matters, and they set out to discipline the ambitious FASE. They forced Eyraud, also the FASE delegate, off the CGAF national committee, while first threatening and then proceeding to cancel the national congress scheduled for Lyon in 1924, convening it instead in Paris. The national committee further decided on a complete reorganization of its southeast sector and temporarily transferred its headquarters from Lyon to Paris. Finally, the CGAF brought a civil suit against Eyraud, accusing him of misappropriating funds meant for artisanal credit.[6] It seems, in fact, that several scandals marred Eyraud's tenure in the southeast. The mutual aid and retirement funds he set up for the FASE had to be liquidated under shady circumstances, and this finally forced Eyraud out of his long presidency.[7] Parenthetically, Eyraud emerged from his troubles a few years later in Paris, where he seems to have gravitated to a group led by a journalist for the right-wing paper, *Echo de Paris*, Jean Delage, backed by the Paris Chamber of Commerce and the Paris Municipal Council, which operated under the name, "La France Artisanale."[8]

The FASE, while protesting its continued faith in the ideal of artisanal unity, not unnaturally bridled at these "villainous" attacks by "those little Napoleons" from Paris.[9] The Lyonnais took their case to the Commission supérieure de l'artisanat, created to oversee the system of artisanal credit. Here the FASE discovered, not for the last time, that the administration placed its confidence in the CGAF. The FASE found, however, that others in the artisanal movement shared their disillusionment with the CGAF leadership. In the summer of 1924, at a meeting in Grenoble, regional artisanal federations from Bordeaux, Toulouse, Montpellier, Limoges, and Dijon joined the Southeast in the new Union des fédérations régionales d'artisans de France (UFRA), which also called itself the Artisan Français.[10]

The CGAF leadership coincidentally provoked a schism with the artisans of Alsace-Lorraine when in 1924 they demanded that the Alsatians abandon their local corporative system and adopt the French syndical model for the sake of the movement's homogeneity and effectiveness. This would have meant expelling from the movement the leaders of the Alsace Chamber of Trades, most of whom owned substantial businesses and were not artisans according to French standards. Words were exchanged between Grandadam and Ley, the chamber's general secretary; the Alsatians ceased, thenceforth, to pay their dues to the CGAF.[11]

The Alsatians hesitated, at first, to join the secession of the UFRA. They wanted to avoid a permanent division of the artisanal movement and still hoped for some kind of reconciliation with the CGAF; however, after several months of accusations and counteraccusations, and finally finding an accommodation with the Confédération impossible, the Alsatians took refuge in the tolerance and regionalism of the UFRA. Schlieffer became the president of the new organization and the heads of the other regional groups its vice-presidents. In less than two years the compromises that had allowed the creation of the CGAF had utterly broken down, and the artisanal movement was breaking apart.

The formal division of the movement inaugurated a period of open warfare for dominance among artisans and for influence with the public authorities. The UFRA challenged the CGAF for equal representation within the Commission supérieur de l'artisanat and on other administrative councils. It lobbied for changes in the legal administration of the artisanat that would allow nonsyndical organizations, like the UFRA, to participate in the creation of cooperatives and the distribution of credit. The UFRA met its greatest success in this area when Schlieffer was named, along with Tailledet, to the newly established National Economic Council (CNE) in 1925,[12] but it never succeeded in acquiring any of those privileges reserved for syndicates. For its part, the leadership of the CGAF applied to the administration for sanctions against the UFRA and contested Schlieffer's nomination to the CNE. The CGAF even brought legal proceedings against the Artisan Français (as the UFRA was officially known) for using a name that was already the title of the Confédération's journal. The courts eventually held in favor of the CGAF, causing the UFRA to change its name to the Union des artisans français (UAF) in 1927.[13]

In the artisanal press, sparks flew between Paris, Lyon, and Strasbourg. The Alsatians' *Gazette des Métiers* and the UFRA's *Artisan* accused Tailledet and Grandadam of the flagrant violation of the Charter of the Artisanat of 1923, of "unification and centralization *á outrance*," and of being "traitors," "parasites," "industrialists," and thinly disguised Bolsheviks.[14] The CGAF's leaders defended themselves against charges of "dictatorship" and reproached the "dissidents" for a nefarious campaign of "calumnies and division."[15]

These vitriolic exchanges discomfited the artisanal movement's allies in Parliament and the administration, who feared that disunity would both weaken the movement and make it more difficult to work with. Petty producers were hard enough to defend when they were not fighting and trying to discredit each other. Robert Thoumyre, who had become president of the Chamber of Deputies' Groupe de défense artisanale in 1924 when Courtier acceded to the Senate, urged the CGAF and the UFRA to find some common ground. Louis Serre, still president of the Senate group, wrote, "Those who are interested in the future of the artisanat consider this unity as the one compensation for the aid they have always given freely."[16]

The minister of labor, Durafour, through his undersecretary, Piquenard, took more concrete action. At the end of 1925 Piquenard cajoled the CGAF and the UFRA into delegating representatives to a series of conferences aimed at patching up the movement. The group first met on December 28, 1925, at the ministry and unanimously adopted a resolution calling for unity. More tangibly, it set up a joint committee to study the means to this end and allowed itself a month to produce such a plan. Both the CGAF and the UFRA promised in the meantime to refrain from polemics and mutual harassment. The committee issued its report on January 9. It envisioned, somewhat optimistically, a division of labor between the two artisanal groups within an inclusive new organization. The CGAF would handle "professional, corporative, and national" problems and the UFRA would occupy itself with regional and interprofessional matters, while the labor minister would preside, in order to enforce a kind of binding arbitration on the unified artisanat (which suggests just how unlikely such a compromise was).[17]

The peace talks dragged on for six months. The parties could reach no agreement on this or any other modus vivendi and soon lapsed back into their old contentious ways. In effect, any agreement ran aground on precisely those differences that had precipitated the regionalist secession in the first place.[18] The regional federations considered local autonomy every bit as important as political effectiveness. For the Alsatians, the CGAF's policies presented a mortal threat to their traditional privileges, a concern for which had drawn them to the movement. The CGAF leadership, meanwhile, never had the least intention of decentralizing their organization. Nor were they willing to share power with a loose agglomeration of regional groups, an organization, as they saw it, which would by its very nature be politically ineffectual and ultimately prejudicial to artisans' real interests. The CGAF admitted the possibility that the prodigal federations might return to its ranks, but it steadfastly refused "to modify in any way [its] federal and confederal statutes."[19]

The split between the two groups was just the beginning of the subdivision of the artisanal movement. It is almost as if the whole movement were subject to the second law of thermodynamics. From the Big Bang of the artisanat in 1922, no grouping could maintain itself. It sometimes appeared, looking at the second half of the 1920s, that the movement would continue to fracture into smaller and smaller groups, and to finish, sometime in the 1930s, where it had begun in 1919: without any national coherence.

The story is difficult to follow in an artisanal press long on invective and innuendo but short on background information. In 1926 the Alsatian leadership inspired the creation of the Union générale des artisans d'Alsace et de Lorraine (UGAAL), representing the 32,000 artisans of the recovered provinces. Schlieffer addressed the founding congress of the UGAAL and announced its intention to remain within the UFRA, which by then claimed to represent some 80,000 small masters throughout France. At the same time, he hinted that at some moment in the near future the UFRA's charter would have to be amended to give to each federation a weight proportional to its membership. Schlieffer contended that this would only make the UFRA a fairer representation of the artisanat *régional*. He did not add, although it was clear to all, that such a system would allow the Alsatians total domination of the UFRA.[20]

The regional federations had left the CGAF to escape the authority of Tailledet; they naturally refused the Alsatians' demands. Thus spurned, the Alsatians quit the UFRA, and this set off another flurry of groupings and regroupings. The rump of the UFRA became the UAF, still headed by Paul Bulnois of the Parisian Association des petits fabricants et inventeurs. For the moment, the other regional federations remained loyal to the UAF, which was having difficulty finding its rationale.[21] It was too diffuse and, without the Alsatians, too small to have much impact on national political affairs; that is, to challenge the CGAF's influence.

What the UAF lacked in purpose and influence it apparently also lacked in cohesion. By 1931 the rump of the UFRA was experiencing its own defections. The Breton federation crossed swords with the union's leadership, once again over the question of organizational discipline. Bristling at the "pride and arrogance" of the UAF leadership, the Bretons resigned from the Union, taking with them the federations from Burgundy, the Franche-Comté, the Midi, and the Southwest. These doubly recalcitrant regional groups then came together in what they called the Confédération artisanale française, a sum wholly subordinate to its parts, with no independent leadership.

With the Confédération artisanale française the regionalist elements reached the apex of disorder: an organization that was, in effect, no organization at all. It could not and did not survive. In the fall of 1932 the artisanal federation of Brittany voted unanimously to return to the UAF, where it would again have access to significant resources, especially loans. Its disappointed leader, Martin, resigned and the Confédération artisanale française was dissolved.[22]

Even the CGAF was forced to accommodate the widespread discomfort among its membership with central control. Obviously under pressure from its constituents, the Confédération decided in October 1927 to make some concessions to regionalist sentiment within its ranks and called an extraordinary session of the general assembly in January 1928 to arrange this reorganization. The new system set up thirty-six action committees, which it endowed with an increased measure of autonomy and responsibility in local artisanal affairs. Each action committee was entitled to elect one delegate to the new national committee. Competition within the new local groups could sometimes provoke as many problems as it solved, however. In the Seine-Inférieure, for example, Baudet, of Le Havre action group, won election to the national committee over Rouen's Albert Dupuis, the old artisanal warhorse. Dupuis thereupon left the CGAF and, shortly thereafter, joined the Alsatians.[23]

As the artisanat developed its organizational and political life, it also began to elaborate a view of France and of history into which its day-to-day activities had to fit. The artisanal *movement* has been continually referred to, yet to take this collection of trades unions, federations, and confederations at its most transparent, it would seem to constitute more an interest lobby than a movement. Indeed, as a quotidian matter, this is exactly how it behaved—flooding the government and the administration with *voeux*, prowling the corridors of the Palais Bourbon in search of lower taxes and cheaper credit—and this is how the various organizations justified themselves to their membership.

Viewed in this way, moreover, the artisanat was hardly a class. Ideally, all master artisans shared the mixed condition of small capital and skilled, manual labor. In economic and social fact, however, the artisanat took in such a universe of particular skills and property arrangements as to have but the slimmest measure of unity. The artisanat was, to use the Marxist formulation, determined in only the vaguest sense. Ideology was therefore crucial. It was, to borrow Sewell's elegant turn, in "construing their inevitably construed experience,"[24] that artisans expressed their solidarity and identified themselves as a class. Simply put, an interest group of *petits artisans fiscaux* could exist without a worldview; the artisanat could not.

Two challenges faced the artisanal movement. It had, first, to manipulate the political system to artisans' advantage so as to assure their survival in the short term. Secondly, it needed to articulate a vision of the future, a historical strategy, a means to help artisans persist against the tide of industrial development, either by carving a niche for the artisanat in the new world or by preserving the old one.

Each of the movement's *groupuscules* represented a particular set of experiences, and each offered a solution to the problems of master artisans that derived from these. We have seen that the primary ideological division within the artisanal movement lay between those whose orientation to politics and society was syndicalist and those whose bent was corporatist. In the rough and tumble of parliamentary politics and bureaucratic maneuvering, the syndicalists of the CGAF and the corporatists, whose main strength lay in the Alsace Chamber of Trades, closely resembled one another. Fiscality, credit, and influence were the order of the day. Their conceptions of the meaning of the organization of artisans, however, did not coincide.

It was Hubert Ley, the erstwhile general secretary of the Strasbourg Chamber of Trades, who most clearly articulated the corporatist position. Ley, reflecting the historical and legal realities of Alsace-Lorraine, conceived the artisanat to be a unique form of production characterized by manual labor, a high degree of skill, and virtually no division of labor. He considered the size of an artisanal enterprise irrelevant.[25] For Ley, the corporation of small masters was united not by interest, narrowly held, but by that whole manner of life implied by the Profession: by the skill, which meant nonalienated work, and by a social fluidity that bound master, journeyman, and apprentice and led to the absence of fixed social boundaries necessary to class formation. Within the Profession, collaboration, not competition, prevailed.

Artisanal syndicalism, on the contrary, fell into a tradition that included Proudhon, Perdiguier, and even, to a degree, Marx. "The nineteenth-century labor movement," as Sewell noted, "was born in the workshop, not in the dark, satanic mill."[26] As defined by its most vigorous spokesman, Robert Tailledet, artisanal syndicalism was a theory both of social differentiation and of conflict. For Tailledet, the artisanat was neither a corporation nor a *stand*. It was a class, determined basically in opposition to other classes, bound together and made an effective political force by the natural development of an artisanal class consciousness, a consciousness conditioned by material factors; that is, by the labor process. Speaking of this solidarity, "this class spirit which is both spontaneous and latent," Tailledet wrote:

> . . . Our task consists of making it conscious and calculated. But, we insist, we have not brought together just any heterogeneous group . . . without a personality and for demagogic purposes. All we have done is to unite individuals who share the same fundamental interests for the sole purpose of giving them the strength to vindicate their existence and to fight for the right to a decent life.[27]

Unlike Ley, for whom the artisanat included large patrons and small, journeymen and apprentices as well as masters, Tailledet saw it as a homogeneous class of small, independent master craftsmen, with homogeneity the crucial component of solidarity. For how, Tailledet wondered, could the cobbler or the goldsmith, working with his wife and his children, have the same interests and the same consciousness as the shoe manufacturer or the jeweler with a shop employing thirty workers and a few foremen? Classes, in the syndicalists' view, always developed in a pluralist society. They inevitably organized to defend their interests; and these clashed necessarily with the interests of other classes.[28] Political institutions might aggravate conflict or facilitate its resolution, but no arrangement could eliminate it. Social harmony—and this was the crux of their disagreement with the corporatists—was a pipe dream. Practically, then, the CGAF searched for a structure that could arbitrate among competing class interests without denying any one the ability to defend itself as it saw fit.

Artisanal syndicalism also distinguished itself from corporatism by its individualist notions of liberty and voluntarist ideas of association. Whereas the corporation—witness, for example, the charter of the Alsace Chamber of Trades—was a creation of the state, argued Georges Grandadam, vice-president of the CGAF, the trade union represented spontaneous, voluntary collective action. Therein lay its virtue and its power. He expressed the dichotomy more tendentiously: the corporation meant "obligation, limitation, and subjection"; the syndicate implied "liberty, affiliation, discipline."[29] More than this, in the corporatists' insistence on the compatibility of employers and employees, *petits* artisans and substantial businessmen, Grandadam saw a blind for the conservative interests of the *petits industriels* who, as we have seen, dominated the artisanat in Alsace. He wrote that,

> the stabilization [of the artisanal regime in Alsace] operates always to the profit of those who have already succeeded, and the maintenance of preconceived ideas [of social organization] serves often hypocritically to support vested interests.[30]

The mass of French artisans, with their smaller businesses and roots in the labor movement, the CGAF argued, would be better served by a syndicalist approach.

And yet, for all the differences in political orientations and all the venom between Paris and Strasbourg, syndicalists and corporatists shared more of a common worldview than either would have liked to admit. At the center of the artisans' ontology was the Profession, "the human activity . . . productive rather than speculative . . . manual, full of personality rather than anonymous, mechanical, and schematized."[31] "By the exercise of a trade," wrote H. Théallier, "each individual takes his place and finds his niche in human society."[32] For the corporatists, the shared skill and holistic work experience was the emotional and social bond of the artisanat. It united employers and employees, and masters of vastly different means. At the same time, the Profession erected a barrier between artisans and the proletarians and nonlaboring bourgeois of industrial capitalism.[33]

The syndicalists also placed the Profession at the base of their political sociology. "When a man exercises a profession for a long time," said Tailledet, "it gives him a certain turn of the spirit, a manner of being and of feeling that situates him, that classifies him, that places him definitively in the world."[34] Georges Chaudieu, butcher and artisanal activist, voiced the matter more vividly:

> All those who have to deal with tradesmen have learned to recognize them, first of all by their hands, which often bear the imprint of the tools or the materials that they use, by their bearing and their conversation. These ex-

terior signs are perceptible in the majority of individuals: blacksmiths, massive and rugged as an oak; wheelwrights, carpenters, furniture-makers, saddlers, boot-makers, carrying on their clothes the scent of wood or leather; hairdressers, precious and foppish, talkative and full of humanitarian ideas . . . artists, lost in their creative meditations, without regard for their material conditions. . . .[35]

Praise for the Profession was always joined to the defense of the family, "an island of order in our world in disarray, a 'land of liberty' closed to directed and aggressive proletarianization." Ask a carpenter or a mechanic why he wanted to be an artisan, suggested the *Artisan de l'Ouest*, and he would reply, "Because I have to live and take care of my family."[36] The movement relentlessly identified the health of the artisanat with that of the family, both practically and morally. "The artisan works at home," wrote social commentator Jean Delage. "He has his shop, his home. Marriage for him is the foundation of his trade. His wife will be his helpmate; his children, too. The more children, the more assistants, and the more his enterprise will prosper."[37] "When you work for yourself," observed a Parisian cobbler, "you can't have too many people whom you have to order around. You can't be everywhere at the same time. My wife is [therefore] my best helper. She keeps my books; she helps me conserve my raw materials. She's my first *compagnon*."[38]

Given this emphasis on home and family, it is clear why so many leaders of the artisanat involved themselves in the crusade to revive French natality. Albert Dupuis, for example, who was president both of the Rouen Chamber of Trades and of the APCMF, served concurrently as chairman of his local Ligue des Familles Nombreuse. Dupuis praised the family not only as the foundation of "a healthy and happy existence" but also as "the best guarantee against revolution."[39]

Reality, it seems, did not always match the artisans' idyll. In some trades (baking, for instance) the family often did form a productive unit, while in others it did not. Generally, the role of family members decreased as the number of journeymen increased.[40]Henri Mourier found a further irony. He referred to a survey conducted by the Ministry of Industrial Production in 1940, which examined some 40,000 artisans in thirty-two departments. The survey discovered that 29 percent of artisans had no children, 34 percent had one child, 22 percent had two children, and only 8.7 percent had more than two.[41]Apparently, the large artisanal family was an exception.

Like most of their contemporaries, artisans' commitment was to a patriarchal model of the family. Their ideal artisan-wife (*artisane*) was no bourgeois stay-at-home but neither was she the equal of a man. Tens of thousands of women might work in hatmaking, dressmaking, and the other so-called *professions féminines*. A wife might help her husband out in the shop or a widow continue to run the family business after her husband's death, yet her role always remained subordinate. Thus the artisanal movement both idealized women and rejected their equality in fact. "The woman," limned Théallier, "finds the full development of her being in the domain of sentiment, the man in his trade."[42] And while Delage insisted on the defense of the "female trades," he also counseled that,

> Women must develop aptitudes consistent with the direction of their nature without seeking to imitate men. Their role in the progress of civilization is higher than the men's. They must not abandon it.[43]

Likewise, Grand'mère, a columnist for *Artisan* (Le Puy), wrote, "the role of the wife is of great importance. She is the soul of the household." Behind any successful business, she continued, is a home that is well-run—not necessarily in luxury, but efficiently and "even with a bit of *coquetterie*."[44] Conversely, observed the *Artisan* of Lyon, "Nothing is more grotesque than a household of which it can be said vulgarly: 'It's the woman who wears the pants.' "[45] Grand'mère captured the flavor of artisanal feminism when she showed firm support for *artisanes'* syndicalism but also for obedience and against the vote for women.

While all the artisanal organizations sought to one extent or another to attract *artisanes* to the movement, their efforts were limited in conception and success. The Alsace Chamber of Trades, for example, had only voted to enroll the "female professions" of dressmaker, milliner, and hairdresser (*modistes*, *tailleuses*, and *coiffeuses*) in 1913. And after the war, when the Alsace Chamber decided to accelerate its recruitment of *artisanes*, it ran into stiff opposition from its male constituents, who wanted to preserve the all-male character of the corporations and the Chamber. The *Gazette des Métiers* reported:

> Employers and journeymen look with skepticism on the intrusion of females in the professional domain. The first fear the professional drawbacks and the moral dangers which the promiscuity of the two sexes might provoke; the second concern themselves especially with the competition [caused by an influx of women assistants].[46]

The CGAF, in its own bid to recruit *artisanes*, in 1926 established a Comité and a Coopérative d'artisanat féminin and named Isabelle Dudit, syndicalist and author, as one of its vice-presidents. Once more, however, the leadership saw this as a question of protecting a "supplement" to the family income and a way of keeping wives in the *foyer*. "We must permit the wife to stay at home," wrote Delage in the *Echo de Paris*. "We must defend the family. We must defend the *artisanat féminin*."[47] In Lyon, Eyraud reported his disappointment at the FASE's inability to appeal to women and at the absence of their perspective from the pages of the *Artisan*. His solution was the inclusion of a home economics column in the journal.[48] The result of these efforts was modest indeed. Neither as individuals nor by way of trades unions did *artisanes* ever achieve a significant role in the movement.

Within the worldview of the artisans, therefore, it was axiomatic that the survival of the artisanat depended largely on the strength of the family and on the time-honored "duties" of its members. It followed reasonably, then, that the movement denounced as immoral or decadent whatever might threaten this delicate division of labor. We can read this fear of immorality and decadence in the pervasive artisanal concern about the *crise rurale* and the demonization of the city—a center, not just of factories, but of "cinemas, dance halls, and other dens of germs and distractions"[49]—with its "influence délétaire" on the nation.[50] Lucien Gelly, a long-time ally of the artisanal movement and one of Vichy's philosophers of rusticism, deplored the tendency of young women to leave their villages for the towns where they would be tempted by consumer goods and "the possibility of an easier promiscuity." Naturally enough, Gelly pined in a brief essay on sexual demography, "The young girls having left [the countryside], the young men follow them."[51] Artisanal social thought was horrified at the prospect of wives and daughters leaving the home to become factory hands, department store salesgirls, or office secretaries, for this implied the disintegration of the most basic of artisanal structures.

The literature of the artisanal movement thus tried to propagate an "ideal type": the Artisanat as the repository of traditional values; the Craftsman as independent, hard-working, and disdainful of the materialism of urban, industrial culture. The *Artisan* romanticized:

> An artisan is honest; he's a man of courage in the fullest sense of the word. He is absolutely incapable of cheating anyone out of even a centime. You could entrust him with your wallet without ever looking inside. . . . The Artisan is the Frenchman most admired in the world.[52]

Isabelle Dudit filled her didactic novel of 1930, *Marbréry: Maître Artisan*, with just such images. The hero, Jean Marbréry, son of Antoine, a carpenter, inherits his father's small workshop. Diligent, talented, devoted to his family and community, Jean soon finds his reward and employs five assistants and trains three apprentices. A friend suggests to Jean that he ought to profit from his popularity and success, expand his business, and become a genuine entrepreneur instead of a mere artisan-patron. Jean demurs, "What?! A factory. So it won't matter how the work is done or who does it? No, thanks. I love my trade, and I love my responsibilities. I leave to others the profits of mass production. Me, I'm satisfied with a job well done."[53]

The transition that Marbréry rejected, from master tradesman to *petit industriel*—that is, to small capitalist—implied more than adding a few workers and a certain division of labor. It meant the use of machinery, and this presented artisans with a dilemma. Historically, technological change had brought with it the degradation of skill and the concentration of production. "The triumph of the machine," offered one exuberant defender of the artisanat, "will lead to world-wide disaster."[54] Yet such innovations as electricity and the internal combustion engine allowed the workshop to multiply its productivity, if not to compete with the factory directly. Thus the issue of mechanization always left artisans ambivalent.

Adelaïde Blasquez captured artisans' wariness of technology in her biography of the locksmith, Gaston Lucas. Gaston remembered how his grandfather, at the turn of the century, reacted to the installation of electricity in his house:

> Never! I don't want anything to do with your so-called progress. Progress is going to kill you all. It'll cut off your arms; you won't be able to work anymore. Machines will do everything. They'll replace you and you'll be worthless.

And later, when Gaston told his father of his intention to begin an apprenticeship as an electrician, his father expressed his skepticism:

> Electricity?! Why that's no profession . . . . Don't you realize what wonderful opportunities there are for locksmiths? Now that's a secure trade. The world will always need locksmiths, but as for electricity. . . . [55]

It was in industrialization—the complete division of labor and mass production that the worker felt as the "amputation de sa personne morale"— that artisans saw the seed of moral and social decline. What does modern production mean? asked Georges Chaudieu, president of the butchers' federation and later Vichy functionary. "Monotony, standardized taste . . . lack of human contact." So unlike the artisan, he continued, who works with "a grain of friendliness, a smile, expressions of humanity and the joy of living."[56] Bernard Laffaille drew the distinction between the typical conversations of tradesmen and factory workers:

> In a group of workers at the factory door at five o'clock in the morning . . . the conversation concerns . . . political events, or a football match, or what's in the paper . . . . In an artisanal workshop the rare conversations center on the work itself—on the quality of the wood, on personal skills and methods, on precise work on a concrete object, on the task at hand. The life of each *compagnon* focuses on the work cycle, on family events, on the health of children. The master artisan, his two or three assistants, his apprentices— all know each other from a human angle.[57]

Here, in contrast to their own lives, artisans found the germ of class conflict: in the profoundly alienating nature of pure machine work, on the one hand, and in ownership without social responsibility, on the other.

In the real economic world, however, a too sincere traditionalism was a recipe for bankruptcy. Thus the spokesmen of the artisanat, while they might have longed for some rosy preindustrial past, also took care to recommend modern business and production methods to their followers. Every one of the movement's journals published regular articles with suggestions about improving techniques and bookkeeping. The *Artisan* of Lyon, while still the voice of blacksmiths, farriers, and wheelwrights, encouraged its readers to use gasoline engines and electricity and to keep careful account books. Indeed, it remarked proudly, the smithy already practices Taylorism; he just calls it "economy of time."[58]

The CGAF also showed its concern with the artisanat's technological development. Pierre de Felice, the CGAF's "expert" on the *artisanat rural*, enumerated the benefits that would accrue to rural artisans from the mechanization of farming.[59] In addition, at its offices in Paris—the "Cité Clémentel," named for the Confédération's great patron—the CGAF installed model workshops and in 1931 set up the Institut National des Métiers (INM). Its aim was to promote the technical modernization of craft production. In the ideology of the artisanal movement, therefore, the workshop of the future coexisted uneasily with the workshop of the past.

Despite their antipathy toward big business and industrial manufacture, however, artisans claimed not to be anticapitalist. The workshop, like the factory, after all, was private property. And it lived on profits, but reasonable profits, honestly earned. What artisans condemned was business without morality and production without humanity; a distinction that led the movement's economic theory to separate "productive" from "speculative" capital. Prosper Convert, addressing an artisanal congress on the problems of the milling industry, explained it this way:

> [Artisanal enterprises] are subject to and follow the . . . natural law of supply and demand. Their profit is but the legitimate remuneration of the work of transformation carried out on the merchandise; [whereas] big businesses, organized in cartels, form a consortium powerful enough to manipulate prices. Their profit is always speculative.[60]

Extending the logic of this analysis, Tailledet equated public and private finances. The financial health of a country, he contended, depended on its savings and on the "multiplicity of personally-run businesses."[61]

Critics of the artisanat, both then and now, have been wont to dismiss their ideology as "antimodern" or "reactionary": a worldview appropriate to a group of "losers of industrialization." This, we see, was partly the case. Insofar as *modern* implied progressive industrialization of the French economy—to the ultimate benefit of tycoons, proletarians, or technocrats, all soulless agents of modernism—artisans opposed it. Their approach to the economy was Malthusian, rather than dynamic. "They simply refuse to believe," wrote François Gresle, "in the inevitability of growth and take neither wealth as their goal nor power as their ideal."[62] Michel Debré agreed: "Their reduced clientele and mediocre profits satisfy them."[63] "What is the artisan's ideal?" asked Pierre Poujade. "To have a little business of his own, all his own." ("Avoir une petite affaire à toi, bien à toi.") We have noted artisans' ambivalence about new techniques, but as a rule, the movement endorsed the new only as a bulwark of the old: for example, the lathe that would turn the farrier into the country machinist, or the enlightened commercial policies that would keep the corner barbershop in business.

Artisans' social ideology inevitably influenced their political philosophy, the core of which was a search for a France in which tradesmen were better trained, professionally secure, and more respected. The artisanal movement saw itself defending a class under attack. Its politics aimed principally to arrest the forward march of industrialism and to contest the political economies of liberalism and Marxism; for both, the artisanal press never tired of reminding its readers, assumed the imminent disappearance of the small, independent producer. The literature of the movement bristled with attacks on laissez faire capitalism as the root cause of the structural deterioration of the economy and of the periodic crises that beset it. Tailledet charged liberalism with causing "social atomization" and "imperialist war."[64] Peter accused it of fostering "anarchy."[65] Of Marxism, the *Artisan* wrote that "its revolutionary, individualist, devastating Idea" makes it "perfectly incapable of conceiving a reconstruction of the social edifice based on the order and harmony of the forces of production."[66] What had these modern philosophies brought France, and what were they likely to bring in the future? A world of "professional incompetence," with "tailors who can't sew and masons [who can't] build."[67] Whether through corporative reforms or protective legislation, the movement's first priority was to break this historical assault.

Artisans' ideological predispositions indicated the broad thrust of their politics yet left the artisanal movement a wide tactical berth on everyday issues. Two of the most contentious of these in the 1920s were the fiscal and financial crisis of the mid-decade and the debate over social insurance that dominated the second half of the 1920s. Each centered on a question of the distribution of wealth; taken together they illustrate both the ambiguities and consistencies of a class torn between its property and its work.

The artisanal press showed little hesitation in assessing responsibility for the inflation and the collapse of the franc in the early 1920s. It launched a populist attack on the "liberal" economic structure and on "parasitical" finance capital in particular. "The money merchants who make their living by so inflating the economy are ennobled in some countries; in France they receive the Legion of Honor," complained the *Artisan Français*. "Circulation, it is said," noted Tailledet, "creates wealth. But it recreates always the same wealth—a ruinous parasitism for the [real] producers."[68]

> It is thus of the greatest urgency that we get rid of the web of finance capital in which we struggle and that we eliminate it from all areas of national activity. We must then turn to all those who work and produce, for it is through them, and through them alone, that the financial stabilization of our country can be achieved.[69]

The CGAF, and even the Alsace Chamber of Trades, refused to follow the government and the conservatives in blaming the crisis on the recalcitrance of the Germans or the recklessness of the working classes and the *Cartel des Gauches*. If Tailledet praised Poincaré's devaluation of the franc, he did so less out of any faith in fiscal orthodoxy than out of the simple fact that, as a group, artisans had little in the way of financial or capital investments and gained more from stabilization than they lost through devaluation.[70]

Throughout the 1920s, the artisanal movement supported policies aimed at increasing social justice in France. The CGAF and the UAF spoke continually in favor of a more progressive tax structure: "We must get the money from those who have it," the *Gazette des Métiers* wrote, not to create a situation of "absolute and suffocating equality," but in order that "the most hard working, the most able, the most frugal ... would be able to rise to higher steps on the social ladder."[71]

The movement had once again to declare itself on the issues of a national system of social insurance and family subsidies. Here again artisans expressed their peculiar existence as both workers and small property owners. All the major artisanal organizations in theory applauded the idea of some sort of assistance to the needy, and naturally they favored subventions to assure the integrity of the family. The law on family allowances (*allocations familiales*) proposed by Poincaré in 1929 and passed by the Parliament in 1932, however, intended that the cost would be borne mostly by employers and the benefits accrue only to employees.[72] It placed artisans with the former.

When artisans referred to the needy, of course, they generally included themselves. Hence, the specific provisions of the law on family allowances, as well as other forms of social insurance, did not meet with their approval. The movement argued as it had in 1923, on the question of the income tax, that artisans, particularly *petits*, differed fundamentally from other *patrons* by the limited size and special nature of their enterprises, and that while the laws recognized artisans' liabilities as employers they ignored their needs as laborers. A master craftsman earned his profits by work, not by some "value-added" speculation; his relations with his *compagnons* were paternal rather than exploitative. His earnings therefore had the moral value of wages, not of a return on capital. Finally, and most practically, artisanal businesses lacked the resources and flexibility of larger enterprises. These new social burdens, artisans warned to no avail in this instance, would crush petty production.

While the artisanal movement expressed its opinions on these matters of national import, its main attentions in these years were turned inward. The perennial squabbling and jockeying for position within the movement entered a new phase in the late 1920s, with the appearance of the first artisanal chambers of trades, the eagerly and long-awaited products of the 1925 Courtier law. Analogues of the chambers of commerce and agriculture already spread across the country, the chambers of trades were supposed to serve as the organs of artisans' economic and professional welfare: to regulate apprenticeship, organize expositions and contests, distribute information to constituents, and in general to act as conduit between the state and its small craftsmen citizens.[73] The Courtier law became an object of some optimism among artisan militants, who saw in the chambers the imminent palliative to a variety of frustrations. The chambers of trades promised to become a focus for artisanal consciousness and unity—especially important for a movement in which disunity appeared to be less a rule than a sacred duty—and a means to the general rehabilitation of artisanal production. A decaying level of skill in France? "Unfair" competition from a flood of foreigners and shoddy manufactures? A state administration forever on the side of the *gros*? The appearance of the chambers of trades would turn the tide.

And so artisans had geared up for the happy day. The Lyon Chamber of Trades, like the others of pre-1925 vintage, prepared to reconstitute itself according to the new guidelines.[74] The CGAF set its local action committees to laying the groundwork. The regional federations made ready to do battle in the new forums. Yet three years after the passage of the Courtier law, the first chambers of trades had failed to appear, and artisans' optimism soon dissipated.

Several things accounted for this delay. The first was the administrative gap that lay between the wish for a chamber and the fact of its establishment. "If there have been hold-ups in the constitution of the chambers," the CGAF complained, "it is because these chambers can be erected only by decrees which are issued only after numerous and necessarily long inquiries and consultations."[75] The enabling decree of April 14, 1928, coming almost three years after the bill itself, required that the request for a chamber of trades first obtain the approval of the local chamber of commerce, the local consultative chambers of arts and manufactures, the departmental and municipal councils, the departmental committee on technical education, the regional committee of applied arts, and the concerned professional organizations.[76] The minister of labor threw up a further roadblock when he ruled that all the preparatory work for a chamber had to be done independently by local artisans, which effectively scotched CGAF plans to lead a national campaign. Tailledet had written to Piquenard directly after the Ministry's decree of April 1928, proposing to facilitate the creation of chambers of trades in the seventy departments where the CGAF had well-organized groups; the action committees stood ready for orders from Paris. The CGAF had also begun its own census of the artisanat in order to speed up the process. The Labor Ministry authorized the census but rebuffed the Confédération's offer to collaborate with departmental officials.[77] Piquenard likewise put off a delegation from the UAF: "It took five years to get the chambers of agriculture going .... So be patient and know that the minister is sincerely with you, and that he will be forthcoming with serious and beneficial programs. But you have to wait."[78]

Going for the new chambers proved toughest, surprisingly, in the old centers of artisanal strength: Lyon, Toulouse, Bordeaux, Grenoble, Limoges, and especially Paris. In Lyon, after getting everything ready for the constitution of a chamber, the Association artisanale du Rhône approached the prefect for final authorization. He refused to give it.[79] In the department of the Haute-Loire artisans had obtained the support of the Departmental Council in 1927 but could make no further progress. In 1934, after a long struggle waged by the Le Puy Chamber of Commerce, the council even reversed its position.[80]

Indeed, the chambers of commerce proved to be the most dogged and effective opponents of the chambers of trades. Just as they had fought the Courtier law itself in the early 1920s, the chambers of commerce now did their best to obstruct its implementation. In front of the departmental and municipal councils, the committees of technical education, the prefects and the ministries, the chambers of commerce contended both that chambers of trades were redundant and that they would contribute to social division and class conflict. The Paris Chamber of Commerce wrote to the labor minister:

> It seems to us a poor idea to give artisans a special representation since a certain number of them are already electors for the chambers of commerce. The division of the Nation into increasingly narrow and specialized classes can only to our minds multiply antagonisms and encourage each one of them to call on legislators for individual privileges.[81]

They continued their battle to limit artisans' autonomy even after the chambers of trades began to function.

On the other side, those who tried to build the chambers of trades had to contend with the hostility of organized labor, which saw the chambers not as the refuge of independent skilled labor but as one more tool of the employers. In some ways this presented artisans with their greatest problems, for the Courtier law had provided that one-third of the members of each artisanal chamber would be made up of *compagnons*. Thus while the chambers of commerce could interfere only from the outside, the CGT could operate as a fifth column within the chambers themselves.

The workers found that they could express their opposition passively. *Compagnons* were considerably less organized than even the masters, which largely accounts for the perpetual difficulty in finding journeymen to stand for election to the chambers of trades. If participation in the chamber election averaged about 20 percent of the masters, it seldom surpassed 10 percent for the *compagnons*.[82] In the election to the Loiret Chamber of Trades in 1934, for example, while the masters were able to field two lists of candidates for each professional section, the journeymen had trouble putting together even one, and none could be found to stand for the food trades.[83]

The best organized *compagnons*, and therefore the most likely to succeed in the chamber elections, belonged to the CGT. At its 1931 national congress, the CGT, which found itself on this occasion the odd bedfellow of the chambers of commerce, ordered its syndical delegates in the departmental committees "to oppose energetically any consideration of the creation of chambers of trades . . . ."[84] In the Pyrénées-Orientales, for example, the journeymen elected to the new chamber of trades resigned en bloc at the first meeting.[85] The exasperated masters even began to discuss amending the Courtier law in order to eliminate workers' representation and counter these obstructionist tactics.[86]

Despite these considerable obstacles, slowly, painfully, artisanal chambers of trades started to appear. A decree of December 31, 1929, established the pioneer chambers in the Haute-Marne, Courtier's home department, and the

Seine-Inférieure, where Blaudy's Comité d'action artisanale de Chaumont and Dupuis' Union départementale de Rouen had combined their efforts.[87] By May 1931, however, only nine chambers had come into operation, while plans for another forty remained lodged in the bureaucratic apparatus.[88]

The trials of those who would create a chamber in the Seine department exemplified the problems artisans faced in the country as a whole. The establishment of a chamber of trades in the capital was crucial to the success of all the chambers, for with 80,000 masters and 15,000 *syndiqués* in the Seine, this chamber would inevitably dominate the others.[89] Artisans in the capital first filed a formal request for a chamber in August 1928, a few months after the enabling decree of April. For four years the Parisian artisans wrestled with the usual bureaucratic inertia and disfavor, as well as with the staunch resistance of the powerful Paris Chamber of Commerce. Working, as ever, through the medium of its parliamentary sponsors, the CGAF eventually prevailed upon the minister of labor to expedite matters, and in December 1932, the Departmental Council of the Seine at last approved the creation of a chamber of trades. Another year and a half elapsed, however, before elections were held. Thus the course of the formation of the most important chamber of trades required almost six years.[90]

Artisans' frustrations with the chambers were not confined to delays in their creation. Much to their chagrin, the leaders of the artisanal movement found that, once in operation, the chambers became anything but the hoped-for focuses of artisanal unity and influence. First, the chambers' practical utility fell far short of expectations. Recall that, in order to get his bill through the National Assembly, Courtier had been forced to eliminate its provisions for artisans' regulation of apprenticeship: a tactical retreat. But in the absence of jurisdiction over apprenticeship the chambers lacked a *raison d'être*. What other function were these institutions, so laboriously obtained, to fulfill? Until war and occupation created the essential job of rationing raw materials, this question went unanswered. As a result, while the leadership of the movement believed them a great victory, the chambers hardly touched the lives of most master craftsmen. Elections impassioned the militants. There is no evidence, however, that they engaged more than a minority of the rank and file. Second, the chambers failed dismally to reconcile competing elements of the movement. Instead, they became one more arena for organizational conflict.

Nowhere did the shortcomings of the Courtier law appear in greater relief than at the summit of the new structure, in the Assemblée des Présidents des Chambres de Métiers de France (APCMF). The 1925 law had provided for the formation of an executive council to coordinate the efforts of the individual chambers and to facilitate communication between these and the state. The APCMF got off to a promising start. The presidents of the first few chambers were invited by the CGAF to its national congress of 1931. There they met for the first time and, several days later, on June 11, joined with the presidents of the Alsace and Moselle chambers to form the APCMF. Its first official meeting was held in Paris, in October, at the offices of the Labor Ministry. Presidents from chambers of trades in the Corrèze, Côte-d'Or, Haute-Marne,

Loire-Inférieure, Pyrénées-Orientales, Seine-Inférieure, Moselle, and Alsace elected Albert Dupuis—who had bested Baudet in the Seine-Inférieure—their president.[91]

The participants saw the formation of the APCMF as a major step forward for the artisanat, one which gave it a symbolic parity with other sectors of French society and a chance to put its professional house in order. But the existence of the APCMF raised more questions than it answered. What place would it occupy in a divided artisanal movement? Would it ally with the Alsatians? Would it become the pawn of the CGAF? Would it be a champion of artisanal federalism or would it be able to chart a course of its own, to become *the* voice of the artisanat? A three-way struggle developed, as the traditional tussle between the CGAF and the Alsace Chamber of Trades was complicated by the APCMF's own claim to leadership.

The CGAF, as we have seen, had worked hard to ensure that the chambers of trades would become a reality and had encouraged the formation of the APCMF. The CGAF's enthusiasm, however, rested on the assumption that its own legions would dominate these institutions and that the whole edifice would enhance its position within the artisanal movement. The leadership in Paris, through the local action committees, attended to the birth of each chamber in order to make certain that this would be the case, even, it seems, opposing the formation of chambers that the CGAF felt would line up with the opposition.[92] For Tailledet and his colleagues, chambers of trades controlled by the allies of Alsace were worse than no chambers at all.

In the event, the CGAF's expectations suffered a rude shock, as it did not manage to control all of the chambers of trades or obstruct those that escaped it. And these included some of the most important: Dijon, Bordeaux, Lille, Grenoble, Orléans, Calais, and Rouen.[93] Furthermore, the CGAF's failures in the local chambers inevitably foiled its plans to dominate the APCMF. Many of the presidents were in fact the confessed enemies of the CGAF's action committees. Even some of those who were *confédérés*, more loyal to their local mandates than to the Paris leadership, saw the APCMF as an independent actor in the movement; or, as representatives of regional bodies, found themselves attracted to the regionalist program of the Alsatians. The CGAF's attempts in 1933 to discipline its member presidents produced a backlash, and only a year's worth of cajoling and threats to remove CGAF subsidies produced the Union des chambres de métiers confédérées at the Chaumont congress of June 1934.[94] The new union aimed to pursue the goals of the CGAF through the medium of the chambers of trades and to defend its point of view in the APCMF. It was led by the Seine Chamber of Trades.

As they developed, relations between the APCMF and the most powerful chamber of trades were, at best, strained and, at worst, hostile. The March 1934 elections to the Seine Chamber of Trades had given the CGAF thirty-two of the forty-eight seats reserved for masters; only the food and construction trades and the *métiers d'art* had voted for the candidates of the UAF.[95] Georges Grandadam, vice-president of the CGAF, became president of the Seine chamber; Bardet, also an officer of the CGAF, its vice-president. The chamber of trades in the capital thus became a virtual extension of the CGAF, a means for it to control the APCMF if it could and harass it if it could not.

In the APCMF's meeting of November 1934, the presidents *confédérés*, seeking to make this control manifest, moved that the Assembly locate its planned secretariat at the Cité Clémentel in Paris, headquarters both of the CGAF and of the Seine Chamber of Trades. They argued that the Cité Clémentel alone offered the kind of facilities that could make the APCMF effective in national affairs. The other presidents recognized that this would result in the de facto subordination of the APCMF to the CGAF and voted to refuse the offer. The Seine chamber, declaring, first, that it had no need for the secretariat's services and, second, that in its present state the APCMF would be ineffectual, left the meeting. Grandadam then informed the assembly that the Seine chamber would take its place only when the APCMF conformed to the following demands: that it establish a functioning secretariat in Paris and that it rescind the resolutions it had passed—sponsored, needless to say, by the Alsace Chamber—insulting to the CGAF.[96]

Encouraged by the presidents *confédérés*, negotiations between the Seine Chamber of Trades and the APCMF proceeded intermittently throughout the 1930s, although for the most part unsuccessfully. A vicious circle developed: The APCMF would make an offer that the Seine Chamber of Trades could not accept; the chamber would counter with a demand that the presidents could not meet. Meanwhile, the two organizations slandered each other in their respective presses, the APCMF hurling the familiar epithets of "tyranny" and "traitor" at the Seine Chamber of Trades and the chamber dismissing the APCMF as irrelevant.

On several occasions an agreement seemed imminent. In the summer of 1936, for example, Grandadam attended a special meeting called by the APCMF to coordinate an artisanal response to the Popular Front social legislation. The following November Grandadam sat in on the regular assembly meetings, though only as an observer because the two sides were still unable to agree on the Seine chamber's financial contribution. By May 1937, however, Grandadam had withdrawn once more. Only in 1939 did the Seine Chamber of Trades and the APCMF finally reach an understanding. The chamber of trades agreed to pay its full obligation of 5,000 francs to the APCMF, but Grandadam still refused to sit on the secretariat or serve on any of the assembly's committees. The compromise was in any case moot, for by 1939 the CGAF had decisively won the battle for leadership of the artisanal movement and the APCMF had ceased to be any threat at all.[97]

At this point it is necessary to digress, for in the early 1930s the attention of the APCMF and the rest of the artisanal movement had shifted to what was the most consuming issue of these years: redefining the Artisanat. Differences of opinion about the boundaries of the class had long been a pea under the movement's mattress, for here the conflict between the sometimes abstract and elusive social visions of the CGAF and the Alsace Chamber of Trades found their concrete expression. Would the movement belong to the *petits* masters represented by the CGAF or to the *moyens* and *gros* businessmen like those who ran the artisanat in the recovered provinces? As a matter of jurisprudence, the multiple definitions employed by the state for taxation and credit indicated the government's thinking on the subject— *artisan* meant *petit*—but they did not decide the issue.

After 1928 the existence of chambers of trade only gave the question more weight without answering it in any definitive fashion. The Courtier law of 1925 had a vague definition of the artisan as a petty craftsman, practicing an "artisanal" trade, taking an active part in the productive process. But how petty? Which trades, exactly? And what constituted an "active part"? The legislature had left these thorny problems for the administration to resolve. In a circular of July 17, 1928, addressed to the impending elections for the chambers of trades, the labor minister issued these guidelines: a master artisan was one who took a "*courante*, constant, and genuinely effective" hand in production. The minister implied that he would go on to fix the maximum number of assistants for each *métier* after a survey of the artisanal professions and hinted that these numbers would be low, which pleased the CGAF. But the minister explicitly added the food trades to the chambers, which displeased the CGAF, because it considered these to be *commerçants*. For the moment, however, the government went no further.[98] The result was widespread confusion and conflict in the original elections for the initial chambers.

In July 1931, Senator Courtier, seeking to force the minister's hand, filed a bill aimed at more rigorously delineating the artisanat for purposes of membership in the chambers of trades:

> By master artisan it is meant independent workers of either sex, exercising personally and in their own behalf, without being under the direction of a patron, a manual trade, justifying their professional ability by a prior apprenticeship and/or prolonged practice of this trade, carrying out this labor alone or with the aid of associates: members of the family, journeymen, or apprentices.
>
> The number of assistants or apprentices is limited to a number set by the necessity that an artisan unite in his person the direction and execution of his enterprise without the aid of a foreman.[99]

Courtier's original proposal of 1931, although it implied some upper limit on the number of *compagnons*, did not set one. He soon amended this and indicated that the maximum would be fixed at ten, though it was understood that the minister of labor would ordinarily set the number much lower, usually at two or three.[100]

Courtier was, in fact, the CGAF's legal councilor, and the two were, as usual, in concert. The confederation had traditionally insisted on distinguishing between *petits*, *moyens*, and *gros* artisans. It had always considered the *petits* the truest members of the class and concentrated on defending their interests. Before 1931, however, the CGAF had always balked at any comprehensive mathematical definition of the artisanat. Indeed, when a proposition resembling Courtier's was introduced at the CGAF congress in 1928,

Courtier himself had replied that such a limit would be impractical and that the issue of assistants pertained only to fiscal and credit questions. For the chambers of trades, Courtier stuck to his 1925 definition: a patron who participated *directly* in production was an artisan. The CGAF leadership at the time concurred.[101]

What then provoked a reversal of CGAF policy only three years later? First, by 1931 the country was beginning to feel the first effects of the world economic crisis and the consequent squeeze on the French budget. Tailledet and Grandadam feared that the government's concern for revenue would lead it to rescind artisans' fiscal privileges. They pointed out at the CGAF congress of 1932 that legislation to this effect had already been proposed. In order to protect the *petit artisan fiscal*, therefore, Grandadam contended that the artisanat needed to define itself more precisely.[102]

The leadership of the CGAF made much of these fears, but they were, in fact, somewhat disingenuous. The attempt to tighten up the definition of artisan really addressed a quite different problem. As the chambers of trades began to come into operation in the early 1930s, the CGAF confronted a new challenge to the dominance of the artisanal movement it had won in the 1920s. In the absence of such limitations on the property of artisans eligible to vote for the chambers of trades, the Confédération, as noted earlier, experienced some embarrassing setbacks.

The most serious of these occurred in the Loiret in 1931, when the CGAF's candidates lost to those from the Union de commerce et d'industrie. This union, led by Henri Huguet, a *gros* artisan—Pégeot, president of the Calvados Chamber of Trades, had accused him in the APCMF of employing twenty-five or thirty workers—and allied to the Alsatians, triumphed despite the CGAF's threats to cut off all subsidies to the Loiret Chamber of Trades if its people lost.[103] The CGAF blamed its failure on the interference of "merchants and industrialists," and appealed the results to the Council of State, which turned aside this complaint.[104] It was in response to events in the Loiret that the CGAF, having lost the game, decided to change the rules.

The immediate result of the CGAF's campaign to redefine the artisanat was a return to the vitriolic exchanges that had characterized the artisanal press in the mid-1920s. The *Artisan*, of Le Puy, labeled the mathematical definition the product of a "conception Marxiste." The Alsace Chamber of Trades, through the *Gazette des Métiers*, cited the circular of 1928 and complained that Courtier's proposal ran counter to administrative precedent. Fernand Peter, the new president of the Alsace Chamber of Trades, and Ley also circulated a pamphlet in which they referred to the CGAF leadership as "egotists" and "plutocrats." "Enough of this Dictatorship!" wrote Peter. The *Gazette* further accused Jean Lerolle, the labor minister in the left-coalition government that had supported Courtier, of trying to turn the chambers of trades into "instruments de classe." At the UAF national congress in June 1933, ten of the fifteen regional federations supported a resolution condemning the restrictive definition.[105] The CGAF returned the fire, accusing the Alsatians of betraying the movement by clinging to their anomalous German statutes.[106]

This bitterness naturally spilled over into the APCMF. It tabled the question of the new definition in its meeting of May 1932, when Peter presented a report that was predictably hostile to the revision of the original Courtier law. He argued that, since the social and economic reality of the artisanat was fluid, the definition should reflect this:

> If in fact the head of the business works himself at his trade, if, by his training and his professional career, he is one of us, if the work that goes on in his workshop is of a manual nature, outside of any specialization and marked automation of the functions and means of production, if it produces for individual orders, then in our estimation this entrepreneur or manufacturer is still an artisan. The fact that he might employ a foreman in no way detracts from his artisanal nature.[107]

It was also a question of political expediency, Peter added. The broader the definition of the artisanat, the larger it would be, the greater would be its weight in national affairs and the more effectively it would be able to fulfill its central role in the renovation of French society. He concluded that it was unfair and counterproductive to exclude some artisans from the chambers of trades simply because they had succeeded too well.

The APCMF did not vote on Peter's resolution on this occasion. It considered the matter again at the assembly's next meeting, in November 1932, and this time Peter's position received the APCMF's endorsement, over the objections of some presidents *confédérés*, but with the support of others. Having suffered a temporary setback, the pro-CGAF forces—those who approved or were supposed to approve of the new definition — prepared for another round. Those presidents *confédérés* who had originally voted for Peter's report were called to syndical order at the CGAF's national congress at Avignon in early 1933.[108] Then, in the APCMF meeting of May 1933, the *confédérés*, led by Pégeot, challenged the previous vote on the mathematical limitation of the artisanat. A lengthy and acrimonious debate followed. Peter reiterated his contention that the *confédérés* would deprive the chambers of trades of their healthiest elements and make it impossible for them to perform the functions for which they were created. Pégeot accused Peter of nefariously seeking "nothing less than the dissolution of the National Artisanat, to the benefit of medium and big business."[109] This time confederal discipline held. A new vote reversed the APCMF's position and recorded a majority vote of 17–10 in support of the new Courtier definition.

Outnumbered first in the legislature and now in the APCMF, on the brink of being evicted from the artisanal movement altogether, the Alsatians began to lay plans for yet one more attempt to seize the leadership of the movement from the CGAF. They intended to bring together all those artisans who objected to the Confédération's goals and methods, united more than ever by the CGAF's latest effort to trim the artisanat to its syndicalist and slightly leftist conception. "The Artisanat," declared Peter to the assembled opponents of the CGAF, "will be regionalist and corporatist or it will not be."[110] "Against the narrow conception of the CGAF," the *Gazette des Métiers* proclaimed, "we support a broad conception. To its purely external and arbitrary criteria [of the artisanat] we propose reasoned and organic [ones]."[111]

A meeting was held in Paris in March 1933 to prepare the formation of the Comité d'entente et d'action artisanales (CEAA), which brought out, according to the *Artisan*, the representatives of some 200,000 artisans.[112] The CEAA convened its first general assembly in Paris in November 1933, coincidental with the biannual meeting of the APCMF. Delegates were present from a number of chambers of trades, led of course by the Strasbourg and Moselle chambers, from the nineteen regional federations of the UAF, and from a variety of local syndicates and artisanal associations—predominantly blacksmiths, bakers, butchers, and groups from Alsace-Lorraine. The assembly elected Peter its president, and distributed the vice-presidencies among other artisanal eminences: Bulnois, president of the UAF; Marlier, president of the Moselle Chamber of Trades; Leleu, miller and president of the Union des Artisans du Nord; Périer, president of the General Syndicate of French butchers; Huguet, president of the disputed Loiret Chamber of Trades; Bergue, president of the Artisanal Union of French butchers; Peillon, president of the National Confederation of blacksmiths, wheelwrights and farriers; and Michel, from the Confederation of pastry and candymakers (*pâtissiers-confisiers*).[113] The CEAA even set up its own parliamentary defense group. Comprising only the deputies and senators from Alsace-Lorraine, however, it never had more than symbolic importance.

The new CEAA won some small victories at first. The places on the CNE formerly reserved for the "consortium" of the UAF and the Alsace Chamber of Trades fell to the disposition of the CEAA, for example. It further enjoyed the usual, but rather meaningless, presence of government officials at its congresses.

This latest attempt to topple the CGAF from the top of the artisanal heap eventually proved no more effective than earlier ones—and as before for reasons of structural weakness and political ingenuousness. The CEAA arranged itself in a loose, decentralized fashion, in self-conscious contrast to the CGAF's top-heavy cohesion. It organized as an association rather than a syndical confederation. This enabled it to include the Alsace and Moselle Chambers of Trades but effectively denied it the many administrative privileges enjoyed by the CGAF.

Questions of procedure and policy soon split the CEAA as they had its predecessor, the UFRA. Secession followed dissension, with the UAF pulling out even before the CEAA's second national congress in 1934, over the issues of proportional voting within the CEAA and representation to the CNE. Besides, the UAF, while it shared the Alsatians' distaste for Tailledet and Grandadam, was composed of syndicalist-minded elements and could never feel completely at home with the CEAA's corporatist disposition. Subsequent attempts to conciliate the UAF came to naught.[114]

All of this looked depressingly familiar, as if the artisanal movement were locked in some compulsive dance, performing the same pointless embraces, spins, and breaks over and over. Yet something essential had changed in the years between the UFRA and the CEAA: the historical context. The distance between those who put the accent on regional freedom and those who stressed the effectiveness of confederal discipline was no wider than it had always been; nor was that between syndicalist and corporatist tendencies. By the mid-1930s, however, the nation's economic and political fabric had begun to develop some noticeable tears. At the moment of the 1934 CEAA congress in Lille, the French economy was already depressed and spiraling downward. The events of February 6, had shaken the foundations of the republic, and Hitler had consolidated his power across the Rhine. Under these circumstances, the CEAA was drawn, in a more immediate way than the UFRA, to questions of national politics. The players were the same, but the stakes of the game had been raised.

Understandably, the contraction of the artisanat met none of the criticism from the chambers of commerce or the CGT that had greeted the first Courtier law in 1925.[115] The bill authorizing the new definition breezed through the Senate in January 1933. In June it received the enthusiastic endorsement of the Chamber of Deputies' Labor Commission, and on January 16, 1934, it was approved by a vote of 558–21, with only the deputies from Alsace-Lorraine in the opposition. On March 27, it became law: "A victory for the CGAF," wrote Hubert Ley, "but a defeat for the Artisanat."[116]

For membership in the chambers of trades, the new law set a theoretical maximum of ten *compagnons* per master artisan, and it established a new Register of Trades to identify those who were eligible. Those artisans sympathetic to the CGAF hurried to offer the labor minister their advice on where to draw the line. The Groupement artisanal de Béziers, for example, considered 150 trades and suggested as many as three journeymen be permitted only in the case of ten; only for quarriers did it think four workers were appropriate to an artisan. The syndicate of *coiffeurs* in the Allier, Nièvre, and Puy-de-Dôme thought four the limit of an artisanal salon.[117] The minister apparently saw things similarly, for in practice he never set the allowable number of *compagnons* above five.[118] As was the case for all legislation on French artisans, the new law left untouched the German system still in force in the departments of the Moselle, the Bas-Rhin, and the Haut-Rhin.

With the restrictive definition the CGAF scored a tactical victory, but reality did not come up to expectations. The artisanat got no closer to a *statut fiscal artisanal*, which the CGAF had hoped would extend to all artisans the benefits until then reserved for *petits*. In view of the government's budget difficulties this could hardly have surprised the law's sponsors. It was a moment for the defense, and not the expansion, of tax advantages.

On the other hand, the exclusion of *gros* artisans did serve to soften the CGT's opposition to the chambers of trades and to increase the CGAF's influence within them. The most telling reversal of fortunes occurred in 1934 when new elections were held for the Loiret Chamber of Trades. With many of those who had cast ballots in 1931 now ineligible, CGAF candidates won fourteen of the eighteen contested places. The Loiret Chamber of Trades sent Monsieur Maillou, a *confédéré*, to replace Huguet at the next meeting of the APCMF.[119]

Meanwhile, new chambers of trades began to appear at an accelerated pace after 1931. There were twenty-seven chambers in 1933, forty-four in 1936, and seventy-six on the eve of the war. Even so, they never remotely became the vehicles of an artisanal revival, for they possessed almost no real authority. They could not control entry into the artisanal professions. They had no power to restrain or punish *travail noir*. Before the enactment of the Walter-Paulin law on apprenticeship in 1937, they had no province even over apprenticeship—which had been the original argument for their existence. With an inadequate revenue base, the chambers lacked the wherewithal to provide needed social services to their constituents.

More chambers of trades meant more artisanal presidents and a growing APCMF. The assembly's budget, 26,000 francs in 1933, reached 125,000 in 1939.[120] As the quasi-official representative of the artisanat, moreover, the APCMF also acquired a minor share of the movement's small influence within the administration.[121] Yet the APCMF continued to be hamstrung by the internecine struggles within the artisanat. Peter and Ley treated the APCMF as an agent of CEAA designs. Conversely, Tailledet and Grandadam considered it, at best, useless and, at worst, a den of Alsatian subversion. They applied themselves to excluding the APCMF from government patronage. Such real power as existed within the movement continued to rest with the syndicates and federations, and these owed their first allegiance to the CGAF or the CEAA. The journals of the regional artisanal groups and professional syndicates, who rarely mentioned the chambers of trades, did not print a word about goings-on in the APCMF. Eventually, the assembly fell into a pattern that betrayed its irrelevance, conducting heated debates and producing piles of redundant and unheeded resolutions.[122]

The CEAA and the APCMF were not the only organizational innovations of the early 1930s. The CGAF and the CEAA adorned their structures with cooperatives, technical services, mutuality funds, and satellite organizations for such special cases as female and rural artisans.[123] The most important of the new auxiliaries was the INM, established under CGAF auspices in 1931. This institute addressed itself to the movement's *cadres*. Its journal, the *Cahiers de l'Artisanat*, sought to educate the artisanat's leadership, not to make propaganda among the rank and file. The INM's goal was a practical one. It aimed to promote collaboration between master tradesmen and the country's elites: doctors, legal experts, economists, scientists, and especially engineers. This, its creators believed, would "permit the leadership [of the artisanat] to have a comprehensive view of all economic, political, and social problems bearing directly or indirectly—and whether one likes it or not*—on the artisanat."[124] As the engineer, Laffaille, explained:

> Even as Industry, the Artisanat, in order to work better, in order to work under the best physical conditions, in a word, to live better, must address itself (without—and God keep us from that—falling into a "technocratism", more dangerous to artisans because each depends so much on his individual personality) . . . to the engineers who have so much to offer it.[125]

The INM established model workshops to stimulate the technical upgrading of artisanal production and offered services, such as the Technical, Artistic, and Commercial Center and the Medical Foundation for the French Artisanat—all of which were located at the CGAF's Cité Clémentel in Paris.[126] The *Cahiers*, published each month between October 1934 and May 1939, carried relevant artisanal statistics, detailed analyses of tax and social security obligations, updates on the condition of artisans in other countries, articles on ideology and organization, book reviews, and special reports on everything from personal hygiene to the use of electricity. For example, its final number, in May 1939, was devoted to the INM's "Week of Plastics and Rubber."[127] All this highlighted a central aspect of the CGAF's grand strategy: to save the artisanat by making it economically viable.

Not content with reinforcing the artisanat's French flanks, the CGAF became involved in organizing the artisanat across European frontiers, a refinement of the old "Petit Bourgeois International." As early as 1923, Tailledet had been present at the creation of the Confédération internationale des classes moyennes (CICM). The CICM, based in Brussels, had supported "private property, the private economy, and independent labor" and combatted "all tendencies which menace the existence and normal development" of small property—by which it of course meant socialism and excessive industrialization.[128] In 1928 Tailledet succeeded in separating artisans from the rest of the middle classes *internationales*. Two years later the Italian government hosted the constituent congress of the Institut International de l'Artisanat. Vincent Buronzo, the Fascist chief of the Italian artisanat presided, while Mussolini himself came out to greet the delegates. The congress scheduled its first regular meeting for Paris in 1931 and decided to place the institute's permanent offices at the Cité Clémentel.[129]

The institute held annual congresses thereafter, hearing reports on the problems of petty producers internationally and in individual nations, lauding artisans as the "soul" of civilization and calling for representation on the League of Nations' International Labor Office (Bureau International du Travail).[130] The international solidarity of the artisanat, however, proved as fragile

---

*An oblique reference to the regrettable need for modern techniques

as the domestic variety. Ideological and political issues soon split the Institut International de l'Artisanat as they had the CGAF. The "class," or syndicalist, approach to artisanal politics internationally drew its inspiration and its strength from the CGAF; it ranged petty producers somewhat to the left of the political center. The "corporatist" orientation of the Alsatians drew them toward the Germans and Italians, far to the right. Predictably, in 1932 the corporatist groups left the Institute to form the Center for the International Artisanat, based in Rome and headed by Buronzo. The Institut International de l'Artisanat remained in Paris, the international agent of the CGAF.[131]

As the artisanal movement established itself in the mid-1920s, it swung back and forth between promise and frustration. On the one hand, the efforts of its missionaries carried the new artisanal consciousness across the country. The number of local unions of tradesmen, departmental action committees, and regional federations multiplied, and these continued to fill the growing ranks of the national groups. In 1924 the CGAF had claimed to have some 100,000 adherents. By 1933, the leading artisanal organizations together put their membership at around 340,000. These numbers probably exaggerate the scale but not the fact of the movement's growth. The parliamentary defense group for artisans flourished under the *Cartel des Gauches*, elected in 1924, and the *Union Nationale*, triumphant in 1928, as it had in the immediate postwar period. In 1930 the group contained more than 350 deputies and senators.[132] Likewise, electoral shifts from left to right did not stem the flow of legislation favoring petty producers. By the early 1930s the Parliament had satisfied artisans' demands for protection of their commercial property against seizure for bankruptcy and inclusion in public works.[133] A large part of the artisanal program remained unfulfilled, but such progress as had been made since 1923 bred optimism within the movement.

On the other hand, the movement splintered as it grew. The apostles of the artisanat had recognized their differences from the beginning but put them aside in the hopes that they could be reconciled; however, this proved to be impossible. Fraternal feeling wore thin against the friction of incompatible perspectives and priorities. Unable to contain this conflict, the movement split and split again. Unity disappeared beneath a cascade of acronyms. Personal rivalries intensified institutional and strategic disagreements. The movement's friends in the government did their best to restore the movement's lost coherence, but unsuccessfully.

A second wave of organization in the early 1930s caused further disruptions. The chambers of trades, in which artisans had put so much stock, began to appear, the assembly of their presidents to function; but these did not bring the expected influence and concord to the movement, just a new set of disputes. The formation of the CEAA in 1933 merely institutionalized old antagonisms; it did not move them any closer to resolution. Even when French artisans reached across national borders they carried their hostility with them. Growth and factiousness threatened to cancel each other out.

Whatever influence the artisanat did enjoy vindicated the tactical and organizational notions of Tailledet and Grandadam, whose CGAF dominated the divided movement. The Confédération's dedication to *petits* artisans lent it a homogeneity and unity of purpose. Its syndicalist structure enabled it to capitalize on the administrative jurisprudence that privileged such formations. In addition, the CGAF's discipline gave the leadership a political leverage that the more diffuse organizations could not match; its concentration on action in Paris lent CGAF efforts a focus and an access to the corridors of power that groups with their headquarters in Strasbourg or Lyon lacked. The CEAA, while it might rival the CGAF in membership, could never compete for political clout.

We have seen, finally, that the artisanal movement was more than unreflective interest politics, that behind the chase after tax breaks and commercial security lay a grander conception of what French society *ought* to be. Recall the parable of the life of Jean Marbréry. It told of paternalism and comradery, of the deep satisfaction of life in a community, of the joy in a job executed with creativity and skill. Different groups emphasized different aspects of this idyll, and the artisanal worldview was only rarely articulated as a whole. Nevertheless, in its journals, its manifestos, and its petitions to the government the artisanal movement constructed a vision of a society in which the middle classes would no longer be the victims of history but rather the "dorsal fin" of the nation, steering a course of moderate change, moderate prosperity, and moderate happiness. Artisans imagined a kind of trades-*Gemeinschaft*, a world of "moral economy" where skill would count for more than productivity, and where *le bon sens* and not utility would be the measure of value. They dreamed of a stable society, based on a loving, dutiful household and an ordered professional life, in which relations between craftsmen and customers would comprise more than the "cash nexus"; a society where, as it existed in the collective memory of the Faubourg Saint-Antoine, "Furniture-makers were considered artists, [and] women wanted to marry them."[134] In the words of Claude-François Bénard:

> In order for harmony to reign in society, we believe that the social scale must have, between the top and the bottom, a series of intermediate steps tying the extremes by degrees more numerous than the spaces between them. Society is not composed of two great categories, rich and poor. Such a dichotomy is full of dangers. The [social] pyramid has to rest on its [broad side], and for that there must be a large and prosperous middle class. Such a class is an unfailing source of progress for the development and the intellectual culture of a people. It is from the middle class that come the men of art, of science, of technology and education. For this reason we declare that the ruin of the middle class would lead without question to the end of intellectual excellence and cultural greatness of France.[135]

To be sure, this was a social philosophy pregnant with political possibilities. In a broad sense, artisans' construction of the moral economy translated to a generic populism: the strange brew of the radical and the reactionary that followed on the celebration of the "community" and of the "little guy" within it. It located the artisanat's natural political home among those who rejected the Darwinian metaphor of liberalism and Marxism. As economic crisis and political immobility descended on France, the artisanal movement was primed to take its place in the national debate on the reconstruction of the republic.

3

Artisans Face the Crisis, 1932–1936

As capitalism ground to a halt in the wake of the crash of the stock market in New York, as banks failed, factories shut down, and soup lines lengthened across Europe and North America, the French economy remained peculiarly buoyant. Unemployment was virtually nonexistent. The index of industrial production reached an interwar peak of 140 (1913 = 100) in 1930.[1] Gold poured into the Bank of France, reflecting the world's confidence in the franc. The French congratulated themselves on their healthy and well-balanced economy.[2]

It was a short-lived reprieve. In the "black year" of 1931 the world depression washed over the Hexagon, in what Julian Jackson has called an "economic Sedan." Industrial production decreased 17 percent, steel production 29 percent, exports 35 percent, employment in large enterprises (more than ten employees) 10 percent, and wholesale food prices 15 percent. The average work week dropped to 44.5 hours, while unemployment quintupled. If the cost of living also went down by 10 percent, in the scramble almost nobody noticed.[3]

By comparison, the French collapse was never as dramatic as those in the United States and Germany. Unemployment in France, for example, did not reach 1 million,[4] as the country, buffered by a modest industrial development, escaped the deep trauma of the more industrialized nations. Unfortunately, as the rest of the world adjusted and took the first steps toward recovery in 1933 and 1934, the French economy, weighed down by a tenacious deflationism and a doting monetary policy, continued to sink.[5]

In order to assess the impact of this economic crisis on master craftsmen, one must look at the overall performance of the French economy between the world wars and at the development of petty production within it. Ac-

TABLE 3.1.   Evolution of *petits* enterprises: 1921–1936*

	Number of isolés and establishments without employees (in thousands)		
1921	1926	1931	1936
4,730.9	4,359.7	4,290.1	4,258.5

Source: Cahen, "La concentration des établissements," p. 846.

*Since these figures include agriculture, with its masses of small holdings and *petits chefs d'entreprise*, it overstates the place of the smallest units in the other sectors of the economy.

cording to François Caron, the French economy has suffered an unwarranted reputation for mediocrity. Beginning in the early years of the twentieth century and continuing through the 1920s, he observes, French industry underwent a large-scale technological and organizational change, a "slow and broken" concentration of the forces of production. It became, in effect, not just bigger but more openly capitalistic.[6]

How did this broad capitalization of the economy affect the situation of the handicrafts in France? Table 3.1 shows how the absolute number of the smallest units of production, those with no employees, decreased throughout the interwar period. Two qualifications must, however, be added: first, that this trend slowed markedly in the early 1930s and, second, that these always remained the immense majority of French enterprises.† The dwindling of the smallest units did not, however, mean that these necessarily declined as a percentage of all enterprises, since the total number of businesses had been falling steadily since the beginning of the century. *Petites entreprises* dropped from 67.9 percent of the total in 1921 to 67.2 percent in 1926, but then climbed back to 68.5 percent in 1931 and to 69.9 percent in 1936. As Table 3.2 indicates, what in fact was happening was that up to the depression the largest and the smallest units both increased their presence in the economy, while the number of enterprises employing from one to five workers diminished.

To further appreciate the degree of concentration within the French economy, we must also look at the number and distribution of the working population up and down the scale of businesses. The total number of wage earners (*salariés*) increased to 9,544,700 (1.08 percent) between 1921 and 1931. Predictably, this expansion occurred unevenly among larger and smaller enterprises. Medium-sized businesses employed 42.1 percent of all workers in 1921 and only 32.9 percent in 1931; however, in 1936 this number leapt to 36.2 percent. Conversely, the largest enterprises, those with more than 500 employees, which employed 14 percent of workers in 1921, had 18 percent in 1931, but only 16.5 percent in 1936.[7] Looking exclusively at the industrial sector (Table 3.3), we see that the number of establishments employing between one and five workers peaked in 1926, a result of the postwar flood into the *petit patronat*,[8] and then fell precipitously until 1936. Larger businesses expanded up to 1931, before shrinking back in 1936. A slightly different

†Within the category of the smallest producers, the number of those identifying themselves as *isolés* was declining, while the number of those identifying themselves as establishments without employees was growing.

TABLE 3.2.   Number of establishments by employees: 1921–1936

Number of employees	Number of establishments (in thousands)			
	1921	*1926*	*1931*	*1936*
1–5	2,064.1	1,939.4	1,775.9	1,689.6
6–10	93.4	97.9	97.5	81.7
11–50	65.1	75.4	79.8	64.8
51–100	8.2	9.4	10.3	7.9
101–500	6.2	7.5	8.0	6.5
> 500	0.9	1.2	1.3	1.0
Total	2,237.9	2,130.8	1,972.8	1,851.5

Number of employees	Number of establishments (percentage of total)			
	1921	*1926*	*1931*	*1936*
1–5	92.2	91.0	90.0	91.3
6–10	4.2	4.6	4.9	4.4
11–50	2.9	3.5	4.1	3.5
51–100	0.4	0.4	0.5	0.4
101–500	0.3	0.4	0.4	0.35
> 500		0.1	0.1	0.05
Total	100.0	100.0	100.0	100.0

Source: Cahen, "La concentration des établissements," p. 848.

pattern characterized the commercial sector (which included such artisanal professions as the hairdressing and food trades) where the number of medium-sized enterprises increased throughout the period 1921-1936, while the larger businesses suffered a falling off after 1931.

Carré, Dubois, and Malinvaud's survey of French economic history confirms Caron's and Cahen's picture of industrial concentration. They found that, whereas in 1926 35 percent of workers were employed in enterprises with from zero to four workers, this figure slipped to 28 percent in 1931 before rebounding to 33 percent in 1936.[9] Cahen notes, completing her analysis of overall concentration, that the ratio of employees to employers in nonagri-

TABLE 3.3.   Evolution of establishments in industry: 1921–1936

Number of employees	Number of establishments (in thousands)			
	1921	*1926*	*1931*	*1936*
1–5	415,785	457,689	394,840	360,556
6–50	76,083	93,219	96,058	74,451
51–500	11,812	13,769	14,530	11,001
> 500	798	1,049	1,107	827
Total	504,478	565,726	506,545	446,835

Source: Cahen, "La concentration des établissements," p. 859.

cultural businesses grew considerably up until 1931, and then declined slightly until 1936.

Thus the French economy in the first third of the twentieth century developed in two seemingly contradictory directions. The first was that of capital concentration. From 1906 to 1931 France contained an increasing number of large firms, larger than ever before. But this by no means signaled the disappearance of the smallest firms. Interwar France remained overwhelmingly a nation of petty producers: nine enterprises out of ten in the watershed year of 1931, excluding the swelling mass of *isolés*. Because of the complex nature of economic growth, however, this was not evident at the time. It certainly was not clear to the artisanal movement, which seemed most often to vacillate between a rhetorical confidence that, as the "soul of France," the artisanat would never die and the fear that industrialization was destroying it.

How many of these *petites entreprises* were artisanal in nature? Not surprisingly, the vagueness of the question and the imprecision of the evidence produced divergent estimates. In late March 1935 Albert Paulin, the artisanat's commander on the parliamentary front, interpellated the government over its planned changes in artisanal fiscality. In figures that he claimed to have taken from a study by the economist Marcel de Ville-Chabrol, Paulin reported that in twenty years the artisanat had lost 1,375,216 enterprises, which was more than one-third of the total.[10]

Paulin's statistics might have impressed his colleagues in the Chamber of Deputies, but it appears that de Ville-Chabrol's numbers were both terribly inflated and overly pessimistic. Compare them, for example, to those of Louis Lagaillarde and Hermine Rabinovitch, who, using the 1921 census, identified 466,066 artisanal workshops and 1,199,511 persons engaged in artisanal production: masters, journeymen, and apprentices.[11]Alternatively, Michel Debré, and others, employing the 1926 census figures, discovered approximately 2.5 million people active in the artisanat. These comprised 1,025,000 artisanal businesses: 465,000 *établissements* of which 35,000 had no employees, 400,000 between one and five, 30,000 between six and ten, and 560,000 artisans *isolés*.[12] Again looking at the 1926 census, the two powers within the artisanal movement, the CGAF and the Alsace Chamber of Trades, found themselves in substantial if temporary agreement on the matter of the artisanat's population. Both, counted approximately 1,300,000 artisanal workshops, with a total working population of some 3,400,000—exaggerations meant to maximize the artisanat's importance in the national economy.[13]

This strategic consensus collapsed in the 1930s. As the CGAF and the CEAA wrestled for control of the movement, their definitions of the artisanat, and therefore their estimations of its size, increasingly diverged. In one ill-tempered debate in the APCMF, Paul Réal (Grenoble) of the CEAA proposed a population for the artisanat of 6,237,000 masters, journeymen, and apprentices. President Didier-Jean (Marne), arguing the CGAF position, counted only 3,572,080.[14] These wildly conflicting figures demonstrate once again that defining and tallying artisans was as much a matter of polemics as of statistical method.

Two points emerge from this array of numbers. First, there existed in France a large and relatively constant population of master artisans for the first forty or so years of this century. Predictions of the demise of petty production missed the mark; the workshop did not disappear under competition from the factory. The most reliable estimates set the number of artisanal enterprises between the world wars at between 850,000 and 900,000.[15] Second, the artisanat by whatever definition remained the province of small masters, its numbers dominated by those who worked by themselves or only with their spouses. For a slightly later period, Mourier calculated that the average artisanal workshop employed only 0.64 *compagnons* and trained but 0.14 apprentices, 8 percent of whom were family members. In economic fact, *artisan* almost always denoted *petit*. The prosperous master with a shop full of *compagnons* and apprentices was the rare exception.[16] The real transformation for an artisanal business was not to cross the threshold of five or ten journeymen, the frontiers of official definitions, but to hire the first employee, bearing out, perhaps, the old wisdom that "the *compagnon* devours the profit." Beneath the apparent stability, however, the artisanat was in constant motion, turning over individuals, professions, sectors, and ultimately the class as a whole. If the artisanat contained the same number of businesses in 1936 as in 1926, this is not to say that they were the *same* businesses. The artisanat resembled a kind of jigsaw puzzle with the shape of the pieces changing constantly.

It is clear then that concentration, while it proceeded and even accelerated in the 1920s, did not fall evenly across the French economy. We have already seen how the capitalization of production as a whole could co-exist with a high degree of "morcellisme." Concentration, moreover, was a sectoral matter, and the balance between large and small enterprise tipped one way or the other depending on where one looked (Table 3.4). The mining and metallurgical industries, for example, were extremely top-heavy. These sectors had only a few medium-sized establishments and no small ones. The rubber and chemical industries, although smaller on average than mining and metallurgy, were well above the French average and were concentrating their production in the 1920s at a rapid rate.[17] In these most heavily capitalized corners of the French economy the artisanat was a distant memory.

All the other sectors harbored some number, small or large, of artisanal establishments, and in these the respective levels of concentration show two quite different situations for handicraft production. Quarrying, ceramics, book manufacture, paper and cardboard manufacture, and textiles experienced a marked increase in the average number of workers per firm. This suggests an overall tendency toward larger units of production. Smaller firms survived for the moment, yet the direction of change was unambiguous. Artisanal manufacture might not completely disappear in these sectors, but it would certainly shrink drastically in scope. In stonecutting, leather and skins, the food trades, clothing manufacture, and the woodworking professions the number of employees per firm remained below the mean, which implied the continued diffusion of production.

TABLE 3.4.   Industrial concentration: 1921–1936

	Mean number of employees per firm			
Sector	1921	1926	1931	1936
Mining	561.0	953.0	1,088.0	996.0
Quarrying	11.8	10.6	12.2	10.6
Food industries	4.0	4.5	4.9	4.7
Chemicals	31.0	35.4	39.4	37.6
Rubber, paper, cardboard	38.5	45.0	47.0	44.4
Book manufacture	13.6	14.9	15.8	13.9
Textiles	24.8	30.7	36.1	38.8
Clothing	3.9	4.4	5.4	5.0
Leather and skins	5.2	6.5	7.1	7.2
Woodworking	4.4	4.7	4.8	4.3
Metallurgy	458.0	502.0	663.0	586.0
Metalworking	11.7	12.0	12.4	10.8
Stonecutting	4.9	5.5	6.2	5.1
Landscape & construction	7.3	6.3	7.7	6.2
Ceramics	25.0	30.4	33.7	28.8
Total	8.7	9.5	10.8	9.6

Source: Cahen, "La concentration des établissements," p. 874.

The figures compiled by Bernard Legru (Table 3.5) give a sometimes paradoxical detail to Cahen's sketch of sectoral diversity. Legru compared the number of artisanal establishments of a given size in a particular sector in 1896 to the situation in 1936. Taking as a rough guide those businesses with fewer than five employees, one finds that overall concentration did not close off a role for petty production. Four different tracks appear. In the relatively concentrated sectors of ceramics and textiles, the part of small enterprise might have declined dramatically between 1896 and 1936; yet in the similarly concentrated industries of paper, book manufacture, and metalworking, petty production remained stable. Conversely, in woodworking, leather goods, and stonecutting, where production was more dispersed, the decline of the artisanat paralleled the general loss of the working population in these industries; whereas the sectors of construction, clothing manufacture, and the food trades gained in absolute numbers without becoming markedly more concentrated.

Legru also points out a few small anomalies. Polygraphics, including the photographic trades, witnessed a positive boom in artisanal businesses in these forty years. In addition, the large number of craftsmen moving into the precious stones and metals professions may have been the result of the state's policy of training the handicapped (*mutilés de guerre*) for such manual trades as *horlogers-bijoutiers*.[18] One also notes in some industries, including those where the overall movement is down, an increase in the category of "several patrons without employees." This suggests two possible changes, only one of which was substantive. First, it might merely reflect the fact that some of those who previously identified themselves for the census as simple "*chefs d'entreprise* without employees" now counted their wives as copatrons. Al-

TABLE 3.5. Evolution of the number of establishments with up to ten workers: 1936 as a percentage of 1896 (base 100)

Sector	Patrons alone	Several patrons without workers	1–5 workers	6–10 workers	All businesses (total % of workers
Mining	–	–	30	69	177
Quarrying	39	57	66	150	98
Agriculture	144	169	85	121	135
Chemicals	136	82	75	136	263
Rubber, paper, cardboard	180	251	125	136	244
Polygraphics	504	512	150	152	177
Textile weaving	22	55	35	81	98
Cloth	76	144	53	53	91
Leather & skins	70	181	46	46	65
Woodworking	80	150	56	82	84
Metallurgy	–	–	83	200	245
Metalworking	308	293	106	204	236
Precious metals	107	475	71	54	79
Precious stones	156	89	37	145	60
Stonecutting	72	57	55	76	74
Landscaping, construction	448	292	107	118	145
Glass, pottery, porcelain	106	48	33	59	111
Personal services	–	69	52	115	–
Transportation	228	340	118	134	–
Straw & feathers	55	103	44	59	–
Retail foods	103	259	145	218	222
Beverages	103	155	76	106	80
Restaurants, hotels	124	208	117	151	157
Clothing manufacture	109	211	122	128	203

Source: Bernard Legru, unpublished article. I would like to thank Professor Jeanne Gaillard for providing me with this information.

ternatively, it might signal a more complicated movement toward informal cooperation among master artisans, especially in lagging sectors like straw and feathers, a pooling of resources to battle an unfavorable market.

In May 1932 the *Gazette des Métiers* published the results of a survey conducted by the Chambers of Trades of Alsace and Lorraine among the artisans within its jurisdiction (Table 3.6). It distinguished between those professions that were continuing to attract apprentices and those that had become undesirable to young people entering the workforce. As an approximate yardstick of the vitality of the various trades, this survey tells much the same story as Cahen's and Legru's figures. By any criteria and at every juncture of the interwar period, a severe crisis afflicted certain trades. In the majority of cases, these were the fields in which artisans found themselves in direct competition with mass production. As measured by their declining population, as well as by the decrease in the numbers of workers they employed and apprentices they trained, such *industries récessives* as cabinetmakers, watchmakers, or rug weavers experienced a radical thinning of their ranks.[19] Conditions, for example, became quite disastrous in the shoemaking

TABLE 3.6.   Professions and apprenticeship in Alsace-Lorraine, 1922–1932

Professions with fewer apprentices in 1932 than in 1922		
Jeweler	Carpenter	Wheelright
Coppersmith	Tinsmith	Blacksmith
Watchmaker	Joiner	Miller
Painter	Paver	Cookwaremaker
Plasterer	Chimney sweep	Sabotmaker
Stonecutter	Locksmith	Tailor
Dressmaker	Rug weaver	Cooper
Glazier		

Professions with more apprentices in 1932 than in 1922		
Baker	Butcher	Pork butcher
Hairdresser	Mechanic	Electrician
Pastry, candy maker	Photo-engraver	Bookbinder
	Metalcutter	

Source: *Gazette des Métiers* 22 (27 May 1932):390.

industries, with their vast but constantly dwindling army of artisans. A Monsieur Barzic recounted to Bernard Zarca how he at one time had worked as an assistant in a cobbler's shop, refitting the heels on women's shoes. Barzic decided to leave the profession when things began to change. Shoes made from new materials, especially plastic, began to flood the market and these could not be repaired, only thrown out. Coincidentally, factories started to turn out even leather shoes at much lower prices. To the misfortune of Barzic and others like him, it became more affordable to buy new shoes than to have old ones fixed.[20] Factory-produced shoes, sold and resoled in retail stores and chains, cornered an ever-increasing share of the market, inexorably driving down the standard of living of master cobblers.[21]

The statistics on concentration, however, can be misleading in this regard. Legru indicates that small businesses were flourishing alongside larger establishments in the paper industry, implying that in a growing sector there was plenty of work for all. Yet a report to the CNE in 1936 pointed to a quite different state of affairs, to deteriorating conditions for artisans in this industry, where outwork was common, the pay low, and living and working conditions unsanitary.[22] Other artisanal professions that were not competing with industry, nevertheless faced disaster as social and cultural changes caused the demand for their particular skills and products to vanish: for example, stonecutters, basketweavers, and especially the rural trades such as coopers, smiths, saddlers, and *sabotiers*.

Artisans in the textile trades, like their colleagues in *chaussure*, felt the heat of industrial competition but in a different way. Textiles had always been a unique area of artisanal production due to the importance of *travail à façon*. The industry, as Cahen shows, experienced a dramatic concentration from 1921 to 1936, when the mean number of employees per firm increased from 24.8 to 38.8 (56 percent). Yet Legru found that the industry contained some 2 percent fewer employees in 1936 than in 1896, and that by far the greatest loss was in the smaller units of production. Not only were artisan-weavers at a comparative disadvantage; they disappeared at a brisk pace.

Maxime Perrin's 1937 study of the economy in the Loire department (Saint-Etienne) noted some of the changes in the famous ribbon- and lace-making industries.[23] Historically, the ribbon industry was composed of a multitude of small workshops working *à façon* for merchants who acted as *chefs d'orchestre*, coordinating industrial and commercial operations. In *rubannerie* those who actually made the ribbons were never those who sold them to the wholesale houses, department stores, or clothing manufacturers. The technical advances of the nineteenth century reduced the role of muscle power and greatly augmented output but did not lead to profound changes in the organization of production. Ribbons relied on an unpredictable and short-term market, heavily dependent on the caprice of fashion, and this inhibited the creation of factories—capital-intensive and inelastic—and encouraged domestic production. The coming of mass fashion in the twentieth century, calling for higher quantity and lower quality, established a stable market for cheap manufactures and finally rationalized the comprehensive switch to factory production.

It was the sad fate of tradesmen in *cordonnerie, broderie,* and other such crafts, like that of the handloom weavers of a century earlier, that led so many to doubt the future of the artisanat—the artisanal movement not least among them. But even in Legru's figures and in the survey of the Alsatian masters it is clear that some professions thrived in a "modernizing" economy. Those cited by the Strasbourg Chamber of Trades for their vigorousness were representative. Radio repairmen, mechanics, electricians, printers, and members of the photographic trades all benefited from emerging markets calling for a high level of technical skill. The hairdressing and retail food trades were able to take advantage of the demography and cultural habits of urbanization.

A third category of artisans were neither riding the wave of new technology nor clinging to one of the capsized trades. Instead, they were engaged in a long and uneven process of adapting their tools, their skills, their markets, and their organization of production to the changing economic environment. Construction, for example, was one of the most volatile sectors. We have seen earlier how Paul Marcelin, at the turn of the century, made the decisive transition from tinsmith to plumber in order to profit from the arrival of the indoor bathroom. Marcelin's career illustrates how the twentieth century, which brought new ways and means of erecting and furnishing buildings, had an uneven effect on the building trades and how, even in a generally healthy sector, some trades outdistanced others. Plumbers, painters, and electricians were in heavy demand, while furniture makers, locksmiths, and masons might have found themselves unemployed.[24] A similar reshuffling occurred in other sectors: metalworking, for instance. In his study of the Stéphanoise, Perrin found that even in so heavily industrialized a region *petites entreprises* continued to dominate the metal trades in 1931: two-thirds employed fewer than six workers and four-fifths employed fewer than eleven. Perrin catalogues the distress of many of the metal workers, yet adds that some—locksmiths, tool-makers, ironmongers (*quincailliers*)—maintained their positions.[25]

François Gresle, in his study of independent petty patrons, reconstructs the elliptical adaptation of artisan-bookbinders to a changing market. There was a time, when trained craftsmen had to bind the books entirely by hand in order to protect their valuable and perishable contents. At the end of the nineteenth century, however, cheap paper and the industrialization of binding produced a professional crisis among *relieurs*. After World War I, says Gresle, the master binders woke up to their predicament. The more astute among them began to progress from manual to machine-binding. This allowed them to exploit a great new market, the state administration, binding reports for the Postes et Télécommunications (PTT), the Treasury, the municipalities and binding newspapers and magazines for libraries. The *métier* survived, but the work was mechanized, intensified, and simplified. For the *compagnons* it probably meant that the workshop more and more resembled the factory. The manual skill did not, however, disappear completely. A small number of establishments remained, specializing in *reliure d'art* or catering to, as Gresle dismissively phrased it, a "clientèle petite-bourgeoise qui cultive la distinction"; that is, a "snob market" of those who were willing to pay artisanal prices for extravagantly bound editions of the classics.[26]

There was much talk between the world wars of a "crise de l'artisanat rural," wherein the rural artisan became an icon, his disappearance a popular theme for social conservatives. Let us return briefly to the arcadian world of Blunay, recreated by Georges Chaudieu. There we encountered the affable and red-nosed blacksmith; the wheelwright, surrounded by a "mattress" of sawdust; the carpenter, repairing houses, fashioning tables and chairs, en-joying a lucrative monopoly on coffins; and the sabotmaker, a key figure in the damp and muddy countryside. In addition to these fixtures of village life there were the itinerant artisans, the bakers, butchers, saddlers, haberdashers, tinkers, and chimney sweeps who traveled around to those villages too small to support full-time tradesmen.[27]

Unfortunately, lamented François-Paul Raynal, this idyll was fast coming to an end:

> In the countryside one scarcely finds today among artisans any but the old timers, still loyal to their anvil, to their mill, to the blond straw and the blue slate. These days, you have to wait a long time for them, because they cannot be everywhere at once when the roof lets in the rain from heaven, when the tumbrel wheel breaks in the rutted road, or when the humidity warps the window frame.[28]

Lucien Gelly also worried over the fortunes of those "who respond so profoundly to the French character," who exhibit such a "deep wisdom" and "robust good sense." "We love [the rural artisan's] individualism," Gelly wrote, "his taste for a job well done, his professional virtuosity and versatility: in short, his humanity."[29]

The disappearance of the rural artisanat was also among the most urgently voiced and frequently studied concerns of the artisanal movement. At the 1927 congress of the UFRA, Boulier, the general secretary of the Moselle Chamber of Trades, read a report complaining that the nation had yet to confront this social hemorrhage. Boulier mentioned the prosaic problems of inadequate credit and the obstinacy of some artisans in holding on to outdated techniques. He also emphasized the moral causes: the parents who only wanted their children to become state functionaries; the eight-hour law, drawing rustics to the city by promising urban workers a leisure unknown on the farm; and the young men lured by high wages and seductive images of the Moulin Rouge.[30]

There is, in truth, little evidence to support this picture of a rural artisanat becoming extinct. Gordon Wright notes, contradicting Gelly's gloomy scenario, that the shift from agricultural to other employment actually slowed down during the depression.[31] The census conducted by the Ministry of Agriculture in 1929 (Table 3.7) counted 287,542 rural artisans, a healthy 30 percent of the entire artisanal population.[32]

At the same time, it cannot be denied that conditions for rural artisans were changing with unprecedented rapidity. Pierre Barral wrote that in the Alpine department of the Isère, the population of the *artisanat rural* decreased by 40 percent between 1896 and 1936. This, however, corresponded to the decline in the general population of artisans in a developing local economy (from 6.2 to 4.9 percent of the working population) and did not, one suspects, outrun the slipping demand for harnesses and wagonwheels. In Picardy, meanwhile, if the per capita number of rural artisans stabilized between 1911 and 1936, the masters increasingly tended to move to the towns and villages and to desert the smaller, completely rural communes.[33]

On the whole, many of the rural tradesmen in this most rural of industrialized nations faced the "same adapt or disappear" imperative confronting their city cousins, though perhaps at a step behind the urban pace. This was especially true of those associated skills that defined the professions of blacksmith (*maréchal-forgeron*) and farrier (*maréchal-ferrant*). The blacksmith was the pivot of the traditional rural economy, which revolved around animals. As the agricultural economy began to modernize, however, these tradesmen found their livelihoods jeopardized. This sometimes took the form of a direct attack on their ancient prerogatives. It has already been seen how French veterinarians invaded the smiths' traditional province of animal health care. The *maréchaux* also felt the weight of demographic and economic developments. The rural exodus left them with a dearth of customers. Where highly capitalized agriculture edged out the family farm, the smiths found that many of their old jobs were being performed by privately employed wage labor.[34] The Institut de Science Economique Appliquée discovered that the population of *maréchaux-ferrants* decreased from 45,698 to 31,921 (30.5 percent) in the forty years after 1896. It found, moreover, that in 1936 the mean age of these artisans was unusually high, which implied a further imminent decline.[35]

Yet as the 1929 survey of rural artisans indicates, blacksmiths retained

TABLE 3.7.   The rural artisanat, 1929

Profession	Number of master artisans
Farriers, blacksmiths	46,951
Tool repairmen	13,669
Toolmakers	2,020
Barrelmakers	9,804
Harnessmakers	14,903
Wheelwrights	33,039
Carpenters, joiners	52,024
Masons	56,061
Roofers	15,315
Sabotmakers	17,210
Woodcutters, sawyers	14,425
Electricians, mechanics	12,121
Total number of rural artisans	287,542
Entire artisanat	900,000
Rural artisanat as a percent of total	31.9

Source: Ministère de l'Agriculture, *Statistique Générale de la France. Resultats généraux de l'enquête de 1929* (Paris: Imprimerie Nationale, 1936), p. 648.

their place in the rural trades. The continued existence of large numbers of *maréchaux*, however, masked a need to redefine the profession, which rested increasingly on new skills. The modern blacksmith, like most rural artisans who survived, was a man of many talents, not a specialist. He could still shoe the occasional horse but he more often found himself acting as a mechanic or an electrician.[36]

Moreover, the crisis in the rural trades as often as not failed to appear even in artisans' own enquiries. At the CGAF's eighth national congress in 1931, Pégeot, president of the Calvados Chamber of Trades, reported on a survey that the CGAF had carried out into the state of the rural artisanat. The communes involved, from eight departments chosen at random (Pégeot did not mention which ones) cited two contradictory problems: first, that a surfeit of similarly skilled artisans in a locality was producing a ferocious competition among them; second, that the craftsmen in rural areas were often lacking experience with modern equipment and could not provide the agricultural communes with the services they needed. Of the 2,571 communes consulted, 763 (or almost 30 percent) said that they needed artisans.[37]

It is hard to know, in view of what Pégeot does not say, how valid his survey was. In any case, its results were contradicted by an inquiry conducted by the Labor Ministry. The Ministry distributed questionnaires to all the rural communes asking them the following: Did they need any skilled, manual workers? In which trades? Could the commune guarantee them housing? Did it want assistance from the departmental placement officers? What kinds of government aid would help to alleviate the problem? Out of 25,869 communes, 18,187 responded, but only 1,704 (0.9 percent) said that they needed a total of 2,129 artisans.[38] In short, while the eclipse of the rural artisan paralleled that of the *petit paysan* in the twentieth century—and for some, unquestionably, this signaled a personal crisis—there was no independent *crise* among the rural trades.

These were the outlines of the evolution of artisanal production. The French economy was moving haltingly and over the long term toward mechanization and the concentration of capital and labor. Shoes, books, and furniture issued from the factories in increasing volume. The automobile replaced the horse and the tractor, the plow. The young left their sleepy villages for the cities. Caught up in this vortex, trades adapted to their changing environment or they became extinct.

To be sure, the economic environment in the 1930s was especially tempestuous, although exactly how tempestuous for artisans is hard to say. Sociologist François Etienne estimated that by 1936 business was so bad that artisans had laid off some 40 percent of their non-family employees.[39] This sounds reasonable, but Etienne does not provide conclusive evidence. In addition, artisans were typically invisible in official measures of economic malaise. Master craftsmen often eluded the government's unemployment figures, partly due to the inadequacies of the figures themselves and partly to the nature of petty production. On the one hand, the statistics counted only those workers who reported themselves unable to find jobs and asked for some kind of succor. Because artisans were considered employers for purposes of unemployment insurance, they were ineligible for most forms of relief and therefore never applied. On the other hand, as self-employed businessmen, master craftsmen were likely to experience the crisis as a loss of business, as underemployment, rather than unemployment, and as increased self-exploitation. The 1930s also witnessed a limited resurrection of cottage industry (*travail à domicile*) as some artisans were unable to maintain their independence and were forced to lease their skills to better-placed entrepreneurs.[40] What is clear is that artisans' markets dried up and that the crisis squeezed artisans more than usual between their dual vulnerability as workers and as small proprietors.

A sharpened competition for those customers who remained to artisans aggravated the contraction of markets for their products and services. Between 1931 and 1936, as Cahen demonstrates so conclusively, the number of people employed in large-scale industry dropped sharply, while that in commerce and small-scale production climbed. Artisans also failed to win their battle against *travail noir*, the "unauthorized" practice of a trade. *Travail noir* logically proliferated during the 1930s, evidently as unemployed and underpaid workers sought to augment their incomes through *bricolage* ("odd jobs") as carpenters, painters, or mechanics, for instance.[41] These "illicit" tradesmen enjoyed certain competitive advantages vis-à-vis "honest" craftsmen. Prosperous or not, an official artisan owed his *patente*, rent, insurance, social security for his employees, a tax for apprenticeship, and a fee for his local chamber of trades. *Travailleurs noirs* evaded these obligations. The artisanal movement made the control of such "unfair" competition one of its primary goals throughout the decade, with paltry results.[42] In most cases, the state

TABLE 3.8.   Effect of the economic crisis on artisans, 1932

Profession	% decline in work	Profession	% decline in work
Shoemaking	20	Musical instruments	50
Hairdressing	15	Construction	50–70
Book manufacture	30	Mechanics and metalworking	56
Leather & skins	18	Electrician	40
Woodworking	30	Ceramic, glass	15
Furnituremaking	40	Jewelry	50
Clothing	10	Decorating, design	50
Clothing accessories	48	Photography	44
Textiles	55	Painting, sculpture	47
Blacksmith, wheelwright	47	Optical and surgical equipment	37.5
Motorcycle, auto repair	37	Basket and ropemaking	56
Bronze, copper	15	Toolmaking	10
Paper	47		

Source: "Situation du travail artisanal à fin avril 1932," Artisan Français 116 (May 1932).

was unwilling to police professional activities. While the chambers of trades did their best to control the invasion of the *travailleurs noirs*, their resolutions and watchdog committees, not backed by the force of law, proved singularly ineffective.

In addition, small businessmen found their situations menaced by the spread of department stores and *prisunics* (French "five and tens") whose volume and merchandising allowed them to undersell the independent masters.[43] The artisanal movement railed against what it called "this bolshevization" of retailing and warned consumers against being "deceived" by low prices and cheap merchandise. In November 1934, for example, the Fédération du petit commerce et de l'artisanat tried to obstruct the opening of a Monoprix in Paris.[44] The *Gazette des Métiers* reported an occasion on which an owner of a *prisunic* in Alsace was convicted of fraudulent business practices. Naturally, the *Gazette* expressed its delight: "A la guerre comme à la guerre."[45] Such moments of satisfaction were rare, however.

The economic crisis did not strike all trades with equal force. Those producing luxury goods or items for export felt the collapse of markets most keenly. Those trades that rested on the most easily acquired skills and required the least investment in capital were most vulnerable to *travail noir*. In May 1932 the CGAF journal, the *Artisan Français* published a report on the state of the artisanat (Table 3.8). From the categories employed, it is evident that the numbers were provided by the CGAF's member trade federations; however, the report contains no information as to how the statistics were gathered or what stands as their base of comparison. They can serve, nonetheless, as a crude measure of the crisis in artisanal production early in the depression. Business was off everywhere, although this varied from the 10 percent slide in the toolmaking trades to the up to 70 percent dip in construction activity.[46]

This last figure makes an interesting point about the way in which conjunctural difficulties could confound the logic of structural development. The depression accelerated the descent of blacksmiths, ribbon- and lacemakers, watchmakers, and especially artisans in the textile trades. A study conducted in February 1932 of unemployment in the artisanal professions in the Pas-de-Calais, for example, discovered that, of 12,039 persons who had been out of work for more than two days, 10,798 were in textiles and clothing manufacture.[47] By the same token, the structurally dynamic professions of electrician, printer, photo-engraver, and mason suffered a more precipitous collapse in the 1930s than did the moribund trades of shoemaking and woodworking. The hairdressing trades provide a further illustration of the anomalous way in which structure and conjuncture meet. To take a strictly structural view, in an increasingly specialized and urbanized France, where fashion was a preoccupation and people did not usually cut their own hair, *coiffeurs* should have prospered. Indeed, the study from Alsace includes *coiffure* as one of the vital professions, and that of the CGAF shows hairdressing as among the least depressed of sectors. It was a trade, however, whose practice necessitated a minimum of training and capital and was therefore especially vulnerable to overpopulation and *travail noir*.[48] In practice, therefore, the line between short- and long-term factors of development is not an easy one to draw, for the latter operated always by way of the former.

To the considerable problems of petty production in an industrializing economy, the depression added a tight conjunctural squeeze. The contours are difficult to draw, but the numbers provided earlier suggest the shape of the crisis and correspond to the logic of the situation. They document the accelerated decline of artisanal production in textiles, metalworking, and other *industries récessives*, and a more anomalous pinch in the more dynamic trades of mechanics, electricians, and construction. One gets the unmistakable impression of traditional customers lost and new competitors found.

In its number of July 1935 the *Artisan du Bois* considered the tragic plight of artisans. In typical fashion, it described the "professional decadence," exacerbated by those "gros patrons" who preferred to hire cheaper, less skilled workers. But "the greatest fault," it concluded, "lay with the public authorities," who had done nothing to protect the integrity of the profession or the dignity of work.[49]

It is doubtful that the French government precipitated the depression by its inattention to artisans. It is generally conceded, however, that the government's response to the crisis lacked both imagination and intelligence. In trying to come to grips with the economic collapse, France's leaders found themselves trapped between two fears: first, of the dislocation and turmoil bound to follow from a devaluation of the franc and the consequent inflation and, second, of the equal instability assured by continuing depression. The Radical governments produced by the 1932 elections, which were the first to confront the new economic problem, sought a solution in balancing the budget and protecting the currency. But their financial orthodoxy continually agitated the Chamber of Deputies' leftist majority and the demands of their constituents, many of whom were the civil servants especially menaced by the government's frugality.

This leftist conundrum evaporated in the wake of the attempted coup of February 6, 1934. The political turnover that led to the installation of the conservative ministries of Doumergue, Flandin, Laval, and the decree powers that the legislature granted them, enabled the government at last to pursue the vigorous deflationism previously carried out only by half measures. Unfortunately, the weakness of this policy had been neither its vigor nor its consistency but its conception: Parsimonious budget-balancing was simply the wrong medicine for a dying patient. While the United States devalued the dollar and Great Britain abandoned the gold standard, while Roosevelt and Hitler built highways, post offices, and war memorial stadiums, Laval continued to pare the salaries of state employees and to defend the "Poincaré" franc. France's political leaders failed to see, writes Sauvy, that devaluation constituted "the true Liberal solution."[50] "In the end," concludes Richard Kuisel, "the French sacrificed the economy to the franc."[51]

French economic thought was deficient in a number of ways. According to Sauvy, policymakers were indifferent to the international economy and monetary balance. They suffered from a "deplorable ignorance" of rudimentary economic facts and theoretical knowledge about the condition and mechanics of the national economy.[52] Quite apart from his unorthodox economic ideas, Keynes remained for the French the man who had so vociferously opposed the Versailles treaty. Then, too, ideology became the enemy of practicality as businessmen and classical political economists saw the depression as just one more, albeit very serious, cyclical "purification" of the free market and maintained their enthusiasm for fiscal and economic orthodoxy. Even the left got caught in the bog of conventional wisdom. The Marxist parties, often joined by the Radicals, called for increased government spending and argued ever more convincingly in favor of structural change. Even the French Socialist party, however, continued to support the idea of the balanced budget.[53] There existed, finally, a widespread anti-industrial bias that led many to view the depression as the inevitable outcome of an uncontrolled multiplication of the means of production. Sauvy cites an admittedly extreme comment from the fascist paper, *Je Suis Partout*:

> It is impossible for me, and for you as well, to drink three hundred cups of Brazilian coffee, to eat ten kilos of bread, to burn electricity all through the night . . . [The problem is] to lower production to the level of consumption.[54]

The *Gazette des Métiers* quoted in this regard the Malthusian wisdom of Joseph Hittler, of the Institut Commercial Supérieur in Strasbourg. "This is rationalization for you," Hittler wrote. "The electric plant that furnishes current to the entire city of Cologne employs . . . only thirty to forty workers. Without [this kind of rationalization] there would truly be no unemployment in Germany."[55] The answer for some lay not in a more just and efficient industrialism, but in a return to lower levels of production.

The widespread hardship among artisans and the state's apparent impotence before it, pulled the artisanal movement out of its tedious organizational disputes and back into the mainstream of national politics. The CGAF and CEAA became reinvolved in electoral politics and counseled their supporters to pay close attention to those politicians who promised to support the artisanal cause. However, the movement's first order of business was to provide some relief to its suffering constituents. The CGAF and the CEAA tried to encourage buyers' and sellers' cooperatives among master craftsmen, seeing these as a step toward the rationalized business practices that might allow artisans to survive in a killing market. Except in Alsace-Lorraine, where cooperatives were the products of state initiative, successful ventures remained rare among master craftsmen. The movement also tried to promote mutualist solutions to meet artisans' expanding social needs, with equally disappointing results.[57] Perhaps, as Michel Debré reflected, artisanal cooperation ran into both material and attitudinal barriers: problems of capital, on the one hand, and an aversion to banks and to collective action, on the other.[57]

A more decisive factor was the lukewarm government support for artisans' self-help projects, especially when it came to hard cash. In the spring of 1932, for instance, Tailledet wrote to the labor minister requesting state subsidies to help the CGAF set up an unemployment fund for its members. The minister responded that, while he favored the idea of artisanal *caisses de chômage*, he felt that they should be financed by the artisans out of their own resources—which was precisely the problem.[58]

As the economy began to flag such pleas for social assistance multiplied. The struggle for unemployment benefits, in particular, became one of the hallmarks of artisans' actions throughout the crisis. Recall that petty producers were disadvantaged under a system of social assistance that treated them as employers. Even those with this coverage, however, found the structure of unemployment insurance inadequate to the dimensions of the problem. French unemployment funds relied almost entirely on financing from the localities, without significant subventions from the national government. Even as it threatened to bankrupt the localities, the reigning system of unemployment insurance offered insubstantial amounts of support to the needy, and then only for a limited period of approximately six months.[59]

Sometimes small groups of master craftsmen took it upon themselves to petition the authorities directly. This scrawled letter from a delegation of handicapped cobblers from the files of the Labor Ministry is one such example:

For some time now we artisan-cobblers of Dunkirk have seen our work diminished to the point where we are in fact reduced to unemployment. Misfortune and misery have taken over our lives, and we can no longer sustain our basic needs. Our wives and children are hungry. The majority among us are "nature's disinherited," handicapped without any pension.

> Everywhere we turn for help we find only refusals . . . . Such a situation cannot endure much longer. We ask only that justice and equity—those great French rights—be accorded to all citizens, and that is why we are calling your benevolent and generous attention to our plight, soliciting, as for all the unemployed without distinction, our registration in the unemployment fund.[60]

In matters of unemployment compensation master artisans found that their interests coincided with those of other *chômeurs*, which often led them into alliances built around the demand for the extension of benefits. Usually, local syndicates of workers and of artisans would unite in favor of joint resolutions calling for expanded public works or form ad hoc "committees of the unemployed" to petition the government for the nationalization of unemployment insurance and for the admission of all *petits* to its rolls. These often received the support of municipal and departmental councils, which found themselves, as the crisis wore on, unable to shoulder the welfare load. In a special session of January 1935, the General Council of the Nord issued the following resolution:

> In view of the disquieting development of the economic crisis, striking at the same time wage earners and all categories of workers, exclusive of the actual regime of unemployment relief, [the Council] resolves that parliament substitute for this unjust and inefficient regime a new organization of a national system of relief for all the victims of the crisis: wage earners of all the corporations and all the communes—workers, intellectuals, artisans, [et al].[61]

If the crisis sometimes led to a tactical coalition of *petits*, conversely it aggravated the conflict between small and large property-holders. While the unemployed and the financially straitened local authorities asked for the extension and the nationalization of social relief, the chambers of commerce flooded the Labor Ministry with resolutions in support of austerity. The Bergerac Chamber of Commerce predicted that,

> the creation of a national unemployment relief fund would be an encouragement to laziness and would lead to a large increase in the number of the unemployed because, if there are those workers who really do their best to find work, there are those on the contrary spending all their efforts to remain on the dole.[62]

Likewise, the Nancy Chamber of Commerce asked the minister to "reduce fiscal and other charges weighing on French industry and commerce." The Bourg Chamber of Commerce complained of "hand-outs" and argued that such welfare only acted as a disincentive to work. "Unemployment will become a popular profession," it warned soberly. And the Rouen Chamber of Commerce offered this curious prescription for the depression: balance the budget, return women to their "proper" place in the home, and send workers back to the land—or at least develop "systems of workers' gardens around the industrial centers."[63]

The CGAF naturally concurred with those who sought to expand state aid to the victims of the depression. But it went further. Two months after the traumatic events of February 6, the CGAF unveiled its plan for national renewal in a new Artisanal Manifesto (Appendix B). The manifesto returned to familiar themes but added a new sense of urgency to artisanal politics. The country, it concluded, had arrived at a moment of truth. France had become fat on "tainted wealth," while allowing the real source of its fortunes, "healthy, respectable capital" and skilled labor, to decay. To recover its greatness, the nation had to restore these elements to prominence. The manifesto proposed a program of public works, easy credit, and the control of economic "giganticism," as the road back to quality production and national sanity. It called for the convocation of an "Estates General of the Nation," to prepare the agenda for reform, and demanded that the artisanat have seat at the table.

Thus it did not take artisans long to make the connection between their old diagnoses and their new troubles. From its beginnings, the artisanal movement had insisted on the material and spiritual bankruptcy of industrial capitalism. "Despite all the victories of modern man in the domain of science and technology," Peter, president of the Alsace Chamber of Trades, wrote, "the century of aviation, of radio, of statistics, and of rationalization finds humanity in an indescribable anarchy . . . at once moral, social, and economic."[64] The artisans in the early 1930s were all but gratified to see that the depression seemed to signal the "twilight of the gods of mechanization and technology," a "divine judgment" on a century of economic development. The movement tried to seize the occasion to enable petty craftsmen once more "to fulfil a function of the highest order" in the nation's economy.[65]

Artisans had been offering more or less the same critique for fifteen years. But now, as the republic's economic and political failures became manifest, the rest of the polity suddenly seemed to fall in behind them. From the perspective of the mid-1930s, postwar history appeared as a woeful tale of "immobility," marked by demographic decline, economic stagnation, irrelevant parliamentary games, and a general squandering of the victory of 1918.[66] From all over the political spectrum came schemes for national regeneration that promised to cure the present crisis and to prevent a relapse. Each one of these hinged on some abandonment of liberal political economy, some step away from the free play of the market and toward the institution of a more rationally conceived and executed economic policy. Perhaps the best example of this was the Marchandeau project of 1935. This bill aimed to impose an obligatory organization on recalcitrant and individualist interests, but it was "buried in the parliamentary sand."[67]

The ground for all this had been prepared by the wartime experience of government stewardship and of labor/capital cooperation and had been fertilized during the 1920s. Charles Maier explained this creeping corporatism as the growth of interest organizations in the early postwar years giving many of these groups a more or less effective veto over what they saw as injurious policies. The legislature, unable to make tough but necessary decisions, created a number of councils and commissions in which these powerful interests could meet, argue, and hammer out compromises under the guidance of the state. (It was noted earlier how artisans were co-opted on to several of these.) The new administrative councils operated under the implicit understanding that, if social conflict could not be eliminated it could at least be bureaucratized.[68]

Social thinkers expounded on these same themes. In the early 1930s, for example, a group of neo-liberal *planistes*, graduates largely of the Ecole Polytechnique and including, most notably, the economist, Sauvy, and the socialist leader, Jules Moch, came together in study groups, such as the "X-Crise," and reviews, like the *Nouveaux Cahiers*.[69] The CGT also drew up a reform plan as did many of the fascist groups. Even the ultra-liberal CGPF thought that, "it might be useful to have, beside political organs and professional groupings, an assembly of a small number of members, judiciously chosen, charged with giving advice on problems of a general order."[70]

Such a rationalization of political economy even won recruits in the unlikely camp of radical-socialism; this was, however, at least for some of its exponents, an oblique strategy for defending the interests of the Radicals' petty-bourgeois and very unmodern constituency.[71] The new wave of Radicals (the so-called Young Turks) hoped to preserve the principles of private property against "collectivism" and to reverse the domination of the "plutocrats" in a new political economy more or less *dirigée*. Serge Berstein quoted from their 1932 platform: "Liberalism is collapsing. Its rules no longer serve to support a capitalist regime, which looks to the state when it is a question of protection and salvation, but which [repudiates] the state when it seeks to put a little order in the most demoralizing of anarchies." "Our party," they concluded, "has always been interventionist."[72] The Young Turks demanded only a more intelligent and self-conscious approach.

As the hold of classical political economy began to weaken in the mid-1930s, corporatism and syndicalism emerged as the leading pretenders to the succession. Modern corporatism (in the sense used here) had grown out of Catholic social thought of the previous century, as expounded by writers like Albert de Mun and La Tour du Pin, and popularized by Pope Leo XIII's Bull, *Rerum Novarum*.[73] Broadly, corporatism aimed to protect property and ease social inequality by restoring discipline and morality to economic activity. More practically, it sought to dissolve conflict by reorganizing society "vertically" into a hierarchy of professional and regional groups. "In opposition to the 'social class' in the Marxist sense that divides society into horizontal groups," read the CEAA's report to the president of the Commission Sénatoriale de la Réforme de l'Etat, "the corporation erects a vertical division of society according to one's trade; for the class struggle it substitutes professional solidarity."[74]

After World War I and the Bolshevik Revolution corporatism also found a new base of support among the fascists. Georges Valois, apostate from the Action Française and founder of the Faisceau, for example, saw in corporatism the social essence of fascism. In 1920 Valois founded the Confédération de l'intelligence et de la production françaises, which in 1927 transformed itself into the Union des corporations françaises (UCF). In 1934, the UCF took a leading part in the establishment of a corporatist think tank, the Institut d'Etudes Corporatives et Sociales, known as Institut Carrel, after its inspirator, Dr. Alex Carrel.[75]

It was logical that corporatist ideas should be associated with the reforming and revolutionary right. If in theory corporatism promised harmony and social peace, in practice it always placed "order before progress, security before liberty, society before the individual, and, most of the time, justice and equality after authority." In the end, it owed its inspiration less to some passion for community than to a fear of Marxism:

> The corporatists, fearing that the syndicates would succeed in shaking the foundations of capitalist society, wanted to integrate them into public corporations, socially heterogeneous and compulsory. In order to avoid social revolution—meaning socialist revolution—they sought social restoration through the Corporation.[76]

The corporatist clamor grew louder until 1940.[77] Despite enjoying a certain intellectual vogue, however, corporatism never translated into functioning institutions in France, at least not before Vichy. This was due largely to the violent opposition of the organized working class, who rightly read into the notion of class collaboration the powerlessness of labor.[78] The CGT rejected liberalism, of course, but proposed instead a syndicalist alternative to laissez faire, an institutionalized version of social conflict characterized, as Georges Dubost put it, "essentially by its economic preoccupations in response to the demands of class struggle." For the reformist wing of the CGT, syndicalism meant above all economic planning and labor/management cooperation in the decisions of production. They saw it as a way of avoiding the recurrent crises of market capitalism and of giving labor some influence over the direction of the economy.[79]

As this national debate developed, the artisanal movement staked out its position or, rather, its positions, for the movement's anti-liberal consensus had never quite reconciled syndicalists and corporatists. These differences in orientation now blossomed into divergent political projects. Consistent with the corporatist and conservative traditions of the Alsace Chamber of Trades, the CEAA imagined a socioprofessional regime that would "tie an anarchic present to a past in which order and discipline reigned...."[80] "We must recognize," said Fernand Peter,

> that our economic regime, referred to as liberal-capitalist, has gone awry in putting technical progress at the service of a purely material civilization and in favoring industrial concentration and overmechanization, abandoning in the name of individual liberty small and medium-sized producers in a battle of murderous competition, and in tolerating class war and professional anarchy.[81]

Accordingly, the CEAA produced a number of programs pointing the way back to "a disciplined and directed economy." Each pivoted on some kind of corporatist reconstruction of French society, where all the members of a corporation, including workers, employers, and technical advisors, would meet and hammer out policy through discussion and compromise instead of through confrontation. The Artisanat would constitute one corporation among several, beside those for Industry, Commerce, Agriculture, etc. Each corporation would bear the responsibility for regulating its own recruitment, development, and social services. Each would be organized at the local and regional level and divided into its constituent professions (in the Artisanat, for example, shoemaking, woodworking, construction, etc.). At the crown of the corporatist structure the CEAA envisioned an interprofessional parliament, which would coordinate corporate affairs at the national level and advise the National Assembly on social and economic legislation. Such a system, the CEAA purported to believe, would lead away from strikes, lockouts, and class war and toward an economic and social policy in the "general interest."[82]

Corporatist theory was forever bedeviled by the problem of making corporate authority consonant with parliamentary sovereignty and individual freedom. Typically, the division of labor between the assembled corporations and the popularly elected legislature always remained ambiguous in the CEAA schemes. Albert Dupuis tried to explain it in the following way:

> The Corporation must not confuse itself with the State. It must not impinge
> on the functions that belong to the State nor allow the State to substitute
> itself for the Corporation in professional matters. . . . To the Corporation the
> role of organizer, and to the State control, arbitration, and the administration
> of decisions in order to give them the force of law.[83]

But this did not settle the matter. If the National Assembly were no more than a rubber stamp of the intercorporate parliament, it could hardly be considered "sovereign." If, on the contrary, the National Assembly were permitted to debate and eventually reject the recommendations of the collected corporations, how could it help but reproduce the old *immobilisme*?

Clearly, corporatism would not easily be married to parliamentarism, nor professional freedom to economic discipline, nor, finally, democracy to authority. Ley, Dupuis, Peter, and the other artisan-corporatists did their best to fudge the issue. "We can only wish," wrote Ley, "that the corporative regime will be realized, and we have the firm hope that it will be realized in a democratic form."[84] Peter seemed less certain: "My most ardent desire is to see democracy . . . put the brakes on Liberalism by the reconstitution of the authority of the State. . . ."[85] The CEAA dreamed of both democracy and order, but it was never clear which was closer to its corporatist heart. In the end, its programs were forced to resort to a Bonapartist (what would later be called Pétainist or Gaullist) solution. They projected the direct election of a powerful president and the use of referenda to overcome the most vexing problems—although this would curtail the autonomy of the corporations.

The leadership of the CGAF also interpreted the depression as history's revenge on industrial capitalism. "The underlying cause of the crisis," wrote Tailledet, "is industrial concentration and all the processes that flow from it: standardization, rationalization—words as barbarous as the things they describe."[86] As he had in the preceding decade, the CGAF's president betrayed his populist tendencies, laying economic disorder at the door of finance capital, the notorious "Two Hundred Families," whose peculations constrained the circulation of money and produced a consequent crisis of underconsumption. The CGAF, as did the CEAA, named the political system of the republic as an accomplice in this disaster. It likewise insisted on the need for a new structure for making national economic policy. The CGAF's model for this, however, was syndicalist. Naturally, artisanal syndicalism differed from the CGT version, taking as its measure the interests of independent petty producers and not those of industrial workers. But the CGAF shared the CGT's commitment to politics-as-conflict and to the trade union as the vehicle for particular interests.

As it laid out its plans in the Artisanal Manifesto, the CGAF imagined a reconstructed CNE at the center of economic policymaking. Here the representatives of the syndically organized interests, along with a leavening of technocratic "experts," could confront each other directly. The CNE would then present the legislature with a pre-negotiated and rationally considered economic program, thereby sparing deputies and senators a task that had heretofore beleaguered them. In the CGAF program, the planned economy emerged as the natural product of controlled struggle and state arbitration among rival interests. Tailledet explained:

> [The planned economy]—the phrase is gaining in popularity. In the face of the anarchy of our epoch we need more order, more method, more cohesion. No one contests this. That things must be planned in order to avoid the jolts to which we have been subjected in the past—agreement is unanimous.
>
> But in this world where people are different, it is also a question of who will direct this economy and in whose interest. Can the State carry out this task, quitting its function as arbiter to enter into the battle over the economy? We don't think so. Is it necessary then to accept the Liberal doctrine and to abandon to private interests a direction that ought to be collective? We believe this even less.
>
> If, on the other hand, one asks professional individuals to get together, to create above themselves organizations which will faithfully represent their interests and their aspirations, and if, having expressed the interests of their constituents, having broached their common interests, these organizations would allow the State to arbitrate, to direct in the *general interest*—that would truly be a controlled, arbitrated, directed economy. And the country would find in this the most healthy expression of a popular economy, one with which, without hesitation, all workers would cooperate [emphasis added].[87]

The CGAF proposed only two major alterations in the CNE as it already existed: investing it with wider authority and giving artisans a greater voice within it. The CGAF believed that such a system would bring France a more coherent and efficacious policy while shielding artisans from the winds of economic change.

As a practical matter, the CGAF's programs had several advantages over those of the CEAA, as indeed syndicalism had over corporatism in general. First, syndicalism rested on an amalgamation of interest groups as they already existed: the syndicates and confederations of workers, employers, farmers, artisans, and the national trade federations. It did not, therefore, require the unlikely professional reorganization implied by corporatism. Second, syndicalism began with a more realistic view of the political process. Whereas corporatists looked to an elusive collaboration among competing interests, syndicalists sought merely to domesticate pluralism, leaving each group to defend itself as it thought best. The CGAF thereby committed itself unequivocally to democracy. "We ask simply," it said, "that our democracy adapt itself to the necessities created by the evolution of the economy and the social transformation [accompanying it]." The CGAF rejected "any authoritarian solution which would sacrifice the individual to a state bureaucracy"—a gibe at the corporatists.[88]

In examining the projects of the CGAF and the CEAA, however, one notices that syndicalists and corporatists shared a revealing artisanal blind spot, which led them both, in the end, to make two dubious and, as it turned out, incorrect assumptions: that artisans would ever be accorded a significant role among more powerful economic and social forces and that, apart from these, the state could function as a neutral arbiter in the general interest. The great irony was that Tailledet and Grandadam had wrestled with successive ministries and numerous administrative councils since 1919. Yet for all their repeated complaints about the neglect of the "little guys," even the hard-headed CGAF leadership failed to see that the kind of rationalization of political economy they entertained would strengthen precisely those forces artisans feared most: big capital and big labor.[89]

This blind spot also indicated a naivity in artisans' ideology that worked fundamentally to constrain their politics. The versions of corporatism and syndicalism propounded by artisans were not merely impractical, they were completely unrealistic. The parliamentary inefficiency of the Third Republic, which had allowed small property to incubate, could generate no answers to the economic crisis. Yet any of the remedies that the artisans proposed was bound to make their own situation worse. Simply put, there was no artisanal solution to the problems of industrial society. The artisanal movement claimed to want a more effective national economic policy, but this would inevitably have buried a substantial part of the artisanat.

The worldview that the artisanal movement had developed in the preceding decade pointed no way out of this predicament. Instead, the artisans' moralistic and romantic reconstruction of the world, the language by which they made sense of it, foreclosed an adequate accounting of the sources and functions of power in twentieth-century France. The political economies of liberalism and Marxism, although these obviously contained their own mythologies, did not operate under the same burdens, or at least not to the same degree. The former could prescribe a system in which capital would be free and where the political dominance of capitalists would follow from their possession of the sources of wealth. The latter could envision a polity dominated by a working class that had seized control of industrial production. Both these ideologies posited the relation of economic to political authority. Neither in its social theory nor in its political practice did the artisanal movement betray a similar grasp of the material basis of power.

Thus were artisans, by way of the artisanal movement, caught in a contradiction between the wish for a world hospitable to handicraft production and the structures of the twentieth century, between the desire to protect their interests and the need to be politically effective. An autonomously artisanal resolution of this dilemma was a patent impossibility, which the movement's corporatist and syndicalist projects recognized implicitly. Craftsmen were able to mourn the disappearance of traditional social virtues and to preach the moral superiority of the family workshop over the factory. The *Artisan* could write, in a moment of nostalgic excess, that "one can live very well without vacations, without cinemas, without dance halls and cafés, without silk stockings."[90] This did not amount to a practicable political program. In the final analysis, neither syndicalists nor corporatists within the artisanat could conjure up a France in which handicraft production would predominate. Both refused to come to terms with basic issues of power, and each retreated to the ingenuous notion of the general interest as artisans' best hope.

It seems appropriate to address the classical historical proposition that links the petty bourgeoisie, of which the artisanat was so eminently a part, to political reaction in general and fascism in particular. Taking their lessons from the analysis in *The Eighteenth Brumaire of Louis Bonaparte*, Marxist scholars have long made the connection. Following in this tradition, Arno Mayer argued some years ago that,

> although it may waver along the way, in the final analysis the lower middle class resolves its ambiguous and strained class, status, and power relations with the power elite above and the underclass below in favor of the ruling class. It is this inner core of conservatism, ultimately revealed in moments of acute social and political conflict, that is common to all segments of the lower middle class and that justifies treating them as a coherent phenomenon and as a significant historical problem.[91]

The not strictly Marxist work of Seymour Lipset and Wolfgang Sauer agrees with Mayer at least in part. They describe a lower middle class hostile to both capitalism and socialist collectivism—an amalgam of attitudes Sauer labeled *antimodernism*—that was driven into what Lipset called the *extremism of the center*.[92]

Each of these political sociologies, Marxist and quasi-Marxist, rests on two propositions. The first is that economic and social disorder radicalized a temperamentally unradical class. This makes an explicitly political assumption and is best pursued in the context of the Popular Front, in the next chapter. The second is that the untenable nature of the petty bourgeoisie's antimodernist outlook led it to such airy ideologies as the *Volksgemeinschaft*—the "people's community," the political system without politics—where material conflicts would dissolve in the solvent of the general interest. This implies that the petty bourgeoisie's attraction to fascism is to be found in its fundamental ideological ingenuousness. In the political sense, because petty proprietors cared more for their property than their autonomy, and because this could only be secured by the repression of those who refused on principle to recognize the general interest, the lower middle classes threw in their lot with those who were willing to impose it on the recalcitrant; that is, the fascists.

Much in the artisans' reaction to the economic crisis bears out this analysis. The artisanal movement's approach to politics *was* deeply naive, as it tried to hold the exposed position of petty producers by way of an optical illusion: the rule of the general interest. We can anticipate its frustration. But when artisans' syndicalist and corporatist offerings inevitably failed to pay dividends, what then?

One is struck, moreover, by the similarities between the language of the artisanal movement, especially of the corporatist element, and the language of fascism. The Jeunesses Patriotes, under a banner of "Order, Hierarchy, and Discipline," promised a war against the "forces of disorder" threatening the family and other "French traditions." Doriot's Parti Populaire Français, in its manifesto of 1932 wrote that "[France's] shopkeepers and artisans are driven to the wall by misery. The middle classes are being ruined." And the Croix de Feu called for "class reconciliation and collaboration. Restoration of national morality. A controlled economy . . . and parliamentary reform."[93]

None of this would have sounded out of place at a CEAA congress or in the columns of the *Gazette des Métiers*. Indeed, it was all part of the language of a lower middle class *enragée*, the generic populism of those frustrated by forces beyond their control, rejecting the economic and political structure that favored *les gros*, but also refusing to follow the working class into collectivist socialism. The dismissal of laissez faire economics, the conservative social vision, the idiom of the general interest were all at the core of artisanal ideology and politics. The depression did not so much create this alienation from contemporary France as bring it to a climax. As the crisis wore on and the republic appeared incapable of decisive action, the artisanal movement naturally reached for a way to staunch the tide of concentration and protect *petites situations*.

The example of the French artisanat suggests, however, that the case, as put by Mayer, Lipset, and Sauer, is overstated and that, between Adam Smith and Karl Marx many kinds of politics were possible. If the artisanal movement shared much of its social agenda with the radical right, so did every other interest and party. Who, after all, called for the disintegration of the family? Who applauded economic disorder? Who wanted to destroy the middle classes? Moreover, while the movement showed itself hostile to economic liberalism, it never abandoned its commitment to political liberalism. It never embraced the authoritarianism that was the sine qua non of fascism. The CGAF, supported by the *petits* artisans who were the bedrock of its membership, pursued a leftish populism, suspicious of the authorities, respectful of the virtue and good sense of the *français moyen*, with a constant eye to democracy and social justice. The artisan-corporatists, led by the Alsace Chamber of Trades, with its Wilhelmine pedigree, more substantial constituency, and intense concern for "professional order," sometimes steered closer to the illiberal edge, but they did not fall off.

Fascism in France, therefore, proved unable to attract even such likely recruits as disgruntled artisans. It never found a mass base and was consigned to the political margin. This examination of French artisans during the depression suggests, briefly, that the economic crisis in France, tempered by the country's large nonindustrial sector, never attained the proportions that it did in Germany or the United States. Its effect, moreover, was regressive, striking the large, highly capitalized producers harder than the small. The economic and psychological threat to middle-class property and status was therefore comparatively moderate. In addition, the French artisans operated within the democratic political culture embedded in both syndical and national traditions. Ill-defined, ambiguous, and unsatisfying, these traditions were decisive. Recall the 1934 Artisanal Manifesto. Exasperated with the deficiencies of the republic and casting about for a better way, the CGAF called not for a führer or a duce but for a new Estates-General.

There was yet one more reason for artisans' general reluctance to pass into the anti-republican resistance. Heeding perhaps Paulin's warning that "Hitler had found an invaluable ally in the misery of the German middle classes," the Third Republic, for all its *immobilisme*, maintained its favored treatment of small property. Take, for example, the survival of the artisanal movement's most precious achievement, the tax exemptions for *petits* artisans. Increasing demands on the national budget and the ministers' determination to balance it, naturally led the government to consider some fiscal reform, which brought the privileges of the *petit artisan fiscal* into question. The Doumergue government, granted the authority to legislate by decree-law in early 1934, proceeded to do just that. Despite what artisans felt were Doumergue's promises to the contrary, the decree-law of July 1934, put into effect by a Finance Ministry circular of January 1935, returned artisans to the regime that pertained before June 1923. It again subjected *petits* artisans' income to the schedule for "industrial and commercial profits" and their businesses to the "turnover tax."[94] The movement and its defenders leapt into action. Paulin rose in the Chamber of Deputies to interpellate the government. The CEAA sent out letters to all deputies, requesting their support on this vital matter. Peter wrote directly to Piétri, the finance minister, warning him once again of the economic and social dangers of the "super-industrialization" promoted by the government.[95] In late March 1935, the artisanal cause prevailed. By a unanimous vote in the Chamber of Deputies, and by a vote of 194–99 in the always less accommodating Senate, the legislature restored the regime of the *petit artisan fiscal*.[96]

The government was also forthcoming with more direct attempts to shelter petty production, even if these had a more symbolic than a substantial impact. For example, the movement called for action against foreigners practicing artisanal trades. "We are submerged by foreigners," Pégeot told his fellow presidents in the APCMF. "It is becoming impossible for the French artisan to survive," added Peter.[97] And in 1935 the Strasbourg Chamber of Trades attempted to deny apprenticeship contracts to foreign born apprentices.[98] Whether such a threat to "native" artisans really existed is unclear. The Lyon Chamber of Commerce found in a 1938 survey that more than 11 percent of the 60,000 businesses in its jurisdiction were owned by foreigners. The professions of mirrormaking and sculpting led with more than 70 percent. Forty percent of shoemakers were "non-French." Yet a similar survey carried out in Caen produced very different results. In a city of 65,000 the Chamber of Commerce found only 107 artisans and merchants *étrangers*.[99]

The authorities proved receptive in the matter of foreign artisans. The decree-law of August 8, 1935 required all non-French citizens who wished to practice a trade to obtain formal authorization from the prefect.[100] The government also responded to other of the movement's demands. It created so-called *marques artisanales*, which were meant to certify the quality of artisanal-made goods, and thus to give them a competitive edge. Laws in January and October 1935 guaranteed artisanal construction businesses a place in public works projects.[101] The Poullen law of March 22, 1936 satisfied a long-standing artisanal grievance when it proscribed "the opening of any retail store . . . designated *à prix unique*."[102] The legislature also granted the artisanal movement's wish for greater representation in the state administrative bodies.[103]

In view of these accomplishments, the artisanal movement might well have congratulated itself and thanked its sponsors. On the contrary, Tailledet, Peter, and others continued to complain that "the government has made no effort to mitigate artisanal distress."[104] This may seem like rank ingratitude or the habitual dissatisfaction of interest group politics. After all, no group ever gets all of what it wants, and pickings were naturally slim during the depression. But it is also evidence of a widening gulf between what one arm of the state promised and the other arm delivered.

The depression hardly cramped the Parliament's old habits of generosity toward *la France moyenne*. At the core of this policy, so far as it stemmed from more than electoral calculation, was a suspicion that, while *petits* might contribute little to the gross national product, they would add much to political and social stability. This was the so-called social approach to the problems of the artisanat, the willingness to tamper with the free market in order to blunt the impact of economic development on petty producers.[105] Juxtapose the social concerns of the legislature against the uneven concentration of French production and it appears as if the fate of the handicrafts depended as much on parliamentary patronage as on the strict logic of industrial progress. That is to say that favorable legislation helped to provide numerous eddies in the French economy where preindustrial forms of production could avoid being dragged under. If this is true, artisans' experience supports the view that the easy pace of industrialization in the Third Republic betrayed neither a failure of will nor a flawed entrepreneurial character but a social contract, one of whose clauses was the preservation of small property.[106]

As public policy, the social approach to petty production had never been without its critics, and the regime's failure to surmount the depression multiplied their numbers. Skeptics saw the republic pursuing Malthusian policies at the cost of overall growth and a more enduring social contract. They proposed instead that the state's treatment of petty producers should be based on more narrow economic considerations.[107] Alfred Sauvy, who was especially insistent on this point, took the regime to task, for instance, for its irrational fiscal structure, which so favored *petits* artisans:

> Conceived for ends other than economic expansion, French tax laws present numerous malthusian aspects. These are often justified by social considerations. Unfortunately, as they protect not persons but activities, these laws only serve to sustain archaic interests.[108]

The so-called economic approach found its most enthusiastic exponents within the state administration and its technocratic phalanx. Here Sauvy, and others like him, sought to co-opt social conflict in institutions such as the CNE, where Smith's "invisible hand," by 1935 so manifestly arthritic, would cede to the rationalizing touch of the social engineer, and where conflict would be buried beneath high production and full employment. As a consequence of the predominance of "big labor" and "big capital" among its members and the "modernizing" bias of its technocratic chaperons, the CNE did not much concern itself with the "backwaters" of national production. Dominated by corporate *cadres*, the CGT, and the advisors from the Cour des Comptes and the Inspectorat des Finances, the CNE prescribed concentration and rationalization as the remedy for every economic ill.

Throughout the interwar years public policy bounced artisans back and forth between these contending visions, one with a cozy place for master craftsmen, one without. In the 1920s, administrative action consistently lagged behind legislative intent. In the 1930s, this became more pronounced. Controls on *travail noir*, foreigners practicing artisanal trades, and the registers of trades went largely unenforced. Public works projects did not open up to artisan masons, carpenters, plumbers, or locksmiths. Tailledet occupied his seat on the CNE, but no one listened to what he had to say.

The state's attempt to reinforce France's weak shoe industry (*chaussure*) illustrates the way this worked in practice. The Poullen law of March 22, 1936, in addition to its ban on the opening of new *prisunics*, also sought to eliminate "unfair competition" in the shoemaking industry.[109] This meant above all protecting uncompetitive domestic manufactures, especially from the power that the Czech firm, Bata, was beginning to exercise on the French market even in the face of high tariffs.[110] Naturally, artisans approved of any policy that would reverse *chaussure*'s sagging fortunes, but they saw things from a uniquely artisanal perspective. The artisanal press joined the chorus against Bata and the industrial practices that enabled it to sell shoes "at prices incomparably lower than ours." In September 1932, after Thomas Bata's demise in a plane crash, the *Artisan* all but blamed his death on his methods of mass production. Logically, then, artisans dismissed a parallel rationalization of shoe manufacture in France because it would "transform France into a communist barracks."[111]

Poullen himself, in his original bill, had not singled out shoemakers for special treatment, but artisans' friends in the Chamber of Deputies repaired this oversight a few weeks later. The Paulin-Fèvre law of April 7, in effect granted artisans a monopoly in shoe repair, by prohibiting all shoe stores or manufacturers with more than six workers from fixing shoes, except for artisan-*cordonniers* working by hand.[112]

The legislation regulating the shoe industry was not self-enforcing. Both the Poullen and Paulin-Fèvre laws had to pass by way of the CNE, which interpreted Parliament's intentions according to its own light. Whereas the legislators had responded to the threat to their constituents' interests, the CNE was more concerned with bringing order and rationality to a sector in disarray.[113] Protecting some elements might make sense, but in the CNE's opinion that was not the crux of the matter.

As individual cases came before it for consideration, the CNE did not distinguish between artisans and other businessmen. For example, in its meeting of April 1937, the tenth professional section (leather and skins) considered the application of the Paulin-Fèvre law. A Monsieur Pichette sought permission to move his business, which manufactured luxury sporting shoes, from Sainte-Rex to Paris and to expand it with the machinery he had bought from a bankrupt firm in Sainte-Rex. The section, according to the recommendation of its chairman—Hannotin, a clerk from the Conseil d'Etat—consented. There followed the case of Monsieur Robert, a manufacturer of sabots and galoshes in Agen. Robert's lease had expired, and he wanted to move his operation, a much smaller one than Pichette's, to a larger and healthier workshop. Again, the councilors gave their approval.[114] Similarly, a few months later Hannotin wrote this response to an application by a Monsieur Gresy:

> Monsieur Gresy, bootmaker, working exclusively by hand with two assistants, desires to move to a larger and better ventilated workshop; this will allow the suppression of domestic production. In these instances, the National Economic Council has always given its authorization. In this sort of manufacture, the increase of production is without danger ... the Section is favorable.[115]

On other occasions, invoking the intent of the Poullen and Paulin-Fèvre laws, the councilors turned down requests to expand or transfer an enterprise. Monsieur Lapierre of Steenvorde (Nord), an ex-foreman in a shoe factory that had fallen into bankruptcy, proposed to open a small workshop where, with the aid of one machine and three workers, he would manufacture shoes out of materials produced for him by twenty *ouvriers à domicile*. The local authorities and the local Chambre syndicale des cordonniers-réparateurs were favorable to Lapierre. Hannotin argued, however, that the question was purely one of political economy. Was the market large enough to support another such business? He thought not, and a majority of the section concurred.[116] In October, the councilors rejected a Monsieur Wassong's appeal to establish an artisanal workshop in Alsace. Due to the usual bureaucratic drag, the shop had already been operating for eighteen months. Nevertheless, the CNE recommended that it be closed.[117] These divergent opinions indicate that the CNE was interested in neither the salvation nor the destruction of the artisanat. It approved those changes which seemed likely to stabilize the market in *chaussure* and turned down those that threatened to increase competition in an already anarchic sector. Over the long run, such a set of priorities would inevitably work against the smallest and most marginal enterprises.

In the early 1930s the depression did not so much shift the emphasis of artisanal politics as increase the urgency with which they were played out. This change can be seen in Tailledet's reaction to the events of February 6, 1934. The president of the CGAF began by denying that the artisanal movement had played any part in the riots aimed at overthrowing the republic: "If Parisian artisans found themselves personally mixed up in the battles that occurred, we don't know what side they were on, or for what ideal, or if they were just curious bystanders." Tailledet's own political commitments prevented his supporting either the rioters' antiparliamentary intentions or their extraparliamentary and violent methods. Yet he expressed his admiration for their courage and wondered along with them whether, in fact, the republic had failed the nation.[118] Above all, the progress of fascism signalled for Tailledet the pressing need for an urgent response to a desperate situation. He recognized that behind the weakness of France's economy lay that of her political structure, and beyond that the fragility of her liberty.

4

Artisans and the Popular Front, 1936–1939

Throughout the first years of the economic crisis, despite their occasional essays on parliamentary reform, artisans' involvement in national politics remained sporadic and parochial. It was the question of definition, not the syndicalist-corporatist debate, that really inflamed the artisanat. This insularity became more and more tenuous after 1936. The victory of Léon Blum and the Popular Front coalition brought the country to a new pitch of intensity and the artisanal movement to a new degree of politicization. It finally forced artisans to choose sides.

The events of that spring were not glaringly prejudicial to the interests of independent petty production, for the "Rassemblement populaire," as it called itself, was a deeply ambiguous alliance. With its roots in the radical center-left as well as in the Marxist left, the Popular Front expressed less a commitment to rearrange the socioeconomic geography than an attempt to make common cause against the fascist and anti-republican right. Despite the spontaneous outbreak of worker action that greeted him, Blum took office formally pledged to guarantee the continued democratic operation of the Third Republic, not to socialize France.[1] The Popular Front stood generally for social justice and against the oppressive, plutocratic, inefficient aspects of French capitalism. Beyond this, the constituent currents of vision and strategy flowed in different directions.[2]

Broadly speaking, Blum's program of economic reflation seemed to promise better times for small businessmen than previous deflationist policies. The newly elected legislature offered equal reason for artisans' optimism. The Groupe de défense artisanale remained under the chairmanship of Albert

Paulin, whose natural affinity for the artisanal cause grew out of his own past as a tailor and his adventures on the Tour de France des Artisans (1895–1899). Paulin's group now included more than 400 members; indeed, the communist deputies had joined en bloc in May 1936.[3] In their first meeting following the election these defenders of the artisanat resolved to grant artisans special treatment in the upcoming social legislation, eliminate *travail noir*, and force the administration to apply the pro-artisanal laws already on the books. For the government itself, Blum and his labor minister, Jean Lebas, personally assured artisans of their benevolent intentions.[4]

The legislation that followed hard on the formation of the first Blum ministry appeared less promising from the perspective of the *petit patronat*. The leadership of the CGPF, frightened by the rash of factory occupations, had consented to meet with the new cabinet and the representatives of the CGT. On the evening of June 6, these parties signed the so-called Matignon accords: paid vacations for all employees; the forty-hour work week; and mandatory collective labor contracts. The government immediately submitted these to the new parliament, and they quickly became law on June 20, 21, and 24, respectively.

In the long run, Blum's failure to extricate France from economic crisis could only have meant a continuing sag in artisanal production. In assessing the direct costs of the Matignon accords for artisans, however, it must be noted that the artisanat was a heterogeneous group and that the impact of the new social legislation depended on the size of a master's business and the number of assistants he employed. If, as noted earlier, the greatest part of artisanal enterprises employed no labor from outside the family, these remained largely untouched by the demands of Matignon, while they perhaps benefited from other aspects of the Popular Front's social program. For the rest, the Matignon settlement meant a steep rise in labor costs that promised to push some small businesses into bankruptcy. The *Artisan de l'Ouest*, voice of the Breton artisanat, estimated that the new obligations would increase these costs by between 31 and 39 percent.[5] The 1938 Artisanal Commission put the figure at 20 percent of the artisanal budget, but admitted that in some cases it might be higher.

This attack on the pocketbooks of employers naturally alarmed the artisanal movement and its supporters. In the Senate, Le Troquet wondered about the dire effects of the Matignon agreement on the neglected elements of French society. "It is important, above all," he said, "to make sure that such accords do not end up uniting big capital and big labor against medium-sized [and] artisanal industry."[6] The *Artisan de l'Ouest* entitled its consideration of the new laws "La fin de tout" ("the End of everything") and contended that the new social obligations would fall on artisans like "a volley of *coups de bâtons*."[7] The APCMF hastily convened a special session in Paris on July 3, which even the apostate Seine Chamber of Trades attended, and condemned the "fatal repercussions that the enforcement of the new social laws will have on the artisanal world."[8]

Yet, on the whole the artisanal movement, at least in the beginning, showed itself to be anxious but not openly hostile. The confederation of master printers, for example, declared its intention to apply the laws "not only with total loyalty, but with the best possible will."[9] The CGAF asked the new government for the right of each person to a job, a measure of professional autonomy, a decent income, protection for his home and family, guarantees against social misfortune, and a decent retirement—a wish-list hardly at odds with the designs of the Popular Front.[10] It also took care to couch its criticisms in such a way so as not to appear "des esprits rétrogrades."[11] Even the CEAA had sounded a sympathetic note when Henri Huguet, its future president, asked the 1935 congress "to not reject our social burdens.... Let us even be proud to support them despite their weight because they are a sign of social progress and civilization, a sign of this fraternity that is part of our national motto." On the other hand, Huguet had pronounced himself unalterably opposed to the forty-hour work week.[12]

Confronted by a new situation, the artisanal movement stuck to its trusted political methods. It lobbied the government for protection from the *travail noir* that it felt would follow the increase in workers' leisure. It asked that artisans be involved in any future negotiations of collective contracts and above all that Parliament grant petty producers a measure of dispensation from employers' new responsibilities. As the CGAF wrote to Blum and Lebas:

> Without wanting to belittle the intentions of social relief underlying the elaboration of [the Matignon] texts, the CGAF, desirous, within the possibilities of artisanal production, of contributing by all means to the amelioration of working conditions . . . is forced to observe that the material means necessary to respond to the envisioned measures are not in fact possessed by the "artisanal class."[13]

The CGAF believed that these additional burdens would deprive the masters once and for all "of the one thing the master artisan really possesses: the capital of his labor."[14] Its attitude is best characterized as yes to the Popular Front but with exceptions for artisans.

On the record, artisans could expect a sympathetic response from their friends in the legislature. Yet perhaps no group knew better than the leaders of the artisanal movement that parliamentary action was only half the battle. Legislation was, as we have seen repeatedly, unfinished law, which had to be given the spark of life by ministerial decree and administrative zeal. This was probably truer of the Matignon accords, as much a declaration of principle as a labor contract, than of any preceding legislation. Thus while the Parliament announced its desires, the process of determining the mode and effecting the operation of the new social regime fell to the administration and, in particular, to the reconstituted CNE.[15]

The idea of an advisory body representing the nation's economic interests had originated with the left, and the CNE had been created in 1925 by the *Cartel des Gauches*. The syndicalist base of the CNE and the *étatisme* it implied led to disputes even within the governing coalition over its form and the

the breadth of its authority. The CNE was established finally by ministerial decree rather than by parliamentary vote, attached directly to the premier's office, and given but minimal contact with the legislature and its committees. During the 1920s the CNE played only a modest part in setting economic policy.[16]

As the parliamentary machine seized up in the 1930s, the old idea gained new life and new support. There followed a number of attempts to remake the CNE, especially to broaden its base of representation and powers. The most fertile of these came in 1933 from the Paul-Boncour government, which revived a Poincaré proposal from 1927. This project, under the stewardship of Paul Ramadier, remained stalled in committee for three years before finally becoming law in March 1936.[17]

The Ramadier reform enlarged the CNE and linked it directly to the Parliament and its powerful committees. The new CNE comprised three parts: the General Assembly, which purported to represent the spectrum of social and economic interests in the country; the Permanent Commission, which acted as a kind of executive committee to the whole; and twenty professional Sections to advise on matters affecting individual economic sectors. Nominally, the minister of National Economy presided over the workings of the CNE. It was effectively dominated, however, by the general secretary, the "Normalien," Jean Cahen-Salvador, and by the vice-presidents drawn from the most powerful interests—men such as Lambert-Ribot, of the Comité des forges; Peyerimhoff, of the Comité central des houillières de France; and Léon Jouhaux, president of the CGT.[18]

Artisans received only a modest representation on the expanded CNE. The chambers of trades were accorded four seats on the General Assembly, compared to the twenty each given to the chambers of commerce and agriculture.[19] Tailledet, as president of the artisanat's "most representative" organization, the CGAF, was given the artisanal spot on the Permanent Commission. The CEAA received one seat in the General Assembly.[20] Artisanal federations obtained places on only four of the twenty professional sections: building and public works (Charles Massé), leather and skins (Gustave Papelard), personal services (Gaston Forestier)—all of whom were from the CGAF—and *artisans d'art*, where Paul Bulnois represented the UAF. The master artisans in such trades as woodworking and textiles, meanwhile, went unrepresented.[21]

Tailledet's and Peter's efforts to broaden artisans' representation on the CNE ran up against determined and well-placed opposition. In its early session of May 1936 the Permanent Commission discussed the artisanal question. Ramadier pronounced himself willing to see a slightly higher profile for small masters but rejected the idea of a separate Artisanal section. Cahen-Salvador was more steadfast. While he agreed that artisans deserved a representation commensurate with their social and economic importance, he insisted that the artisanat was a style of production and not a separate corporation. He added that he feared that the creation of a *section artisanale* would introduce into the CNE a class struggle of *petits* versus *gros*—precisely the sort of thing that the CNE was designed to avoid. The forces of big business were even more firmly set against the artisans' demands. Lambert-Ribot rejected out of hand any artisanal representation in the section for metallurgy. And Peyer-imhoff argued that,

> Any increase in the seats reserved for the artisanat would give this form of activity, of which the social importance cannot be denied, an influence far in excess of that which it enjoys in the work of the nation as a whole.[22]

Yet the push for an independent artisanal section enjoyed a critical meas-ure of support. Speaking in the Senate, Edouard Néron pointed out that the artisanat comprised fully one-fifth of the working population of France. He criticized the absence of a *section artisanale* and added that the practical effect of this scattering would be to drown the artisanat in a sea of industrial interests. Néron called the creation of an artisanal professional section "logically in-dispensable," because in his words, artisans were a key element of "order, equilibrium, and peace." Paul-Boncour concurred that artisans deserved spe-cial treatment less for their economic significance than for their "moral im-portance and for the long French tradition they represent."[23]

As so often in the past, on this issue artisans were eventually granted the form of their demands without acquiring the substance. The decrees of June 14 and November 12, 1938 expanded the CNE from twenty to twenty-five professional sections and satisfied the masters' demands for one of their own.[24] The CGAF controlled seven of the ten seats in the *section artisanale*. Bulnois still represented the UAF, Pierre Manoury the recently formed Confédération de l'artisanat familial (CAF), and Mademoiselle Wrignard, a milliner, the CGT. The APCMF and the CEAA, neither of which fit the syndical model for membership, found themselves shut out.[25]

The *section artisanale* held its inaugural session on January 13, 1939. Cahen-Salvador greeted the new representatives and graciously accepted his defeat. He even proposed that artisans be permitted to attend the meetings of the other professional sections when their interests were addressed.[26] The *section artisanale*, however, was just one more empty triumph. By 1939 the great debates over the Popular Front had been overtaken by Daladier's pursuit of *retranchement* and by the growing threat of war. There is no record of the artisanal section ever meeting for a second time.

The wage increases and paid vacations were, for the workers at least, the payoff of the Matignon agreement, but the keystone of the new labor policy was the provision for mandatory collective conventions, for it was by way of the latter that the former became reality. France already enjoyed legislation on collective bargaining, dating back to 1919. The old law provided that a binding convention would take effect only if a preliminary agreement existed between the parties. That is, it was voluntary rather than compulsory. In practice, suspicion and mutual hostility between workers and patrons made such conventions rare and limited in scope. On the contrary, the 1936 text gave the labor minister the power, if called upon by either side, to convene a *commission mixte* of employers and employees in an industry in order to negotiate a collective convention, to compel collective bargaining. Such contracts had by law to be concluded between the "most representative" organizations of *patrons* and workers, which most of the time meant the CGT and the CGPF. Furthermore, the minister, by issuing an appropriate *arrêté*, could make these agreements obligatory for all the members of a given profession and region.[27] The CNE became involved in this process as disagreements arose over the application of the conventions.

Many in the artisanal movement had at first applauded the new policy on collective contracts because it seemed to invite artisanal participation; yet the masters' hopes for a leading role in the politics of the economy were consistently frustrated. On the contrary, as the CNE began in the autumn of 1936 to put the Popular Front into operation, the artisans received a long, bitter lesson about their marginal position in the process. On the one hand, the masters met the opposition of the larger *patrons* to any special privileges for small producers. On the other, they confronted the determination of the workers—who remembered patronal foot-dragging in the matter of the forty-eight hour work week—to prevent any exceptions to the letter of the Matignon accords.[28] As Tailledet confessed to his readers: "I have gotten used to being beaten [in the CNE] since I'm always beaten."[29]

The usual course of events was as follows: A group of artisans would approach the CNE with a grievance about being subjected to a collective convention negotiated strictly between industrial employers and workers. The masters would demand a separate agreement for themselves and their *compagnons*. The appropriate professional section would first discuss the matter and then would summon all the parties in the dispute to Paris to meet with the CNE. The members of the professional section—workers, patrons, and "experts"—would listen to the artisans' complaints and promise that, in the future, syndicates of master artisans would be asked to participate. The artisans would agree to abide in the meantime by the original convention. Long-standing protests by artisanal syndicates were repeatedly placated and agreement reached once the CNE brought all sides together for mediation.

The CNE took up a typical case on January 19, 1937. The ninth professional section (construction and public works) met to decide whether or not to extend a convention signed between the Chambre syndicale des entrepreneurs and the Union départementale des syndicats ouvriers du bâtiment of the Haute-Savoie to all construction businesses in the department. This particular accord had resolved a strike of June 1936.[30] The convention was challenged by the Union départementale des syndicats des maîtres-artisans of the Haute-Savoie, affiliated with the CGAF, which insisted rather that relations between themselves and their journeymen be regulated by a separate contract. When they failed to receive satisfaction from the labor minister, Lebas, the artisans appealed their case to the CNE.

The masters found sentiment in the ninth professional section to be generally unsympathetic, or at least hostile to establishing any sort of exclusionary principle for *petites entreprises*. Cahen-Salvador recommended, and the section provisionally accepted his idea, that the CNE ought to approve the extension of the convention at issue unless the Union des maîtres-artisans could demonstrate that they, and not the Entrepreneurs, were the "most representative" group of patrons.[31]

In June 1937 Lebas reversed his earlier decision and ruled that, because the artisans represented the greatest percentage of construction businesses in the Haute-Savoie, a new contract, explicitly including master artisans, had to be negotiated. But the Union des maîtres-artisans and the minister soon found themselves at odds with the prefect, who claimed that the figures provided by the masters were greatly inflated and that, in fact, the original parties to the convention constituted the "most representative" elements. This occurred in October. On November 10, the question again came up in the CNE. The Entrepreneurs protested that the artisanat had not yet come under the terms of the convention and that the larger establishments were being hurt by this competitive disadvantage. The artisanal union and the patrons exchanged conflicting figures to support their positions. Ivan Martin, a *maître des requêtes* at the Conseil d'Etat, was the government administrator who presided over the proceedings. He leaned toward the artisans, but suggested that it would be best to call the several parties to Paris to settle the matter.[32]

On November 19, a delegation of artisans, workers, and patrons from the Haute-Savoie presented themselves at the CNE. Tailledet, as a concerned member of the Permanent Commission, also attended. Saccani, the president of the Union des maîtres-artisans, said that artisans merely resented having been presented with a fait accompli but were ready to cooperate in negotiations for a new agreement. Tailledet added his own disappointment with the condescension with which masters had been treated; yet he also agreed to withdraw his opposition to the old convention if artisans could be assured that they would participate in drawing up a new one. Rulland, president of the Chambre syndicale des Entrepreneurs, and Blandin, secretary of the Union des syndicats ouvriers du bâtiment, quickly gave their assent.[33]

In this same fashion, when the CNE directly consulted with artisanal groups, the latter were easily persuaded not to oppose the collective conventions. It seems likely, therefore, that much of the masters' recalcitrance had less to do with the details of the contracts themselves—although, as we will see, these, too, were a source of conflict—than with their frustration at being ignored. It was an opposition largely of principle: even small employers wanted to be consulted about the economic and social regime under which they had to live, a voice denied them in the usual course of events.[34] This is not to say that artisans' reluctance to submit to collective contracts signed between business and labor was *primarily* symbolic. The masters sought influence, not for its own sake, but because they thought that they would negotiate a better deal with their own *compagnons* than the larger employers would with the CGT. This became clear in the direct confrontations between artisans and their workers that arrived at the CNE for arbitration.[35] Later, this will be examined more closely in the hairdressing industry.

Unable to defend the interests of petty producers in the CNE, the movement had to look elsewhere for redress. The CGAF worked, as ever, with its friends in the National Assembly to force the authorities to recognize artisans' special circumstances.[36] Nevertheless, its efforts paid only small dividends. Family labor was not subjected to the same strictures as hired labor, and *petits* employers in the metalworking trades were granted, for two years, an extra hour of work per week.[37] Otherwise, *compagnons* had a right to the benefits enjoyed by other workers.

The CGAF also undertook to negotiate directly with the CGT. It had, first of all, philosophical reasons to cooperate with the Popular Front. As Paulin wrote in the *Cahiers de l'Artisanat*:

> We should not fool ourselves into believing that the artisanal class could, by virtue of its own efforts alone, realize a truly humane economic regime. . . . The artisan, who is an independent worker, is very near the non-independent worker because both of them have the same adversaries: anonymous capital, trusts, occult masters of finance.[38]

The CGAF also hoped that these negotiations would preempt a more unfavorable application of the Matignon accords to the artisanat. On September 19, 1936, the CGT and the CGAF signed their own collective convention (see Appendix C), initialed by, among others, Léon Jouhaux and René Belin for the CGT and Tailledet, Grandadam, and Forestier for the CGAF.[39] This convention was not meant to be definitive but merely to draw the guidelines for agreements between artisanal and worker federations, which remained to be hammered out by region and trade. A few of these were indeed signed; in the shoemaking and hairdressing industries, for example.[40] The incidence of strikes involving artisans, the frequent recourse to CNE arbitration, and the small number of "artisanal" *conventions collectives* that were actually worked out, however, all testify to the limited success of the CGAF's strategy.

Not all artisanal organizations proved so willing to go along with the Popular Front. The more conservative groups set themselves against what they perceived as a working class "powerfully organized, installed in power, and determined to realize its ends by any means possible, legal or not." The *Artisan de France*, voice of the CAF, wrote that the Matignon accords jeopardized "the life and the future of the artisanat."[41] Blum understands, remarked the *Artisan de l'Ouest*, that the concentration of production is a necessary prelude to socialization, and that his government intends to fulfill the prophesies of the *Communist Manifesto*. The journal roundly denounced this "syndicalisme révolutionnaire" and called instead for the reinforcement of "corporative liberty."[42] Hubert Ley, of the CEAA, also blasted the convention signed between the CGAF and the CGT, which he saw as a ruse to separate artisans from their real allies and "to divide the patronal world in order to finish it off more quickly."[43] In fact, Ley feared that France had reached the moment of the "final conflict between collective and private property," and he called for the constitution of a "bloc des classes moyennes." "Today, at least, the artisan knows who he is. He is a *small* employer. But he is an *employer*." [emphasis added][44]

The CEAA consistently objected to any sort of legislation that would infringe on employers' "property rights": automatically sliding wage scales and compulsory arbitration, for instance. It demanded instead "a profession organized from the top to the bottom of the social scale."[45] And when directly confronted with "disorder" the CEAA cried "Bolshevism!" and made some very menacing noises. Witness Peter's reaction to a 1937 strike in the Paris hairdressing industry:

> If the government is unable or unwilling to give the assurance that it will stop this attack on our professions, the CEAA will be obliged to examine plans for an organization for the protection of these trades. And I promise you, Mr. President of the Council, that more than a million French artisans are ready to defend their livelihoods with a will all the more firm as their professions are for them more than a mere job.[46]

The CEAA thus tossed off the cloak of the "social buffer" and took its place with the forces of order.

For those who agreed with Ley and Peter it was a small and predictable step outside the artisanat proper and into the renascent organization of the *classes moyennes*. The political order of the middle classes was of a modest vintage. The first Association des classes moyennes, based on the Belgian model, was founded in 1907.[47] Not much was heard from what Crossick called the "petty bourgeois International" in the 1920s, but the depression brought it back to life. In 1934 Armand Pugi, a veteran of the cause, set up the Bloc du Petit Commerce. Pugi hoped to wield his new weapon to challenge "the planned economy, nationalizations, and state monopolies" promoted by the left.[48]

But it was the Popular Front that really energized the movement of the middle classes. Suddenly, middle class organizations began to appear everywhere. In the wake of the Matignon accords, as the Radical party began to take its distance from the Blum government, a group of deputies, led by the former *enfant terrible* of the Radicals, Edouard Daladier, formed a Groupement des classes moyennes in the Chamber of Deputies. In October, this group presided over the creation of a larger organization, the Confédération générale des classes moyennes (CGCM). The CGCM turned out to be the least conservative of the new organizations of the *classes moyennes*. It did not set itself completely against the new social legislation but merely insisted that the middle classes receive a fair share of state largess.[49]

At about the same time, the Comité confédéral des syndicats des classes moyennes was formed "to defend the middle classes as a part of the Nation whose existence is imperiled by the economic and social evolution of our era." In January 1938 this committee linked up with the Groupement général des classes moyennes, led by another of the Radicals' Young Turks and the editor of *La Voix*, Emile Roche, to create the Confédération générale des syndicats des classes moyennes (CGSCM). In October of that year the CGSCM received a place on the CNE. A month later it celebrated the adhesion of the Union fédérale des anciens combattants to its cause. At one point the CGSCM claimed to have some 2.5 million members. That figure is certainly much too high and is, in any case, no indication of any broad representativity.[50] The organizational spree of the middle classes continued with the founding of the Confédération générale des associations des classes moyennes (CGACM) in early 1938. A diffuse group, unable, because of its non-syndical structure, to aspire to a place on the CNE, the CGACM had to content itself with a general campaign for tax reform, family allowances, and other social perks for the middle classes.[51]

As a matter of form, the various middle class organizations proclaimed their political neutrality, by which they meant their antipathy to social conflict and their faith in class collaboration. "The movement of the middle classes in no way represents a self-serving defense of vested interests," wrote Gaston Lecordier.[52] Most groups subscribed to a vaguely corporatist program of reform. That is to say, their rhetoric was obsessively anti-Marxist and their practical policy a point by point opposition to extended benefits for employees and support for the retrenchment begun under Chautemps and continued under Daladier and Reynaud. The CGCM suspected the influence of foreigners in the economy and required that all its members be French citizens.[53]

The movement of the middle classes attracted several prominent figures from the artisanal movement. The CAF officially joined the CGSCM in January 1939, and its general secretary, Pierre Manoury, sat on its board of directors.[54] Henri Huguet, former president of the Loiret Chamber of Trades and Peter's successor as head of the CEAA, was part of the "study commission" of the CGSCM and chairman of its Artisanal Section. Georges Chaudieu, president of the National Butchers' Federation, a member of the CEAA's national council, and future Vichy functionary, was a CGSCM secretary. René Serre, head of the butchers' syndicate in Paris, was one of its most "eminent" members. Dejeante, president of the UAF, served as a vice-president of the CGCM.[55]

The solidarity of the middle classes was not a new idea. The novelty in the 1930s was in the breadth of the new organizations and in their frankly conservative appeal. Historically, the *classes moyennes*, like the artisans, had set themselves against both big capital and big labor—the twin bogeymen of industrialization. As often as not, they pointed to finance and industry as the greater menace, as Tailledet had done in the crisis of the mid-1920s. Only after 1936 did this social neutralism dissolve and the middle classes fix on Marxism and the working class as the chief threat to small property, to the virtual exclusion of the "Trusts." For a group like the CEAA, concerned with the need for "loyalty in production and order in society," it was an easy shift to the right and into the movement of the middle classes, where it could pursue its mission to protect artisans from the Marxist doctrine supposedly preached by the CGAF.[56]

"The defense of the middle classes is the order of the day," wrote Tailledet in February 1937.[57] Yet the CGAF accepted the concept of the "middle classes" with reservations and carefully kept its distance. Its syndicalist leadership felt that despite impressive lists of members and high-placed sponsors, the new movement would achieve few concrete results:

> To proclaim loudly a will to defend the middle classes is not, in our opinion, sufficient. It is necessary in reality to go further and to take, for each of the distinct groups that comprise the middle classes, precise measures, taking into account its particular needs. . . .[58]

It was felt that such a broad movement, with such diverse interests (which were often at odds with one another) could never achieve more than rhetorical successes. The "middle classes" were a pleasant enough notion, but practically speaking artisans should defend artisans. The CGAF perceived, moreover, in this politics of the middle classes, as it had all along in corporatism, a disingenuousness and species of demagoguery aimed at manipulating petty producers for ends that were ultimately not their own.

Just as the Popular Front galvanized the *classes moyennes*, it also produced what can be characterized as a critical moment for the organization of the artisanal movement. From the beginning, the formation and evolution of the movement had depended on a series of just such critical moments: the Astier law, the appearance of the Alsace Chamber of Trades in France, and the elaboration of the income tax. In the 1930s, artisans were coaxed further out of their traditional isolation, first, by the economic crisis and, second, by the Matignon accords. The effect of these critical moments on the movement is easy enough to measure. Having been organized only in 1933, the CEAA reported 160,000 members, including the UAF, by April 1935. A year later it claimed to have 175,000 members, which escalated to 200,000 in some 1,500 affiliated groups by June 1936.[59] The CGAF had counted 100,000 members in 200 affiliated syndicates in 1929. These figures climbed to 180,000 in 332 syndicates in June 1933 and to more than 200,000 members by 1935.[60] The agitation over the Blum reforms gave both the CEAA and the CGAF an organizational jolt that lasted through 1937 and brought the movement to the pinnacle of its fortunes, uniting some half-million master artisans.[61]

For all the activity at the top of the artisanal movement, however, it seems that the surge in organization came primarily from the bottom up. For most masters, their initiation into the artisanal movement was by way of their local trade syndicate, where the great questions of national import took second place to more immediate and parochial concerns. Often the local syndicates were merely elaborations of existing mutualist societies, which extended their fields of operation to cover new troubles. Artisans' most common motivation was the desire to establish some kind of price discipline in their localities, usually at *le minimum vital*, for the worst-placed tradesmen. "Syndicalization" represented the attempt to turn around the market forces unleashed by the decline in business and increase in businesses; it was, first of all, a commercial

and not a political act. "Il faut adopter un tarif," wrote a cooper from the
Ille-et-Vilaine, "il faut un syndicat."[62] "For us," said the *Artisan de France*,

> the trade is not just a group of independent individuals without any ties
> between them; a trade is a small society where [some] authority must reign
> . . . [and] which has the power to impose its decisions on all [its members]
> for the good of all. . . .[63]

Subsequently, as local organizations proved only minimally effective at protecting the interests of their constituents, local trade syndicates were more
and more drawn to larger groups such as the regional and national trade
federations and unions of master artisans.

The tradesmen were also recruited into the artisanal movement through
their participation in the chambers of trades lately being formed throughout
the country. Representation in the chambers was apportioned by profession.
Once elected, however, members of the chamber were forced to think about
the artisanat as a whole. In addition, the compilation of the trades registers,
following the decree-law of 1934, helped to bring the chambers into closer
contact with their constituents.

In this sense, the artisanat was once again the child of government action,
yet it remains true that at every level the making of the artisanat depended
on the vision and dedicated activity of a few personalities. We have already
seen the critical efforts of Tailledet and Grandadam for the shoemakers;
Chaudieu, for the butchers, and Rebé, for the blacksmiths, played a similar
role in stimulating syndical activity. At the local level, the development of
the artisanal movement reflected the work of men like Eyraud in Lyon, Albert
Dupuis in Rouen, Louis Bourrières in the Lot, André Jeannin in the Cher,
and of course the ubiquitous energies of Peter and Ley. Across the country,
as presidents of local syndicates and mutualist societies, of the chambers of
trades, and of the regional unions of artisans, the same names appeared over
and over. If the state was the architect, these were the *batisseurs* of the
artisanat.

Some of this is visible in the process that led to the appearance of a major
new contender in the ranks of the artisanal movement: the CAF. The Matignon accords, it appears, drew artisans from the West to their trade syndicates in unprecedented numbers and, through these, to the departmental
unions of artisans. The Union artisanale of the Charente-Inférieure, for example, counted 250 adhesions in the first month of its existence, December
1936.[64] The Union artisanale from the Ille-et-Vilaine reported 1,255 new
members in 1936, and that from the Maine-et-Loire, more than 1,500. The
Union artisanale de la Manche signed up 1,600 artisans in the last four months
of 1936 alone. In the Finistère, the union artisanale quadrupled its membership (from 500 to 2,000) in the second half of that year.[65]

The progress of the artisanal movement in Brittany owed much to the
proselytizing efforts of Christian-inspired tradesmen of this traditionally Catholic province and to the patronage of Church officials like the Abbé Vallé,

of the Manche. Many of the Breton unions of artisans, with their regionalist and conservative perspective, had originally joined the CEAA. Few were attracted to what the *Artisan de l'Ouest* called the "syndicalist-fascists" of the CGAF. They apparently objected to the centralization and lack of regional autonomy in the CGAF and were clearly horrified by its willingness to deal with the CGT. Yet Breton artisans yearned for something more syndical, coherent, and explicitly Catholic than the CEAA.[66]

In March 1937 the "spontaneous" grouping of these "Christian" syndicates produced the CAF. This confederation began immediately to pick up support among the petty tradesmen of the northwest, and by the time of its first national congress, in June 1937, the CAF could claim to represent some 35,000 artisans in fifty-two departmental unions.[67] The CEAA predictably condemned the intrusion of the *arrivistes* of the CAF; however, under the leadership of its president, A. Ewald, and its energetic general secretary, the chandler, Pierre Manoury, it proved to be the most dynamic element in an artisanal movement that was beginning to level off. In less than two years, the CAF managed to bring some 50,000 artisans into its fold and to win control of a number of chambers of trades.[68] When the CNE created its "Artisanal section" in 1939, Manoury was given a place.

The CAF resembled the CGAF in its strictly syndical organization. Its doctrine of "Christian socialism" brought it closer to the CEAA in its regionalist bent and sympathy for corporatism. The CAF was also animated by the recognized need for *services practiques*, and its program repeated the routine demands for tax relief, easier bankruptcy laws, and the control of *travail noir*—"especially," as Maurice Boulland, a confederation officer from the Ile-de-France, put it, "among foreign employers (and I might add, without being anti-Semitic, *les Israélites*, French or not)."[69] Its corporatist perspective led the CAF to regard class conflict as artificial, as the product of a distorted *régime économique*.[70] It therefore sought to replace classes, "the source of weakness and division," with a "harmonious hierarchy," where social distinctions would be reduced to a "mésure légitime" and where social antagonisms would disappear.[71] The CAF's was a largely moral crusade, "mystical" rather than materialist, against the "demagogic politics and the untrammelled pursuit of pleasure" that suffused modern France.[72] The love of family, the joy of work, the pride in one's region "that certain people find backward because factory chimneys are rare, but [that] the artisan finds healthy and vigorous because the family, instead of serving industry, serves work": these were the principles of the new confederation.[73] The *Artisan de France* counted the CAF officers' contribution to the French family: Ewald, the president, had eight children; Prévost, the vice-president, had nine; Manoury, the general secretary, had only three, but he came from a family of ten and would presumably prove more prodigious in the end.[74]

The hairdressing trades (*la coiffure*) are not typical of the artisanat; no one trade really is. The coiffeur is not the salt of the earth like the country cooper; he does not possess the exquisite skills of the goldsmith; his corporation does not enjoy the *ancienneté* of the masons, or the watchmakers, or even the printers. There was a time, of course, when *perruquiers* ("wigmakers") and *tonsureurs* ministered to the *toilettes* of the rich and eminent. The modern hairdresser, however, thrived in an urban, industrialized world and under the habit of popular fashion.

At the same time, the sector of *coiffure* stands out for the overwhelming dominance of the smallest establishments. Marcel de Ville Chabrol found in 1906 that of 56,784 hairdressing businesses, 56,478 employed fewer than ten assistants. Figures from the 1936 census reveal that this pattern changed little in the first third of the century. Approximately 98 percent of all hairdressing establishments were artisanal, at least in size. Eighty-three percent of all assistant *coiffeurs* worked in these tiny salons. Some 52,000 employees were divided among 30,364 enterprises, of which only 698 had more than 5 assistants, and only 124 more than 10. Two establishments alone employed more than 50 workers. Naturally, the larger salons were clustered in Paris. In departments such as the Vaucluse or the Lot not one salon employed more than 5 assistants. The census also discovered some 26,000 hairdressers *isolés*.[75] Still, while the hairdressing trades are not exactly microcosmic, they are instructive. It is therefore useful to take a closer look at the experiences of *coiffeurs* and *coiffeuses* as they ran parallel to those of other independent petty producers.

Problems in *coiffure* did not begin with the election of Léon Blum. The profession's fortunes had waxed and waned since the beginning of the century. In 1906 there were already some 75,000 hairdressers.[76] Over the next fifteen years the profession prospered. The number of hairdressers decreased at the same time as postwar fashion dictated short hair for women—truly a *bonne affaire*. The *Coiffeur-Parfumeur* of Bordeaux even went so far as to express its anxiety about the shortage of trained hairdressers,[77] and, indeed, the early 1920s subsequently came to be considered a kind of "golden age" for the trade.[78]

Bad times soon followed the good, however, as *coiffure's* reputation attracted young workers and the supply of hairdressers caught up to demand by the mid-1920s. The *coiffeurs* no longer enjoyed an open field. In fact, according to Monsieur A. Presle of Moulins, the advice, "Become a hairdresser; that's a great trade," terrorized them.[79] Henri Janvier, writing for the workers' *Coiffeur Confédéré*, estimated that every year between 4,000 and 5,000 people tried to establish themselves as hairdressers.[80] Only after 1926 did work begin to pick up and prices to stabilize once more.[81]

The on and off troubles in the profession convinced *coiffeurs* that safety lay in some kind of unity. Hard times stimulated the expansion of syndicalism among the masters and led them to focus more sharply on the defense of *petits patrons*.[82] Once more it is interesting to note that although the rising consciousness among master *coiffeurs* coincided with the growth of the artisanal movement itself, the two were only tenuously connected. Sometimes, it is true, trade concerns came together with artisanal consciousness. The most significant instance of this convergence in *coiffure* came in 1925 when the Union fédérale des syndicats des maîtres-artisans coiffeurs decided to hitch its wagon to the CGAF. Tailledet invited the hairdressers to the Confédér-ation's congress in August of that year. There the hairdressers *fédérés* pro-ceeded to rewrite their statutes, elect new officers, and commit themselves at least to the principle of artisanal solidarity.[83] It is not possible to conclude, however, that some grass roots demand compelled the Union fédérale initi-ative. Local *coiffeurs* continued to pursue a rigorous economism, their or-ganizational drive fueled by narrow professional concerns. The local syndicates seemed to know little and care less about the artisanal movement.

Let us examine the course of events in Bordeaux. In late 1922 the Syndicat des maîtres coiffeurs de Bordeaux combined with the Association syndicale to form the Syndicat des maîtres-artisans coiffeurs (SMAC).[84] The master hairdressers of Bordeaux thereby sought to transform what had been a means for professional training, cooperation, and mutuality going back to 1849 into a shield more appropriate to the challenges of the 1920s.[85] Among the most serious of these was the imminent application of the forty-eight hour work week, passed by the National Assembly in 1919. Indeed, in the spring of 1920 the profession had experienced a strike over precisely this issue.[86] It was true, the *Coiffeur-Parfumeur* admitted, that some *coiffeurs* had shamelessly ex-ploited their workers, making them spend fifteen or sixteen hours a day in the salon. And it was precisely this sort of abuse that had "furnished the workers' organizations with their pretext for intervention and the principle argument that moved the public authorities to action." Yet the SMAC ob-jected that the eight-hour law would bring "the gravest perturbations" to the profession.[87]

In fact, hours in the hairdressing industry were generally longer than in most. It was routine in Bordeaux for masters and their assistants to put in a sixty-hour work week. Work in the salon, after all, was irregular, "porous," nothing like the continuous hum of the factory. Throughout the day customers might stop by in crowds or not at all, and an hour of leisurely snipping and *bavardage* might be followed by an hour with nothing to do. It was only after the shops and factories closed during the week or on the weekends that clients began to wander in for their haircuts and shaves. How then could a patron reasonably be forced to close at 7:00 P.M. or shut his salon on Saturday afternoon and all day Sunday—the so-called *semaine anglaise*?*

Indeed, the administration recognized this peculiar schedule in its decrees of August and October 1921, which ameliorated the forty-eight hour work week for *coiffure*.[88] This did not, however, resolve the matter. The workers' federation condemned the decrees as "excessive benevolence toward the em-ployers."[89] Negotiations for a collective convention between employers and employees continued, and became the fulcrum of the very intense dispute

---

*The *semaine anglaise* could mean either a half-day Saturday and a day off Sunday or a half-day Sunday and a day off Monday.

over hours. Another strike in the hairdressing trades in Bordeaux at the end of 1923 produced a convention that satisfied many of the workers' demands. The agreement broke down, however, because neither the workers nor the SMAC had the means to enforce it. Refractory masters who did not belong to the employers' syndicate (maybe a majority, certainly a large number) did not consider themselves party to the pact, which remained a principle rather than a fact.[90]

The case of the maverick employers raises an interesting point. If the collective contracts were in one sense the occasion for bitter conflict between workers and patrons, in another sense they brought the two sides together against a common enemy: the so-called *baissiers*. These were *coiffeurs*— either hairdressers without employees or employers who refused to respect the conventions—who insisted on their right to stay open as long as they liked and charge whatever prices could guarantee them business. Given that the public was not likely to pay higher prices than necessary, the existence of the *baissiers* made the collective agreements virtually impossible to enforce. The syndicates looked to the state for help, and sometimes the *inspecteurs du travail* intervened. For instance, in July 1925 the *Coiffeur Confédéré* reported that the labor inspectors took action against a Monsieur Lhoummeau, who was discovered by an inspector to have two of his employees working at 12:30 on a Saturday, when, according to the collective contract in Paris, they were supposed to be at lunch. Nor did Lhoummeau have his hours posted in the window of his salon, as the law required. The Tribunal of Prud'hommes, supported by three workers' and one employers' syndicate, ordered Lhoummeau to pay a 160 franc fine as well as court expenses, and, of course, to obey the law in the future.[91]

The syndicates of workers and employers complained constantly about such infractions and, to judge by the number of reports to the minister, the labor inspectors stayed busy hunting down those who violated the rules; however, there was little they could do. The law prevented an employer from keeping his workers past the agreed upon hours, and the inspectors generally reported that despite a certain amount of confusion the law was being respected. Nothing, however, stood in the way of an employer himself or an *isolé* working whatever hours he liked. In order to close this loophole, the syndicates asked for the application of a *horaire unique* for all salons, employees or not, but the administration refused to comply. That is, the state, while agreeable to controls on employees' hours, hesitated to interfere with what it considered to be freedom of commerce.[92]

It would be misleading, therefore, to portray the struggle in the hairdressing trades as a simple tug-of-war between workers and their employers. A prosperous and well-organized *métier* had benefits for both sides. At the same time, their frequent tactical cooperation against the *baissiers* hardly softened the conflict between masters and *compagnons*. The *Coiffeur Confédéré* continued to lash out at the employers' "rapaciousness" and "absolute intransigence."[93]

Marcel Jonca, editor of the *Reveil des Coiffeurs*, characterized the early

1930s in the hairdressing trade as "the years of the lean cows" because there were salons without work, workers without employ, *baissiers*, competition from beauty parlors in department stores, and new laws restricting hours and extending employees' social benefits.[94] The *Artisan Coiffeur* described the situation in the region of the Centre: "Giant salons, *travail noir*, poorly skilled workers charging starvation prices."[95] One can only guess at the true dimensions of the depression in *coiffure*. The logic of economic crisis and the weight of the evidence, circumstantial as it is, would place hairdressers in the classical vise. It seems evident that even in so fashion-conscious a place as France, a trip to the barber or the beauty parlor would be one of the first items to disappear from a shrinking budget. Hairdressers, in this sense, were in a less favorable situation than, say, bakers or others in the non-luxury food trades. Yet aside from the Union fédérale's estimate of a 15 percent drop in activity (see Table 3.8), there are no figures.

Faced with the prospect of empty chairs and empty pockets, hairdressers across the country tried to think of ways to bring customers back to the salons. One popular idea was to encourage a return to the fashion of short hair— *mode à la garçon*, it was called—that had so profited the profession in the Roaring Twenties. Monsieur Lesourd, vice-president of the *coiffeurs'* syndicate in the Centre, for example, proposed that the patrons ask all their female employees to cut their hair short as an example to the customers.[96] One hairdresser suggested that *coiffeurs* learn the art of tricking their customers by telling them that short hair would help to prevent head colds and thus require the client to return soon for his own health.[97] The Chambre syndicale of master *coiffeurs* in Paris went so far as to establish a propaganda commission "to study all effective means to revive the fashion of short hair."[98]

The *coiffeurs* also sought to recapture their old monopoly on the sale of toiletries, a highly profitable territory lately invaded by bazaars, pharmacies, and grocery stores. To this end, Marcel Destephan, from the little town of Bègles, urged his colleagues to require that their suppliers refuse to deal with other retailers. "La parfumerie aux coiffeurs!" he demanded.[99] Lesourd thought that a bit of salesmanship might go a long way:

> Tell the client, "Take Brand X . . . it's better," and buy your supplies only from those manufacturers who sell exclusively to *coiffeurs*. [That way] you will be sure that tomorrow the same customer will come back to you, because she will be able to find her favorite fragrance only at the hairdresser's *salon*.[100]

The same kind of boycott, the *Artisan Coiffeur* suggested, could be used against hairbrush manufacturers, to "control the sale of [their] products and to suppress certain unqualified vendors who, what is more, do not respect the prescribed prices."[101]

Paradoxically, if the hairdressers fretted over their declining fortunes, *coiffure* retained its reputation for easy work and decent money. Thus while business fell off, the working population continued to increase. Between 1931 and 1936 some 30,000 new salons opened their doors. Lesourd reported that in 1914 Nevers had been home to twenty-four hairdressers; twenty years later it had fifty-seven, not counting the six who worked out of their homes and "le travail noir incontrôlable."[102] Presle wrote that whereas the Allier department had barely 250 *coiffeurs* in 1920, by 1937 it had nearly 600.[103] The Chambre syndicale of Versailles complained that in this city of 70,000 there were 70 *coiffeurs*, while there was enough work for only 45.[104] The *Coiffeur-Parfumeur* remarked disparagingly that in a mining community not far from Bordeaux, the unemployed miners had begun to set up small salons at home, cutting their neighbors' hair and selling the perfumes and pomades that were the *coiffeurs'* usual commercial fare. Hairdressers from the local syndicate brought the matter to the attention of the authorities, who received them politely but did nothing.[105]

On the matter of professional overcrowding, unions of both workers and employers agreed that the glut of *coiffeurs* and *coiffeuses* encouraged cheating against the labor conventions, depressed prices, and frustrated mutual efforts to "put the trade in order." Who was responsible for the surplus? Both *compagnons* and masters pointed to the independent "schools" of *coiffure*, the so-called *écoles privées*.[106] These private operations, capitalizing on the profession's reputation, made a profit on every hairdresser they trained, and so they generated as many as they could. François Magnien, general secretary of the Fédération ouvrière, painted this unsympathetic picture: A child leaves school at age thirteen or fourteen years. His parents want him to find a trade. The child naturally has a preference, but in these days of economic crisis there are no jobs to be found there. Then the parents notice an advertisement for an *école privée de coiffure*, which promises to train the child in three months and to guarantee a placement thereafter. The parents pay their money; but, said Magnien, this amounts to a kind of confidence trick. A person does not become a *coiffeur* in three months. In fact, the national collective convention signed in 1938 required an apprenticeship of eighteen months for *salonniers* and two years for *coiffeurs-dames*. So the "graduate" cannot find a job in a reputable establishment. What does he do? (And, Magnien added, this concerns "hundreds of victims.") He gets himself all the equipment of a hairdresser and sets himself up at home or in some basement under the most miserable conditions. There he works at cut-rate prices, with the inevitable consequence of a widespread instability in rates and salaries. The level of professional competence declines. The general business climate worsens as the more competent and honest tradesmen are undermined and forced into bankruptcy. "Pushed to the wall," concluded Magnien, "our beautiful trade is now the despair of the true professionals who are ashamed to be *coiffeurs*."[107] The syndicates looked to the public authorities again and again to close down the *écoles privées*. As in the case of *baissiers*, however, the state was reluctant to get involved.

The unions, both worker and patronal, found another cause of over-crowding to be the influx of foreigners to the hairdressing trades—"especially Greeks, but also Jews, Poles, Italians, etc."[108] Even the *Coiffeur Confédéré*, affiliated to the CGT, demanded that "the entry of all foreign workers in our profession be totally prohibited throughout France." Ironically, it appeared just below the journal's masthead: "Proletarians of all countries, unite!"[109] Monsieur E. Bénazet, secretary of the Fédération des patrons coiffeurs artisans in Montauban, also found foreign workers a likely target. "I have recently seen," he wrote, "a salon run by a Portuguese and a Spaniard, employing a Polish worker—what you might call a 'Salon International.' There you have it, three rogues who get along perfectly in the matter of prices and hours. These are the fellows who are the 'Kings of France.' "[110]

There is no reason to believe that there was any truth to this assertion or that immigrants comprised an unusually large percentage of *coiffeurs*. The investigation by the Lyon Chamber of Commerce revealed that some 17 percent of salons were operated by foreigners, which was below the mean for all professions. The Grenoble Chamber of Trades found that less than 12 percent of *coiffeurs* in its jurisdiction were *étrangers*. Magnien told a gathering of workers that foreigners made up 15 percent of Parisian hairdressers.[111] Nevertheless, the government proved more open to the beau geste here than on the question of *écoles privées*. The labor minister, Adrien Marquet, issued a decree of July 20, 1934, effecting the law of August 10, 1932. Marquet set the maximum number of foreigners in *coiffure* at 10 percent in the Paris region and slightly higher in the frontier regions. There is no indication, however, that the government consistently enforced this decree.[112]

Whether or not the *écoles privées* and immigrant *coiffeurs* were the cause, the excess of workers willing and able to cut hair did indeed complicate labor relations in the profession. The workers' syndicates, either those connected to the CGT, or those attached to the Confédération générale des travailleurs unitaires (CGTU), a communist union, held to their insistence on higher wages and shorter hours. Until the summer of 1936 they remained committed to a complete application of the forty-eight hour work week. The patronal syndicates, or at least a fair number of them, did not reject these demands unconditionally. They merely pointed out that as long as there existed a population of *baissiers*, who would not abide by any collective convention, employers could not charge the prices necessary both to satisfy the workers and to turn a profit.

The patrons' syndicates therefore spent the greatest part of their efforts trying to obtain the *horaire unique* and to enforce some kind of price discipline. The SMAC of Bordeaux, for example, warned that low prices would bring on professional decadence and "specialized machine work." It tried to lift its readers' spirits by declaring that high prices would produce a competitive advantage among those clients who reasoned judiciously that, "The work of this *coiffeur* must certainly be superior if he doesn't follow the example of his price-cutting colleagues."[113] The fédérations ouvrières understood the employers' dilemma and joined them, as we have seen, in petitioning the government to do something about *baissiers*. Yet the workers were not willing to suspend their demands. As a consequence the profession experienced endemic labor troubles over both the form of collective conventions and the substance of the forty-eight hour work week.

Naturally, Paris was at the center of this particular trouble. Throughout the 1920s, workers and employers in the capital had wrestled over the questions of wages and the eight-hour work day. In the spring of 1926 a ten-day strike proved inconclusive.[114] Nevertheless, hours in *coiffure* gradually decreased and the *semaine anglaise* was established as the theoretical norm. Finally, in May 1932, thirteen years after the legislature had made the forty-eight hour work week law, a group of syndicates representing both patrons and employees signed a collective accord. It provided for a fifty-two hour work week in Paris and a fifty-five hour week in the surrounding region. At the same time, it established the principles of closing on Sunday and the *semaine anglaise*.[115] The new convention did not, however, produce any lasting concord. According to the usual schedule of administrative action, the ministerial decree imposing the new agreement only appeared eighteen months later, in October 1933. Moreover, while the employers saw the new schedule as a great compromise on their part, the workers considered it to be an interim arrangement. They had their sights firmly set on forty-eight hours.

The 1932 convention complicated the politics of *coiffure* in another way. It had been co-signed by the Chambre syndicale of master *coiffeurs*, affiliated with the Union fédérale des maîtres coiffeurs and the CGAF, and by the local Fédération ouvrière, connected to the CGT. Many of the Paris employers, especially the owners of the larger salons, were implacably opposed to the new agreement, which they saw as a sellout by the Chambre syndicale. These renegade masters thereupon set up a new group, the Syndicat indépendant des patrons coiffeurs (SIPC), in the hope of derailing the new agreement, which, in the words of the SIPC's president, Marcel Bagnaud, would steer the profession toward "le socialisme d'état."[116] The SIPC insisted that, "We do not consider the workers our enemies...."[117] But both the Fédération ouvrière and the Union fédérale considered the independent patrons, as the SIPC were known, to be exactly that. Indeed, Bagnaud himself declared, "We are patrons-*coiffeurs* and we address ourselves to other patrons."

Bagnaud's career was an unusual one for *coiffure*. A native of Rambouillet and graduate of the Ecole Normale in Saint-Cloud, he was a decorated veteran, a *grand mutilé de guerre*, and an officer in the Légion d'honneur. Invalided out of the army, Bagnaud went to work for the paper, *L'Intransigeant*, which gave him intimate connections to the political right and to the organizations of *anciens combattants*, which he maintained even when he changed professions. In the early 1920s, Bagnaud married a *coiffeuse*, moved to the capital, and began a successful career in *coiffure*. His shop, the Maison Marcel became renown in the capital for being exceptionally modern, clean, and comfortable; the *Semaine de la Coiffure* called it a veritable "usine de coiffure" ("hairdressing factory").[118] Indeed, the *Artisan Coiffeur* of Moulins described him as "one of the great magnates of *coiffure*."[119] Bagnaud became active in commercial affairs and Paris politics, was named a secretary of the Paris Chamber of Commerce and, in 1934, an Inspecteur départemental de l'enseignement technique[120]—an appointment that Henri Janvier of the *Coiffeur Confédéré* thought inappropriate for "the worst enemy of the working class in hairdressing."[121]

Almost immediately the independent patrons became involved in a violent confrontation with the workers. On September 22, 1932, the SIPC met in the back room of a café at Place Victor Hugo, in the sixteenth *arrondissement*, to plan its strategy. A section of workers learned about the meeting and arrived in force. They took issue with the patrons' presentation of the facts, demanded the floor to rebut these "calumnies," and were refused. Shouts were exchanged but not punches, thanks, according to the *Coiffeur Confédéré*, to the solidarity and cool-headedness of the workers. When the workers began to leave, they were greeted outside by a cordon of police, called in by one of the patrons. In the end, the public order was maintained, but so were the antagonisms.[122]

It is not therefore the case that the social legislation of the summer of 1936 dropped into *coiffure* like a pebble into a tranquil pool. The particular issues of the Popular Front quickly integrated themselves into a pattern of ongoing disputes within the hairdressing profession. What the Matignon accords did, however, was to crank up both worker militancy and employer paranoia. Like its parent confederation, the CGAF, the Union fédérale tried to mix a general support for social justice with demands for special consideration for small businessmen.[123] The SIPC and the journal, *Reveil des Coiffeurs*, raised the banner of class war. The independent patrons minced no words in condemning this "syndical dictatorship," this "intrusion of [Bolsheviks]" in professional affairs.[124] The *Reveil* wrote that the Blum ministry, "in defiance of all natural laws," had shaken the national foundations. "The class struggle," it continued, "threatens to shatter the harmony of our civilization. The [new] social laws, under the pretext of rights and of justice, have engendered economic disequilibrium and social anarchy."[125]

These fears were confirmed by the spate of labor actions that accompanied the signing of the Matignon accords. In only two days during that June, claimed the Chambre syndicale of master artisans of Nantes, the *coiffeurs compagnons* created a new syndicate in the city. On the third day, they launched a strike against the patrons.[126] Nevers, Roanne, and Moulins also experienced strikes and workers' occupations of *salons dissidents* in that hectic summer of 1936.[127]

Meanwhile, labor turmoil reached a new pitch in the Paris salons. The Chambre syndicale was the capital's and the country's largest organization of *maîtres-coiffeurs*, and in June 1936 it reached a quick if fleeting accommodation with the workers (the CGT and CGTU unions had recently patched up their differences). But this collective convention satisfied neither party and left the Chambre syndicale in an ultimately untenable position. On the one side, the workers kept up their insistence on the five-day, forty-hour regime in *coiffure*, which the June agreement did not grant. On the other, the Chambre syndicale had to suffer the Independent patrons'* accusations that it had given in to the "Marxists' " demands and had betrayed the interests of the patrons. The workers' determination to have the substance of the Matignon agreements and the CPC's equal determination to wreck them left the Chambre syndicale with little room to maneuver.

The parties to the new convention recognized that higher wages and a shorter work week in *coiffure* depended on establishing some kind of price floor within the profession. Even the CPC concurred on the need to repress *baissiers*. Masters and workers gave form to this consensus in late July, when they held a giant rally at the Gymnase Japy in Paris. Ten thousand *coiffeurs*, according the Chambre syndicale, reiterated the demand for government action to protect the trade against those who would undercut agreements on prices and hours.[128]

The syndicates mixed two tactics of dealing with *baissiers*. The first of these was direct and often violent action. In February 1937, for example, 500 workers and patrons gathered to denounce these *baissiers*. When the parade of angry *coiffeurs* reached the rue Drouot, reported the *Semaine de la Coiffure*, things got out of control. A group of "idlers" and "troublemakers," to the cry of "collective contract everywhere!" began hurling coal at the windows of the Maison Gendre, a notorious *baissier*. The leaders and the police had trouble restoring calm. The crowd, which had by then reached 3,000, succeeded in "convincing" the reluctant Gendre to announce his intention to respect henceforth the syndical guidelines. In another demonstration, "bombs" were thrown and windows broken by one of the "vigilance committees," formed in order to ensure compliance in the city's *salons*.[129] "Before the fear of starvation," warned a Monsieur Guillon, "nothing will stop those artisans and workers who defend their livelihoods."[130]

Such confrontations also served to buttress the second of the *coiffeurs'* tactics, to convince the parliament of the need to enact the so-called Law 900. Law 900 derived from similar legislation that had been passed to protect other threatened trades. The Union fédérale had first approached the CGAF, which then pressed its supporters in the Chamber of Deputies for a bill that would limit access to and regulate prices in the profession. Albert Paulin introduced such a law on July 30, 1936. The Chamber of Deputies voted it without debate in January 1937 and passed it along to the Senate. Here the *coiffeurs'* demands ran into a stone wall.[131]

Without such a price floor and a *horaire unique* the conditions of professional consensus were not met, and the "Front Japy" could not hold. The regime agreed to in June 1936 was never generalized, and both sides began

---

*In October 1936 the SIPC expanded its organization and renamed itself the confédération patonale des coiffeurs de France et des colonies. Henceforth, it will be referred to as the CPC.

to agitate for a renegotiation of the collective convention, a new edition of which was signed on February 8, 1937.[132] This second accord, however, proved no more conclusive than the first. The workers remained unhappy with its provisions for a forty-eight hour work week in the capital. The CPC, not party to the pact, held out for a more flexible regime. Finally, even the Chambre syndicale, finding that its strategy of accommodation with the CGT was beginning to alienate its members, refused to be bound by the terms it had just initialed.

In March the labor minister issued his enabling decree to impose a forty-six hour work week in Paris and its suburbs; forty-eight in large cities; fifty in middle-sized cities; and fifty-two in towns. The workers' federation was unable to accept the minister's decision. It demanded the full application of the forty hour work week and a 20 percent wage increase, and threatened to strike if it did not receive satisfaction by Pentecost.[133] The Chambre syndicale, also unhappy with the new regime, closed ranks with the CPC in a "patronal front" against the workers' "unreasonable" demands. The profession, in a word, began to slip toward a confrontation.

Both sides prepared for a strike. The patrons, who enjoyed the full support of the CGAF and the CGPF, met to coordinate their resistance to a work stoppage with mass meetings on April 29 and May 3 and 10. In an apparent gesture of defiance, the employers voted to keep their salons open all day May 1. When joint talks at the Ministry of Labor failed to produce an agreement, 1,200 workers held their own rally at the Gymnase Jaurès on May 11 and, on the eve of the Pentecost holiday, decided on a strike by voice vote.

The call for the strike seems to have met with limited support.[134] In Paris, the newspapers reported that only 20 percent of the workers stayed out on the first day of the strike, May 13. Ninety percent of the 13,000 salons in the department of the Seine continued to do business about as usual, though the response was a little better in the suburbs. One *salonnier* even expressed his satisfaction that his employees had walked out. Now, he told the *Figaro* reporter M.-P. Hamelot, he would go back to working by himself and at last begin to make some money. He would never take back his two assistants, and he thought that many of his colleagues would do the same. The owner of another larger shop, however, declared the strike "catastrophic." He explained that on the previous afternoon his employees had begun an oil treatment on the head of one of his best clients, a rich American woman. Now, he fretted, the woman was stuck with a head full of oil—or at least she would have to find some other salon to finish her treatments.

Most vexing to the employers was that the striking workers started to organize *salon volants* ("mobile shops") in the cafés of the "red belt" and to advertise their willingness to cut customers' hair for free. The CPC complained of "outside agitators" and threatened to take legal action against the *salons volants*. Some of the employers tried to break the strike by forcing their employees to sign individual labor contracts. The Fédération ouvrière adopted a conciliatory posture, claiming that it understood the particular problems of *petits patrons* and wanted to help them out, but that the *petits* had allowed themselves to be led astray by "certains gros patrons agents directs du fascisme."

By the standards of the period the strike was not exceptionally contentious. The newspapers and the police noted only a few violent incidents. On Friday, the day after the strike began, a group of workers marching from the Opéra and the Madelaine to the Place de'Etoile, and singing the "Internationale," threw rocks at open shops and became involved in skirmishes with the police. Three policemen were hurt and six demonstrators arrested. The next day a group of approximately 100 workers, leaving the offices of the Fédération ouvrière on the rue Darboy and passing down the avenue de la République, began to break the windows of an open salon. Several of these rioters later appeared on the boulevard Magenta and again had to be dispersed by police.

The strike lasted one week and resolved none of the differences between workers and employers. On May 20 both sides accepted a government offer of arbitration. The employees, assured that there would be no retribution by the patrons, went back to work. Matters were then placed in the hands of an arbitrator, Ivan Martin of the Conseil d'Etat. Martin decided on a compromise: a 10 percent salary rise above the June 1936 convention, half of what the workers had asked, and a compensatory price increase for the patrons. A ministerial *arrêté* in August made the new regime obligatory for all hairdressers, *syndiqués* or not. The Chambre syndicale reported in September that 75 percent of its members were applying the Martin ruling, which suggests that the syndicates and the government had yet to find a way to bind all *coiffeurs* to official decisions.[135] Meanwhile, a mixed commission, including Tailledet, Grandadam, and Gestalder for the patrons and Magnien for the Fédération ouvrière, continued to talk about a new collective convention.

The CPC and the Union fédérale had been brought together by the strike in Paris. Their entente could not survive the substantial philosophical and political differences that separated them, and the two groups soon regressed to their old antipathy toward one another. Of the two, the Union fédérale, founded in 1905, was by far the greater organization. In 1937, it calculated its forces at some 25,000 members in 178 syndicates and 18 regional federations.[136] A year later the union derisively compared the 60 syndicates claimed by the CPC (which it said was an exaggeration) to its own expanded population of 210 syndicates of master *coiffeurs*.[137] The most powerful element within the Union fédérale was the Chambre syndicale in the capital, which could trace its own origins to the republic's legalization of trade unions in 1884. In the critical summer of 1936 the Chambre syndicale numbered approximately 6,000 members, up from 5,000 the previous year. The Popular Front benefited recruitment here as well. On the eve of the strike, for example, the eleventh section of the Chambre syndicale reported that its population had doubled, to 300, since January 1936; that in Juvisy had grown from 33 to 73 in the same period.[138] By the beginning of 1937, the Chambre syndicale estimated its strength at over 7,000 adherents in 80 local sections in and around Paris, far in excess of the CPC's 300 members.[139] The state recognized the Union fédérale's dominance when the CPC appealed to the Conseil d'Etat against the August 1937 decrees, meant to enforce Martin's decision. The Conseil d'Etat rejected the CPC's *démarche* and reaffirmed the Union fédérale's position as the "most representative" artisanal and commercial organization of hairdressers.[140]

Bagnaud's staunch resistance to the demands of the Fédération ouvrière nevertheless appealed to many of the *petits* patrons. Indeed, since the obligations imposed by the Popular Front and subsequent collective contracts burdened small employers more than large, Bagnaud, despite his doubtful credentials, could pose as the defender of *petits*. That is, the CPC threatened to occupy the territory traditionally held by the CGAF and its member syndicates. In Moulins, for instance, the CPC's unflinching opposition to the workers' demands caused the local artisan *coiffeurs* to waver in their commitment to the Union fédérale.[141] In Paris, it unquestionably helped to push Lamy and Dallant, the presidents of the Chambre syndicale, into a harder line in their negotiations with the workers.[142]

Those involved with the CPC and their allies at the *Reveil des Coiffeurs* apparently dabbled in the politics of the far right. Bagnaud, of course, with his position in the Paris Chamber of Commerce and his links to the *Intransigeant*, had friends in the capital's conservative circles. It seems clear that he and his collaborator, Louis Tison, were involved with, if they did not actually belong to, Colonel de la Rocque's Parti Social Français.[143] The *Coiffeur du Sud-Ouest*, voice of the Union fédérale in Montauban, even accused the *Reveil* of having close ties to Maurras and the Action Française.

When the Bordeaux syndicate that published the *Coiffeur-Parfumeur* joined the CPC camp, it began to carry a column by Paul Darconnet, who preached an antiparliamentary and corporatist message. Darconnet called for a compulsory syndicate in *coiffure*, policed by artisans themselves and backed with "draconian sanctions," to regulate the hairdressing trades and to do away with liberalism and "professional egotism." The *Coiffeur-Parfumeur* subsequently became involved in a bitter, if cryptic, exchange between Louis Tison, owner of a large salon in Paris and vice-president of the CPC, and François Magnien, president of the Fédération ouvrière. Magnien had written an article in the *Hebdo-Coiffure* in which he accused Tison of belonging to a party of the "extreme right" and of addressing one of its rallies in the capital. Magnien added that Tison was a partisan of a program more apt for "the other side of the Alps or the Rhine" than for a democratic France.[144] Tison replied that Magnien was a "born enemy" of the artisanat. Although he admitted to attending a conference on the artisanat sponsored by this "extreme right" group, Tison held that he was sent there by the CPC. Besides, he said, everyone knew that he belonged to this party.[145]

The Popular Front, then, had several direct effects on the hairdressing trade. First, it drove masters out of their localism and into the national organizations of *coiffeurs*. The SMAC in Bordeaux, as we have seen, had flirted with the Union fédérale in the 1920s and early 1930s.[146] The Bordelais hairdressers simply could not bring themselves to abandon their comfortably local perspective or, for that matter, to pay the dues that the Union fédérale required of its members. With the spreading labor troubles of the spring and summer of 1936, however, the SMAC's splendid isolation seemed less idyllic. That December the Bordelais, in a compromise between opposed factions, voted for "partial" affiliation to the Union fédérale. At the same time, when the masters found that an overcrowded trade could not hold the line on prices they bailed out of the labor agreement they had signed in July.

The SMAC was ready for the confederal plunge but of two minds about the Union fédérale. Perceiving his opportunity in the Bordelais' ambivalence, Bagnaud traveled to Bordeaux to romance the SMAC. In a meeting in March 1938, the SMAC reversed opinion and voted to join the CPC. A Monsieur Reuil argued in defense of the decision that the affiliation would not cost the Bordelais a *sou* more in dues. But it seems that, in the end, the SMAC opted for the CPC for political reasons: the Union fédérale had come to appear too ready to appease the workers. In the CPC, Reuil wrote, one finds "real patrons to defend real patrons." It was at this point that the *Coiffeur-Parfumeur* veered sharply to the right and began printing the corporatist and antiparliamentary diatribes of Darconnet and Tison.

The SMAC's drift to the avowedly conservative CPC was a plausible response to the political pressures of the Popular Front. The case of the Fédération des patrons-coiffeurs de Guyenne-Gascogne-Languedoc-Quercy (FPC du Sud-Ouest), however, was more typical.[147] The artisan-hairdressers of the Southwest had created their federation in the spring of 1932 with hours, prices, and the monopoly on toiletries as their major concerns. In 1935 the FPC du Sud-Ouest celebrated the adhesion of the Toulouse federation of *coiffeurs*.[148] The federation's reaction to the Matignon accords was the usual one. "I am in favor of the workers' demands," wrote E. Bénazet, the federation's secretary, "but on the condition that everyone shares the compensation." The *coiffeurs* of the Southwest were subsequently wooed by both the Union fédérale and the UAF. In January 1937 the executive board of the federation traveled to Paris to meet with the leaders of the national organizations. The board was divided: The president, Beaumont, favored the UAF; Bénazet and Robert Vidieu, the Union fédérale. One year later, after extended discussions about the Union's fédérale's 25 franc dues, the FPC du Sud-Ouest brought its 500 members into the Union fédérale. Vidieu became the new president, and Beaumont left to found his own Syndicat des coiffeurs in the Southwest.

The hairdressing trades provide an object and ironic lesson in the effects of the Popular Front on the artisanat. The Matignon accords raised the expectations and diminished the patience of workers in *coiffure*. They did not, however, produce much in the way of tangible benefits. The latest national schedule prescribed a work week of forty-six hours in Paris and its *environs*;

forty-eight in the larger provincial cities; fifty in the towns; and fifty-two elsewhere. On the other hand, in Bordeaux, Toulouse, Montauban, Moulins, Paris, and other towns events galvanized the *petit patronat*. Endemic labor disputes and economic crisis encouraged syndical action among local master *coiffeurs*. Yet the Matignon accords did not hurt the masters so much as scare them. By explicitly linking economic to political questions the Popular Front added a new, volatile element to professional affairs. It helped to draw local syndicates into the national federations; it pushed some *coiffeurs* to the political right. The fears of employers proved to be every bit as radicalizing as the misfortunes of employees.

While *coiffeurs*, masters and employees, continued to wrangle over control of the corporation and the forty-hour work week the ground began to shift beneath them. The index of industrial production (1929 = 100), which had been 78 in 1936, crept up to 82 in 1937.[149] The Popular Front had ameliorated the condition of wage earners but had failed to pull France out of the depression, to placate the middle classes, or to confront the gathering international crisis. In February 1937, Blum announced a "pause" in the push toward economic and social justice, and in June, denied decree power by a hostile Senate, he resigned. Blum ceded his place to the old Radical war-horse, Camille Chautemps, who turned the pause into a stall, and in the spring of 1938 to Edouard Daladier, who moved the stall into a retreat.[150]

The artisanal movement, decisively split in its attitude toward the Popular Front, was similarly divided over retrenchment. The CEAA applauded the decrees that repaired "the gross errors committed since 1936." The CGAF, meanwhile, suspected that the government's new conservatism would bring little relief to petty producers and would serve only what Grandadam called "Corporate France" (La Société Française). The CGAF further chafed at the Reynaud tax laws of November 1938, which it condemned as a "flagrant injustice" and a step backward from the progressive income tax.[151]

In the autumn of 1937 the Chautemps government convened a number of commissions of inquiry on national production as a basis for the revitalization of the French economy. Artisanal leaders interpreted this as the preparation for a new, less radical round of Matignon accords and were again disappointed to discover themselves sitting on the sidelines. The CGAF approached its parliamentary friends and asked them to provide a place for artisans in this "national effort." Chautemps proved amenable, and in January 1938 the premier announced the creation of a "Commission on the current state of the Artisanat." The work of the new commission was remarkable only for its predictability. In its composition the commission mirrored the similar groups formed since 1923, bringing officers of the artisanal movement together with state secretaries and technocrats. Chautemps' gesture also gave the CGAF another opportunity to demonstrate its privileged access to patronage. The commissioners spent several days listening to representatives from the CEAA, the CAF, and the APCMF; however, these groups did not have seats on the commission itself.

The commission's recommendations, issued in September 1938, bore an official stamp but covered familiar and infertile ground. They stressed the artisanat's need for more fiscal, financial, and social benefits, control of "unfair competition," and lighter charges on artisanal employers. The CGAF incorporated these saccharine findings in the Plan de Redressement Artisanal that Paulin put before the Chamber of Deputies in December 1938. Whatever would have been their fate under other circumstances, (and experience suggests it would have been dim) these proposals, coming less than one year before the war, were doomed to failure.[152]

Meanwhile, the artisanal movement was running out of steam by the late 1930s. Membership, which had surged in 1936 and 1937, had leveled off in 1938. The CGAF, the CEAA, and the UAF were all losing members. Only the new CAF continued to attract new recruits. The Parliament had ceased to pass significant new legislation to protect artisans, the proposals of the 1938 commission notwithstanding. It was clear, finally, that the leading artisanal organizations had not managed to formulate an adequate response to any of the major problems of the decade.

The fading fortunes of the CGAF and the CEAA did nothing to reduce the bitter competition between them. The CGAF, for example, used its connections to close the CEAA out of participation in the Paris Artisanal Exposition of 1937.[153] The two organizations even found ways to pursue their combativeness when they were in substantial agreement. Thus in 1937 both groups introduced legislation to restrict *travail noir*, Paulin for the CGAF and Walter for the CEAA. The two bills did not disagree in any fundamental way. No principles were at stake, only a habit of opposition and a battle for credit within the artisanal movement. The lack of real differences, however, did not prevent the *Artisan Français* and the *Gazette des Métiers* from exchanging the harshest invective. The Strasbourg journal accused Paulin of sabotaging artisans' struggle against *travail noir*. Paulin countered with his own low blow, linking the Alsatians not just to the enemies of the artisanat but to the enemies of the republic. The CEAA, he wrote to the premier, represents,

> an Artisanat that is Catholic, connected to the [clericalists] and the Christian syndicates, autonomist, composed of professional associations issuing from the opposition movements and constituted at the instigation of powers that I have no need to specify, except to say that they are always found among the militants of [De la Rocque's Parti Social Français] and other such organizations.[154]

The CGAF added to these insinuations when it commented on the CEAA's participation in an International Artisanal Exhibition held in Berlin in 1938, noting that the Alsatians had allowed themselves to be referred to as *Vogesendeutsche* ("Germans from the Vosges"). The CEAA, of course, denied this.[155]

The most heated exchanges occurred when the CGAF initiated a campaign to further limit the definition of *artisanat* to masters employing no more than five assistants and apprentices. This newest effort originated in the legislative discussions over tax reform in December 1936 and the CGAF's desire to obtain finally a *statut fiscal unique* for artisans. This new definition fit neatly with administrative practice since 1934 and had the additional advantage of undermining the CEAA within the movement. The CEAA retorted that the new definition would gut the chambers of trade, and it named Tailledet and Paulin as the leaders of a Marxist fifth-column within the artisanat.[156]

The new definition came into force with the Daladier decree-laws of May 2, 1938. These, which were followed by further decree-laws later that month and the following November, were a mixed bag for artisans. They imposed an 8 percent "supertax" but extended the exemption from the *patente* to all masters without *compagnons*, tightened restrictions on foreign-born artisans, excepted those on the registers of trades from the tax for the chambers of commerce, and broadened the financial base of the chambers of trades. The government did not, however, come through with a comprehensive artisanal fiscal regime. As far as petty producers were concerned, thought Pierre Manoury, Daladier's policies added up to "not much."[157]

Surprisingly, the divided forces of the artisanat managed to cooperate over the issue of apprenticeship. Recall that the Courtier law of 1925 had in theory attributed the regulation of apprenticeship in the artisanal trades to the chambers of trades but that it had provided no means to this end. As the chambers of trades began to grow in the 1930s, the artisanal movement pressed for a law that would formalize the masters' control over professional training. In their accustomed fashion the sympathetic deputies came through. In 1934, Paulin introduced a CGAF bill; Walter, the leader of its *groupe parlementaire*, a CEAA version. The two, amazingly, were similar enough to allow a compromise, and in March 1936 the Walter-Paulin project cleared the Chamber of Deputies. One year later the Senate gave its assent. On March 10, 1937, it became law.

Specifically, the Walter-Paulin law made apprenticeship obligatory for the exercise of an *entreprise artisanale*. It prohibited apprenticeship before the required years of schooling were completed and created a *service d'orientation professionnelle*, through which all apprentices had to pass. The chambers of trades gained the power to conduct professional examinations of competence and in general to regulate apprenticeship in their jurisdictions.

The premise, for exponents of artisanal apprenticeship, was that it should be a mixture of professional and moral training. Under the guidance of a master craftsman, a young man would learn to be a husband, a father, and a productive member of the community. Charles Kula had written in 1929 that only professional training under the aegis of the artisanat could forge a "civilization based on the duty to produce." And Kula compared this to the technical education that a young man received in a state school, a training that would inevitably produce an "unwholesome mentality" and "transform a people of farmers and artisans into a people of bureaucrats, functionaries, and parasites." A young man formed under these circumstances would inevitably belong to the "dangerous classes."[158] It was such a concern for the moral fiber of the young worker that led the APCMF, when considering the Walter-Paulin law, to insist on the following strict rules about who would *not* be able to train apprentices:

1. Those of recognized professional incapacity
2. Those under twenty-four years of age
3. Those having been convicted of a crime or having spent three months in prison
4. Those convicted for some moral offense.

The APCMF also proposed that unmarried masters and widowers should not be able to take young women apprentices into their households.[159]

The evidence, and most of it is anecdotal, suggests that the state of apprenticeship in the artisanat was chaotic at best. Laurent Azzano, for example, entered the furniture shop of Monsieur Jaquin, where his father worked as a *compagnon*, without an apprenticeship contract or any other quid pro quo.[160] Gaston Lucas remembered that the practice in *serrurie* prescribed three to four years of apprenticeship at the parents' expense. Gaston's father, however, managed to find a master locksmith willing to train his son in only two years—and on very satisfactory terms.[161] Isabelle Bertaux-Wiame's study of the baking trades in the 1930s substantiates this picture. None of the apprentices she interviewed had ever been party to an apprenticeship contract. Bertaux-Wiame found, moreover, that young apprentice-*boulangers*, far from receiving a valuable professional and ethical education, formed the most exploited element of a highly exploited workforce. A young man typically worked twelve hours a day, either from midnight to noon or from 7:00 A,M, to 7:00 P.M. Night work, in fact, was the most bitterly contested issue in the profession. It had been forbidden by the Commune in 1871 and the Third Republic had suppressed *travail de nuit* in 1919. Bertaux-Wiame discovered, however, that neither these nor any other regulations were reliably enforced. The apprentice, like the *compagnon* normally worked seven days a week. A collective contract signed in 1934 cut this back to six, a situation which only became generalized during the Popular Front.[162]

Usually an apprentice received food and lodging. Sometimes he was paid a nominal wage. A Monsieur L. told Bertaux-Wiame that at first he had earned 20 francs per month and then 60 when he quit his apprenticeship at nineteen years of age. A Monsieur G. explained that he had earned 30 francs and a Monsieur D. 100.[163] The Walter-Paulin law almost crept into *boulangerie* through a *règlement d'apprentissage* incorporated into a 1939 collective contract. This regulation fixed the length of apprenticeship at two years, plus one year as an *ouvrier débutant*, and dealt with hours and holidays. Unfortunately, it was no more applied than previous legislation.[164]

The biannual meetings of the APCMF and the congresses of the great confederations would give the impression that artisans were impassioned by the question of apprenticeship. The truth appears rather that most masters harbored only a tepid enthusiasm for training apprentices. What the artisanal movement saw as a social and professional imperative, the individual master considered an economic liability. "They're expensive," wrote one cobbler. "They ruin the material. They cost me time. And as soon as they're old enough to go into a factory they take off."[165] In the APCMF most of the discussion of the Walter-Paulin law centered on the question of money. How much was all this regulation going to cost the chambers of trades? How much, if anything, should apprentices—who were after all students—be paid? Henri Mourier in 1944 found that only 14 percent of artisanal establishments had apprentices. Thirty years later Bernard Zarca estimated that only 12 percent of artisans trained apprentices.[166] There are no parallel figures for the 1930s, but there is no reason to think that masters at that moment had displayed any greater zeal for forming a young *cadre*, especially in a time of economic hardship.

In any case, the Walter-Paulin law was a dead end. Many in the movement objected that the law did not go far enough toward granting artisans hegemony within their corporation. According to the logic of the Walter-Paulin legislation, a certificate of professional aptitude, and ultimately a *brevet de maîtrise*, would be required before a worker could advertise himself as an artisan. It did not, however, prevent anybody who wanted to do so from setting up shop as a tradesman. A *brevet* was not the equivalent of a medical certificate, for example. Predictably, the Walter-Paulin law's most serious shortcoming was the lag between legislation and application. It waited on the administrative stamp of approval that would bring it to life. Alas, the never-applied and by then anomalous Walter-Paulin law was formally abrogated in March 1962.[167]

By the beginning of 1939 the possibility of war had edged the Popular Front off the top of the political marquee, and the artisanal movement, despite its disappointments, did its best to prepare artisans for the national defense effort. In 1938 alone the CGAF leadership held more than forty meetings with its member syndicates in order to alert them to the imperatives of defense work. It launched a census of its constituents as a means of facilitating their integration into production for war, and the *Artisan Français* copiously treated all these matters in its columns throughout 1939.

When war finally came, it necessarily wrought major changes in the personal and professional lives of artisans. Like other Frenchmen, the masters had already been subjected to new taxes: a "National Contribution" and a special armament tax levied in 1938. With the outbreak of hostilities, official decrees raised the work week to sixty hours, imposed an additional tax of 5 to 15 percent, and rigidly controlled prices. The artisans particularly welcomed the law of September 9, 1939. Meant to protect the interests of those who had been called away to service, this legislation enforced a moratorium on the opening of any new enterprises or the expansion of existing ones.[168] Meanwhile, tradesmen found themselves drafted out of their workshops, either taken into the army or conscripted to work in factories. For those artisans who remained in their workshops, supplies of crucial raw materials soon ran short. Complaints on this account in the artisanal press were just the first indication of what was to become a major grievance during the Occupation.

The artisanal movement had continually maintained that independent skilled tradesmen could play a critical role in the war effort. Bernard Laffaille, an engineer and a member of the Institut des Métiers, paraphrased the artisanal position: "Give me the raw material, allow me decent workers, send back as a special measure such *compagnons* as are absolutely essential to me, and I will furnish [the means to fight]."[169] Tailledet and Grandadam met with the labor commission of the Chamber of Deputies in October 1939 and received assurances that artisans would be given an important place in war production. Yet they soon became disenchanted with this place and feared that the war economy would mean the end of artisanal production. Laffaille, too, worried that "under the pretext of national defense, there can be no question of destroying the Artisanat."[170]

The minister of armaments, Raoul Dautry, dealt with these problems in his circular of November 21, 1939. Dautry acknowledged the artisans' unease, reassured them of his benevolent intentions, and stated his readiness to work with all those "of good will."[171] He encouraged independent masters to cooperate among themselves in order to rationalize their methods and directed the prefects to involve the presidents of the chambers of trades in all these efforts. Dautry even authorized 50 million francs to help finance war production in small and medium-sized enterprises. To the consternation of Laffaille among others, however, all this money went to the chambers of commerce, leaving the chambers of trades with their ambitions but without resources.[172]

It is striking, in view of the circumstances, how much of the old artisanal program remained on the table. The CAF was forced to admit that war constituted the major problem of the day but counseled that it was not the only one. The *Artisan de France*'s headline of June 1939 illustrated the marriage of patriotism and interest: "The armament tax, so be it! But also the Family Allowances and the repression of *Travail Noir*."[173] From September 1939 to June 1940 the *Artisan Français* conscientiously informed its readers about wartime legislation; it regularly carried Grandadam's and Tailledet's editorials on the question of artisans in war production. At the same time, the CGAF kept up its call for a reduction in artisans' tax burdens and its demand that masters recruited into the factories be returned to their workshops. The CGAF continued to press for the enactment of its Plan de Redressement artisanal.

Perhaps, like so many of their compatriots, artisans had fallen into the complacency of the *drôle de guerre*. The *Artisan Français* of June 1940, which reached its readers as the *Wehrmacht* reached Paris, carried the usual array of articles on rent, paid holidays, the fiscal regime in construction. In a corner of the front page, however, was a small notice: "URGENT APPEAL," it read, "To all artisan refugees, French and Allies. . . ."[174] This alone betrayed the fact that life had changed since January 1923.

5

Vichy: The Broken Promise

In June 1940 the Third Republic voted itself out of existence. Artisans, like a majority of their compatriots, waved farewell, not too sadly, and got on the bandwagon to Vichy. Albert Paulin, the socialist champion of artisanal causes in the Chamber of Deputies, cast his vote for Marshal Pétain and was rewarded with a place on Vichy's new National Council. Albert Coustenoble, president of the APCMF, was also asked to join the Council and accepted. Indeed, the bulk of the artisanal movement greeted Pétain's National Revolution with optimism. Tailledet wrote characteristically, "We have no doubt that the Marshal's government will realize those aims that for twenty years have been but a dream for artisans."[1]

And why not? The National Revolution promised after all to recast French society by eliminating class conflict, resolving the "rural crisis," and protecting the *classes moyennes*. It offered a social conservatism rooted in the values of the peasant and the artisan. The watchwords of the new order—Patrie, Famille, Travail—had been the artisans' own. "The Artisan," said Pétain in his May Day speech of 1942, "is one of the vital forces of our nation, and I attach special importance to its development, its conservation, and its perfection."[2] Other social commentators echoed Pétain's sentiments. "At the root of all things is work," wrote André Demaison. "No existence could be worthwhile, no spiritual or material joy exalted, no labor, no happiness could survive outside of Work—in regularity, discipline, and the love of creative effort."[3] After decades of perceiving that the Third Republic had regularly sacrificed their interests to those of Capital and Labor, artisans had reason to believe that Pétain would treat them more kindly. "Who would dare hope that the defeat could be beneficial," asked Paul Réal in the *Artisan des Alpes*, "and that it would have a more salutary effect on the Country's destinies than the victory of 1918? And yet," he replied, "that is exactly what I think in all sincerity."[4]

The Vichy era thus marks an ironic postscript to the Third Republic, as the Republic's demise left the shape of French society to be redefined. To take Pétain at his word or to read through the volumes of quasi-official social theorizing (of which Demaison is a perfect example)—the regime leaned toward the kind of Malthusian social and economic policies that had always been close to the artisans' hearts. Its authoritarian cast suggested that neither the working class nor the *gros* bourgeois would be able to obstruct these intentions, as they had under the old parliamentary regime. Such was the pretense, but was it the reality? Pétain preached corporatism and a secure place for artisans in the National Revolution, but what did his government practice?

"What are you talking about?" Charles-Hubert Poissonard chided his wife, Julie, in Jean Dutouard's novel, *Au bon beurre*. The horrors of occupation, he explained, could never be what they were in the dark days of the Franco-Prussian War. "Good God," he said, "we're in the twentieth century. We'll never lack for butter in France."[5] Poissonard, of course, was tragically mistaken. The military debacle of 1940 quickly translated into an economic crisis, although the precise contours of this crisis are hidden by the absence of reliable data. Carré, Dubois, and Malinvaud in their study of French economic growth, estimate that the French gross national product decreased to 80 percent of its 1939 level by 1946. Alfred Sauvy drew an even more somber picture. The index of industrial production (1939 = 100) dipped to 54 in 1941, to 45 in 1943, and to 33 in 1944. François Caron confirms Sauvy's bleak analysis. He adds, however, that these overall numbers can hide vast discrepancies between sectors. For example, while textiles plummeted to a fifth or a quarter of what it had been before the war, steel production dropped only 18 percent between 1938 and 1943 (though by 1943 most of the steel was going into the German war effort). Private building activity, meanwhile, all but disappeared.[6] Food was the most serious problem. Agriculture fell to an index of 89 (1938 = 100) by the Liberation, as vegetable production dropped 11 percent and animal production 30 percent. By comparison with the mid-1930s, wheat production was down 37 percent, potatoes 28 percent, and sugar beets 44 percent. By June 1944, inflation had added to consumers' woes, as the index of prices for 135 controlled articles increased to 222 for agricultural products and 300 for industrial goods. Those in a position to take advantage could supplement starvation rations and other shortages on the black market, but the prices were many times their official level. In the conditions of shortage, noted Poissonard, his vast stocks made the *crémier* a kind of king.[7] And Sauvy remarks that "the baker or the miller never lacked for bread." On the other hand, the regime proved fairly successful in controlling wages, which Caron calculated fell in real terms by at least 40 percent between 1940 and 1944.[8] Whatever the exact degree of deprivation, the facts of war and occupation—

the missing prisoners of war, the lack of coal and food, the collapse of transportation, and the cost of hosting a part of the *Wehrmacht*—meant that the immediate future would be bleak for artisans and other French.[9]

The political situation was disturbing as the economic situation for petty producers. The suicide of the Third Republic and the Armistice resulted in the suppression of parliamentary politics and free syndicalism. Syndicates of local masters and trade federations were not immediately dissolved, but their field of operations was greatly reduced. As the syndicates and the Chamber of Deputies had been the chief weapons of artisans' self-defense before the war, this augured poorly for the future. Everything depended on Pétain's being true to his word.

"It is worse," commented Jean Bichelonne, Pétain's minister of National Production, "for a country to lose all its strength than to choose the wrong side."[10] Even as defeat washed over France, people like Bichelonne began to act to assure the economy's survival in the midst of massive dislocation and to lay the foundation for future reform and development. The government took the first step toward economic reconstruction in the summer of 1940. The law of August 16, 1940 nominally placed all production under the direction of the state and set up a series of organization committees. Patterned on such administrative bodies as the Conseil Supérieur de l'artisanat or the CNE, the organization committees brought together patrons, workers, and technocrats and grouped them by professional "families"—one for metallurgy, one for construction, etc. The organization committees, subdivided by region and profession, tended to multiply over time; by 1945 there were 231 functioning committees covering some 1,800,000 enterprises, each charged with facilitating the control of production and distribution within its orbit. The government loaded its new economic bureaucracy with a number of responsibilities: the census of enterprises, productive forces, stocks of materials, labor, the elaboration of a program for national production, the establishment of operating procedures for business, and the setting of prices. A companion law of September 10 created the Office central de répartition des produits industriels (OCRPI) to preside over the acquisition and distribution of raw materials to the various organization committees.[11] While the committees and the OCRPI were encouraged to promote local and professional initiative, the government explicitly warned them against becoming the agents of labor, industry, city, or province. Rather they were mandated to serve the population in "all spirit of justice."[12]

The architects of economic reconstruction meant it to serve long-range political and social aims as well. General Maxime Weygand, less an architect of the new system than a vandal of the old, stated the problem as many in the regime conceived it:

> The old order of things, that is to say a political regime of masonic, capitalist, and international compromises has brought us to where we are. . . . Class struggle divided the country, prevented all profitable labor, permitted all the

excesses of demagoguery. The recovery of France through labor cannot be realized without the institution of a new social regime founded on the confidence and collaboration of workers and patrons.[13]

Weygand was a traditionalist in social and economic matters. Even those Vichyists with a more dynamic view of the future, however, saw politics and economics as intimately linked. They sought to employ the "vertical" restructuring of the organization committees to erase class boundaries, root out social conflict, and establish state control of the economy.[14]

Pétain had promised that the economic reorganization would repair the abuses of the prewar system. "I intend," he said, "that our country will be relieved of its most contemptible tutelage, that of wealth."[15] Much to their disappointment, however, artisans received no special place in this largely ad hoc structure. From the *coiffeurs*, for example, Marcel Bagnaud was named president of the organization committee for *coiffure* and *parfumerie*. Bagnaud, along with several of his old associates in the CPC, Louis Tison and Robert Maigre, later became involved in the "aryanization" of hairdressing salons and perfume shops.[16] The CPC, however, had been the creature of the *gros coiffeurs* and had represented commercial interests. The hairdressers of the more artisanal Chambre syndicale of master *coiffeurs* did not share in this patronage.

On the whole, the artisanat saw itself divided up and apportioned to the organization committees by sector and profession; that is, plumbers to construction and public works, tailors to textiles, and so on.[17] As in the case of the CNE of 1936, representative of artisanal syndicates sat among other employers, where they were more or less buried by the more powerful interests and by the technocrats who considered them irrelevant to macroeconomic problems. Léon Bossavy, acting president of the APCMF, complained, "We must with regret remark the almost total absence of the artisanat in the new professional mechanism [in place] since August 1940." He reported that only 19 of the 658 members of the departmental organization committees were artisans.[18] The CAF's *Artisan de France*, now published in Paris, grumbled that artisans were treated as "poor relations" and were given only "crumbs from the table."[19]

The government, however, did not ignore artisans completely. A Ministry of Production circular of November 28, 1940 established the Artisanal Service, which soon became a prime example of Vichy ambivalence about how to handle its petty producers. The force behind the Artisanal Service was Jean Bichelonne, whom Richard Kuisel describes as a "model technocrat [and] a brilliant graduate of the Polytechnique."[20] A convinced advocate of economic modernization, Bichelonne felt that the future of artisanal production and its ability to contribute to the national wealth lay in the renewal of its technical capacities and that this required the government's help. As director of the new Artisanal Service, Bichelonne chose Pierre Loyer. The choice appears paradoxical. Bichelonne, the arch-polytechnicien, saw society in terms of production and economic value; whereas Loyer was a social conservative, a

monarchist, and a devout Catholic. Throughout the 1930s he had been involved in the ultra-conservative Ligue Franc Catholique and had been principal director of the Ligue anti-Judéomaçonnique. Here Loyer applied himself
to a crusade against the sinister influence of Free Masonry, which he blamed
for, among other things, the French Revolution, the League of Nations, the
Great Depression, the Stavisky scandal, and Adolf Hitler.[21] Loyer held a
romantic view of petty production:

> It is certain that it is [within the artisanat] that the most beautiful family
> traditions are preserved. . . . If our people, despite years of nefarious prop-
> aganda, is able to give proof once more of its profound virtues, is it not
> because the artisanat has formed a good part of its children?[22]

Thus he conceived the artisanat as a fundamentally social and ethical entity,
an "institution naturelle," as he put it. While he did his best to upgrade the
conditions and the techniques of master artisans, his ideas owed more to
moral than political economy. Loyer was a true believer.

However intensely Loyer was dedicated to his mission, he found that the
newly created Artisanal Service lacked both adequate personnel (it had only
about one dozen agents for the entire country) and specific statutory power;
its responsibilities went largely unfulfilled. A law of April 30, 1941 provided
the Service with a formal existence and enabled it to expand its corps of
regional delegates. A decree of August 22, 1941 gave the Service effective
hegemony in artisanal affairs. More significantly, this decree transferred the
authority for all artisanal matters, which had hitherto been shared among the
Ministries of Labor, Industry, Commerce, and Technical Education to the
omnivorous Production Ministry. Here was more evidence that, whatever its
corporate patter, the regime assigned petty production to the most forthrightly
technocratic of ministries.[23]

"A harmonious organization of professional life," explained Loyer, "is
inconceivable if artisans cannot find their niche in the structure set up by the
law of 16 August 1940."[24] And he responded to artisans' contention that their
concerns were being systematically overlooked in the organization committees
with a circular of July 1941, which provided for the creation of the Groupes
Artisanaux Professionels (GAP). The GAP were small groups of master
artisans, organization subcommittees, which would represent their professions
in the organization committees and act as the conduits between the economic
bureaucracy and the mass of petty tradesmen. The state did not envision the
GAP, of which there were more than 2,000 by the end of the war,[25] as
permanent institutions. They were intended, like the organization committees
themselves, as a temporary arrangement until a more comprehensive structural reform could be set in place.[26]

The expansion of the artisanal *apparat* continued in the fall of 1941 as the
Artisanal Service began to encourage the formation of Bureaux Artisanaux
des Matières (BAM). Meant to improve the flow of raw materials to petty
producers, the BAM operated, in effect, as the local and artisanal arms of

the OCRPI. They were attached directly to the chambers of trades and made responsible for the census of artisanal production, the determination of its needs, and the direct distribution of resources. A circular, signed by François Lehideux in the spring of 1942, specified that the OCRPI would allot a mass of material to the BAM for each profession. Then under the guidance of the GAP, the BAM would deliver goods only to those artisans who possessed "ration cards" (*cartes d'acheteur*) issued by the chambers of trades through the syndicates.[27] In fact, the whole system of distribution remained in flux, with some trades provisioned through the chambers and others directly through the organization committees, throughout the war.[28]

While it pursued this slapdash approach to economic reorganization and distribution, the government also claimed to be working on a more systematic application of its corporative principles. Finally, in October 1941, Vichy unveiled its plans for the new order with the publication of the Labor Charter. The regime and its supporters hailed the Charter as the successor to the so-called liberal society, a system in which cooperation among diverse social elements would replace the old conditions of class war. The Labor Charter, wrote Maurice Bouvier-Ajam, would found its corporative system on the syndicate, "thanks to the Marshal," and thus would end the old quarrel between syndicalists, usually thin on theory, and corporatists, whose elaborate plans often neglected practicalities.[29]

Yet the content of the Labor Charter once more manifested the regime's schizophrenia. It traced the ideological and tactical division between the conservative exponents of corporatism and the advocates of a more dynamic system of social negotiation and production (who had ordinarily been attracted to syndicalism or some form of "planisme"). In effect, this was a split between the Loyers and the Bichelonnes. In 1940, Pétain had vetoed two early drafts of the Labor Charter because he found their implications too syndicalist. The version that became law was, according to Jacques Juillard, neither fish nor fowl (see Figure 5.1).[30]

If the regime was of two minds in its positive vision, it was united in its negative ones. Both corporatists and Vichy syndicalists (like René Belin, former vice-president of the CGT and author of the Labor Charter) could agree on the destruction of free trade unionism; on the elimination, that is, of groups explicitly committed to interest-group politics. Belin, for example, asserted that the Labor Charter would "suppress the conflict and antagonisms between classes" and promote within each profession "the harmonious organization of all its elements."[31] In fact, notes Robert Paxton, "[It] was clearly designed to break the back of the trade unions in France." Sauvy calls the Labor Charter a "législation de classe," which forced workers to collaborate without granting them "indispensible liberties."[32] Replacing the scattered associations of the past, born of the syndical laws of 1884 and 1920, the Labor Charter created a series of state-sponsored unions. In contrast to those they replaced, the Vichy syndicates were "singular so as to be simple, compulsory so as to be strong, supervised so as to be loyal."[33]

To accomplish its broad goals, the Labor Charter provided for the dis-

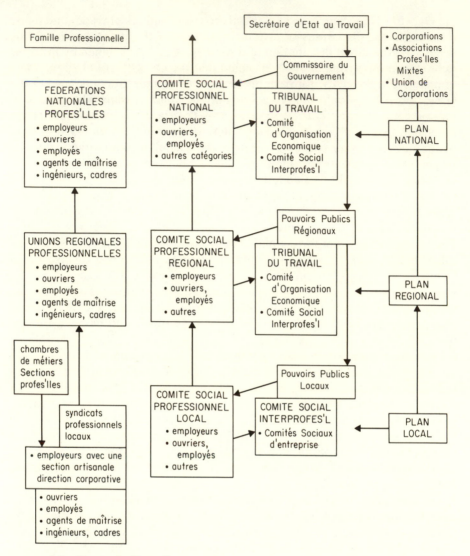

FIGURE 5.1. Charte du Travail.

Source: *Artisan Français* 320 (1 December 1941).

solution of the old trade unions and handed their funds and property over to the new *syndicats uniques*. It prohibited interprofessional unions, such as had been one of the bases of the artisanal movement. In keeping with its notion of "vertical" reorganization, the charter established mixed commissions (*comités paritaires*) by enterprise and sector. To look after a profession's internal needs, it set up social committees (*comités sociaux*). These also rested on a joint council of workers and employers and concerned themselves with such matters as pay, training, and social security. As a final measure to eliminate conflict, the Labor Charter outlawed strikes and lockouts, and put an end to direct government arbitration. Any disputes that the mixed commissions themselves could not resolve were to be submitted to the newly created Labor Tribunal, with its members drawn almost exclusively from the ranks of employers and administrators.[34]

As a practical matter, the Labor Charter brought little real change in artisans' conditions. The GAP, for example, received a formal legal status, but they remained starved for funds and only marginally successful in energizing local artisans. Moreover, the Charter was a social project; it left artisans' economic fortunes in the hands of the organization committees, where they continued to be greeted with disinterest or contempt. Even the efforts of the Artisanal Service availed little against the bureaucratic weight of the organization committees, for while the service had authority over artisanal affairs, it had none over raw materials. When the masters complained of being denied their share of available resources, the organization committees insisted on their fairness in the matter and resisted the Artisanal Service's attempts to intervene. One example will suffice. In February 1944 Loyer wrote to several organization committees requesting a more generous cut for artisans in state-directed production programs. A typical reply came from the director of the committee responsible for textiles and leather: "Artisans have generally been removed from the distribution of production orders as a result of their feeble productive capacity and the lack of any central authority able to direct the efficient distribution of tasks."[35] As often as not, the Artisanal Service's demarches led merely to jurisdictional squabbles with other elements of the administration. They seldom affected decisions about allocation and almost never satisfied the artisans concerned.[36]

From the publication of the Labor Charter, artisans, it seems, began to suspect the regime's good intentions. They were unhappy, first of all, at not having been consulted. Only one artisan had sat on the committee charged with drafting a charter.[37] This meant that, as usual, the whole operation was in the hand of *les gros*. President Colomer, of the Pyrénées-Orientales Chamber of Trades, normally a reliable supporter of Pétain, reported that business interests in Perpignan were trying to set up the new *syndicats uniques* without giving artisans their "special sections," as provided for in the Labor Charter.[38] Louis Bourrières, head of the CAF of the Lot, made the same observation, and advised his readers to reject overtures from the *patronat* that threatened artisans' autonomy and identity. He approvingly quoted a response from a group of artisan-electricians in Provence to those who would set up a *syndicat unique*: "Your project for a corporative Charter does not correspond to our feelings on the subject. . . ."[39]

This is to say that, whereas the government offered the Labor Charter as something new, the artisans saw it as merely another version of the professional sections of the old CNE or of the organization committees. As Bourrières remarked acidly, "The Artisanat, treated as a star ("mise en vedette") in the Press and on the Radio, is ignored when it comes to practical action."[40] It was the old fear of being absorbed by the larger interests that led the remnants of the CAF to support syndical pluralism and to insist that "le syndicalisme unique obligatoire" would mean the "end of the artisanat."[41] Needless to say, the government was less than pleased with Bourrière's criticisms, and the *Artisan de France* of November 15, 1942 carried the following notation from the official censor on its front page: "As the peasant plowing his field, the artisan must pursue his efforts along the straight line laid down by the Marshal."[42]

Obstruction on the part of the various interests effectively stalled the *mise en operation* of the Labor Charter. Artisans' hesitations joined the hostility of the workers' unions and the "polite indifference" of the *patronat*.[43] Maurice Bouvier-Ajam perceived in all this the nefarious activities of "a minority hostile to all evolution, all conciliation, and, in a word, to any French national revolution."[44] Perhaps the government's own ambivalence paralyzed it, or circumstances just made any kind of plan irrelevant. In any case, the reorganization foreseen by the Labor Charter proceeded slowly and incompletely. A very few *syndicats uniques* began to take shape. A Labor Ministry decree of December, 5 1942 created a Butchers' corporation; the *cordonniers* also tried to organize their profession.[45] In 1944, however, François Chasseigne could still write that the "rapid [sic] establishment of *syndicats uniques* is our primary task."[46]

Despite its minimal impact, the publication of the Labor Charter marked a turning point in artisans' relations with the regime. Many small producers had originally been attracted to the National Revolution for the practical reason that they expected better treatment from the solicitous Marshal Pétain than they had received from the Third Republic. We have seen artisans express their disappointment when the laws of the summer of 1940 seemed to follow the precedent of the defunct republic—Pétain's flattery notwithstanding. Throughout, petty producers continued to hope, and the government constantly reassured them, that it would soon carry out more considered, permanent reforms truer to Vichy's social vision and more favorable to master artisans. The Labor Charter proved otherwise. Parsonneau, of the Charpentiers, Menuisiers, and Ebénistes, put the rhetorical question: "1943 . . . What's new in professional organization? Nothing!"[47]

Expressing this growing sense of disillusion and, even more, doing something about it, was another matter. The artisanal movement, as it had developed between the wars, had unraveled under the strains of mobilization, occupation, and censorship. Its political godfather, the Chamber of Deputies, had disappeared without compensation. Artisanal confederations had no place in the organization committees or on the OCRPI. Their relations with the Artisanal Service were ambiguous.

The old CEAA, with its center of gravity in Alsace-Lorraine, was gutted with the Germans' reannexation of the provinces. The rump of this conservative, corporatist committee was attracted to the like-minded Loyer and his Artisanal Service. The voice of the CEAA, the *Information Aristanale*, consistently showed itself the most loyal to Vichy of all the artisanal papers. And many of the CEAA's leaders, such as Huguet, Chaudieu, and Coustenoble, took quasi-official positions in the new order. As Loyer sacrificed his ideological purity to the practicalities of Vichy politics, this support became more tepid. The Catholic-inspired CAF, which shared in such large part the Vichy social agenda, showed itself to be more active and critical than the CEAA. Here agreement on ends largely ran aground on the question of means. Despite its conservative social ideas, the CAF was firmly committed to free syndicalism. While the CAF was willing to cooperate with the Artisanal Service, it never accepted the "coordination" of the artisanat.[48]

In the absence of decisive evidence, it is difficult to know what went on within the CGAF, the group, on its record, least likely to stand behind Pétain. There is no record of any CGAF activity during the war. Its parliamentary strategy was now moot and its left-leaning syndicalism clearly out of step with the National Revolution. The *Artisan Français*, after its number of June 1940, ceased publishing for thirteen months. It returned in August 1941 and continued to appear until December 1942. Not surprisingly, it had in the interim revised its editorial policy. Tailledet, now without his long-time collaborator, Grandadam, paid the obligatory obeisance to Marshal Pétain and expressed optimism about the artisanat's future in the New France. Yet the *Artisan Français* maintained a critical edge in its comments. The paper punctuated its general support for the regime with pungent remarks on the government's alleged "back-to-the-land" policies. The exodus of people into the countryside and the regime's announced intention to fight unemployment by training more craftsmen, wrote Pégeot, the *confédéré* president of the Calvados Chamber of Trades, was resulting in a ruinous competition for rural masters.[49] Tailledet, again between the lines of support, objected to what he perceived as the creeping *étatisation* of artisanal institutions and the government's efforts to concentrate production at the expense of the *petits*. Finally, the journal printed regular articles describing the dearth of materials available to the artisanal trades.

The shortages of necessary raw materials were by far the most frequent and insistent of the complaints heard among artistans. At a conference in Montpellier in March 1942, Monsieur Bourdet of the OCRPI gave a general accounting of resources: In 1942, as compared to 1938, France suffered a decrease of 67 percent in ferrous metals, 84 percent of lead, 24 percent of pewter, 28 percent of zinc. Only 20 percent of the usual inventory of textiles remained, 8 percent of gasoline, and 25 percent of lubricating oil. Coal stocks were only 60 percent of what was needed. The "relatively privileged" construction trades received 40 percent of their requirements.[50] Under these conditions a tradesman's survival rested on his ingenuity and ability to recycle materials.

This naturally led to what president Estivals, of the Aveyron Chamber of Trades, called the "hunt for raw materials which are becoming unceasingly rarer."[51] This letter from the Allier typified the masters' conundrum: "I repair agricultural machines and bicycles. I live in a remote area and can find no materials where I am. My village being badly provided for, I have only my little truck to allow me to obtain provisions. However, since September [1941]

I have had no gasoline."[52] The *Artisan des Alpes* reported devastating shortages of cement and paper in its region.[53] A Breton cobbler and father of four
wrote to the *Artisan de France* that he could not find enough leather to make
shoes. And a blacksmith complained that, "We know that we cannot have
the finest quality coal, but what we do get is nothing more than dust."[54]

The pro-Vichy *Information Artisanale* painted a much brighter picture of
the situation in petty production. In its March 1942 number, the journal
printed an OCRPI survey of the various sectors. The OCRPI estimated that
artisans were receiving 50 to 60 percent of their coal needs, while industry
obtained but 30 percent. The situation was the same in rubber, textiles,
leather, and fats. The most serious shortages, the *résumé* noted, were in
metals. But even here artisans were getting a better deal than most. "Far
from being forgotten or disadvantaged in distribution," it concluded, "the
artisanat has not ceased to benefit—whether one considers their consumption
[of materials] from before the war or compares what they now receive to
what is currently allocated to big industry—from an equitable, and even in
numerous cases, privileged treatment."[55]

Which was it? Were artisans being fairly treated or systematically *désa-
vantagé* by the organization committees and the OCRPI? It is impossible to
say for certain. Jean Bichelonne had said that "the sole concept which can
guide the apportionment [of resources] is that of the public interest."[56] But
of course Bichelonne's technocratic perspective was unlikely to coincide with
that of petty producers themselves. In view of artisans' lack of representation
in the policymaking apparatus and the economic pressures on the government,
there is no reason to believe that petty production was especially well provided
for. The truth is probably that artisans were receiving a reasonable part of
dwindling resources, but even this produced disaster for most masters as it
did, after all, for almost everybody.

When the government had dissolved the CGT and the employers' Confédération nationale du patronat français in November 1940, it had left the
artisanal confederations alone. Whether this signaled some kind of official
favor or merely a recognition that the artisanal movement was politically inert
is not clear. In either case, the regime changed its mind (or corrected its
omission) and, by a decree of May 1942, put an official end to the CGAF,
CEAA, CAF, and UAF.[57] The professional federations, departmental unions,
and local trade syndicates continued to function, but the movement had been
stripped of its national, interprofessional organizations with the exception,
that is, of the APCMF. The APCMF had been in existence for a decade but
was long overshadowed within the artisanal movement by the older, more
dynamic, and more influential syndical formations. The elimination of the
artisanal confederations, however, left the APCMF for the moment the sole
collective voice of the artisanat. The subsequent experience of the APCMF
provides something of an object lesson in the evolution, or rather the deterioration, of relations between the Etat Français and its artisans.

In the beginning these relations seemed harmonious enough. A necessarily truncated version of the APCMF met in Clermont-Ferrand at the end of August 1940. Many of the presidents of the departmental chambers had been trapped in the occupied zone and were unable to attend. Albert Coustenoble, of the Nord, the president of the APCMF, had been caught up in the invasion the previous year and was marooned in Brittany.[58] A second and more fully attended meeting took place in Lyon in March 1941. It opened with the most florid expressions of confidence in Pétain and his National Revolution. Loyer, representing the government, responded in kind and backed up his solicitous sentiments with a small measure of policy. He announced the regime's intention to put into effect the Walter-Paulin law on apprenticeship and to place the BAM under the chambers of trades' jurisdiction. Loyer even arranged a meeting between several of the presidents and Marshal Pétain himself.[59] Once back home, however, even the most sanguine presidents found themselves harangued by their constituents, unable to ignore the distance between Pétain's promises and the policies of the organization committees. Future APCMF meetings became less genteel affairs.

The presidents' complaints continually turned to the essential question of raw materials. Echoing what we have heard elsewhere, the APCMF reported shortages in every region and trade. Papasseudi, of the Alpes-Maritîmes, noted that painters in his chamber could get neither the linseed oil nor the turpentine they needed to mix their paint. In 1942 the presidents learned that the minutes of their previous meeting would be unavailable because the printer, lacking both gas and coal, had been unable to operate his business. These examples were multiplied endlessly. Moreover, as Hunault, of the Hautes-Pyrénées, remarked, even allocation in principle was not synonymous with delivery in fact.[60]

Loyer responded to these tales of woe with calls for patience yet admitted that he could do little to remedy the situation. Resources simply did not exist in sufficient quantities, the operations of the organization committees and OCRPI were outside his province, and the Germans were pressing the French for the funneling of precious materials to the most efficient—that is, the most concentrated—manufacturers. At their meeting of June 1942, Loyer informed the presidents that materials available to artisans in 1943 might be only 15 percent of what they required and predicted that some trades could lose up to 80 percent of their effectives.[61]

This was understandable; however, the presidents began to see their afflictions as a consequence of Vichy's imperfectly administered social policies and, in particular, of the composition of the organization committees and this angered them. Castéras, president from the Haute-Garonne and the APCMF's most outspoken critic of the regime, quoted Pétain to the effect that, "The economy will be organized and controlled. The state's coordination of private activity will take in hand the power of the trusts . . . and give greater justice in distribution."[62] Castéras continued ironically that in fact the National Revolution had changed little: "It's the trusts that control things and not the middle classes as we have been promised."[63] He went on to say:

> Take the Comité des Forges. This Comité has been, so it would appear, dissolved. Yet we see it revived under the cover of the organization committees. Certainly, we don't see the same people [sic], but we see that the activity of these organization committees is directed in the same manner— which is to say, to the advantage of trusts and big business and to the more or less progressive suffocation of the artisanat and of small and medium-sized production.[64]

The presidents complained that artisans never reached leadership positions alongside the businessmen and technocrats who seldom shared their opinions. Even when the presidents volunteered their assistance, the committees ignored them. For example, in the spring of 1941 the general secretary of the APCMF, Poilblanc, wrote to sixty organization committees proposing collaboration with the assembly. He reported that three responded favorably, two evaded the question, two explicitly refused, and fifty-three never bothered to reply.[65]

Alternatively, the presidents sought to detach the artisanat from the purview of the organization committees. To this end, they demanded control over the registration and installation of new artisans—in other words, a closed and autonomous corporation. Loyer sympathized. "I regret it as much as you," he told the presidents, "but I am obliged to tell you that you cannot prevent [those who are not true artisans] from setting up in business."[66] Loyer also defended the integrity of the organization committees, and further promised that the government was already at work on an artisanal statute that would fill the gaps in the legislation of 1940 and the Labor Charter.

At the same time, the Artisanal Service tightened its grip on the chambers of trades and the assembly of their presidents. The Courtier law of 1925 had provided for the free election of the chambers and their officers; but such democracy in a quasi-public institution was clearly not acceptable to the Vichy regime. With the laws of January 21, and November 17, 1941, the state appropriated for itself the direction of the chambers and subordinated the entire system to the Artisanal Service in order, it claimed, to compensate for wartime disorder.[67] Loyer now reserved the right, through the prefects, to name new members to the chambers "after consultation with local professional groups." The Service also appointed the officers to each chamber and had the authority to demand the resignation of any artisanal functionary "who proves lacking in his charge."[68] Loyer's deputies became omnipresent, sitting in at APCMF meetings, setting up local GAP, arranging artisanal expositions, and surveying the technical progress of petty production. Formally, these delegates, drawn almost exclusively from the technical *cadres*, stood between the state and the master artisans. In fact, they were responsible to their chief, Loyer, and not at all to their artisan constituents.[69]

The Artisanal Service used its new authority to reorganize several chambers of trades that were "lacking in their charge"—apparently a political as well as an administrative matter. Consider the reorganization of the chamber in the department of the Seine. From its creation in 1933 the Seine Chamber of Trades had been one of the cornerstones of the CGAF and of artisanal syndicalism. After the Armistice, its old president, Georges Grandadam, disappeared from the editorial staff of the *Artisan Français* and probably from the Seine chamber, too. In December 1941, the production minister, Lehideux, dissolved the old chamber and appointed a new one. Henri Bardet, tailor and former vice-president of the CGAF, was named the new president. It seems that the new chamber proved no more satisfactory than the old, because in August of 1943, concurrent with the publication of the Statute of the Artisanat, Bardet resigned, to be replaced by a more politically dependable president, Louis Tison, general secretary of the Parisian syndicate of *patron-coiffeurs*, who in 1938 addressed a rally of the Parti social français and in 1941 was a candidate to administer "aryanized" salons.[70]

A few presidents, true believers in the National Revolution, endorsed the new order with enthusiasm. Most appear to have made a sincere effort to accommodate themselves to political realities, either out of resignation or a genuine desire to cooperate. Louis Bourrières, president of the Lot Chamber of Trades, seemed to express the general feeling when he said to his colleagues, "I am sure that on this point we are all in agreement. If you are supported by the minister your authority will be that much greater."[71] Yet the presidents were not willing to become the pawns of the administration.

Many of those in the APCMF had been less than distressed by the government's "coordination" of the syndicates and confederations, for it raised the chambers of trades and the APCMF to the leadership of the artisanal movement. As the greedy hand of the state began to reach to the chambers and the assembly itself, however, the presidents became increasingly restless and cantankerous. The question of who, indeed, would control the organized artisanat first surfaced at the APCMF meeting of August 1941. The Artisanal Service insisted that its delegates be allowed to attend such meetings in order to provide the presidents with important information, to answer their questions, and to "guide" their decisions. For their part, the presidents objected less to the participation of the delegates than to being ordered to receive them—to being treated as "poor relations," Ollier (Puy-de-Dôme) put it.

By the middle of 1941, therefore, and despite their continued protestations of loyalty to Pétain, the members of the APCMF had begun to affect an air of opposition. This grumbling cannot be taken for a general critique of Vichy politics. The presidents expressed no nostalgia for the Third Republic; they made no open reference to the lack of political liberties, nor did they squarely reject the regime's posture of collaboration with the Third Reich—even though the prewar attitudes of some of the presidents suggested the existence of such private sentiments. Their horizons started and finished with the artisanat.

This mood of discontent in the APCMF finally produced a confrontation at the meetings of June 1942 held in Nice. The assembly's committee on professional organization lit the fuse with a letter to Pétain, which reminded the marshal of the presidents' enduring devotion to the National Revolution, but sharply criticized the actual policies of the administration. Naturally,

Loyer, presiding over the discussions, was annoyed by what he perceived as both a personal attack and a breach of protocol. His mood darkened when there followed an extremely negative report on the GAP. Although the presidents thought the GAP a good idea in theory, they complained that they relied too heavily on the Artisanal Service and ignored the chambers of trades and the presidents in practice. "The one thing I will not accept," proclaimed Rabier (Haute-Savoie), "is that a member of a GAP would meet me on a staircase and say: 'Who is this fellow I've never seen before?' "[72]

The explosion occurred following a lengthy report on the BAM. Hunault, of the Gard, first reviewed the problem of material shortages for petty producers and then pursued the issue of relations between the chambers and the Artisanal Service. "Little by little," he said, "we see this Service substitute itself for the natural authority of the presidents of the chambers of trades and the other qualified representatives of the Artisanat." President Charlin complained that the BAM were no more than "mailboxes" for the OCRPI. The committee demanded the reconstitution of the BAM as artisanal organization committees. Castéras, who had previously expressed his unhappiness with these organization committees, punctuated the report by describing the regime's artisanal policy as "twenty months of bankruptcy" and by accusing the Artisanal Service of subverting the chambers of trades.

Silence. A moment of tension. Then Loyer rose to respond. "The tone of this report is unacceptable." He was only trying, he pleaded, to do his best by artisans and by the nation, and the presidents had to recognize that the state could accomplish some tasks better than the artisans themselves. He was disappointed, moreover, to see that the presidents had not truly understood the National Revolution. They were backsliding into self-centered, class-conflictual patterns of behavior. Loyer finished with a concise lesson in Vichy political science:

> The power your chambers enjoy has been given . . . by the State. I ask you
> to remember this because the Marshal has said that authority flows from the
> top. If you have received [any authority] the State is responsible, and you
> have no right under the circumstances to adopt a systematically critical attitude, as if back under the old parliamentary regime.

Loyer's rebuke threw the meeting into disorder. Some presidents traded recriminations across the floor. Others called for restraint and deference. Coustenoble, in the chair, refused to put the committee's recommendations to a vote and left the room in a panic. The tumultuous session finally adjourned amid calls to forego "these useless discussions" and move on to less controversial business. Thus the APCMF broke up, not to meet again until after the Liberation.

As a formal matter, a ministerial decree of February 11, 1943 put an end to the APCMF's existence. The official notice accompanying the decree read:

> [The APCMF] has proved, at its recent congress, that it has not given up
> the sterile habits and discussions appropriate to the old parliamentary as-

semblies. It has been a nest of intrigues, inspired more by personal ambition than by any genuine interest in artisans.[73]

The elimination of the APCMF was not merely punishment for its sulky behavior. By June 1942 it remained the last remnant of an independent, national artisanal movement. Its passing, as Castéras perceived, seems therefore part of a process of *étatisation* that would have caught up to the APCMF sooner or later, however well it behaved. It was not in the first instance an act of spite or censorship but a part of the organic reform of the artisanat. Accordingly, the decree of February 11 noted that the minister of production had already convened a consultative committee to help the government draw up its Statute of the Artisanat. Several of those who had sat on the defunct APCMF now took their place on the *comité consultatif*—Coustenoble, Bourrières, Jeannin, Pégeot, Bardet, among others. The government also brought in representatives of the various professions: for example, Tison, for the hairdressers, and Kergoat, for the electricians. The committee even included two *compagnons*.[74]

The consultative committee worked on and off from the fall of 1942 through the spring of 1943, trying to give shape to those vague and contradictory ideas that had been the artisanal social program since 1919. Bichelonne, now the production minister, and Loyer kept the committee on a tight leash in order to make sure that its work conformed to the contours of the National Revolution. In August of 1943, Bichelonne finally published the Statute of the Artisanat. Here at last, he said, was the concrete manifestation of the Vichy social Idea, the long-promised artisanal corporation.[75] This was indeed the case, but not exactly in the way that Bichelonne meant. Like so much of the National Revolution, the Statute of the Artisanat remained an architectural blueprint rather than a finished edifice. Nevertheless, by the incompleteness of its corporatism and the degree of state control it envisaged, the Statute demonstrated perfectly both the regime's conflicting intentions and the practical limits of corporatist reorganization.

Structurally, the Statute was complex (see Figure 5.2). It divided the artisanat in two parts. For those professions that were more or less exclusively artisanal in nature (blacksmiths, for example), the Statute erected Communities of Trades (*Communautés de Métiers*): mixed syndicates of masters, *compagnons*, and the heads of those few larger and not truly artisanal enterprises. These functioned as independent organization subcommittees. The state denied a similar autonomy to the second group, composed of those professions in which artisanal production coexisted with industrial (such as masons and shoemakers). Masters in these trades found themselves as before united in the GAP and then integrated into the organization committees, where they constituted a subsection of artisanal *commissions mixtes*. In keeping with the Vichy political principle, the state maintained a firm hand on the direction of the Communities of Trades and the GAP. Both were led by *syndics*, artisan-administrators jointly appointed by the Artisanal Service and the artisanal syndicates. The Artisanal Service, of course, had the final word.

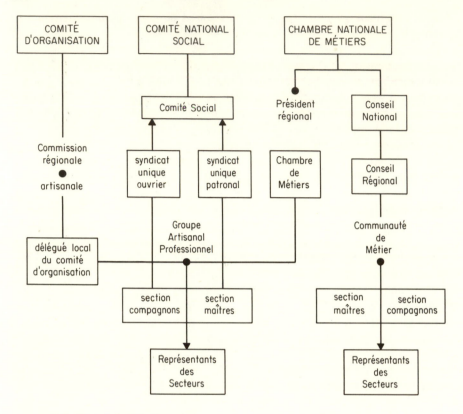

FIGURE 5.2. Statut de l'Artisanat.

Source: Jean Bichelonne, *Le Statut de l'Artisanat, Extrait du Journal Officel*, 25 August 1943 (Clermont-Ferrand: Imprimeries Paul Vallier, 1943), p. 4.

For interprofessional matters the Statute of the Artisanat retained the chambers of trades but lashed them more tightly to the state. The chambers of trades kept most of their old functions: regulating apprenticeship, distributing certificates of competence, and supervising the registers of trades. In some sense, the greater presence of the state even enhanced the chambers' efficacy in these tasks—at the cost, however, of their independence.[76]

At the apex of the new structure, the Chambre Nationale des Métiers replaced the fractious APCMF. The Chambre Nationale united the *syndics* of the Communities of Trades, the presidents of the local chambers of trades, and *compagnons* selected from each profession and region. In fact, it virtually reconstituted the consultative committee, and Coustenoble stepped neatly from the presidency of the APCMF, to the chair of the *comité consultatif*, to the head of the Chambre Nationale.[77] Responsible for coordinating the hierarchy of professional groups and the chambers of trades, the Chambre Nationale operated under the direct supervision of the Artisanal Service and the Production Ministry. Once again, the new differed from the old less in its organization and functions than in its locus of power.[78]

The Statute of the Artisanat, like the Labor Charter before it, changed artisans' lives but little. The artisanat remained without corporate unity and independence, and without effective control of resources.[79] Even its modest reforms, moreover, met a very mixed reception. Pierre Lucius, in *Le Moniteur de la Mécanique Rurale* praised the Statute as "a new and important victory for corporate liberties over the statism and marxist syndicalism of the old regime."[80] Most of the artisanal syndicates seem, on the contrary, to have been decidedly cool. All the syndical organizations in *coiffure* approached the Artisanal Service with a resolution opposing the application of the Statute to their profession. The furriers, harness and saddlemakers, wheelwrights, and shoemakers expressed similar sentiments.[81] The Statute of the Artisanat was likewise condemned by the organization committees, threatened with a loss of jurisdiction, and by the organizations of *compagnons*, who would have found themselves separated from their fellow workers in industry and abandoned to the Communities of Trades dominated by masters.[82] Even Hubert Lagardelle, the labor minister, offering Loyer his opinion on the impending Statute, wrote that he did not recognize any "problème de l'artisanat" or any need for such a statute. It would only lead, he continued, to "both regrettable administrative confusion and heavy financial burdens."[83] Not surprisingly, the Statute of the Artisanat never functioned to any significant degree before the Liberation put an end to it.

The publication of the Statute of the Artisanat marked the climax of artisanal legislation in Vichy but not the end. In January 1944 the government created the Centre national de la coopération artisanale in an attempt to unify and coordinate artisanal cooperatives. The next month it resuscitated the INM, this time under close state supervision. Shortly thereafter the Production Ministry set up the Société centrale pour le développement de l'artisanat. Like so many of Vichy's plans for master artisans, these found little support either within the administration or among the tradesmen. They disappeared with their sponsors, leaving scarcely a trace.[84]

As far as artisans were concerned, therefore, the National Revolution brought little that was revolutionary. Administrative policy, except for the imperatives of war and penury, followed the patterns established between the wars. In the areas of credit to small business, taxation, and social assistance Vichy simply carried over or extended what the Third Republic had begun. It even maintained the controversial (and certainly not corporatist) mathematical definition of *artisan*.[85] Neither did the regime grant artisans the kind of authority within their corporation they had so long desired. The Statute of the Artisanat, for example, entitled the chambers of trades to refuse a place on the register of trades to people who lacked proper professional training, which would appear on the surface to have given the chambers crucial control over the market. As the law operated, however, a person shunned by his chamber of trades could simply register himself at the chamber of commerce and operate as a *commerçant*.[86] Perhaps the most important bit of social protection for small business was a law that prohibited the opening of new enterprises without the explicit consent of the government. But this had been passed by the old Parliament in September 1939 to protect those small proprietors called away to war. Besides, for the Vichy administration this law served not for corporate self-regulation but for strict government control.[87]

The regime's social posturing produced no notable turning of artisanal fortunes. There was, for example, no surge in the population of small masters during the war. Alain Rodet, using the register of trades first published in 1936, recorded that 130,000 new names appeared on the registers in 1941 and another 93,000 in 1942, while only 27,000 were dropped from the rolls. Rodet thus concluded, mistakenly, that the artisanat leveled off during the war at about 1 million enterprises.[88] Henri Mourier, however, explained that the inscriptions on the registers reflected instead the need for official status in order to obtain raw materials. They did not signify any real increase in the number of artisanal businesses, which Mourier puts at 700,547 enterprises, according to a 1944 census (Table 5.1). These employed some 352,000 *compagnons* and trained 98,154 apprentices. Mourier's figures were depressed by the German annexation of Alsace-Lorraine and the absence of large numbers of prisoners of war.[89]

The National Revolution also failed to transform the internal make-up of the artisanat. Mourier's breakdown of *compagnons* per trade (see Table 5.2) reveals a by now familiar pattern. Printers, those in the construction and food trades, and mechanics were above the mean of 0.52 *compagnons* per enterprise. The rural trades of blacksmith, saddle-, and barrelmaker as well as the troubled cobblers, fell below the average. Of course, some trades simply required more hands than others, and the number of *compagnons* therefore does not always correspond to economic vitality. In the case of tailors, the large number of journeymen reflects a situation of widespread *travail à domicile*. In contrast, it is the nature of the watchmaker, however prosperous, to work alone.

A better indicator of a hale trade is its coefficient of renewal; that is, the number of *compagnons* and apprentices ready to become masters (Table 5.3). And here again, the National Revolution wrought no real structural changes. The war years were relatively good ones for contemporary trades, such as automobile repair and sheet metal work. Prosthetists were especially in demand. Most of the *industries récessives*, such as sabotmakers or basketweavers, continued their slide into quaintness. A number of irregularities do appear in these figures, however. Some of the rural trades, such as farriers and blacksmiths, were attracting young workers during the Occupation, whereas before 1940 they had been avoided. Conversely, several of the more dynamic trades, especially those connected to construction, contracted during the war years.[90] The robust health of the rural trades and the crisis in construction reflected the distortions of a war-devastated economy, rather than any long-term revival of the market for horseshoes and wagonwheels.[91]

More dramatic, if perhaps less disastrous for the individual, was the National Revolution's impact on the organized artisanat; that is, the process of *étatisation*. Herbert Lüthy characterized Vichy as little more than a state apparatus "deprived of its democratic and republican facade", or as Pierre

TABLE 5.1. 1944 Census of the artisanat by sector and profession

Metals and Mechanics (18.5%)		Construction (17.8%)	
Auto mechanics	17.176	Masons	40,726
Bicycle mechanics	8,944	Roofers	10,920
Carriagemakers	1,504	Plumbers	10,332
Wheelwrights	9,210	Locksmiths	8,136
Agricultural mechanics, blacksmiths,		Painters, glaziers	21,523
farriers	45,783	Plasterers	3,347
Metalworkers	16,095	Fireplace installers	1,336
Electricians	13,519	Quarriers	1,629
Watchmakers	7,140	Stonecutters	1,082
Gunsmiths	422	Tombstonemakers	1,560

Wood (12%)		Textiles and Clothing (18.8%)	
Cabinetmakers	8,926	Dressmakers	59,321
Chairmakers	1,009	Tailors	17,364
Joiners	20,881	Lingeriemakers	2,615
Wheelwrights	13,746	Milliners (women's)	12,217
Carpenters	11,153	Milliners (men's)	617
Sabotmakers	11,152	Laundrymen, laundresses	10,398
Barrelmakers	4,303	Ironers	2,189
		Dyers	2,140
		Furriers	2,322

Leather Goods (10.7%)		Food Trades (10.8%)	
Shoemakers	48,970	Butchers	24,414
Saddlemakers	12,815	Pork butchers	12,100
Luggagemakers	841	Bakers	32,000
		Pastrymakers	6,245

Diverse Trades (11.4%)	
Hairdressers	43,600
Jewelers	1,209
Basketmakers	2,240
Printers	2,343
Photographers	3,794
Rugmakers	3,751
Mattressmakers	1,750

Source: Henri Mourier, "L'artisanat, sa structure et son intégration dens l'économie moderne." Thèse en droit (Paris, 1952) p. 103–6.

Nicolle put it, a bureaucratic dictatorship "on the march."[92] Artisans certainly would have agreed. Undoubtedly, Loyer himself was motivated by a genuine desire to improve the lot of small masters. He worked diligently against the combined forces of bureaucratic confusion and outright opposition to put the artisanat on more solid economic and social ground as he conceived it. But the main result of his efforts was less the amelioration of petty production than a profound change in the nature of what had been the artisanal movement. The interprofessional confederations that had been the backbone of the movement since 1922 were dissolved. The chambers of trades and the APCMF were remade into state bureaucracies. Along with this, the National

TABLE 5.2.　Coefficient of compagnons per enterprise, 1944

Profession	Coefficient	Profession	Coefficient
Tailors	0.97	Hairdressers	0.51
Printers	0.87	Carpenters	0.49
Pastrymakers	0.72	Rugmakers	0.47
Roofers	0.70	Blacksmiths	0.44
Agricultural machine repairmen	0.69	Milliners	0.39
Cabinetmakers	0.67	Dressmakers	0.36
Pork butchers	0.63	Barrelmakers	0.26
Masons	0.63	Saddlemakers	0.26
Auto mechanics	0.61	Upholsterers	0.25
Butchers	0.55	Watchmakers	0.22
		Cobblers	0.17
	Mean 0.52		

Source: Henri Mourier, "Essai de statistiques artisanales," *Annals du droit economique. Aspects de l'artisanat en France et à l'étranger*, n.s. 4 (1953):83.

Revolution effected a certain circulation of elites within the artisanat. The predominant figures of the prewar period—Tailledet, Grandadam, Peter, Ley, and Manoury—disappeared from the lists of those brought in to collaborate with the government and others such as Tison, Bossavy, Coustenoble, Chaudieu, and Jeannin took their places.

Paradoxically, while the political artisanat was immobilized, the base of the movement expanded during the war years. The regime worked to set the chambers of trades on a firmer foundation, even if it compromised their independence. The trades registers, as Mourier noted, swelled, and even the local trades syndicates found new members.[93] This did not signify any popular enthusiasm for Vichy's ideological and social designs. The rank and file of master artisans seem to have greeted the Labor Charter and the Statute of the Artisanat with, at best, a yawn and, at worst, a jaundiced suspicion. After the war, Ollier, president of the Puy-de-Dôme Chamber of Trades ridiculed the masters' response to the *brevets de maîtrise*, which the chambers were authorized to distribute. Of the 14,000 artisans in his department fewer than 1,000 ever turned up to claim their *brevets*, despite a vigorous propaganda effort.[94] Rather the artisanat organized itself in response to its material needs. The chambers and the syndicates, through the BAM and the GAP, controlled access to critical resources.

Vichy intentions did not translate into social and political reality. The domination of the organization committees and the attempted *étatisation* of the artisanal movement produced a kind of passive resistance within the artisanat. The APCMF showed itself more and more obstreperous, while individual artisans ignored the questionnaires of the organization committees and declined to cooperate with the Artisanal Service. The masters rallied slowly, if at all, to the GAP and the BAM.[95] The beefed up local syndicates and federations enjoyed their new popularity. Yet they continued to insist on their autonomy and, as we have seen in the case of the Statute of the Artisanat, dragged their feet when it came to more elaborate reorganization.

TABLE 5.3. Coefficient of renewal in the Artisanat, 1944: compagnons and apprentices becoming masters

Profession	Coefficient*
Dressmaker	2.43
Prosthetist	2.34
Auto mechanic	1.69
Coachbuilder	1.38
Metalcutter	1.28
General mechanic	1.26
Sheet metal worker	1.24
Milliner	1.22
Cabinetmaker	1.21
Pastrymaker	1.14
Farrier	1.14
Wheelwright (metal)	1.11
Hairdresser	1.06
Blacksmith	1.05
Carpenter, joiner	1.03
Coppersmith	1.00
Printer	1.00
Electrician	0.96
Tailor	0.93
Radio repairman	0.91
Engraver	0.90
Wheelwright (wood)	0.85
Luggagemaker (leather)	0.85
Jeweler	0.80
Plumber	0.74
Plasterer	0.71
Heating installer, repairman	0.70
Saddle- and harnessmaker	0.67
Embroiderer	0.66
Pork butcher	0.63
Roofer	0.62
Dry cleaner-presser	0.62
Bootmaker	0.62
Chairmaker	0.60
Carpenter (wood)	0.58
Corsetmaker	0.57
Painter	0.55
Watchmaker	0.55
Mason	0.55
Stovesetter	0.54
Linenmaker	0.53
Barrelmaker	0.53
Hatter	0.51
Sabotmaker	0.49
Rugweaver	0.49
Tinsmith	0.45
Cobbler	0.45
Tinker	0.35
Quarrier	0.35
Cutler	0.34
Basketweaver	0.23

Source: Mourier, "Essai," p. 91.
* > 1.00 = being adequately replaced; 0.75 = a grave crisis; < 0.60 = risks a disappearance.

Indeed, as the *Information Artisanale* remarked with some remorse, corporatism in practice looked more and more like the old syndicalism:

> Oriented originally towards an authoritarian corporatism, the "Statute of the Artisanat" tended to be applied within the context of a pre-existing syndicalism. . . . Generally desired [sic], the corporation proved to be the exception.[96]

Artisans' own unwillingness to go along thus helped to derail the regime's program of social reconstruction. But the program itself was flawed, full of logical inconsistencies and contradictory intentions. Yves Bouthillier, Pétain's one-time finance minister, once remarked that Vichy represented the "primacy of administration over politics."[97] The history of petty producers in this period suggests that Bouthillier was half right, for administration and politics were not incompatible in practice. While the Etat Français was probably administered to a greater degree than the Third Republic, this turned out to be merely politics by other means. But what sort of politics?

At first glance Vichy social and economic thought appears ambivalent, with corporatists, like Loyer, on one side and modernizing technocrats, like Bichelonne, on the other. Pétain's official pronouncements, stressing authority, traditional social forms, and the profession *organisée*, displayed an affinity for the corporatists. His coterie, as distinct from his governments, was dominated by like-minded conservatives. These often fretted about the regime's failure to move quickly or decisively enough in a corporatist direction; yet they enjoyed their limited victories, most notably in aspects of the Labor Charter in 1941 and in the overthrow of the "technocratic" Darlan government in 1942.[98]

Among the corporatists artisans had their special pleaders. These had traditionally gathered around the Institut d'Etudes Corporatives et Sociales, established in 1934 to perfect and to publicize corporatist social theories. The National Revolution, of course, brought corporatism into vogue and gave the Institut a new measure of prestige and influence. In 1942 the Institut gave birth to the Ecole des Hautes Etudes Artisanales (EHEA). Patterned after the other *hautes écoles*, the EHEA was meant to prepare the future administrative elite of the artisanat. It offered courses and diplomas in the history of trades, the artisanal economy, and the administrative law of the artisanat. Seventy-seven students in 1942 were pursuing their artisanal studies in residence, while another 127 took their degrees by correspondence.[99] The EHEA was staffed by many of those "new men," pushed to the top by the fresh political currents: Maurice Bouvier-Ajam, Maurice Avril, André Jeannin, and the Ecole's president, Georges Chaudieu.

If the corporatists had Marshal Pétain's ear and enjoyed a novel access to government patronage, they nevertheless found themselves engaged in a running battle with the businessmen, financiers, and technocrats who directed the economic ministries, the organization committees, and the OCRPI. Both groups wanted, above all, to rid the country of the withering social conflict of the 1930s. The modernizers—or neo-liberals, as Kuisel calls them—like Bichelonne, thought to buy national harmony with increased consumption, which meant structural economic reform and state direction. The corporatists, too, believed in a strong state. Essentially they looked to eliminate class hostility by defining class out of existence—that is, by designing a system in which big capital, small property, and labor would have the *same* interests. But authority would serve if society refused to cooperate.[100]

It would be a mistake, however, to infer that the competition between these "idéologies patronales," as Caron and Bouvier call them, involved a parallel ambiguity of policy, and still less an ambiguity in the regime's historical impact. First of all, as Robert Paxton notes, these competing policies overlapped in fundamental ways. Both fought the same enemies: laissez faire economics, parliamentary government, and independent trade unionism. Neither challenged the sanctity of property and each defended the virtues of social order.[101] Yet, as the emptiness of corporatist restructuring of the artisanat suggests, when these two strategies clashed over concrete economic policy, the modernizers usually prevailed.

This, so far as artisans were concerned, was the great deception of Pétainism. Despite the decentralizing logic of its corporatist posturing, Vichy daily stoked the fires of state control. And it used this enhanced power to concentrate and rationalize the economy. Even after the government had chased its most vocal modernizers—Bouthillier, Lehideux, Pucheu—the process of rationalization and concentration continued under the auspices of the organization committees, the OCRPI, and the Production Ministry.

All this marked but a minimal rupture with the prewar evolution of political economy in France. The institutional models for the Vichy administration already existed in the councils and commissions, some of which included artisans, set up between the world wars. The organization committees served then as the perfect transition from the CNE of the 1930s to the Commissariat du Plan of the 1950s. The committees, writes Claude Gruson, lacked the resources but not the aim of planification: "It could not be a question of conceiving and executing investment programs or renovation projects [during the war]. But it was possible to dream about them."[102] Bichelonne, saw it all very clearly. He said,

> the economy *dirigée* is destined to place a powerful means of action at the service of the economy . . . and, in this respect, it must continue after the war is over. . . . Instead of the disorder of the prewar years, the peace will bring coordination and rational management. . . .[103]

Continuity existed in personnel as well as policy. Of the chief economic policymakers, Pucheu and Lehideux had been executives in the steel and automobile industries, respectively; Bichelonne, a prize graduate of the Ecole Polytechnique and Bouthillier, a former inspector of finance and protégé of Paul Reynaud. At a lower level, the Vichy *cadre* filled up with graduates of the *grandes écoles*, important members of the business world, even anticom-

munist officers of the CGT, like Belin. What was true of the ministries was
even more true of the organization committees. "In some cases," wrote Kuisel, "especially in heavily concentrated industry, [the organization commit-
tees] merely reconstituted existing employers' associations and cartels."[104] Of
the seventy-six directors of the organization committees in 1942, reported
Henri Russo, 80 percent were *patrons* and 20 percent were *technocrats*. In
fact,

> It was almost always the same men, the same enterprises, representing, in
> each professional branch, the same interests, that controlled the destiny of
> their sector before, during, and after the war.[105]

The practical effect on petty producers of an administration dominated
by big businessmen and graduates of the *grandes écoles* had been mitigated
before the war by the political system. First, the popularly elected Parliament
of the Third Republic inevitably represented a less "progressive" constituency
than the administration and acted to restrain the modernizing impulses of the
neo-liberals. Second, the direct participation of workers' groups, and especially the independent syndicates and the CGT, curbed the administration's
natural management/capitalist bent. Both of these buffers disappeared in June
1940. Those artisans who applauded the National Revolution missed the point,
and this is the great irony of Vichy. The "anarchy" of the parliamentary
system, with its universal manhood suffrage and its weak executive—its benevolent *immobilisme*, if you will—was the best guarantee of the survival of
independent petty production.

President Castéras was essentially correct then, when he complained to
the APCMF that the National Revolution had failed in its basic promise to
artisans: to free them from the hegemony of *les gros*.[106] Pétain did not replace
political with moral economy, nor did he substitute profession for class as the
determinant social reality. Instead, the pressures of war and occupation intensified the politics of economy and, except perhaps for the individual victories won on the black market, accentuated their bias against petty
production. Even Loyer, who began with such high corporatist hopes, had,
by the end, sacrificed these to the imperatives of the system.

Within the artisanat, the true believers of 1940 became the cynics of 1944—
but only in a certain way. Many maintained their faith in Pétain and in the
possibility of the petty "bourgeoisification" of the French economy through
corporatist reorganization. Their disappointment was with tenacious plutocrats and duplicitous administrators: a matter, that is, of bad faith, not of the
Idea itself. It seems, on the contrary, that the shallowness of the Vichy social
revolution was perfectly foreseeable. In fact, the right-wing corporatism that
informed the National Revolution was an empty doctrine, its promises to
artisans and other *petits* meaningless or dishonest. The vertical restructuring
of society could not succeed in either of its basic aims: to break the link
between economic and political power or to reconcile inherently opposed
interests. In practice, therefore, corporatism inevitably degenerated into

repression dressed up as consensus.[107] Robert Paxton's observation that "every important decision about establishing corporatism turned in favor of big business," only confirms the fact that in Vichy France, as in other self-styled corporatist regimes, *les gros* continued to dominate.[108] In the authoritarian regimes with which it was inevitably associated, wrote Jacques Juillard, corporatism played "an essentially camouflaging role."[109]

In one of his more disingenuous moments, Loyer described the Statute of the Artisanat as "an audacious measure of decentralization."[110] It was, of course, just the opposite. By its policy of "coordinating" the artisanat, by stripping the syndicates, the confederations, and the chambers of trades of their independence—by, in effect, turning the notion of representation upside down—Vichy claimed to make these organizations embodiments of "the Trades themselves" rather than of individual tradesmen. Here again we find the fiction of the "general interest" obscuring the real suppression of particular interests. Loyer's dissembling logic goes to the heart of the National Revolution, where "audacious decentralization" meant the co-optation of formerly free institutions and the sacrifice of lesser interests to those better able to wield state power. The artisanal movement learned, or should have learned, that while liberty may vanish, politics never do.

6

Epilogue:
Artisans in the New France

Laurence Wylie returned to Chanzeaux in the early 1960s for the first time in ten years, and was astonished by the dramatic changes that had overtaken this Breton village—not the least of which was the transformation of the local artisanat. Wylie found, for example, that Georges Davy, a local blacksmith, had given up shoeing horses and was now repairing automobiles. Another Chanzeaux native, Monsieur Bertrand, the son of a blacksmith, had first become a bicycle mechanic and then operated a motorbike station.[1] The social and economic "miracle" of the 1950s had similarly left its mark on the Vaucluse bourg of Roussillon. Retracing his steps in the first years of the Fifth Republic, Wylie could not help but notice how traditional skills and their practitioners had drifted to the periphery of the village economy. By the mid-1970s the *sabotier*, the harnessmaker, the blacksmith, and all the old artisans were gone. In their place, Wylie discovered tractors, tourists, and a new, more optimistic sense of the future.[2]

Wylie's observations are a measure of the progress that France had made in the fifteen years after the war, the period in which the country finally began to break out of the "stalemate society." Automobiles, televisions, country vacations, or even running water and electricity—without a doubt the "third industrial revolution" brought leisure and material comfort to the majority of French citizens. But what of those for whom "stalemate" had meant survival?

With the end of the war the country began to look to the economic future, and artisans once again heard talk of the inevitable "disappearance of small workshops" from most sectors of a rebuilt economy.[3] In the short term,

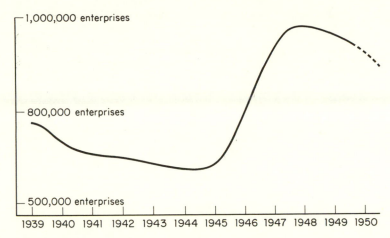

FIGURE 6.1. Number of Artisanal Enterprises, 1939–1950.

Source: Mourier, "L'artisanat," p. 101.

however, decadence posed a lesser problem for many trades than did over-crowding. The population of the artisanat probably reached its twentieth-century peak in 1948, with slightly more than 1 million enterprises (Figure 6.1). In 1946, as the prisoners of war and conscripted workers returned to France, some 150,000 artisans added their names to the registers of trades. The next year the registers inscribed another 40,000 businesses encouraged by the inflation that made small shops such an attractive investment. Most of these new enterprises remained tiny and fragile; many of the new entre-preneurs had not the least experience in *gestion* ("management"). The pro-liferation of *petites entreprises* naturally increased the level of competition among them, a situation intensified by the drastic decline of inflation at the end of the decade. As in some Malthusian population curve, this brought the expansion of the artisanat to an abrupt halt.[4]

As calculated either by the census of artisanal enterprises or by the number of masters eligible to pay the tax for their local chamber of trades, the pop-ulation of the artisanat then began a slow steady decay that spanned the rest of the Fourth Republic. Table 6.1 reveals a considerable erosion of the ar-tisanal population. Adding the calculations of the commissions of the Third and Fourth Plan to those provided by the APCMF, we find that the artisanat lost more than 189,000 enterprises between 1948 and 1960, a decrease of almost 19 percent. The aggregate number of establishments, moreover, greatly understates the real amount of turmoil within the artisanat, for a small change in the size of the artisanat hides a great coming and going of individual artisans.[5]

While artisanal workshops were becoming fewer, those that remained exhibited a tendency to increase in size (Table 6.2), at least in the second half of the 1950s. The Commission for the Fourth Plan noted that while the number of master artisans diminished by 7 percent between 1955 and 1960,

TABLE 6.1. Artisans subject to the tax for the chambers of trades, 1947–1957

Year	Number taxed	Loss from preceding year	Loss from 1948
1947	998,082		
1948	1,011,633		
1949	992,379	19,254 (1.9%)	
1950	950,653	41,726 (4.20)	60,980 (6.1%)
1951	939,686	10,967 (1.15)	71,947 (7.10)
1952	924,975	14,711 (1.55)	86,658 (8.55)
1953	913,729	11,246 (1.20)	97,904 (9.65)
1954	905,025	8,704 (0.95)	106,608 (10.6)
1955	879,760	25,265 (2.80)	131,873 (13.1)
1956	860,487	19,273 (2.20)	151,146 (15.0)
1957	845,287	15,200 (1.75)	166,346 (16.5)

Source: Assemblée des Présidents des Chambres de Métiers, circulaires 59/10/SG/8, 1959.[6]

the number of workers was leveling off (704,169 in 1955 and 706,821 in 1960). The statistics can also be read as testimony to the striking durability of petty production. The Commission for the Fourth Plan estimated that the artisanat comprised approximately 1,600,000 masters and workers in 1960, which still amounted to some 8 or 10 percent of the working population. This varied, of course, by region. The Tarn had the highest concentration of artisans, 20 percent of the "population active"; Basse-Normandie the lowest, with 8 percent.

The continued existence of such a vast artisanal sector also helps to sub-stantiate one of Carré's ironic comments about the shape of economic ex-pansion in France, which he finds remarkable precisely for the dominance of small and medium-sized businesses and the relatively modest contribution of giant firms to the "economic miracle." "Postwar French growth," he writes, "took place without substantial change in the degree of concentration of industrial production in effect at the beginning of the century or earlier."[8]

A second look at Table 6.1 shows that the decrease in the population of the artisanat was continuous but far from uniform. Structural factors dictated the direction, but conjunctural variables determined the pace. We see an accelerated decline in 1950 and again in 1955-1956. The precipitous drop in 1950 probably measures the delayed effect of the end of postwar inflation and a subsequent weeding out of the feeblest new businesses. The years to 1954

TABLE 6.2. Number of artisanal establishments by size

Number of employees	Number of establishments	
	1955	1960
1	493,988	465,617
2	241,930	253,308
3	87,883	87,919
4	31,725	39,119
5	15,723	16,142

Source: Commissariat général du Plan de modernisation et d'équipment, Quatrième Plan, p. 13.

were a period of moderate growth and price stability, in which the decline in the population of the artisanat leveled off. The decrease of artisanal businesses in 1955–1956, unlike that in 1950, occurred in a time of low inflation and healthy but not phenomenal growth, and it is harder to account for. Perhaps it owed something to the impact of the new tax laws on artisanal businesses. More likely, it reflected the compounded effect of structural change in the French economy and the push (nudge might be more appropriate) toward rationalization. In any case, it does not appear that the population of the artisanat correlated exactly with movements either in the rate of inflation or in the index of industrial production. The latter, for example, had increased briskly in the late 1940s, as the artisanat continued to expand.[9] There is another possibility that the disappearance of enterprises from the artisanat might in fact represent prosperity. The artisanat might have experienced upward mobility, as vigorous businesses added employees and hence left the registers of trades for the registers of commerce.

It is likely that all these theories are true, which means that it is necessary to study the parts in order to understand the whole. Economic survival for an individual artisanal enterprise depended on a complex combination of both professional and personal factors. First, the successful master required sufficient capital. Leborgne Lafont reported the results of a study by the Institut National de la Statistique et d'Etudes Economiques (INSEE) in 1962 of the major construction trades, which found that a master's income increased geometrically with the size of his business. A patron with from one to five employees more or less doubled the revenue of an *isolé*. A patron with six to nine workers doubled it again. Whether an artisan flourished or slipped back into the wage earning classes owed as much to his business acumen and working capital as to his trade skills.[10]

In addition, an artisan's commercial success depended on adequate social preparation. Unfortunately, precise biographical and intergenerational data do not exist for the pre-INSEE era (before 1950). Those few extant studies of the origins and the social destinations of artisans since then, however, lead us to several observations (Table 6.3). The first is the insecurity of petty production. From 1955 to 1970, according to Zarca, fewer than nine of ten artisans remained independent craftsmen for a period of ten years. Of those who left the artisanat, 12.9 percent moved up to become *industriels*, while 70.1 percent went into the working class. Intergenerational mobility was even less assured. Of the sons of master artisans, 16 percent became artisans themselves and 55 percent become *employés*. Zarca notes, moreover, that the most stable enterprises were run by the sons of artisans, the least stable by the children of workers. He found further that professional stability varied with age. Upward mobility tended to occur before a person's early thirties, while downward mobility decreased with age; that is, the collapse of an enterprise usually occurred within the first few years or not at all.[11]

Second, the artisanat was not a juncture of unrestricted social movement. In the large majority, artisans came from and went back to the lower middle class and especially to the skilled working class. The flow to and from the liberal professions and the bourgeoisie was negligible. Interestingly enough, artisans and *artisanes* traced different social trajectories. The women tended to come to the artisanat from the commercial and white-collar sectors, the men from the skilled and semi-skilled working class.

A tradesman's business prospects depended on not only his personal qualities and financial resources, but also on the particular trade he practiced. The rapid economic evolution of the 1950s more than ever separated those trades offering good opportunities from those promising a dismal future. This worked two ways. A profession that could not attract young workers would wither away; but few with any talent, ambition, or just plain good sense would undertake an apprenticeship in one of the notorious *industries récessives*.

Many in the artisanal movement continued to fret over the decline of apprenticeship, and the Commission for the Third Plan looked into the question. Its findings confirmed in part the artisans' premise but not their inference that this signaled some social or economic peril. The Commission's inquiry in the department of the Sarthe, for example, found a total of 9,500 artisans, of whom 3,902 had trained at least one apprentice in the last ten years. Two out of three masters, however, declared that they would be unwilling to do so in the future because apprenticeship constitutes a "charge trop lourde." All the same, the Commission, although it regretted the low educational level of the apprentices, concluded that the artisanat overall was training enough young people to ensure its reproduction. Indeed, it was training too many, for only one in three apprentices actually entered the artisanat whereas the other two became, in effect, skilled industrial workers.[12]

One can obtain a panoramic view of the state of the various sectors of the artisanat by examining the survey of "population and replacement" carried out in 1956 by the Third Plan's Commission for the Artisanat (Table 6.4). The Table confirms the fact that the Fourth Republic's great leap forward did not cause any great shift in the long-term development of the artisanat. It merely accelerated those trends that had been in operation since the turn of the century. Construction, the assorted food trades (bakers, butchers, confectioners, and *charcutiers*), the electrical trades, and those businesses subcontracting or producing for industry tended to be the larger enterprises and to have the highest ratio of workers to establishments and the most trainees. Meanwhile, those professions (the textile and garment trades, woodworking, and shoemaking) whose fortunes had been sinking since the beginning of the century continued to do so. Cobblers' extremely low replacement coefficient, for example, suggests not just crisis but annihilation. "Many [shoemakers]," wrote the Commission for the Third Plan, "abandon their profession while others live miserably." Paul Hunsinger counted the sabotmakers in Alsace: from 460 in 1904 to 229 in 1948 and to only 43 in 1963. The Société Savante reported a diminution of 36.6 percent between 1947 and 1960 among Alsace's master tailors. The Institut de Science Economique Appliquée in 1946 announced the almost complete "proletarianization" of braiders and trimmers.[13]

Population and replacement are not, however, perfect indicators. For instance, while a high replacement coefficient implies a healthy trade in one

TABLE 6.3.   Artisans' social origins and mobility

Socio-Economic Background (1970)		
	% of children who became artisans	
Sector	Sons	Daughters
Agriculture	3.68	11.30
Large scale commerce, industry	5.00	0.33
Small scale commerce	5.40	17.30
Artisanat	18.25	3.40
Liberal professions, upper-level bureaucrat	8.98	1.45
Middle-level functionary	7.87	13.87
Lower-level functionary	7.70	25.72
Foreman	3.80	0.33
Highly skilled worker	20.43	1.90
Moderately skilled worker	12.00	7.80
Unskilled worker	2.86	1.70
Domestic worker	—	8.60
Other services	1.30	5.48
Other categories	2.03	0.32
Total	100.00	100.00

Source: François Etienne, "L'artisanat et L'Education, 1921–1970." Thèse en sociologie de l'éducation. Paris: Université de Paris, 1977) p. 662.

Background of artisans' apprentices (1955)	*Percent*
Sons of farmers	20
Sons of workers	28
Sons of white-collar workers	16
Sons of artisans and shopkeepers	36
Total	100

Source: Commissariat général du Troisième Plan, p. 39.

Socio-Professional Origins	
Sector	*% of the Artisanat*
Farmers	14.4
Merchants and artisans	33.1
(artisans alone)	(28.2)
Industriels	1.4
Large merchants	0.9
Liberal professions	1.2
"New" bourgeoisie	2.5
Popular classes	38.5
Total	95.0

Source: Bernard Zarca, "Situation et positions sociales de l'artisanat et du petit commerce," in the unpublished minutes of the Equipe de recherche sur les problèmes de la petite entreprise, 6e séance, 12 April 1975. I would like to thank Philippe Vigier for providing this information.

TABLE 6.4.   Population and replacement in artisanal trades, 1956

Profession	Number of establishments	Number of employees	Totals	Number of trainees	Replacement coefficient
Mechanic, turner, adjuster	9,736	10,094	19,830	5,226	26.3
Radio installer, repairman	9,369	6,559	15,928	5,559	34.7
Locksmiths, iron workers	7,819	8,226	16,035	3,562	22.2
Auto mechanic	26,909	30,713	57,622	9,328	16.1
Electrician	2,111	2,097	4,193	638	15.1
Baker, pastry-maker	58,449	68,771	117,220	16,305	13.9
Coppersmith, sheet metal worker	5,430	5,254	10,594	1,478	13.9
Carpenter, joiner	48,601	35,601	84,202	10,939	11.6
Butcher, pork butcher	69,988	56,668	126,646	11,866	9.3
Tailor, dress, linenmaker	86,731	63,094	149,825	13,758	9.1
Bicycle, motorcycle mechanic	15,418	6,217	21,365	1,961	9.0
Hairdresser	55,506	29,620	85,126	6,287	7.3
Luggagemaker	3,163	3,654	6,817	474	6.9
Plumber, zinc worker	29,058	26,377	55,435	3,471	6.2
Mason, plasterer	66,902	65,915	132,817	8,112	6.1
Jeweler	3,914	3,370	7,274	310	4.2
Farmer, blacksmith, wheelwright, agricultural machinery repair	57,366	22,868	80,234	3,329	4.1
Watchmaker, repair	9,807	3,285	13,092	450	3.4
Painter	49,154	37,045	86,199	2,636	3.0
Cabinetmaker, carpenter	51,764	40,738	92,502	2,036	2.2
Cobbler	43,503	13,707	57,210	755	1.3
Totals					
Number of establishments	710,608				
Number of employees	546,273				
Total	1,240,441				
Number of trainees	107,380				

Source: Commissariat général du Plan de modernisation et d'équipement, p. 35.

respect, it does not measure the amount of business available to the members of that trade. It has already been noted how overcrowding disrupted the hairdressing trades between the wars; *coiffure*'s troubles, it appears, persisted into the Fourth and Fifth Republics.[14] Likewise, according to the 1956 coefficient, the trades of bicycle and auto mechanic clearly were not on the brink of disappearing. In fact, the market was growing, but the number of mechanics was growing even faster. As a result, the Commission for the Fourth Plan reported that 7,000 establishments went out of business and 2,800 employees lost their jobs between 1955 and 1960.[15]

The experiences of masons and plasterers shows us the other side of the coin, for despite the low replacement coefficients, construction was a sector in *plein expansion*. Thriving in a lively economy and a country beginning to rebuild after half a century of disrepair, the professions of *bâtiments et travaux publics* increased by more than 15,000 establishments and 20,000 *salariés* between 1955 and 1960. The Société Savante of Alsace claimed that construction accounted for fully 30 percent of the enterprises and 50 percent of the employees of the Alsatian artisanat in 1965.[16] There was plenty of work for everybody, except, it seems, for locksmiths, yet they enjoyed the third highest replacement coefficient among artisanal trades.

No group of master artisans felt the effects of the "economic miracle" more sharply than those who worked in the countryside. We have seen that the artisanal movement had long bemoaned the "flight-from-the-land," but it was the demography of the 1950s that finally gave substance to these fears. The rural exodus, which had slowed down during the depression of the 1930s and again during the Occupation, picked up momentum after 1945 and doubled between 1944 and 1951.[17] The number of agricultural holdings in France decreased throughout the 1950s, while the percentage of the labor force engaged in agriculture fell from 32.5 (1929) to 29 (1949) to 27 (1954) to 18.5 percent (1963).[18]

Actually, the "rural revolution" confronted tradesmen in the countryside with two complementary but separable difficulties. The first was rural depopulation, which simply reduced the potential number of customers for artisans' skills, and whose consequences can be gauged by the absolute decline in the size of the *artisanat rural*. Alongside this demographic movement the revolution in French farming also brought a technical overhaul of agricultural production, and this had a more complex impact on those petty craftsmen who served the sector. Although different sources give different figures, the outline of this mechanization of agriculture is clear. Between 1946 and 1956 the number of tractors in France increased from approximately 44,000 to 400,000. It doubled again from 1956 to 1964, while the number of mechanical cultivators, reapers, and harvesters in use expanded almost geometrically.[19] In contrast to depopulation, about which little could be done, mechanization presented rural artisans with a different and not altogether intractable problem.

Those artisans most directly affected by changes in agricultural production were engaged in the trades called *auxiliaires de l'agriculture*: blacksmiths, farriers, wheelwrights, carpenters, sabotmakers, coopers, toolmakers, saddlers, and agricultural machinists. Compare the numbers provided by the 1929 survey by the Agricultural Ministry (Table 3.7) with those from the report of the Third Plan. In twenty-seven years, the population of artisans *auxiliaires de l'agriculture* had plummeted from close to 200,000 to between 70,000 and 80,000. Most of these were artisans working alone rather than substantial businesses; the Third Plan recorded only 35,000 employees for 70,000 enterprises. The Fourth Plan mapped the further decline of this sector: from 77,000 enterprises in 1956 to but 66,000 in 1960. The *artisanat rural* at this last date made up only 7 percent of the artisanat as a whole. Furthermore, two-thirds of rural artisans were now *isolés*. Their 25,000 employees accounted for only 3.5 percent of the artisanal total.[20]

The dilemma was not that there was no place for petty tradesmen in the new agricultural economy, but that so many of the artisans had the wrong skills and lacked the resources to acquire the right ones. *Sabotiers* and coopers were indeed fated to disappear from the economic scene. In Chanzeaux, Wylie noted that by 1961 the *sabotier*, Uzereau, and the harnessmaker, Bonnerot, had retired without successors; rubber boots and tractors had made their skills superfluous.[21] At the same time, the spread of farm machinery dictated the need for trained mechanics and repairmen, whom farmers often found to be unavailable. It was precisely this problem of training and equipping the rural artisanat that occupied both the artisanal movement and the public authorities in the 1950s.[22]

Gérard Pelsonnier, in his study of the rural artisanat in Burgundy revealed another curious aspect of the rural revolution. Pelsonnier noted the relative shortage of mechanics, but he also stressed the need for more artisans in the construction trades. The modernization of agriculture, it seems, was accompanied by a widespread renovation of rural habitations. While the strictly agricultural trades decayed, masons, carpenters, and electricians were set to work building new houses and rehabilitating old ones.[23]

To summarize, even while engaged in a dramatic bout of modernization, the French economy remained open to *petites entreprises*. The process was much as David Schoenbaum describes it for Germany: "Thrust back into the winds of industrial society the artisan was conceded a role in repair and installation and service industries, particularly in the country. But his chances were linked to his capacity for reducing prices and increasing efficiency."[24] By way of "fitting in," however, artisanal production tended to lose some of its historical uniqueness. It began to resemble capitalist business for the successful and wage labor for the unsuccessful.

In 1945, however, as the *Wehrmacht* abandoned France to the forces of the Resistance, the years of 5 percent annual growth and mass consumerism still lay in the future. At the Liberation France faced the consequences not only of four years of occupation but of seventeen years of economic stagnation, a worn-out population, and an aging productive structure. In May 1945, the index of industrial production (1938 = 100) bottomed out at 42. It did not reach prewar levels until the late 1940s and even then was below what it had been in 1929.[25] Moreover, as the gross national product recovered, consumer production lagged substantially behind industrial production, while the defeat of Mendès-France's austerity plans and the victory of René Pleven's easygoing monetary policies added rampant inflation to consumers' woes. By 1949 prices had multiplied seventeen times since 1938. The new statistical service, the INSEE, estimated that the cost of living increased threefold for a *famille modeste* between 1945 and 1949.[26]

Penury and pessimism, then, was the birthright of the Fourth Republic. This meant that for artisans, as for other producers and consumers, the first order of Liberation business was much like the last order of Vichy business: to find the means of subsistence. In addition, artisans found that, for the moment at least, this required working through the wartime economic administration. The Liberation government had repudiated the Statute of the Artisanat in the summer of 1944,[27] but rationing remained, and the OCRPI, the organization committees, and the Service centrale artisanale des matières (SCAMA) continued to control the flow of resources to artisans.

The presidents in the reassembled APCMF expressed their unhappiness in the clearest terms. They distinctly failed to recognize any improvement in the postwar economic situation and expressed their fervent wish to have done with the whole state structure of distribution. Indeed, the presidents described what amounted to a spontaneous strike against the organization committees in various parts of the country. For example, Guillaume reported that the chamber of trades and the syndicates in his native department of the Cher had advised their constituents to stop paying their dues to the organization committees. Similar incidents occurred in the Isère, the Drôme, and elsewhere.[28] Why, asked president Fouillet, should artisans contribute to the organization committees when they received nothing in return? "Let's call these things what they are," he said. "Robbery!" His colleague, Fernoux, called the entire system of distribution a joke. The whole job of the apparatus is to allocate materials, he said, and these just don't exist, except on the black market.[29]

In February 1945 René Lacoste, the socialist minister of production, reorganized the organization committees as *offices professionnels*, with the expressed aim of streamlining and democratizing the operation of *répartition*. By changing the names, Lacoste sought to wipe away old and unfortunate associations. Hardly anyone, it seems, was placated by the *offices professionnels*, and in 1946, as imports began to arrive and the material situation to ease, the Gouin government dismantled these offices and transferred responsibility for allocation to the Ministry of the National Economy.[30] As far as the APCMF was concerned, however, little had changed. President Ouvrière sounded much like Castéras, who had leveled the same accusation at Pétain when he proclaimed, "The organization committees and the offices professionnels have been dissolved, but their personnel, their methods, and their politics persist."[31] On this occasion the APCMF called for a return to the free market. In 1948, as the economy recovered its strength and the flow of material to artisans improved, the volume of such complaints naturally diminished. Instead, economic competition brought a new set of constraints for petty producers.[32]

Artisans understood implicitly that the country was reconstructing its political economy in these years and that, if they wanted to be a part of it, they would have to rebuild the artisanal movement. Yet the situation was quite different from what it had been in 1919. Two things explain why the architects of the New France were less open than ever to the demands of independent, petty producers. First, the nation—or at least those in a position to make policy—had adopted a new set of priorities. Gone was the strategy of the *tampon social*. In its place stood the determination to give France a more dynamic economic structure; that is, the old administrative formula of social peace through high production and consumption. Second, the master craftsmen also had to confront the unsavory reputation bequeathed to them by

Vichy's ideological predilection for artisans and peasants. We have seen that regime's practical commitment to *petits* lagged substantially behind its sentiments and that artisans did not collaborate to any extraordinary degree with the National Revolution. Nonetheless, to many in France artisans bore the mark of Pétainism, and this more or less discredited their projects.[33]

Vichy's half-hearted and unsuccessful social revolution had never really succeeded in co-opting the artisanal movement. At the same time, the wartime administration had directed the flow of resources to petty producers through the chambers of trades and the local syndicates. As a result, it had sent tens of thousands of independent masters flocking to their quasi-official representatives. The number of artisans *syndiqués* doubled from the beginning of the war to a figure of 400,000, about 45 percent of the artisanat. The contribution of rationing to organization can also be seen in the decline of artisans' syndicalism in the late 1940s, as economic controls were removed. Between 1946 and 1949 the number of artisans *syndiqués* decreased by 25 percent. Over the next ten years it remained steady at about 30 percent of master artisans.[34]

Nevertheless, Vichy's attempts at reform meant that the artisanal movement emerged from the National Revolution somewhat changed in character. Unlike the local syndicates, which had continued to function throughout the war, or the APCMF, which quickly reconstituted itself in 1945, the great prewar artisanal confederations were all shattered in 1942. The old leadership slipped into retirement or some other form of obscurity. Tailledet, Grandadam, Peter, Ley, Huguet, and Manoury—not one of them remained prominent in the movement after the war.[35] A new version of the CGAF, now under the presidency of Jean-Jacques Stefanelly, a radio-electrician from Paris, reoccupied its old offices on the rue des Vinaigriers, but it never recaptured anything like its old influence and was consistently left behind by more powerful professional and political currents in the 1950s. The CEAA and the CAF never did reorganize themselves. Many of their old militants, however, reappeared in 1947 in the Confédération nationale de l'artisanat (CNA). The CNA was probably the most representative of the postwar confederations. It occupied that vast territory on the center-right of the artisanal movement and was secure in its moderation until its right flank came under attack from the Poujadists.[36] Parenthetically, artisans seem to have had little contact with the new, self-styled representative of the middle classes, Léon Gingembre's Confédération générale des petites et moyennes entreprises (CGPME), which aimed at a slightly higher class on the social ladder.[37]

There were several attempts, at both the national and departmental levels, to profit from the fluid postwar conditions in order to unify the artisanal movement and to repair the divisions that many felt had crippled the movement between the wars. In May 1946 President Jeanselme reported to the APCMF on his efforts in this direction. The rank and file, he told his colleagues, were alienated by the battles between the various confederations, while these, consumed by their petty quarrels, paid little attention to what the mass of artisans actually thought. He concluded sadly that artisanal unity was not likely to occur and that the movement would fall to those who represent "tendances."[38] In this Jeanselme proved to be a fine prophet.

Before the war the Parti communiste français (PCF) had displayed little interest in recruiting artisans to the proletarian revolution. "As Marx has clearly demonstrated," said Maurice Thorez, "the middle classes, so far as they represent economic forms inherited from the past, are very likely to adopt [politically] reactionary positions."[39] It is true that Tailledet often spoke of "classes," and that his opponents liked to accuse him of harboring Marxist sympathies. And it would not be surprising if some of those in the CGAF had exhibited a more than passing interest in the revolutionary left. Yet, for all the interwar period, there seemed to be only one self-confessed Marxist within the artisanal ranks: a Monsieur Cartier, president of a bicycle and auto-mechanics' syndicate in Paris. Cartier sat on the CGAF's National Committee and was apparently well-respected by his colleagues. Politely listened to on the National Committee, Cartier never convinced the others that artisans were genuine proletarians and ought, therefore, to throw in their lot with the other Marxist elements.[40]

The Resistance, however, opened the PCF to the possibility of broader social alliances, to a popular front of the *petits* against the *gros*, and the Liberation witnessed an attempt by the communists to organize their own artisanal confederation, the Confédération générale unifiée de l'artisanat (CGUA).[41] To this end, the PCF held a meeting in the Salle Wagram in March 1945. "How to rescue petty commerce and the artisanat?" was the theme, and the party rolled out its heavy artillery for the assault. Thorez himself did not appear. André Marty, deputy and party official presided instead; however, Waldeck-Rochet was there as were Gaston Auguet, Albert Rigal, and Jacques Duclos, all of whom sounded a note more reminiscent of Tailledet than of Lenin. Rigal began with a defense of the sullied reputation of the petty bourgeoisie. The Vichy regime, he said, had belonged to the "Two Hundred Families," and the trusts. Despite the recent campaign of "odious calumnies" against them, shopkeepers and artisans had been victims in their turn. The other speakers expanded this attack on the capitalists, "always the masters . . . always omnipotent." Duclos excoriated those, like Pierre Mendès-France, who maintained that France suffered from a surfeit of tiny shops and *ateliers*. Rather, he and his colleagues submitted a program designed to demonstrate that the Communist Party was "the best defender of individual property." They promised, in effect, to keep taxes low and retail prices high.[42] It does not appear, however, that the party was making much progress. Their furthest advance into the artisanat came in the chambers of trades elections of 1946, when the CGUA managed to capture but two of the approximately ninety chambers: the Seine and the Lot-et-Garonne.

The communists' influence in the Seine Chamber of Trades provoked considerable dispute among the masters. The elections of 1946 were bound to have a sharp political edge, if only because the Seine Chamber of Trades had been the object of a Vichy coup during the war and therefore had to be purged in a way that the provincial chambers, less brutally coordinated by the regime, did not. In January 1946, the prefect had suspended from their functions all those elected to the chamber before September 1939 or appointed since. He replaced them with a group of artisans chosen from the Comité de libération de l'artisanat.[43] Paris was also a place where artisans' political consciousness was more pronounced and more partisan. The 1946 elections produced two notable results. The first was the complete absence of the CGAF, which had practically monopolized the chamber until 1942. The second was the success of CGUA candidates who, along with those *compagnons* belonging to the CGT, now held a majority. They combined to elect a suitably communist executive bureau, with the CGUA's Emile Delanoë as president.[44]

Those masters now in the minority were bitterly opposed to the communists' control and especially to the recent assertiveness of the journeymen, whose high profile in the Seine Chamber of Trades marked another remarkable about-face. Before the war the CGT had always refused to cooperate with the chambers of trades; those *compagnons* who did participate had represented only a handful of votes and exercised no discernible influence. The PCF's renewed interest in the petty bourgeoisie, however, apparently caused the CGT to change its position. After the 1946 elections the journeymen held the balance of power in the Seine Chamber of Trades. The *compagnons* served on the executive bureau for the first time and even sat on the chamber's finance committee, where the prospect of their spending the masters' funds clearly horrified their opponents.

The communists' hold on the Seine Chamber of Trades proved to be brief. The government, noting irregularities in the 1946 balloting, annulled the elections and submitted the matter to the Conseil d'Etat. Delanoë's administrative practices also came under attack. Kergoat, a former member of Vichy's consultative committee on the artisanat and now the leader of the CNA group in the Seine Chamber of Trades, accused Delanoë of the misuse of funds, irregular bookkeeping, and running the chamber as a "veritable charity" for his friends and their pet projects. The public authorities apparently found evidence of some malfeasance, for in May 1950 they closed down the chamber's various social services, removed the executive bureau, reduced the influence of the *compagnons*, and scheduled new elections.[45] The new vote put the CGUA-CGT coalition in the minority. Kergoat was elected president. The two groups continued to feud for the next several years, with the communists aiming to regain control of the chamber and the CNA masters, who were soon to pitch their tent in Poujade's camp, to expel the *compagnons* from the chamber altogether.

Politics also infected the operations of the APCMF. The Assembly of Presidents, terminated in 1943, had reconvened in April 1945, even before the end of the war. Some of the most vocal critics of the National Revolution had been removed by Pétain's government and did not make it to Paris in November 1945 for the Assembly's meeting.[46] Others, like Seguinaud, of Bordeaux, and Louis Tison, installed as president of the Seine Chamber of Trades in the 1943 coup, were too compromised by collaboration and had been purged at the Liberation. Still others who had been uncomfortably close to Pétainism—Bourrières (Cahors), Réal (Grenoble), Jeannin (Cher)—left no evidence either of having been purged or of returning to the APCMF. They may have been present in 1945 and merely kept quiet (hence they do not appear in the minutes). In any event, they played no part in the postwar APCMF. On the other hand, Léon Bossavy, who had served as acting president of the APCMF in 1941 and had sat on Vichy's *comité consultatif*, again took the chair, from which he argued that the past was best forgotten.

At the next several meetings tempers remained short and remarks angry. Some presidents suggested banning from the chambers any who had "collaborated" with Pétainism. Others simply refused to pay their dues to the APCMF until it was "cleaned up." President Merriaux (Pas-de-Calais) felt compelled to warn Bossavy against his habit of telling fond stories about Pétain, which only compounded the artisans' image problems.[47]

In view of this inquisitorial atmosphere and the general sense of renewal, it is remarkable how easily the APCMF slipped back into its old habits. It is hard to avoid a distinct sense of déjà vu from the telegram that the presidents sent to DeGaulle in November 1945:

> The Presidents of the Chambers of Trades assure [General DeGaulle] of their full cooperation in the great work that the Fourth Republic has undertaken. . . . They desire only that the Artisanat should receive its appropriate place in the country's economy and ask only for the benevolent support of the public authorities in the pursuit of their responsibilities.[48]

Indeed, to read through the minutes of the APCMF's sessions in the late 1940s is to imagine that the 1930s had never come to an end. Debates droned on to little effect. Each meeting saw the same reports on the same issues covering the same ground that had proved to be so barren in former days. Bossavy demanded the application of the 1937 Walter-Paulin law. Voisin complained of foreigners practicing the artisanal trades in the Haute-Savoie; Mériaux that the labor inspectors in the Pas-de-Calais were lax in the suppression of *travail noir*; Richard that the artisanat du bâtiment was being systematically excluded from public works; and Gaillard that small producers had no access to affordable credit. The presidents defended their programs by allusion to the tattered but familiar maxim that the artisanat "fills an important role in quality production" and as a useful social buffer.[49]

Problems over *travail noir* or credit were chronic rather than immediate. They became a kind of "white noise" in the APCMF, while more pressing concerns dominated the presidents' attention. The worries about raw materials that had been prominent immediately following the Liberation, faded as materials came back on the market in the late 1940s. Instead, the APCMF spent most of its time considering the implications of the welfare state for artisans. Time and again, the presidents returned to questions of social security and tax reform.

Prewar programs of social insurance had mostly benefited employees, while leaving employers and the self-employed to their own devices. Vichy had intended to expand social security to the lower middle classes, but it lacked time and resources, and its efforts predictably came up short. After the war, the Fourth Republic again took up the reform of the social security system, but it began with a new principle: to bring everyone under the same umbrella, rather than to separate contributors and beneficiaries by social class. Sentiment in the APCMF ran strongly against this proposal. Laulhère referred to it as *escroquerie* ("robbery"). The presidents suspected that the government wanted to use the funds of the middle classes to subsidize the needs of others—the working classes, in particular. They were amenable to social welfare but wanted artisans to enjoy their own system run by and for artisans through the chambers of trades.

The APCMF was not unanimous on the subject. This became clear when it discussed the report of its committee on social security in June 1947. Delanoë, unveiling his communist sympathies, spoke in defense of a system "where rich and poor are placed together, where they contribute according to their means and where each one is certain of a future under the same conditions." Of course, a majority of the committee was hostile to such collectivist schemes. It endorsed the principle of the *caisse artisanale* and rejected a system that would, as Fouillet (St-Etienne) put it, "float on the back of the middle classes." This image earned Fouillet the retort of "cagoulard" and "fascist" from Delanoë. Hunault shot back that Delanoë's friends in the Communist party and the CGT "have always been hostile to [the Assembly's] decisions and to [artisans'] programs." Eighty-nine of the presidents voted with Fouillet and Hunault. Only the chambers from the Alpes-Maritimes and the Lot-et-Garonne joined Delanoë in opposition.[50]

In May 1956, the APCMF took up the perennial question of fiscal reform. Voisin, from the Haute-Savoie, scolded those of his colleagues (almost all) who implied that artisans should not have to keep careful accounts, and he disagreed with the general feeling in the APCMF that tax audits (*contrôles*) should be eliminated. Without *contrôle*, Voisin continued, there is fraud, to the detriment of the state and of those artisans who do pay their taxes. Voisin's intervention earned him neither popularity nor respect among the other presidents. Charre (Gard) called him "Père Noël," and wondered cynically if the *contrôleurs* did not themselves cheat. Circaud, of the Rhône, went further by maintaining that doing business "off the books" was a necessity, even an obligation, for artisans burdened with "extremely heavy" taxes. Charre's and Circaud's remarks provoked loud applause from the assembly.[51] "It is said," concluded Vergne (Hérault), "that the artisanat has to change with the times, and I favor this. But how is this to happen if its profits are taxed away?"

On the whole, the Fourth Republic made artisans' fiscal situation more complex without making it much more onerous.[52] The level of taxes was generally increased, though the whole thrust of tax reform in the 1950s was to indirect taxation, which encumbered the consumer rather than the producer. In 1954 the new value-added tax (TVA) was substituted for the old turnover tax on businesses. But the TVA was meant to be collected for the state and passed on to consumers; it was more an accounting problem than a real fiscal burden. The smallest enterprises, moreover, were exempt. The legislature also maintained the category of *petit artisan fiscal*, which in 1954 included 42 percent of all artisanal enterprises. Fiscal reform had a greater impact on medium-sized artisanal businesses, who generally paid their taxes according to the new *régime forfaitaire.* In this the individual entrepreneur negotiated a figure with local tax authorities based on his anticipated business activity. It usually produced a "considerable undervaluation" of income.

French tax law nonetheless left independent businessmen in a relatively unfavorable tax situation. Compared with wage earners, *indépendants* were subject to a steeper and more complex schedule of payments. In 1956, according to Jean-Pierre Rioux, two in three shopkeepers needed the assistance of a tax accountant. New policies in the early 1950s, moreover, brought more frequent government audits and an increased use of *contrôleurs* from outside the locality of the audit.[53] While there is no compelling proof then that fiscal restructuring had any of the predicted dire effects on handicraft production, it did produce a political backlash.

Taxes proved to be "the best of recruiters" for the new Union de défense des commerçants et artisans (UDCA). Maurice Lauré made the connection in his description of the situation of the "average" artisan in the department of the Lot:

> His taxable profits only went up by 16,000 francs between 1951 and 1953, going from 195,000 to 211,000 francs, whereas the taxes he paid in those same years rose from 4,280 francs to 10,400: an increase of 6,120 francs. How is this man, whose business is slowing down, not to believe that he is the victim of a greater tax burden, when he sees that he now has to pay two and a half times more on a relatively stable income? It is hardly astonishing, then, that a protest movement of taxpayers has appeared in the Lot at Saint-Céré.[54]

In a similar fashion, Maurice Nicolas, one of Pierre Poujade's confederates, explained his own commitment to the UDCA by telling of the tragedies that tax reform had visited on the nation's *petits*. Nicolas submitted as evidence the case of Oscar Velot, of the Marne, whom the tax authorities had caused to hang himself in his barn and of José Garay, of Handaye (Basses-Pyrénées), who on October 12, 1953 was slapped with "a tax increase of 2,400,000 francs plus a fine of a further four million francs. Immediately following the audit, M. Garay contracted a case of neurasthenia . . . and asked for a delay in payment, which the administration refused. On the eve of the anniversary of this audit . . . [M. Garay] threw himself under a train *heading for Paris.*"[55] [emphasis added] "Work! Save!" Poujade recalled his thoughts:

> But that's all we do. And the more we [work and save] the less we have to show for it. Now I no longer have the right to my 30 percent deduction. No more social security. Not even any family allowance. Well, am I no longer

the same person? Because I wish to be independent by working like a madman
must I suffer *déclassement*?[56]

The Poujade Movement began as a revolt against the tax laws and the
contrôleurs, yet as it expanded the movement revealed itself as something
more, as the protest of those being left behind by the "economic miracle."
A "modern jacquerie," the magazine *L'Express* called it. "[Poujadism]
emerges from the natural evolution of economic progress that, especially since
the end of the war and the halting of inflation, has progressively reduced the
margin of subsistence for shopkeepers and rural artisans, whose activities are
no longer profitable."[57]

It all began in the town of Saint-Céré (department of the Lot) in late July
1953, when the bookstore owner, Pierre Poujade, led a group of local citizens
who had decided to obstruct tax audits planned for the town. The antitax
movement quickly spread among the *plus petits* of the villages and small towns
of the Massif central, and from there to the country as a whole.[58] Poujade
himself was hardly a political neophyte. Son of a Maurassian father, young
Pierre had joined the Doriotists at the beginning of the Spanish Civil War.
At first an ardent Pétainist, Poujade's anti-German sentiments soon led him
into the Resistance, where he fought in North Africa for the Free French.[59]

Poujade's earlier political affiliations, his Mussolini-like public style, and
his antiparliamentary positions often earned his movement the epithet "fascist." Alexander Werth called him "the big-mouthed successor of Doriot."[60]
And Roland Barthes, in a brief essay on Poujade's language, proposed that
"Pierrot's" caddish anti-intellectualism and contempt for "culture" were the
very essence of the fascist mentality.[61] Many of Poujade's associates did indeed
have very dubious political backgrounds. Yet as the UDCA moved across
the country in 1953 and 1954 it picked up support from the left as well as the
right.

Rather than being specifically fascist, the Poujade Movement situated itself
in the long history of the angry, politicized petty bourgeoisie in France. André
Desqueyrat wrote that Poujade reminded him of Maurice Colrat, who had
helped to found the Association de défense des classes moyennes in 1907,
and that the UDCA brought to mind the Bloc du petit commerce more than
the Parti populaire français.[62] The Poujadists looked not to an authoritarian
dictatorship but to "la République de la Boutique." "La République rétro,"
Rioux called it.[63]

Poujade identified what he saw as an attack by international finance—by
"anonymous and vagabond capital"—against the "real France." This sordid
conspiracy was abetted by "the System": that is, by politicians, intellectuals,
and technocrats. Poujade stood up for "les hommes libres." He emphasized
"the utility of small industry and small commerce as a factor of prosperity
and social equilibrium."[64] He demanded a "future where technical progress
is at the service of men, and not men its slaves."[65] "The common people, the
genuine people; a world of the small and the humble. A whole people for
whom common sense is the most important value" was the Poujadists' social

ideal. If this echoes the rhetoric of the fascist leagues, remarks Dominique Borne, it sounds even more like the traditional litany of those whom Poujade castigated as "crooks and thieves"; that is, the Radicals.[66]

We might add that this philosophy could as easily have come from the journals, congresses, and manifestoes of the artisanal movement. Indeed, Poujade wrote of the artisanat that, "[its] beauty and poetry . . . raises in the heart of every Frenchman a crowd of memories. . . . The perfection of labor, the satisfaction of creative work [is now being] crushed by the infernal rhythm of over-production, by machines and automation."[67] Jean Marbréry could not have said it better.

This philosophical convergence, along with its "fiscal obsession" made the artisanal movement perfect grist for the Poujadist mill. In the beginning, the UDCA cut across the traditional political divisions within the movement. For example, Poujade's first colleague in the movement, Frégeac, a fellow municipal councilor in Saint-Céré, was a farrier, a communist, and an ex-partisan from the Francs-Tireurs of the Resistance.[68] Also within his native Lot, Poujade found a confederate in Leyge, who was a departmental vice-president of the UDCA, president of the Fédération des syndicaux artisanals du Lot and of the chamber of trades, and a communist.[69] The CGUA showed a lively interest in Poujade, at least in the beginning. Because he had attracted so many formerly unorganized *petits*, the communist CGUA thought that Poujade could be "especially favorable to the reinforcement of our syndicates."[70] When Poujade made his triumphal visit to the capital in January 1955, his host and choreographer was Vignaud, a grocer, who was also president of the Syndicat d'épicerie française and a member of two communist front groups, the Confédération générale du commerce et de l'industrie (which had ceased to operate in 1951) and the CGUA. Christian Guy reported that when "Pierrot" arrived in Bordeaux, the CGUA was the only organization to welcome him.[71]

As Poujade's politics became more explicitly rightwing, however, his movement appealed more to the conservative elements of the artisanal movement, though largely for reasons internal to the movement itself. In the Paris Chamber of Trades, for example, it was the adherents of the conservative CNA who went over to the UDCA. The forces of the CNA had managed to break the CGUA's control of the chamber in the early 1950s, following the government's censure of the former leadership. They then proceeded to launch a full-scale campaign to oust the workers from the chamber. First, Duhamel, the leader of the CNA masters, began to challenge the credentials of the so-called *compagnons*. Many of these, Duhamel claimed, were either working outside the artisanat (like Landres, who worked for the large firm, Hermès) or were union functionaries and not workers at all (such as Basset, who worked for the Syndicat des ouvriers-boulangers). Ultimately, the administration did strike several of the leaders of the *compagnons* from the rolls of the Seine Chamber of Trades.[72]

In fact, the government went further. A decree of May 20, 1955 introduced a number of important changes in the structure and operations of the chambers of trades, the first since the Courtier law of 1925. Some of the reforms were of minor significance and always enforced laxly; for instance, the introduction of the *brevet de maîtrise*, which would give its bearer the right to train apprentices. Much more fundamentally, the decree expanded the number of categories for the masters from four to six and halved the representation of the journeymen in the chambers. Under the Courtier structure, masters had enjoyed two places in a chamber for every one occupied by a *compagnon*; the new decree raised that ratio to four to one. The government's rationale for this change was that the chambers were having difficulties finding enough journeymen to stand for election and to serve in the chambers. Perhaps this was true in the provinces, but it obviously was not in Paris. The new rules, in any case, were not likely to convince journeymen that the masters either needed or wanted their cooperation.[73]

The May decree also delayed the elections to the chambers of trades due in 1955 until these changes could be sorted out and new electoral lists prepared. Elections for the almost 1,800 places in the reorganized chambers were held in December 1956, and they provide the best measure of the penetration of Poujadism into the artisanat. The first consequence of Poujadist activity, according to Bruno Magliulo, was a heightened level of professional and political consciousness among artisans. As evidence of this, Magliulo cited the masters' greater participation in the elections for the chambers, which increased from under 30 percent in 1949 and 1952 to almost 40 percent in 1956. It is impossible to be certain of the exact figures. Jules Jeudon, the president of the APCMF contended that only 25.6 percent of eligible masters (215,742 of 844,512) had cast ballots in 1956.[74]

What is clear, despite Jeudon's attempts to play down its significance, is that the chambers of trades elections represented an impressive endorsement of the Poujadist message. The newspaper, *Le Monde*, had estimated participation in the chamber elections of 1952 at 14 percent of masters and only 3.5 percent of *compagnons*. In 1956 it reported that while the number of *inscrits* did not increase, the Poujadists attracted the votes of those who had habitually abstained from the chamber elections.[75] The UDCA managed to field a slate of candidates in fifty-seven departments. Magliulo writes that the UDCA won 45.1 percent of the vote. (Jeudon put the figure at 47 percent, although he took care to point out that this represented only 12 percent of master artisans in France.) In fact, this translated into a majority of the available seats: 772 of 1,380 for the masters and 104 of almost 400 for the *compagnons*. In the system in which election was by a plurality, the unified UDCA list could win 55 percent of the seats with 45 percent of the vote. Its success was particularly striking in Paris (Table 6.5), where the Poujade lists received a majority in the categories of food and personal services (the most powerful group in the CNA was the Fédération des coiffeurs), and a plurality everywhere.

Because only half the places in each chamber of trades were at stake in the 1956 election, and because the Poujadist vote was distributed so unevenly from department to department, the UDCA did not gain control of a majority

TABLE 6.5. Voting for the Chamber of Trades of the Seine 18 December 1956

Category	Regist.	Voting	UDCA	CGUA	Others
Food	795	290	270 (?)	–	–
Construction	2,000	840	356	212	258
Wood	1,408	686	311	131	135 (CGAF)
Metal, mechanic, electricity	2,900	1,300	661	291	351
Textiles	3,000	1,100	368	–	794
Leather, misc.	–	1,353	588	–	765
Hygiene, personal serv.	2,200	1,000	727	161	92

Source: CCIP II 5.413, "Réorganisation de la Chambre de Métiers de la Seine, 1950," report from the Prefecture of the Seine.*

*These figures obviously do not match. I merely present them according to the prefect's report.

of chambers or dominance in the APCMF. Of the forty-seven new presidents who came to the assembly meeting of February 1957, twenty were avowed members of the UDCA, but they quickly discovered that many of the old presidents sympathized with their cause. The UDCA opposition within the APCMF could count on thirty-three or thirty-four of ninety-four votes.[76]

Poujadism represented a new constellation within the artisanal movement, one that at first—recall its early success among the militants of the CGUA—correlated poorly with the traditional left and right. Apparently, that had changed by 1956, not just in the Paris Chamber of Trades, where Duhamel, the nemesis of the communists, headed the successful Poujadist group, but across the country. The votes for the UDCA seem to have come mostly at the expense of the lists of the CNA, which formerly stood for the conservative majority of artisans, and they expressed the frustration of the artisanat with its leaders. The Poujadists' passion and their promise of action eclipsed the CNA's commitment to "politics as usual." Tone and tactics, not principles, were the difference between the old artisanal politics and the new. Dominique Borne went to the heart of the matter when she wrote that Poujadism was not an ideology but a revolt.[77]

Jean Cluzel, in an analysis of the Poujade Movement, remarked that it met its greatest success in areas of rural depopulation.[78] This agrees with the conventional picture of Poujadism as a violent rejection of modernization by those who felt themselves to be its chief victims. A comparison of three maps, however, leads us to question Cluzel's assertion. Figure 6.3 identifies those departments with chambers of trades that sent UDCA presidents to the APCMF in 1957. It corresponds very closely to the map of the vote, by department, for the UDCA in the parliamentary election of 1956,[79] and shows Poujadism to be very much a regional phenomenon of the South, the Massif Central, and the West. The inconsistent fit between support for Poujade among artisans and the depopulation of the artisanat appears when we compare Figure 6.3 to Figure 6.2, which charted the relative loss of artisanal population from 1948 to 1957 by department. Poujadist chambers of trades in 1956 can be found both in departments where the decline of the artisanat was dramatic, especially in the West, and in departments where that decline

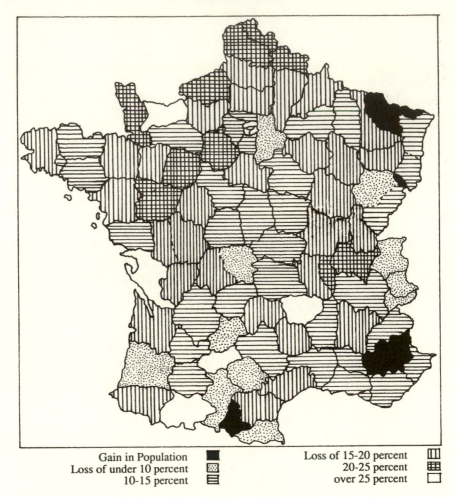

Gain in Population	■	Loss of 15-20 percent	⊞
Loss of under 10 percent	⊡	20-25 percent	⊞
10-15 percent	☰	over 25 percent	☐

National Average = 16.4 percent

FIGURE 6.2. Changes in the Population of the Artisanat by Department, 1948–1957.

Source: "Nombre des artisans payant la taxe pour frais de chambre de métiers," APCMF, Circulaires, 59/10/SG/8, 1959.

was well below the national average. The Vaucluse, where the UDCA polled a national high of 22.4 percent in the parliamentary elections, witnessed a fairly light assault on the artisanat in the 1950s. In the Lot, the decline in the artisanat was well under half the national average. The Poujadists won a majority in the Vaucluse Chamber of Trades but not in the Lot chamber. Conversely, the UDCA gained control of the Chamber of Trades in the Haute-Loire, where the artisanat lost almost one third of its population between 1948 and 1957. Two observations can be made. First, support for the Poujade Movement did not simply express the antimodern reflex of *petits indépendants*; it was also a function of regional political culture. Second, those artisans

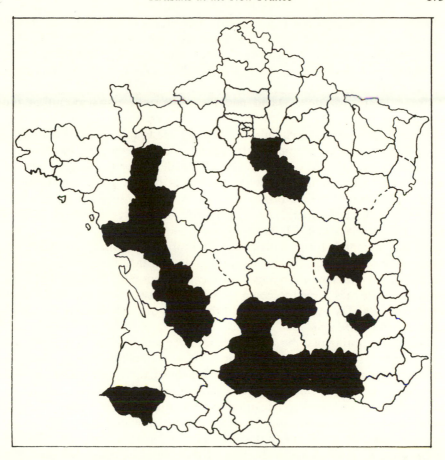

FIGURE 6.3. Poujadist Chambers of Trades, 1956. Darkened areas represent depart-ments with a UDCA majority in the chamber of trades.

Source: APCMF, Assemblée générale extraordinaire, 18 février 1957, Paris.

drawn to the Poujadist revolt against things modern were often the least affected by them. The fear of social decline proved to be as radicalizing as the fact of change itself.[80]

The UDCA presidents elected by the chambers of trades in 1956 saw themselves as the vanguard of the artisanal movement and their electoral success as a mandate to replace the tired functionaries of the syndicates and the APCMF. They arrived at the assembly's special session in Paris in Feb-ruary 1957 ready to seize the future. "Our country needs a revolution. Rev-olutions are always made by the middle classes, and artisans should place themselves at the head of these combatants," proclaimed the Poujadist pres-ident, David (Aveyron).[81] This was, in effect, David's campaign speech, for the UDCA men had decided to challenge Jeudon for the presidency of the APCMF and David was their candidate. They hoped, in view of their minority status, to force the APCMF to give them a seat on the executive board. These expectations were dashed in the closest vote ever within the APCMF. Jeudon was re-elected president by a vote of 59–33, and the Poujadists then failed to capture any of the places on the APCMF's *bureau* or on its important commissions.

Angry and frustrated, David and his supporters marched out of the APCMF. A few weeks later they set up a new organization, the Union des délégués et présidents des chambres de métiers de France. Jeudon contacted Poujade himself in an attempt to arrange a truce between the two groups of presidents. Both the APCMF and the Union des délégués designated representatives to a *commission des sages* to work out an agreement between them. While they negotiated, however, the APCMF suspended its subsidies to the secessionist chambers, which Denoue (Deux-Sèvres) condemned as "a classic case of blackmail." Jeudon, for the majority, continued to reject the Poujadists' demands for proportional representation within the APCMF executive and committees.[82] The two sides finally arranged a compromise, ratified by the *commission des sages*, in the late summer and early fall. The Union des délégués agreed to come back to the Assembly and to make good their past dues. The APCMF accepted that three of the Poujadist presidents could sit on the *bureau*.[83]

It is worth noting that the Poujadists retained an influence in the APCMF well after they had ceased to be relevant to national politics. The government had once again altered the election rules for the chambers of trades in 1959, when a decree of November 19, 1959 substituted *collèges syndicaux* for the old trade categories and restructured the balloting around these. The new system provided the larger trade syndicates with an even greater role in the elections and conversely made it more difficult for a minority list, like that of the UDCA, to win seats.[84] The Poujadists once again presented their own list in the elections for the chambers of trades in 1960 and lost approximately 15 percent of the vote they had garnered in 1956. They nevertheless managed to hold on to several chambers of trades and even to win control in the Allier and in the Ardèche. The UDCA maintained as well its representation on the APCMF's executive *bureau*.[85]

The residual support for the Poujade Movement among artisans came as a particular disappointment to Jeudon, who had made it his mission as president of the APCMF to bring the artisanal movement into line with the New France, and especially to escape from the overarching concern with taxes. "Fiscal protectionism," Jeudon told his colleagues, "has for too long been the artisanat's exclusive concern. This has helped to sterilize and to diminish the productive capacity of our workshops, to destroy the taste for risk and the spirit of enterprise among master artisans."[86] For Jeudon, and those who thought as he did, Poujadism represented the survival of a "retrograde" mentality that both caused artisans public relations problems and kept them from reaching their economic potential. Throughout his long tenure, Jeudon sought to impose a degree of order on the APCMF's proceedings and bring to heel its most arcane discussions. He achieved this to an admirable degree, but the presence of the Poujadists made his task more difficult.

The UDCA represented an enduring atavistic reflex within the artisanat that seemed inevitably to reappear from time to time. In the late 1960s and early 1970s, for example, a new revolt of *petits* artisans and shopkeepers occurred under the leadership of Gérard Nicoud and his organization, Comité d'information et de défense-Union nationale des travailleurs indépendantes (CID-UNATI).[87] It cannot be denied, however, that the social and economic revolution of the 1950s involved the artisanat as well and left such revolts increasingly out of step with the polity as a whole and the artisanal movement in particular.

In fact, by the end of the decade, the artisanal movement was ceasing to be a "movement" at all. This meant, first of all, that the nature of artisans' syndical life was evolving and becoming, in the words of Henri Mourier, more realist than doctrinaire.[88] Jacques Francillon estimates that by 1959 some 275,000 masters (more that 30 percent of the total) belonged to a trade syndicate.[89] At the same time, support for the CGAF, the CGUA, and the CNA waned throughout the decade of the "economic miracle." These throwbacks to the early days of the artisanal movement continued to exist but were increasingly marginal to the syndical and political life of the artisanat. Most tradesmen now gravitated toward the new professional confederations: the Confédération nationale de l'artisanat et des métiers (CNAM), the Confédération nationale des artisans ruraux (CNAR), the Confédération de l'artisanat et des petites entreprises du bâtiment (CAPEB), and the Confédération générale de l'alimentation du détail (CGAD). These formations were more administrative than political.[90] They no longer occupied themselves with "big" political questions, and even as the Fourth Republic crumbled, they avoided replaying the great debates over political reform that had exercised the CGAF and the CEAA in the 1930s or the CGUA and the CNA in the early 1950s. In fact, the crisis of the republic left no imprint at all on the artisanal movement.

As artisans adjusted to diminished state paternalism and to their more thorough integration into the market, they simply became part of the general "rationalization" of political economy pursued by the Fourth Republic and institutionalized in two new bureaucracies: the Commissariat général du plan (CGP) and the Conseil économique. "Radical pragmatism" fed by a "productivist myth" is how Stephen Cohen described the ethos of the CGP, which brought together those of a technocratic bent who shared the goal of the "general interest" and the belief in a dominant role for the *hauts fonctionnaires*.[91] The apparatus of planification took shape after the Liberation under the leadership of Jean Monnet. Between the wars planning had been very much an *idée de gauche*, but under Monnet's leadership the CGP concerned itself with economic growth rather than justice. It assumed that prosperity was the most potent medicine for social ills.[92]

Beneath the thin *cadre* of the CGP itself, much of the work of planning

occurred within the so-called modernization commissions. These were composed overwhelmingly of the representatives of big business, ranking civil
servants, and "experts." Their social profile, then, did not depart very much
from that of Vichy's organization committees, although Kuisel notes that there
was little overlap in personnel. The trade unions, unorganized small business,
consumer groups, and agricultural interests were all but excluded from the
planning apparatus. Not surprisingly, of the great confederations, the CNPF
applauded the Plan and the CGT warily opposed it. The CGPME first approved the Plan, then denounced it as the work of "technocrats," and finally
wavered between requests for a share of the spoils and condemnations of any
form of *dirigisme*.[93] Parliament, which was supposed to operate in the "third
stage" of planning, remained largely irrelevant to the process. The First and
Third Plans never came before it for consideration. The Second Plan was
presented to the National Assembly only two years after it had been in
operation. This was a measure of how little faith the CGP had in the political
structure, but it was logical, Cohen writes, for a system where "a government's
longevity depended greatly on its ability to avoid confronting the National
Assembly with issues of consequence."[94] This skepticism worked both ways,
however. Especially under the Second and Third Plans, the government utterly failed to coordinate its own fiscal and economic policies with the priorities
of the Plans.

Planning held little appeal for the artisanal movement for two reasons.
First, a policy of modernization *à outrance* could offer only insecurity to the
large number of petty producers whose livelihoods depended on a Malthusian
economy. Second, and more directly, the CGP provided virtually no artisanal
input to the elaboration of the plans. Cohen gives this breakdown of the social
backgrounds of the members of the modernization commissions for the Third
Plan: Businessmen, 206; Civil servants, 136; Bankers, 13; Trade unionists,
57; Technical experts, 134; Miscellaneous, 66.[95] The artisanat finally received
some recognition with the formation of the Commission de l'artisanat for the
Third Plan (1957). For the preparation of the Fourth Plan (1961) handicrafts
were granted their own modernization subcommission, which contained a
number of representatives of artisanal organizations. By no means, however,
did artisans' role in the planning administration correspond to their presence
in the French economy.

The Economic Council was created by the government after the war in
order to satisfy those (the trade unions and the reformist Catholics, in particular) who wanted some kind of corporate parliament to advise on social
and economic policy. The new council was much like the old CNE, except
that the arbitration functions that had made the latter such an integral part
of the Popular Front were not continued in the former. Artisans were granted
ten seats on the council, divided up among the leading artisanal confederations
and the APCMF. The specific distribution of seats provoked an occasional
dispute, but on the whole artisans expressed little interest in the council.
Seldom consulted by the government or the CGP, the Economic Council
never cut a significant figure in Fourth Republic politics.[96]

The National Assembly continued to be the state institution most responsive to petty producers. It retained, for example, a sizable group for the defense of the artisanat into the Fifth Republic.[97] Even so, the parliaments of the Fourth Republic found the argument of the *tampon social* less compelling than formerly. The parliamentary defense group managed to preserve the *petit artisan fiscal*, but the 1950s saw no new round of legislation to protect small, independent craftsmen. The National Assembly admitted to an interest in helping these people to improve their training and to adjust to a changing market; it showed no enthusiasm, however, for restraining that market.

We can read the sentiments of the legislature in the various proposals for an updated Statute of the Artisanat that came and went in the 1950s, but that finally emerged as the comprehensive reform of 1962. The artisanal movement began asking for a new statute in 1944, with the abrogation of the Vichy system, and in fact five different bills were introduced between 1946 and 1956. None of them became law. In October 1956, the government issued a decree-law that sought to complement the decree of May 1955 on the reform of the chambers of trades. The 1956 decree tightened up the rules on professional qualifications and mandatory apprenticeship in some trades. The new rules hardly amounted to a comprehensive reform, however, and, as usual, they were applied indifferently.[98]

This was a grand *pas de deux*, the same one the artisanal movement had danced with the state since the beginning. The movement would make a demand. The public authorities would give the appearance of a response. And very little would change. But it was not the same at all. The Fourth Republic was nominally less solicitous of *petits indépendants* than the Third Republic had been. The real difference, however, lay less in the political system than in the world around it; that is, in the accelerated development of the French economy. The absence of positive state action in favor of artisans now meant, not Malthusian drift, but modernization.

The APCMF came to realize at the end of the 1950s that it faced a stark choice—which finally became no choice at all. It could either opt for institutional efficacy, which meant to place itself directly under government tutelage, or it could fight to maintain its autonomy, which would lead, among other problems, to imminent bankruptcy. In November 1957, Jeudon expressed his support for the so-called Klock proposition, which aimed to make the APCMF into an *établissement public* and to bring the chambers of trades into line with the state's new policy of regional development. He contended that the creation of the European Economic Community, which would increase competition in French markets, necessitated a closer reliance of the APCMF on the public authorities. The other presidents agreed reluctantly.[99]

The government of the Fifth Republic took the next logical step in March 1962, when it carried out a complete overhaul of the regime under which the chambers of trades had operated since 1925. The new system was intended to delimit the artisanat more precisely in order to make it more accessible to government aid, but this also meant reshaping it according to the state's conception. The general thrust of the 1962 decree-law was to shift the point

of definition from the individual to the enterprise. The state no longer occupied itself with the question, what is an *artisan*? Instead, it dismissed the
whole matter of essences, over which artisans had battled for forty years, and
settled for the form. If a business produced a specified article, performed a
specified service, or employed the specified number of workers, that was
enough. The artisanat was reincarnated as the *secteur des métiers*.

The new system claimed at the same time to respect the freedom of
commerce and to reinforce the qualification necessary for obtaining the title
of *maître-artisan* and the privilege of training apprentices. It granted the
chambers of trades a more effective control over administrative functions
within the *secteur des métiers*, while it established the absolute *liberté d'exercice
des métiers*. The decree-law of 1962 unambiguously promoted both the operation of the free market and state oversight. It represented the opposite of
corporate autonomy.[100]

The 1962 decree thereby marked the defeat of the artisanal project as it
had existed since 1919. Insofar as the artisanal movement incorporated one
idea above all others, it was that the best way to save independent, skilled
masters was to give them power over their own circumstances. Only such
autonomy, the movement had argued, could bring real meaning to any protection that artisans might receive. Without it, even fiscal exemptions would
be but a recipe for mediocrity. This premise had suffused the original demand
for the chambers of trades and the continuing calls for a statute of the artisanat.

It had been from the start a forlorn hope. This determination to achieve—
or to recapture, as the sustaining myth had it—artisanal autonomy, having
been repeatedly disappointed by the Third Republic and the National Revolution, received the coup de grâce from the economic and administrative
revolution of the 1950s. When the title of *master-artisan* became a kind of
advertising tool and ceased to be a social fact, when the artisanat became the
secteur des métiers, it indicated that the long battle was over. The APCMF
and the syndicates that had once constituted the artisanal movement approved
the 1962 reforms. They thereby ratified the demise of that movement and of
the Idea that had animated it.

7

Conclusion

I have tried here to retrieve one of the forgotten elements of twentieth-century French society: independent master artisans. As I tracked these petty trades-men through the history books and the public records, I was struck by the condescension with which they have been treated—when they have been treated at all. Sometimes despised, often romanticized, usually ignored, ar-tisans have seldom been taken seriously. I hope to have done them that justice.

The history of the artisanat in twentieth-century France raises several broad questions. The first is the special nature of French economic devel-opment. From the end of the nineteenth century through the Fourth Republic the French economy underwent a long-term process of industrial expansion and concentration, punctuated by periods of crisis and stagnation. Industrial-ization, however, did not prove to be, as many predicted, the nemesis of handicraft production. The artisanat lost approximately one quarter of its total population in this period and experienced a notable reshuffling of trades and businesses. Yet France remained, in large part, a nation of *petites situations*.

Second, the case of artisans presents us with a specific instance of the general proposition: class. We have seen that skilled, independent tradesmen enjoyed a rough sort of unity shaped by their shared experience of work and small property. An artisan possessed some degree of professional know-how. His workshop was a modest place, where production proceeded on a scale and according to a rhythm that distinguished it from the factory. Yet the artisanat was an approximation, a suggestion, an area of probability rather than a fixed point in the socio-economic field. At one end the humblest of petty producers, *façonniers* and domestic workers, blended into the world of wage labor. At the other end prosperous masters imperceptibly became *petits industriels* ("small capitalists"). Moreover, everyone on this scale was in motion. A master might employ six assistants in good times and only two or three in bad; a downturn in the economy might force an independent craftsman to find temporary employment in a factory or to resort to piece work in order to make ends meet. Most observers have been willing to grant the existence of the artisanat, but there has never been any consensus as to where it began and ended.

I have argued an additional point about class, that the transformation from abstraction to political reality did not happen spontaneously. There were artisans in France long before there was an artisanat, which only appeared when independent tradesmen came to believe in their distinctiveness and solidarity. This *prise de conscience* occurred following World War I and originated in a number of places more or less simultaneously: the syndicates of master craftsmen, the Alsace Chamber of Trades, the Chamber of Deputies, and among those who envisioned the rationalization of political economy; Etienne Clémentel, for example. The artisanal movement began as the brainchild of a few syndical and political leaders. Perhaps the rank and file were animated by the tireless propaganda of these men; they were certainly given good practical reasons to associate themselves with the nascent movement by the actions of the legislature and by the ferment within the trades themselves.

As it began to articulate its *raison d'être*, the artisanal movement developed a worldview composed of a number of common themes, all of which rested on a fundamental belief in the virtues of "smallness" and of the integration of work into life in general. Artisans rejected as a product of industrial alienation the notion that work could or should be separated from family or from a general sense of self-worth. Historical treatments of the petty bourgeoisie have often taken for granted that the consciousness of the lower middle classes is distorted by an aggravated sense of economic insecurity and social inferiority; but these seem to have left a tiny imprint on the ideology of the artisanal movement. To be sure, most artisans, especially those who performed services for their customers, must sometimes have felt the sting of social indignation. Paul Marcelin recalled how his father, a tinsmith in Nîmes at the turn of the century, was once summoned to the home of one of his bourgeois clients to perform some repairs on the plumbing. The valet introduced him to the patron; "Sir, this is *Monsieur* Marcelin." "No," the bourgeois corrected his man, "just *Marcelin*."[1] And when artisans expressed their disenchantment with liberalism and Marxism, this stemmed from their sense of being dismissed as an anachronism. Yet it does not appear that the artisanal movement fed in any basic sense on "the politics of resentment."

This was a worldview that proposed an elitism of *les petits*, and it naturally translated into a political orientation that was resolutely populist. But populism, it seems, could work two ways, and the movement early on divided into a left and a right wing: on the left, old-fashioned radicalism, economic justice by and for all *petits*; on the right, an emphasis on the interests of small and medium-sized property (what eventually merged with the conservative politics of the *classes moyennes*).

As it turned out, extremist politics never made much headway within the artisanal movement. It is true that a handful of artisanal leaders were attracted to the far right in the 1930s and that a much greater number threw their lot in with the National Revolution. It is also true that after the war both the communists and the Poujadists received a sympathetic hearing among master craftsmen. But the Communist party appealed to artisans only when it ex-changed its Marxist categories for the rhetoric of *petits* versus *gros*, and Poujade gained support primarily because his was the shrillest voice of protest against taxes. Petty producers were willing to listen to whoever told them what they wanted to hear. Quite a few of them listened intently to some questionable characters. There is no reason, however, to point to the artisanal movement as an incubator of any form of political extremism.

This leads us to a reconsideration of the classical proposition that fascism found its social base among elements of the "old" petty bourgeoisie, artisans in particular. The artisanal movement shared many of the conservative social values of the far right and their distaste for Marxist revolution. But then a faith in the virtues of small property and the family were hardly the monopoly of one party or *tendance*. When we move from ideological fellow-traveling to concrete political commitment, moreover, we find absolutely no indication that significant numbers of artisans lined up with the fascist leagues and parties. Indeed, such weak links that have been uncovered suggest that those in the artisanal movement who flirted most egregiously with Maurras and de la Rocque were the most "patronal" elements (men like Bagnaud who owned considerable businesses). The more overtly fascist groups, such as the Doriotists or the "cagoulards," made no mark at all on the artisanal movement.

To what can we attribute this distaste for political adventurism among independent, master artisans? It has sometimes been proposed that the benign populism of the Radical party served to draw support away from the more pernicious champions of the petty bourgeoisie, and I have found a number of connections between the leadership of the artisanal movement and the Radicals—more, in any case, than between artisans and the radical right. Given the limited possibilities of electoral sociology for France, however, it is impossible to test this proposition with much precision. I have further suggested that artisans may have been steered away from the political fringes by the relatively moderate threat to small property in twentieth-century France. The depression brought hard times and a sense of national malaise, but it did not "proletarianize" the lower middle classes or raise the specter of communist revolution.

If small property in France did not find itself on the brink of ruin, this is largely the result of the country's imperfect industrialization, a situation that, in part, reflected the political system's response to the needs of its petty bourgeois constituents. One of the conventional interpretations of the Third Republic is that it sealed a compromise between the bourgeoisie and the petty bourgeoisie against the perils of monarchism and socialism—although those who accept the truth of this do not necessarily agree on its consequences. André Siegfried, for example, found in small property the key to the nation's social and political good health, while Herbert Lüthy saw these *petites situations acquises* as an "albatross" around the country's neck. I am not sure that the history of the artisanal movement allows us to choose between these conclusions. It does, however, support their presumptions.   From its inception the movement enjoyed an intimate, if not wholly satisfactory, relationship with the institutions of the state. The legislature was the most responsive to *la France profonde*, doubtless a matter of electoral calculation and a genuine belief in the social and political value of small property. The pro-artisanal legislation that surged in the 1920s and abated in the 1930s can be read as so many clauses in the social contract; however, its premises were already unraveling. After 1919 concessions to petty proprietors threatened to be swallowed up both by structural economic development and by conjunctural collapse. By the mid-1930s a consensus, of which, paradoxically, artisans were a part, had been reached to the effect that the contract of the republic needed to be renegotiated.

Meanwhile, a more powerful labor movement was searching for its own quid pro quo with the state, and this presented a second challenge to the Jeffersonian compromise of the Third Republic. It was not at all clear that the parliament could maintain its special commitment to small property and at the same time accommodate the demands of the working classes. As a result, and we have seen it reflected in the experience of the artisanal movement, parliamentarians promoted the artisanat as a social buffer at the same time as they increasingly passed on difficult economic and social decisions to the administration.

The administration—from the *grands corps*, to the ministries, to the ad hoc commissions and councils, to the National Economic Council—bore their own prejudices; not those of *le français moyen*, but those of big business, big labor, and the *Grandes Ecoles*. Whereas the Parliament was solicitous but increasingly ineffectual, the bureaucracy of the new political economy was unsympathetic to the Malthusian interests of the artisanat. The artisanal movement recognized that it was being more or less read out of the social contract, yet it was unable to find an adequate response. In fact, it is not clear that such a response even existed.

Artisans appear to have supported the Third Republic to its military end. Nonetheless, they were attracted to the National Revolution because it promised to retrieve "the good old days" when, among other things, small property was secure and respected. My own reading of Vichy is that this promise was, in part, disingenuous and, in part, made impossible by circumstance. In any case, it was not kept. What followed after the war was an acceleration of industrial growth and the rationalization of political economy. The artisanal movement in the 1950s tried to parry this development with two incompatible tactics. On the one hand, it tenaciously fought for its old conception of autonomy and protection for *petites entreprises*; on the other, it struggled to integrate itself into the New France. The first of these roads brought artisans to the Poujade Movement, the second to a rethinking and a reorganization of the artisanal movement. The latter course finished in an acceptance of the reform of 1962 and an end to the artisanat as it had been conceived and set in motion in the early 1920s. Artisans did not completely give up their vision of a France with a special place for handicraft production, nor did the state wholly abandon *petits* to the market. But in the Fifth Republic what had once been a movement became merely an interest.

It is tempting to conclude that the artisanat, as embodied in the artisanal movement, was doomed in twentieth-century France. At the very least, in order to save the cobbler, the blacksmith, or the cabinetmaker the majority of French people would have had to rearrange their historical priorities, to forego high consumption and world power. Even by 1919, therefore, the kind of world artisans sought to preserve, if it had ever existed, was beyond recovery. The logic and apparent ineluctability of this process, however, did not make it any less painful for those who were its victims. Men and women who were proud of their skills and jealous of their independence and who were honest and hard-working, gradually found themselves without work and unable to pay their rent or support their families. As they were able, they fought back against capitalists, industrial workers, technocrats, and despite political economists. The artisanal movement was above all the story of artisans' battle against their own irrelevance.

Appendix A

Charter of the Artisanat

All the artisans of France, affiliated with the General Confederation of French Artisans, conscious of their rights and duties, affirm the following principles:

1. The Artisanat is the social class intermediate between capital and wage earners. Consequently, it must be recognized as such by the state and, as such, provided with organs of legal representation [i.e., artisanal chambers of trades].
   The legal representation of the profession must join all those who participate in it—masters and journeymen—and it must be directed by them;

2. The Artisanat trains its own apprentices in its workshops, with professional courses that it organizes and directs itself;

3. The Artisanat does not support the depreciation of wages. Its virtue lies in the quality of production and not in low prices; the professional know-how of its masters and *compagnons*, being the principal factor, ought to be remunerated at its just value;

4. The Artisanat recognizes individual private property and, therefore, the fair and legitimate return on capital;

5. The Artisanat has to facilitate however possible the accession of journeymen to masters, the goal of the apprentice being to become a *compagnon*, and of the *compagnon* to become a master;

6. The Artisanat must assure its independence through cooperation, in all its forms: local, regional, and national professional syndicates; cooperatives for purchasing materials, for production, for distribution, and for credit;

7. Artisanal production having an individual flavor, finding its source usually in the locality, the Artisanat is therefore regionalist and will cooperate in all efforts at decentralization;

8. The Artisanat unites its members outside of any political or religious concerns.

It will, however, get involved in the political arena each time that it finds its professional interests engaged.

Artisan Français 6 (June 1923).

Appendix B

Artisanal Manifesto Aux Français!

Grave events have occurred, and others are imminent; in any case, France's situation—from an economic, political, and social point of view—remains tense.

The CGAF—representing the country's 1,300,000 independent master artisans whose small businesses provide for more than 8 million inhabitants (a fifth of our population)—present a program on which all men of good will may agree.

The Origin of our Misfortunes

One finds everywhere tainted wealth—acquired without exertion or even, in some cases, by theft and deceit.

However, Remember That

—there is only one healthy and respectable form of capital: that created by work and conserved through saving.

—work is a right and a duty; to pursue it fruitfully one must have a profession and know one's trade. That, for everyone, is the basic capital;

—the *métier* must be recognized and defended by the organized collectivity, that is by the delivery of a certificate of ability after a period of study or compulsory apprenticeship.

—welfare does not resolve the problem of unemployment; it degrades the individual, because it is a humiliating form of charity and a great loss for the community.

It is Thus Urgent

1. To purify and to revive economic activity through:

    a) a democratic reorganization of credit;
    b) a modern transportation system;
    c) a limitation of the number of large enterprises;
    d) the execution of a program of useful and profitable public works—
with the goal of putting the country back to work.

2. To put the brakes on overproduction by returning to quality production in industry and agriculture.

3. To supervise and maintain this quality by the creation of trade *syndics*, charged with defending consumer interests—in requiring the producer to deliver good merchandise.

What do Artisans Want?

—to collaborate in the renovation of the country—in their proper place, alongside all the other productive forces of France—in order to make it an example of a balanced civilization in a topsy-turvy world.

—to unite in independence and strength, the better to serve.

To This End

—artisans have to make their voices heard—they demand the creation of an organ of professional representation, with the full power of law, where all producers will confront the interests *en cause*, under the sovereign eye of a rejuvenated parliament.

Before the Gravity of the Situation

The CGAF demands the convocation of the ESTATES-GENERAL OF THE NATION to permit the organized forces of Agriculture, the Artisanat, Commerce, Industry, Intellectuals, and the *Salariat* to arrive at the bases of great reforms and to submit them to Parliament—which might, without delay, give them the force of law.

LaCGAF

Appendix C

Accord Général: Confédération générale du travail-Confédération générale de l'artisanat français

Article 1: The contracting parties hereby commit themselves to invite their respective syndicates to conclude collective labor agreements according to the following terms:

Article 2: Respect for the laws being imperative for all citizens, artisan employers recognize the freedom of opinion, as well as the workers' rights to join freely and to belong to a professional trade union, constituted according to Book III of the labor code.

Article 3: Mixed commissions, composed in equal parts of representatives of organizations of syndical artisanal confederations and of confederal workers' organizations, will be set up in order to establish collective labor contracts for each profession and professional category, nationally and by region and locality.

Article 4: The real wages in force for all workers and apprentices will be at least equal to those established by the wage schedule in effect in the majority of enterprises in each profession and similar professions according to region and locality.

Article 5: The contracting parties to a collective agreement will each designate, in equal numbers, representatives to form a commission charged with resolving the conflicts which might emerge between master artisans and workers over the application of the said collective agreement.

The decisions of the commission will not prejudice a resolution in those cases amenable to normal legal and administrative procedures.

Article 6: It is compulsory for the artisan employers and workers to observe the guidelines of the labor code, the laws on welfare and insurance, and all measures pertaining to or having to do with work.

Article 7: Artisan employers are prohibited from employing workers apart from the legally prescribed hours and from hiring workers and apprentices already engaged in other employ.

Article 8: Workers of both sexes are forbidden to engage in remunerative or nonremunerative labor either on their own behalf or on that of another outside of their normal hours of employment.

Article 9: The CGAF and the CGT will make every effort to obtain legal measures prohibiting to any individual the exercise of an occupation, remunerated or not, for any employer or on his own account, outside his normal hours of employment.

Article 10: Apprenticeship within the workshop of a master artisan will be effected in conformity with legal dispositions.

Article 11: Organizations of syndical artisanal confederations and organizations of confederated workers commit themselves to seek, by common agreement, the obligatory extension, according to the terms of article 31 of the law of 24 June 1936, of collective labor conventions concluded between them.

Article 12: Organizations of confederated artisans and organizations of confederated workers should be guided insofar as possible, in the establishment of their own collective labor contracts, by the models previously established by the national federations of confederated artisans and confederated workers, which are annexed to the present accord.

Signed: Paris 19 September 1936

For the CGT: Jouhaux, Belin, Racamond, Frachon, Brenot, Buisson, Bothereau

For the CGAF: Tailledet, Grandadam, Forestier

Notes

Chapter 1

1. André Siegfried, *Qu'est-ce que l'artisanat? Son rôle dans le passé, dans le présent, dans l'avenir* (Paris: Horizons de France, 1941), p. 3.

2. Cited in Hubert Ley, *L'Artisanat: Entité Corporative* (Paris: Dunod, 1938), p. 55.

3. Laurent Azzano, *Mes joyeuses années au faubourg: souvenirs du faubourg Saint Antoine* (Paris: Editions France-Empire, 1985), pp. 12, 20.

4. Azzano, *Mes joyeuses années*, p. 51.

5. I do not want to join the debate as to whether *class* exists apart from its self-consciousness. Yet I employ the word because it is convenient and descriptive, because it implies a social and economic component that more neutral words such as *group* and *stratum* do not, and because it is so much a part of everyday political language. At the same time, *class* is vague and often polemical; different groups use it to mean different things. To define *class* too exactly in the beginning and according to my own purposes would preempt everyone else's meaning. I seek, moreover, to approach *class* empirically rather than theoretically. That is not to say that I begin from theoretical ground-zero; obviously, to focus on independent skilled craftsmen is already to prejudge the matter somewhat. It means only that *class* is the premise and not the conclusion of this study. My object is precisely to discover its content as reflected in the behavior and thought of master artisans. For similar views on the question see William Reddy, *Money and Liberty in Modern Europe: A Critique of Historical Understanding* (Cambridge: Cambridge University Press, 1987), p. 193; and Max Weber, "Class, Status, and Party," *From Max Weber: Essays in Sociology*, ed. H.H. Gerth and C. Wright Mills (New York: Oxford University Press, 1958), p. 181.

6. Edgar Hector, *La législation actuelle de l'artisanat: Commentaire et jurisprudence*

(Paris: Librairie du Recueil Sirey, 1939), pp. 7–40, discusses the various definitions of the artisanat.

7. See, for example, Michael Hanagan, *The Logic of Solidarity*: *Artisans and Industrial Workers in Three French Towns, 1871-1914* (Urbana, Illinois: University of Illinois Press, 1980); Bernard Moss, *The Origins of the French Labor Movement, 1830-1914*: *The Socialism of Skilled Workers* (Berkeley, California: University of California Press, 1976); Donald Reid, *The Miners of Decazeville*: *A Geneology of Industrialization* (Cambridge, Mass.: Harvard University Press, 1982); and Joan Scott, *The Glassworkers of Carmaux*: *French Craftsmen and Political Action in a Nineteenth-Century City* (Cambridge, Mass: Harvard University Press, 1974). On the question of the labor aristocracy see Eric J. Hobsbawm, *Laboring Men*: *Studies in the History of Labor* (London: Weidenfeld & Nicholson, 1965), p. 273.

8. La Société Savante d'Alsace et des Régions de l'Est, *Artisans et Ouvriers d'Alsace* 9 (Strasbourg: Librairie Istra, 1965), p. 268. The national census did not, for example, identify artisans as a separate socio-professional category before 1963. Artisanal establishments therefore have to be deduced according to the sector and the size of an enterprise. Moreover, these criteria do not distinguish independent craftsmen from fully dependent domestic workers or from *petits industriels*, businesses with a small number of employees but a different organization of labor. Was a furniture establishment with a patron and five assistants a part of the artisanat? The census figures do not say.

9. Charles Kindleberger, *Economic Growth in France and Britain, 1851-1950* (Cambridge, Mass.: Harvard University Press, 1964), p. 93.

10. Geoffrey Crossick and Heinz-Gerhard Haupt, "Shopkeepers, Master Artisans and the Historian: the Petite Bourgeoisie in Comparative Focus," pp. 3–31, *Shopkeepers and Master Artisans in Nineteenth-Century Europe*, ed. Crossick and Haupt (London: Methuen, 1984), p. 13.

11. Cited in François Caron, "Dynamismes et freinages de la croissance industrielle," *Histoire économique et sociale de la France*, ed. Fernand Braudel and Ernst Labrousse, tome 4: *L'ère industrielle et la société d'aujourd'hui (siècle 1880–1980)*. vol. 1: *Panoramas de l'ère industrielle (années 1880–années 1970)*; *Ambiguités des débuts et croissance effective (années 1880-1914)* (Paris: Presses Universitaires de France, 1979), p. 243. See also Yves Trotignon, *La France au XXᵉ Siècle*, Tome 1: *Jusqu'en 1968* (Paris, Brussels, Montreal: Bordas, 1968), p. 39.

12. Michel Debré, *L'Artisanat*: *Classe sociale. La notion d'artisan. La législation artisane* (Paris: Librairie Dalloz, 1934), pp. 12–34 passim; Ley, *L'Artisanat*, pp. 197–200; Jean Robert, *L'artisanat et le secteur des métiers dans la France contemporaine* (Paris: Armand Colin, 1966), p. 10; Marc Durand and Jean-Paul Frémont, *L'Artisanat en France* (Paris: Presses Universitaires de France, 1979), p. 19; Fernand Peter, "La situation de l'Artisanat en Europe" (presented to the fourth national congress, Comité d'entente et d'action artisanales, Paris, 1937); François Etienne, "L'Artisanat et l'Education, 1921–1970" (thèse en sociologie de l'éducation, Université de Paris-René Descartes, 1977), pp. 2–3.

13. Michelle Perrot, "Les classes populaires urbaines," *Histoire économique*, Tome 4, vol. 1: 510.

14. Lucienne Cahen, "La concentration des établissements en France de 1896 à 1936," *Etudes et Conjoncture* 9 (September 1954): 846.

15. François Caron, *An Economic History of Modern France*, trans. Barbara Bray, *Columbia Economic History of the Modern World*, ed. Stuart W. Bruchey (New York: Columbia University Press, 1979), p. 164.

16. On the artisanat in the building trades see Kindleberger, *Economic Growth*, p. 307; for a survey of the building trades from 1880 to 1914 see Caron, "L'extension des infrastructures et des équipements et l'intensification des échanges de marchandises," *Histoire économique*, Tome 4, vol. 1:138–43. Georges Grandadam discusses the distribution of the artisanat in the various economic sectors in "Conseil National Economique," *Cahiers de l'Artisanat* 18 (April 1936): 8; see also Siegfried, *Qu'est-ce que l'artisanat?* p. 27.

17. Maurice Levy-Leboyer, "Innovation and Business Strategies in Nineteenth- and Twentieth-Century France," ed. Edward C. Carter II, Robert Forster, Joseph Moody, *Enterprise and Entrepreneurs in Nineteenth- and Twentieth-Century France*, (Baltimore and London: Johns Hopkins University Press, 1976), pp. 97–100.

18. Heinz-Gerhard Haupt, "The Petite Bourgeoisie in France, 1850–1914: In Search of the *Juste Milieu*," *Shopkeepers and Master Artisans*, ed. Crossick and Haupt, p. 107; Perrot, "Les classes populaires urbaines," p. 510.

19. Jean Le Laouanq, "La mobilité sociale dans le milieu boutiquier parisien au XIXe siècle," *Le Mouvement Social* 108 (July-September 1979): 93; Bernard Zarca, "Survivance ou transformation de l'artisanat dans la France d'aujourd'hui" (thèse en sociologie, Institut d'études politiques de Paris, 1983), vol. 2: 451.

20. Haupt, "The Petite Bourgeoisie," p. 98.

21. Pierre Barral, "Le monde agricole," *Histoire économique*, p. 369; Paul Roux, *Monographie d'une commune rurale de l'Auvergne*. Bibliothèque de la Science Sociale, Edmond Demolins, fondateur (Paris: Bureau de la Science Sociale, 1912), pp. 60–62.

22. Quoted in Michel Gervais, Marcel Jollivet and Yves Tavarnier, *La fin de la France paysanne: de 1914 aa nos jours*, ed. Georges Duby and Armand Wallon, *Histoire de la France rurale*, 4 vols. (Paris: Editions de Seuil, 1976), 4: 323.

23. Caron, *An Economic History*, pp. 121–22, 125.

24. Georges Lefranc, *Le mouvement syndical sous la Troisième République* (Paris: Payot, 1967), p. 220.

25. *Artisan* (Lyon) 23 (July 1921).

26. Georges Chaudieu, *Au temps des charrues. Basse-Brie - Montois - Bassée Morvois - Sénonais nord - Gâtinais français* (Etrepilly: Presses du Village, 1983), p. 85.

27. G. Olphe-Galliard, *Les industries rurales à domicile dans la Normandie orientale*, (Paris: Bureau de la Science Sociale, 1913), pp. 19–20.

28. Alain Cottereau, in his introductory essay to Denis Poulot, *Le Sublime, ou le travailleur comme il est en 1870 et ce qu'il peut être* (Paris: François Maspero, 1980), p. 70.

29. Lee Shai Weissbach, "Artisanal Responses to Artistic Decline: The Cabinetmakers of Paris in the Era of Industrialization," *Journal of Social History* 16 (1982): 68. For a more general consideration of this process within the skilled trades see Leonard Berlanstein, *The Working People of Paris, 1871–1914* (Baltimore: Johns Hopkins University Press, 1984), pp. 15–21 and 79–84.

30. Quoted in Haupt, "The Petite Bourgeoisie," p. 102. See also Philip Nord, *Paris Shopkeepers and the Politics of Resentment* (Princeton: Princeton University Press, 1986, pp. 82–84.

31. Perrot, "Les classes populaires urbaines," pp. 457–58.

32. Marilyn J. Boxer, "Women in Industrial Homework: The Flowermakers of Paris," *French Historical Studies* 12 (1982): 407. The percentage of women working at home increased from 25 percent in 1896 to 38 percent in 1906.

33. On the evolution of the textile trades in the region of the Centre-Est see Jean-

Pierre Jobard, *Les disparités régionales de croissance*: *Analyse économique des dé-partements situés dans le Centre-Est de la France, 1801-1962*. Fondation Nationale des Sciences Politiques. Service d'étude de l'activité économique. Recherches sur l'écon-omie française (Paris: Armand Colin, 1971), pp. 165-71.

34. On the cotton, wool, and linen industries in Normandy see Olphe-Galliard, *Les industries rurales*, pp. 13, 30-33, 74. For the situation in Lyon see Caron, *An Economic History*, pp. 153–54; and Jobard, *Les disparités*, pp. 165–71.

35. Jacques Lefebvre, *L'évolution des localisations industrielles*. *L'exemple des Alpes françaises* (Paris: Librairie Dalloz, 1960), pp. 24–26. See also Robert Goetz-Girey, "Stimulants et propagation de la croissance dans le 'pays de Monbéliard,' " *Revue Economique* 11 (January 1960): 1–16.

36. Caron, "La croissance industrielle," pp. 313–14.

37. William H. Sewell, Jr., *Work and Revolution in France*: *The Language of Labor from the Old Regime to 1848* (Cambridge: Cambridge University Press, 1980), p. 161.

38. Paul Marcelin, *Souvenirs d'un passé artisanal* (Nîmes: Anciens Etablissements Chastenier Frères et Bertrand, 1967), pp. 15–16.

39. Peter H. Merkl, *Political Violence Under the Swastika*: *581 Early Nazis* (Prince-ton, N.J.: Princeton University Press, 1975), p. 75. Christine Jaeger offers a similar analysis in *Artisanat et Capitalisme*. *L'envers de la roue de l'histoire* (Paris: Payot, 1982), p. 13.

40. Geoffrey Crossick, "La petite bourgeoisie britannique au XIXe siècle," *Le Mouvement Social* 108 (July–September): 30–34; Geoffrey Crossick, "The Emergence of the Lower Middle Class in Britain: A Discussion," *The Lower Middle Class in Britain, 1870–1914*, ed. Crossick (London: Croom Helm, 1977), pp. 12–13.

41. Caron, *An Economic History*, p. 166.

42. Haupt, "The Petite Bourgeoisie," p. 100.

43. Caron, *An Economic History*, p. 258.

44. Richard F. Kuisel, *Capitalism and the State in Modern France*: *Renovation and Economic Management in the Twentieth Century* (Cambridge: Cambridge University Press, 1981), p. 11.

45. Henri Mourier, "L'artisanat, sa structure et son intégration dans l'économie moderne," (thèse en droit, Paris, 1952), p. 8.

46. Edgar Hector surveys the vast wasteland of artisanal fiscality in *La législation*, pp. 118–44; see also Joseph Hamel and Léon Buquet, directeurs, *Le crédit artisanal en France et à l'étranger*. Institut de Droit Comparé de l'Université de Paris. Publi-cations du Centre International d'Etudes de l'Artisanat I (Paris: Sirey, 1958), especially "annexe: Le régime fiscal de l'artisanat en France," pp. 78–106.

47. See, for example, *Artisan* (Lyon) 12 (September 1920).

48. *Artisan* (Lyon) 35 (July 1922).

49. Lucien de Chilly, "La classe moyenne en France après la guerre: 1918–1924. Sa crise: causes, conséquences et remèdes" (thèse en sciences politiques et écono-miques, Faculté de Droit de Paris, 1924), p. 10. On the Radicals' patronage of *petits* see Gil Alroy, "Radicalism and Modernization: The French Problem," (Ph.D diss., Princeton University, 1962).

50. Marius Coulon, *L'artisan devant l'impôt* (Lille: Douriez-Bataille, 1943), p. 10.

51. *Artisan Français* 11 (November 1923).

52. For a discussion of the motivations behind the parliament's solicitude see Demondion, *L'artisanat dans l'état moderne* (Paris: F. Lovitan, 1941), pp. 124–27, 155–57.

53. Jean Caro, "Le régime des artisans en matière d'impôts directs" (thèse en droit, Université de Rennes, 1953), p. 19.

54. *Journal Officiel*, Senate, 6 July 1922.

55. *Journal Officiel*, Chamber of Deputies, Thoumyre recounted the history of the issue in the debate of 18 January 1923.

56. *Journal Officiel*, Chamber of Deputies, 18 January 1923.

57. See the background discussion in the *Journal Officiel*, Senate, 17 January 1923.

58. On the population of the Chamber of Deputies' Groupe de défense artisanale see *Gazette des Métiers* (hereafter cited as *Gazette*) 46 (17 November 1922): 556; 48 (1 December 1922): 578. *Artisan Français* 4 (April 1923) carried a list of those deputies who had joined the group.

59. On the Left's patronage of *petits*, artisans included, see Tony Judt, *La reconstruction du parti socialiste, 1921–1926* (Paris: Presses de la Fondation des Sciences Politiques, 1976), p. 112.

60. *Journal Officiel*, Chamber of Deputies, 18 January 1923.

61. *Journal Officiel*, Chamber of Deputies, 19 January 1923.

62. *Journal Officiel*, Senate, 17 January 1923.

63. *Journal Officiel*, Senate, 17 January 1923. Courtier countered by citing de Lasteyrie to the effect that of the 490,000 artisans who might be affected by the proposed changes, 478,000 did a business of less than 50,000 francs a year. The impact of these exemptions on the public treasury, therefore, would be minimal: *Journal Officiel*, Chamber of Deputies, 19 January 1923.

64. *Journal Officiel*, Chamber of Deputies, 29 June 1923.

65. *Artisan* (Lyon) 47 (August 1923).

66. For example, see *Artisan* (Lyon) 53 (February 1924); and 59 (August–September 1924). See also Courtier's attack on the restrictive way that the government was applying the law of 30 June 1923: *Journal Officiel*, Chamber of Deputies, 27 November 1923.

67. On the credit law of December 1923, see Pierre Demondion, *L'artisanat dans l'état moderne*, p. 109; Hector, *La législation*, pp. 144–69.

68. Debré was particularly skeptical of the *petits* artisans' ability to profit from the new availability of credit: *L'Artisan: Classe sociale*, p. 227. See also the reports from the artisans in the southeast: *Artisan* (Lyon) 69 (July 1925); and 88 (February 1927).

69. "The [syndicate]," explained Gabriel Daty, "is a moral entity in public law, whereas the association is a moral entity in private law." The association, organized under the law of 1901, was more heterogeneous and did not have the same standing in law and the same privileges and responsibilities as the syndicate, regulated by the laws of 1884 and 1920: Gabriel Daty, "L'Artisanat en Alsace" (thèse de droit, Paris, 1933), p. 64. See also Debré's discussion of the difference: *L'Artisanat: Classe sociale*, p. 120.

70. *Artisan* (Lyon) 40–41 (January–February 1923); *Gazette* 51 (22 December 1922): 615.

71. *Journal Officiel*, Chamber of Deputies, 14 December 1923.

72. Hector, *La législation*, pp. 341–42.

73. *Artisan* (Le Puy) 1 (January–February 1938); *Artisan Français* 255 (20 January 1938); 258 (20 February 1938).

74. On the political history of master artisans see Maurice Agulhon, *La vie sociale en Provence intérieure au lendemain de la Révolution* (Paris: Société des études robespierristes, 1970), p. 305; Robert Darnton, "Workers Revolt: The Great Cat Massacre of the rue Saint-Séverin," *The Great Cat Massacre and Other Episodes in French*

Cultural History (New York: Random House, 1985), pp. 75–104; Tony Judt, *Socialism in Provence, 1871–1914: A Study in the Origins of the Modern French Left* (Cambridge: Cambridge University Press, 1979), p. 196; Jacques Rancière, "The Myth of the Artisan: Critical Reflections on a Category of Social History," *International Labor and Working Class History* 24 (1983): 1–16 (with "Responses" from William Sewell and Christopher Johnson); Sewell, *Work and Revolution*; Albert Soboul, *The Sans-Culottes: The Popular Movement and Revolutionary Government, 1793–1794*, trans. Rémy Inglis Hall (Princeton: Princeton University Press, 1980).

75. Annie Kriegel, "Histoire ouvrière aux XIXe et XXe siècles," *Revue Historique* 235 (April–June 1966): 459; William M. Reddy, *Money and Liberty in Modern Europe: A Critique of Historical Understanding* (Cambridge: Cambridge University Press, 1987), p. 162.

76. Zarca, "Survivance ou transformation," p. 59.

77. *Enquête sur l'artisanat* (Paris, Institut de Science Economique Appliquée, 1946): "Maréchal-Forgeron," p. 31; see also the scattered commentaries on the Darlot law and the blacksmiths' opposition in the *Artisan* (Lyon) (1920 and 1921).

78. Zarca, "Survivance ou transformation," p. 1043.

79. Crossick and Haupt, "Shopkeepers," p. 9.

80. Archives Nationales, F22 21, "Aude: Bâtiment-Aude"; this whole series is a national survey of local professional groups.

81. The social profile of the "new right" has been a difficult riddle to solve. Many have pointed at the lower middle classes, but no one has really been able to be more precise. See, on this question, Paul Mazgaj, *The Action Français and Revolutionary Syndicalism* (Chapel Hill, N.C.: University of North Carolina Press, 1979); Nord, *Paris Shopkeepers*, p. 5; Peter Rutkoff, *Revanche and Revision: The Ligue des Patriotes and the Origins of the Radical Right in France, 1882–1900* (Athens, Ohio, and London: Ohio University Press, 1981), p. 108; Robert Soucy, *French Fascism: The First Wave, 1924–1933* (New Haven and London: Yale University Press, 1986), Chapter 1, pp. 1–26 passim; D.R. Watson, "The Nationalist Movement in Paris, 1900–1906," *The Right in France, 1890–1919: Three Studies*, ed. David Shapiro, St Antony's Papers, no. 13 (Carbondale, Ill.: Southern Illinois University Press, 1970), pp. 68–69, 79–80, 84.

82. The quote is from Crossick and Haupt, "Shopkeepers," p. 4; see also Crossick's essay, "The Petite Bourgeoisie in Nineteenth-Century Europe: Problems and Research," *Arbeiter und Arbeiterbewegung im Vergleich: Berichte zur internationalen historischen Forschung* (Munich: R. Oldenbourg Verlag, 1986), p. 227.

83. On the prewar organizations see Haupt, "The Petite Bourgeoisie," pp. 95, 108–9; François Gresle, "Indépendants et petits patrons: perennité et transformations d'une classe sociale," (thèse, Université de Paris V, 1980), p. 76.

84. The expression is Rancière's in, "The Myth of the Artisans," p. 2; see also Haupt, "The Petite Bourgeoisie," p. 110.

85. Marcel Bris, *Le compagnonnage: à la recherche de sa vocation, 1900–1946* (París: Librairie du Compagnonnage, 1984), pp. 11–12.

86. Jean-Pierre Duroy, "Le compagnonnage: initiateur de l'économie sociale" (thèse en économie sociale, Université de Maine, 1982), p. 91. For a personal history of *compagnonnage* in the twentieth century see Abel Boyer, *Le Tour de France d'un Compagnon du Devoir* (Paris: Librairie du Compagnonnage, 1957).

87. Emile Coornaert, *Le compagnonnage en France du moyen age à nos jours* (Paris: Editions Ouvrières, 1966), p. 125.

88. Coornaert, *Le compagnonnage*, p. 122.

89. Bris, *Le compagnonnage, 1900–1946*, p. 29.

90. Coornaert, *Le compagnonnage*, p. 123.

91. Bris, *Le compagnonnage, 1900–1946*, pp. 31–37.

92. *Le Compagnonnage*. Journal mutualiste, professionnel, philosophique et littéraire. Organe mensuel de propagande fédérale des groupements et sociétés compagnonniques du Tour de France, 1 (August 1919).

93. Bris, *Le compagnonnage, 1900–1946*, pp. 29–31.

94. *Gazette* 40 (30 December 1921): 362.

95. Marcel Barraud, *Les chambres de métiers en France* (Paris: Librairie Générale de Droit et de Jurisprudence, 1925), p. 148.

96. Bruno Magliulo, *Les Chambres de Métiers* (Paris: Presses Universitaires de France, 1985), p. 18; Daty, "L'Artisanat en Alsace," p. 93; la Société Savante d'Alsace, *Artisans et ouvriers d'Alsace*, pp. 267–68; Zarca, "Survivance ou transformation," pp. 1050–51.

97. See C. Caillard, *Chambres de métiers et conseils de métiers* (Paris: Librairie de l'Enseignement Technique, 1920), Chapters 2 and 3 on the Alsace Chamber of Trade.

98. Alphonse Daniel, *Les chambres de métiers en France* (Rennes: Presse de la Bretagne, 1922), p. 57.

99. David Blackbourne, "The *Mittelstand* in German Society and Politics, 1871–1914," *Social History* 4 (January 1977): 422; also see Shulamit Volkov, *The Rise of Popular Anti-Modernism in Germany: The Urban Master Artisans, 1873–1896* (Princeton, N.J.: Princeton University Press, 1978), pp. 53–54.

100. Blackbourne, "The *Mittelstand*," p. 410; Robert Gellately, *The Politics of Economic Despair: Shopkeepers and German Politics, 1890–1914* (London: Sage Publications, 1974); Volkov, *The Rise of Popular Anti-Modernism*, pp. 311, 319; Heinrich August Winkler, "From Social Protectionism to National Socialism: The German Small Business Movement in Comparative Perspective," *Journal of Modern History* 48 (1976): 1–14.

101. Noël Metton, *Brève histoire de l'artisanat en France, 1925–1963* (Lyon: L'Artisan de la Métallurgie du Rhône, 1964), pp. 2–3.

102. Jacques Francillon, "Chambres de métiers et syndicats d'artisans: les éléments d'une symbiose" (Chambres de Métiers de la Haute-Savoie, 1962), p. 34.

103. *Gazette* 20 (19 May 1922): 235.

104. This cast some doubt on Peter's position "between capital and labor," as Tailledet noted in *Artisan Français* 142 (15 August 1933).

105. *Gazette* 5 (3 February 1922): 51.

106. Metton, *Brève histoire*, p. 3.

107. Maurice Bouilloux-Lafont, *Les chambres de métiers: comment nous les concevons* (Paris: Payot et Cie., 1919), pp. 88–89.

108. *Gazette* 52 (29 December 1922): 628. See also Blackbourne's comments on participation in the German chambers, "The *Mittelstand*," p. 425.

109. Barraud, *Chambres de métiers*, p. 86.

110. Caillard, *Chambres de Metiers et conseils de métiers*, p. 39; Daniel, *Chambres de métiers en France*, pp. 109, 111; Etienne, "L'Artisanat et l'Education," p. 30.

111. On the Lyon conference see René Dumontier, *Un apôtre de l'artisanat et de la famille: Albert Dupuis, artisan-maître, 1873–1937. Sa vie et son oeuvre* (Yvetot: Imprimerie Commerciale, 1946), p. 139; also the reports in *L'Artisan* 27 (November 1921).

112. Zarca, "Survivance ou transformation, p. 1051. I cautiously accept Zarca's information on Tailledet, first, because I have been able to find almost no evidence

on his background and, second, because it accords with what I was able to glean from conversations with Georges Chaudieu, François Magnien, and Jean Malassigne, veterans of the artisanal movement.

113. *Artisan Cordonnier*. Organe officiel de la Fédération nationale de la petite industrie de la chaussure de France et Provisoirement de la CGAF 1 (30 April 1922): 5. Zarca, in "Survivance ou transformation," p. 1051, writes that the FPIC was founded in 1917.

114. Robert Tailledet, *La doctrine de classe de l'artisanat moderne* (Paris: Institut National des Métiers, 1937), p. 12.

115. On Clémentel see Etienne, "L'Artisanat et l'Education," p. 27; Kuisel, *Capitalism and the State*, pp. 39–56; Charles S. Maier, *Recasting Bourgeois Europe: Stabilization in France, Germany, and Italy in the Decade after World War I* (Princeton: Princeton University Press, 1975), pp. 74–76; Roger Priouret, *Origines du patronat français* (Paris: Editions Bernard Grasset, 1963), p. 232.

116. Henry W. Ehrmann, *Organized Business in France* (Princeton: Princeton University Press, 1957), p. 20.

117. Kuisel, *Capitalism and the State*, p. 56; Maier, *Recasting Bourgeois Europe*, p. 84.

118. *Artisan Français* 8 (October 1926).

119. Quoted in *Artisan* (Lyon) 34 (June 1922).

120. *Artisan Cordonnier* 1 (30 April 1922): 1.

121. For a report on this first congress see *Gazette* 17 (28 April 1922): 194–96.

122. *Gazette* 19 (12 May 1922): 220.

123. *Gazette* 20 (19 May 1922): 236.

124. *Gazette* 13 (31 March 1922): 146.

125. *Gazette* 9 (3 March 1922).

126. *Artisan* (Lyon) 34 (June 1922).

127. *Gazette* 48 (1 December 1922): 578; 50 (15 December 1922): 603.

128. *Gazette* 26 (19 June 1922): 281.

129. Quoted in *Artisan Français* 6 (June 1923).

130. Etienne, "L'Artisanat et l'Education," pp. 31–32, 44.

131. Reproduced in *Artisan Français* 2 (February 1923); and *Gazette* 52 (29 December 1922): 630.

132. *Gazette* 46 (17 November 1922): 556.

133. *Artisan* (Lyon) 40–41 (January–February 1923).

134. *Gazette* 37 (15 September 1922): 446–47; 44 (3 November 1922): 530.

135. *Artisan Français* 5 (May 1923).

136. *Gazette* 33 (18 August 1922): 398.

137. For summaries of the Bordeaux congress see *Artisan* (Lyon) 46 (July 1923); *Gazette* 26 (29 June 1923): 418–19; 27 (6 July 1923): 435–36; and 28 (13 July 1923): 452.

138. Mourier, "L'artisanat," p. 1.

139. Barraud, *Chambres de métiers*, p. 7.

140. Bouilloux-Lafont, *Chambres de métiers*, p. 102.

141. *Le Campagonnage* 44 (February 1921): 2.

142. *Journal Officiel*, Chamber of Deputies, annexe 265, report on the Verlot proposition by Emile Marot, 10 July 1924.

143. On the Astier law see Barraud, *Chambres de métiers*, pp. 23–24; Bouilloux-Lafont, *Chambres de métiers*, pp. 31–32; Jean-Jacques Charles, *L'artisanat: Sa si-*

tuation. See besoins (Clermont-Ferrand: F. Sorlet, 1941), pp. 43–46; Daniel, *Chambres de métiers en France*, p. 24; Magliulo, *Les Chambers de Métiers*, pp. 24–26.

144. On the Verlot proposition see Marot's report in *Journal Officiel*, Chamber of Deputies, annexe 254, 10 July 1924; also *Artisan Français* 4 (April 1924); Barraud, *Chambres de métiers*, pp. 347–59; Caillard, *Chambres de métiers et conseil de métiers*, pp. 108–10; Daniel, *Chambres de métiers en France*, pp. 137–44; *Gazette* 22 (26 August 1921): 206; 31 (28 October 1921): 286; 33 (11 November 1921): 306; Magliulo, *Les chambres de Métiers*, p. 31.

145. "Exposé des motifs," *Journal Officiel*, Chamber of Deputies, annexe 5399, 1922, p. 180.

146. Chambers of trades existed in Limoges, Angers, Laval, Le Mans, Tours, Poitiers, Nîmes, Clermont-Ferrand, Nancy, Nice, Angoulême, Montpellier, Rennes, Troyes, and Roche-sur-Yonne: see Barraud, *Chambres de métiers*, pp. 170–322; Bouilloux-Lafont, *Chambres de métiers*, pp. 106–11; Caillard, *Chambres de métiers et conseils de métiers*, pp. 39–59; Daniel, *Chambres de métiers en France*, pp. 108–22; *Gazette* 33 (17 Auguest 1923): 533; 35 (31 August 1926): 570; Metton, *Brève histoire*, pp. 2–3.

147. Roger Picard, "Les chambres de métiers," *Les Documents du Travail* 61 (May 1922): 152.

148. Barraud, *Chambres de métiers*, pp. 188–93, 289.

149. Daniel, *Chambres de métiers en France*, p. 90.

150. Barraud, *Chambres de métiers*, pp. 193–94; Daniel, *Chambres de métiers en France*, p. 97.

151. Barraud, *Chambres de métiers*, p. 389; Picard, "Les chambres de métiers," p. 157.

152. *Gazette* 22 (1 June 1923): 356.

153. *Gazette* 11 (16 March 1923): 173–74.

154. *Journal Officiel*, Chamber of Deputies, documents parlementaires, report by the Labor Commission on the Courtier proposition, 13 November 1924.

155. *Journal Officiel*, Chamber of Deputies, see the Labor Commission's supplementary reports on the Verlot project, 12 February 1925 and 12 March 1925. Tailledet discussed the passage of the Courtier law and the CGAF's responsibility for it in *Artisan Français* 4 (April 1925) and 7 (July 1925).

156. The text of the law appears in the *Journal Officiel*, Chamber of Deputies, laws and decrees, 30 July 1925. For several considerations of the law, its gaps, and its promises see Assemblée Permanente de Chambres de Metiers, "Etudes sur le droit rélatif á l'exercise des métiers," 1963, pp. 1–3; Hector, *La législation*, pp. 271–331 passim.

157. Mourier, "L'artisanat," p. 167.

Chapter 2

1. *Artisan Français* 2 (February 1924).

2. *Artisan Français* 1 (January 1925); 6 (June 1925); 9 (September 1925); Metton, *Brève histoire*, p. 7.

3. Hubert Ley estimated 250,000 artisans *syndiqués* in the *Gazette* 1 (6 January 1928): 3. *Artisan* (Lyon) 99 (January 1928) reported the same number; however, in his report, in June 1928 to the Congress of the Crédit Populaire d'Annecy, Ley said there were only 150,000 syndicated artisans, some 17% of the population: *Gazette* 27

(6 July 1928): 422. Three years later he reported that only one artisan in eight was *syndiqué*: *Gazette* 23 (5 June 1921): 373. I cannot explain Ley's inconsistency on this matter, but I doubt that he ever wanted to convey the impression that organization among artisans was waning in this period.

4. *Gazette* 33 (15 August 1925): 494; Daty, "L'Artisanat en Alsace," pp. 43–56.

5. *Artisan* (Lyon) 58 (July 1924).

6. *Artisan* (Lyon) 56 (May 1924). The report on litigation appears in *Artisan* 57 (June 1924).

7. *Artisan* (Le Puy) 11 (December 1929); and 3 (March 1932).

8. *Artisan* (Le Puy) 7 (August 1929).

9. *Artisan* (Lyon) 62 (December 1924).

10. *Artisan* (Lyon) 58 (July 1924).

11. *Gazette* 6 (6 February 1925): 82–83; see Tailledet's defense of the CGAF action in *Artisan Français* 9 (September 1925).

12. The CNE provided for two participating and four auxiliary members from the artisanat: *Gazette* 40 (20 October 1925): 587.

13. For a general discussion of the CGAF counterattacks see *Gazette* 39 (25 September 1925): 572. In the beginning of this squabble the *Artisan Français* preferred to say nothing about its rival. On the CGAF lawsuit see *Artisan* (Lyon) 62 (December 1924) and *Gazette* 2 (14 January 1927): 19. Other court cases launched by the CGAF against its challengers are reported in *Artisan* 92–93 (June–July 1927); and 4 (April 1930).

14. *Artisan* (Lyon) 62 (December 1924); 64 (February 1925); *Gazette* 10 (6 March 1925): 149; 34 (3 September 1926): 582.

15. *Artisan Français* 68 (August 1928); *Gazette* 45 (5 November 1926): 793.

16. *Artisan Français* 1 (January–February 1926).

17. *Artisan* (Lyon) 75 (January 1926); *Gazette* 17 (23 April 1926): 258–59.

18. *Artisan Français* 63 (March 1928); 66 (June 1928).

19. *Artisan Français* 4 (May 1926).

20. *Gazette* 24 (11 June 1926): 350; 33 (13 August 1926): 554–57.

21. *Artisan* (Le Puy) 4 (April 1930).

22. *Artisan* (Le Puy) 11 (November 1932); 12 (December 1932); 1 (January 1933).

23. *Artisan Français* 61 (January 1928); 62 (February 1928); 63 (March 1928).

24. Sewell, *Work and Revolution*, p. 11.

25. *Gazette* 20 (19 May 1922): 235.

26. Sewell, *Work and Revolution*, p. 1. Bernard Moss writes similarly that the notion of "trade socialism" was the inspiration for the French labor movement in the nineteenth century. He writes, "The belief that workers could only end their exploitation through their acquisition of the means of production [was] a form of socialism that would preserve the autonomy and the integrity of the trades" in Moss, *The Origins of the French Labor Movement*, p. 156.

27. Tailledet, *La doctrine de class*, p. 14.

28. Tailledet sets forth his philosophy in his essays on "Doctrine," which appeared each month in the *Cahiers de l'Artisanat* (hereafter cited as *Cahiers*). These were later edited and published as *La doctrine de classe*.

29. Grandadam, "Corporation et Syndicat," *Cahiers* 13 (November 1935): 1–7.

30. Robert Tailledet, "Plan d'organisation d'une chambre de métiers," *Cahiers* 1 (October 1934): 8.

31. *Artisan* (Lyon) 72 (October–November 1925).

32. H. Théallier, et al., *Hommes et Métiers* (Paris: Editions 'Je Sers', 1941), p.

82. See also the remark of the sociologist Bernard Zarca: "The men of trades are complicit because they adhere to the same norms of professional excellence and social success," in "Survivance ou transformation," p. 59.

33. Ley, *L'Artisanat*, p. 33.

34. *Cahiers* 4 (January 1935): 6.

35. Georges Chaudieu, *De la gigue d'ours au hamburger, ou la curieuse histoire de la viande* (Chennevières: La Corpo, 1980), p. 103.

36. *Artisan de l'Ouest* (Saint-Brieuc) 22 (March 1937). For a contemporary re-statement see Jean Malassigne, "L'artisanat: vestige du passé? utilité économique? nécessité sociale?" *Droit Social* 12 (December 1966): 614–16.

37. Quoted in *Artisan Français* 1 (January–February 1926). For another consideration of the family and the artisanat see André Siegfried, *Qu'est-ce que l'artisanat?* pp. 16–19.

38. *Information Artisanale* (Paris). Publication mensuelle de l'Office Commercial et Technique de l'Artisanat, n.s., 32 (March 1944).

39. Dumontier, *Un apôtre de l'artisanat*, p. 199. On the political content of family ideology and on the popularity of that ideology in Nazi Germany see Jill Stephenson, *Women in Nazi Society* (London: Croom Helm, 1975), esp. Chapter 2, pp. 37–56.

40. Zarca, "Survivance ou transformation," pp. 22, 391–99.

41. Mourier, "L'artisanat," p. 108.

42. Théallier, *Hommes et Métiers*, p. 10.

43. From a review of a book by Dr. Alex Carrel in *Cahiers* 16 (February 1936): 31.

44. See Grand'mère's columns in *Artisan* (Le Puy) 10 (October 1931); 7 (July 1932).

45. *Artisan* (Lyon) 2 (November 1919).

46. On the question of women in the Alsace Chamber of Trades see *Gazette* 7 (17 February 1922): 76–78; 9 (3 March 1922): 100; and 45 (10 November 1922): 543–44.

47. Delage cited in *Artisan Français* 2 (March 1926). See also the comments in *Artisan Français* 7 (September 1926).

48. *Artisan* (Lyon) 45 (June 1923).

49. *Artisan* (Lyon) 59 (August–September 1924).

50. Henri Mougin, "Un projet d'enquête sur les classes moyennes en France," *Inventaires III: Classes Moyennes*, ed. Raymond Aron, et al. Publications du Centre de Documentation Sociale de l'Ecole Normale Supérieure (Paris: Librairie Félix Alcan, 1939), p. 338.

51. Lucien Gelly, *L'Artisanat rural: ses problèmes actuels*, Institut d'Etudes Corporatives et Sociales (Joigny: Paillard, 1944), pp. 38–39.

52. *Artisan* (Lyon) 68 (June 1925).

53. Isabelle Dudit, *Marbréry: Maître-Artisan* (Paris: Editions de la CGAF, 1930), p. 4.

54. *Artisan* (Le Puy) 2 (February 1932).

55. Adelaïde Blasquez, *Gaston Lucas, sérurrier: chronique de l'anti-héro* (Paris: Plon, 1976), pp. 24–25.

56. Georges Chaudieu, *Artisans et Commerçants* (Paris: Editions C.I.E.M., 1982), p. 24.

57. Bernard Laffaille, "L'artisanat et la défense nationale," *Politique* 3 (March 1940): 182.

58. *Artisan* (Lyon) 2 (November 1919); 3 (December 1919); 23 (July 1921); and 95–96 (September–October 1927).

59. Pierre de Felice, *L'Artisanat Rural* (Paris: Jouve, 1930), p. 27.

60. Comité d'entente et d'action artisanales (hereafter cited as CEAA), 3e Cong. Nat., St. Etienne, 1936, p. 73.

61. *Artisan Français* 102 (June 1931).

62. Gresle, "Indépendants et petits patrons," p. 950.

63. Debré, *L'Artisanat: Classe sociale*, p. 227.

64. *Artisan Français* 100 (April 1931); *Cahiers* 9 (June 1935): 7.

65. See Peter's remarks in "La situation de l'artisanat en Europe," p. 2; Hubert Ley, "The Battle against Unfair Competition," CEAA, 1er Cong. Nat., Lille, 1934, p. 63; and *Gazette* 32 (11 August 1922): 388.

66. *Artisan* (Le Puy) 1 (January 1932).

67. *Artisan* (Le Puy) 1 (January–February 1936).

68. *Artisan Français* 9 (September 1923); 1 (January–February 1926).

69. *Artisan Français* 2 (March 1926).

70. *Artisan Français* 8 (October 1926).

71. *Gazette* 10 (7 March 1924): 147.

72. See the article, "Etudes: Les Allocations familiales," in *Cahiers* 8 (May 1935): 9; Lefranc, *Le mouvement syndical*, p. 300; Alfred Sauvy, *Histoire économique de la France entre les deux guerres*, 3 vols. (Paris: Fayard, 1967), 2 (1931–1939): 44.

73. On the functions of the chambers of trades see *Cahiers* 28 (February 1937): 48–52; Demondion, *L'artisanat dans l'état moderne*, p. 155; Dumontier, *Un apôtre de l'artisanat*, p. 112.

74. *Artisan* (Lyon) 61 (November 1924); 74 (December 1925); 87 (January 1927).

75. *Artisan Français* 101 (May 1931).

76. *Artisan* (Lyon) 102 (April 1928); Hector, *La législation*, p. 271.

77. *Artisan Français* 88 (April 1930); Francillon, "Chambres de métiers and syndicats d'artisans," p. 39.

78. *Artisan* (Le Puy) 10 (November 1929).

79. *Artisan* (Le Puy) 4 (May 1929).

80. *Artisan* (Le Puy) 5 (May 1933); 2 (February 1934).

81. Quoted in *Artisan Français* 101 (May 1931). On chamber of commerce obstruction see also Etienne, "L'Artisanat et l'Education," p. 57; and Metton, *Brève histoire*, p. 5.

82. Magliulo, *Les Chambres de Métiers*, p. 55.

83. *Artisan du Loiret*. Organe des artisans confédérés d'Orléans, de Pithiviers et du secteur administratif de Gien, 3 (December 1934).

84. Quoted in *Artisan Français* 105 (September 1931).

85. *Artisan Français* 103 (July 1931).

86. *Artisan Français* 105 (September 1931).

87. *Gazette* 3 (17 January 1930): 38–39.

88. *Gazette* 18 (1 May 1931): 286.

89. For the artisanal population of the department of the Seine see the Archives of the Chambre de Commerce et d'Industrie, Paris (hereafter cited as CCIP) II 5.413, "Apprentissage. Organisation. Chambres de Métiers et d'Apprentissage, 1929–1949," letter from the prefect of the Seine to the Chamber of Commerce, 30 June 1930.

90. *Artisan Français* 131 (15 January 1933); *Gazette* 14 (6 April 1934): 238; Dumontier, *Un apôtre de l'artisanat*, pp. 133–34.

91. Dumontier, *Un apôtre de l'artisanat*, pp. 133–34; *Gazette* 8 (19 February 1932): 132.

92. *Artisan* (Le Puy) 12 (December 1930); *Artisan Français* 140 (30 June–15 July 1933); Dumontier, *Un apôtre de l'artisanat*, p. 141. It seems that the CGAF also engaged in electoral fraud: see the report by the Paris Chamber of Commerce's Service Technique Etudes, in CCIP II 5.413, "Apprentissage."

93. Assemblée des Présidents des Chambres de Métiers (hereafter cited as APCMF), minutes of the meeting of 23 May 1933, p. 29. See also the report on the elections in the Loire-Inférieure, in *Coiffeur Nantais*. Bulletin trimestriel de la Chambre syndicale des maîtres et artisans coiffeurs de Nantes et Région 7 (July 1934).

94. On the creation of the Union des chambres de métiers confédérées see *Artisan Français* 161 (30 June–31 July 1934) and 162 (15 August 1934); Dumontier, *Un apôtre de l'artisanat*, p. 143. For the protest against the CGAF's heavy hand with its own supporters see APCMF, 22 May 1933, pp. 80–83.

95. *Gazette* 14 (6 April 1934): 238.

96. APCMF, 15 November 1934, pp. 48–50, 60.

97. For the story of these negotiations see APCMF, 26 November 1935, pp. 31–37; 17 November 1936, pp. 118–19; 15 November 1937, pp. 17–20; and 15 May 1939, pp. 16–18.

98. *Gazette* 4 (27 January 1933): 50. The circular itself was reprinted in Alfred Gutersohn, "Nature et importance de l'artisanat dans l'économie publique moderne," *Annals de droit économique. Aspects de l'artisanat en France et à l'étranger*, ed. J. Hamel and H. Bye, n. s. 4 (1953): 8. It read:

> The patron remains an artisan insofar as the number of auxiliaries he employs does not prevent him from participating personally in the material work of his trade. This personal participation in the manual labor of the trade must be *courante*, constant, and genuinely effective.
>
> The number of his assistants is then only one of the elements that must be taken into account to assess the quality of an artisan; it furthermore cannot be fixed in a uniform fashion for the entire range of trades and for every individual business. In one profession the patron would be an *industriel* with a small number of workers, in another he could remain an artisan with a relatively important number of journeymen.
>
> These, in sum, are questions to which the practical experience of each trade will have to respond and which, if this is impossible, will be decided by the [local] tribunals.

99. *Artisan Français* 118 (31 May 1932).

100. *Artisan Français* 139 (31 May–15 June 1933).

101. *Artisan Français* 67 (July 1928); see also the article by A. Broulliard, "Doctrine de classe," *Artisan Français* 83 (November 1929).

102. *Artisan Français* 118 (May 1932); Demondion, *L'artisanat dans l'état moderne*, p. 110.

103. APCMF, 23 May 1933, p. 75; *Artisan du Loiret* 2 (November 1934). The affair also produced a nasty exchange of letters between Marc-Edouard Morgaut, the secretary of the Loiret Chamber of Trades, and the local Fédération artisanale, loyal to the CGAF, which can be found in the Archives of the Chambre de Métiers du Loiret, obtained for me by Madame Chantal Cresson of the Assemblée Permanente des Chambres de Métiers, Paris.

104. *Artisan Français* 108 (December 1931); *Gazette* 8 (24 February 1933): 119; 10 (9 March 1934): 161.

105. For comments see *Artisan* (Le Puy) 6 (July 1933); 1 (January 1934); *Gazette* 14 (7 April 1933): 228; 6 (9 February 1934): 97.

106. *Artisan Français* 144 (15 September 1933).

107. *Gazette* 33 (12 August 1932): 699.

108. *Gazette* 5 (3 February 1933): 66.

109. APCMF, 23 May 1933, p. 71.

110. Fernand Peter, "L'Artisanat sera Régionalist et Corporatif ou il ne sera pas!" report to the CEAA, 3e Cong. Nat., Saint-Etienne, 1936, p. 85.

111. *Gazette* 14 (7 April 1933): 226.

112. *Artisan* (Le Puy) 4 (April 1933); *Gazette* 13 (31 March 1933): 210.

113. *Gazette* 47 (24 November 1933): 887; and 49 (8 December 1933): 921–23.

114. For the secession of the UAF see CEAA, 1er Cong. Nat., Lille, 1934, pp. 21–22; 2e Cong. Nat., Toulouse, 1935, p. 26.

115. See the report to the Paris Chamber of Commerce by Jules Loebnitz, "La réforme de l'artisanat," 18 November 1930 in CCIP III 4.13, "Artisans, 1925–1934."

116. *Artisan* (Le Puy) 2 (February 1933); and 13 (1 January 1934).

117. *Artisan*. Organe mensuel du groupement artisanal de Béziers et arrondissement de Béziers-Saint-Pons, 4–5 (April–May 1934); *Artisan Coiffeur*. Organe des syndicats des patrons coiffeurs des départements de l'Allier, de la Nièvre et du Puy-de-Dôme (Moulins), 49 (November 1936).

118. Dumontier, *Un apôtre de l'artisanat*, pp. 168–69. See also the minutes of the meeting of the Commission de l'Artisanat, 1926–1936, in Archives Nationales F^{12} 10230. See also the pamphlet by the president of the CGAF, Jean-Jacques Stefanelly, "L'artisanat, a-t-il sa chance dans le monde moderne?" (unpublished, 1955), which can be found in the Bibliothèque Nationale, Paris.

119. APCMF, 26 November 1936, p. 13; *Artisan du Loiret* 3 (December 1934); and 10 (March 1936); *Artisan Français* 170 (15 December 1934).

120. Léon Bossavy, the APCMF's treasurer, opened each of the biannual meetings with a report on the budget.

121. APCMF, 15 November 1937, p. 9; 23 May 1938, p. 10.

122. See Albert Dupuis' complaints about the Assembly's treatment by the state in APCMF, 26 November 1936, p. 16. Dupuis' successor, Coustenoble, repeated these complaints and also tried unsuccessfully to put an end to the byzantine discussions and resolutions: APCMF, 15 May 1939, pp. 20–21.

123. Archives Nationales, F^{12} 9404, "Association pour la Renovation Artisanale Rurale." For the CEAA auxiliaries see CEAA, 1er Cong. Nat., Lille, 1934, pp. 50–51; 2e Cong. Nat., Saint-Etienne, 1936, pp. 12–15.

124. *Artisan Français* 166 (15 October 1934); *Cahiers* 4 (January 1935): 22, 27.

125. *Cahiers* 36 (November 1937): 310.

126. *Cahiers* 36 (November 1937): 299–304, 309–10.

127. *Cahiers* 53 (May 1939); see also the reports given at the third national congress of the INM in *Cahiers* 16 (February 1936): 28–29.

128. *Gazette* 43 (26 October 1923): 682–83.

129. See the "Rapport sur l'activité et la réorganisation de l'Institut International de l'Artisanat," *Cahiers* 32 (June 1937): 162–66; *Gazette* 41 (10 October 1930): 729–30.

130. *Artisan Français* 78 (June 1929); 100 (April 1931); *Gazette* 37 (13 September 1929): 662; 44 (28 October 1923): 907.

131. *Cahiers* 32 (June 1937): 167–69; CEAA, "La situation artisanal en Europe," presented to the 4e Cong. Nat., Paris, 1937, p. 2.

132. *Artisan Français* 66 (June 1928) discusses the parliamentary defense group; see also "Le groupe de défense artisanale de la Chambre des Députés," *Cahiers* 28 (February 1937): 62–63.

133. The easiest way to get a general grasp of the mountain of laws, decrees, and ministerial *arrêtés* and circulars touching the artisanat in the interwar period is to look at the summary of government action in favor of the artisanat since 1919, "Essai d'un plan de redressement artisanal," *Cahiers* 49 (January 1939): 1–6.

134. Azzano, *Mes joyeuses années*, p. 34.

135. Claude-François Bénard, *La notion d'artisan dans la loi et les faits* (Paris: Librairie Ernest Sagot, 1927), p. 165.

Chapter 3

1. C.-J. Gignoux, *L'économie française entre les deux guerres, 1919–1939* (Paris: Société d'Editions Economiques et Sociales, 1942), p. 88. Gignoux's book was a compilation of lessons he had given during the winter of 1941–1942 at the Ecole Supérieure d'Organisation Professionnelle.

2. Kuisel, *Capitalism and the State*, p. 93.

3. Alfred Sauvy, *Histoire économique* 2: 25; Jacques Néré, *La Troisième République, 1914–1940* (Paris: Armand Colin, 1967), p. 117; Trotignon, *La France au XXe siècle*, pp. 135–36.

4. J.-C. Asselin, "La semaine de quarante heures, le chômage et l'emploi," *Le Mouvement Social* 54 (January–March 1966): 187–91; Julian Jackson, *The Politics of Depression in France, 1932–1936* (Cambridge: Cambridge University Press, 1985), pp. 29–30; Institut National de la Statistique et d'Etudes Economiques (INSEE), *Mouvement économique en France de 1944 à 1957* (Paris: Presses Universitaires de France, 1958), p. 55, puts the highest figure at 864,170 in March 1936; see also the report on world unemployment by Edouard Châtillon in 1934 in Archives Nationales F^{22} 677.

5. Kuisel, *Capitalism and the State*, pp. 96–97.

6. Caron, *An Economic History*, p. 258.

7. Cahen, "La concentration," p. 851.

8. Debré, *L'Artisanat: classe sociale*, p. 110.

9. Carré, et al., *French Economic Growth*, pp. 162–63.

10. *Journal Officiel*, Chamber of Deputies, 26 March 1935; see the description of Paulin and Jean Lerolle's spirited defense of artisanal interests on this occasion in Paulin's article, "Glane parlementaire: l'artisanat à la Chambre," *Cahiers* 8 (May 1935): 28.

11. Lagaillarde's figures appear in *Artisan Français* 72 (December 1928); see also Hermine Rabinovitch, "L'évolution récente de l'artisanat et ses problèmes," *Revue International du Travail* 17 (1928): 875.

12. P. Audibert, "Les Artisans," *Informations Sociales* 12 (1977): 18; Debré, *L'Artisanat: Classe sociale*, p. 110; Demondion, *L'artisanat dans l'état moderne*, pp. 28–30. Lagaillarde and Rabinovitch used the CGAF's preferred definition, including only those in the so-called artisanal professions with five or fewer employees. Debré, cited by Demondion, counted enterprises with up to ten *compagnons*; he eliminated from his figures *travailleurs à domicile* and the *métiers d'alimentation* (butchers, bakers, etc.) and added *coiffeurs*.

13. *Artisan Français* 66 (June 1928), report by Georges Grandadam to the seventh national congress of the CGAF; *Gazette* 23 (5 June 1931): 382.

14. APCMF, 15 May 1935, p. 110.

15. Henri Mourier, "Essai de statistiques artisanales," *Annals de droit économique. Aspects de l'artisanat en France et à l'étranger*, n. s., 4 (1953): 74–75.

16. Mourier, "Essai," p. 83.

17. Cahen, "La concentration," pp. 867–70, especially the graphs.

18. Mourier, "L'artisanat," p. 110.

19. Paul Bachelard, *Industrialisation de la région Centre: Transformations économiques et socio-politiques* (Tours: Gilbert-Clarty, 1978), pp. 75, 81.

20. Zarca, "Survivance ou transformation," pp. 175–85.

21. Archives Nationales, F^{12} 8792, report by Boissard, Inspecteur des Finances, to the CNE, 12 December 1931.

22. Archives Nationales F^{12} 8792, report to the Council by Charles Ettori, Maître des Requêtes au Conseil d'Etat, 27 April 1933, pp. 8–9.

23. Maxime Perrin, "La région industrielle de Saint-Etienne. Etude de géographie économique," (thèse pour le doctorat ès-lettres, Paris, 1937), pp. 273–318.

24. Bachelard, *Industrialisation de la région Centre*, p. 134; L.-A. Vincent, "Population active, production, et productivité dans 21 branches de l'économie française (1896–1962)," *Etudes et Conjoncture* 2 (February 1965): 84–85.

25. Perrin, "La région industrielle," pp. 236–38.

26. Gresle, "Indépendants et petits patrons," pp. 205–9.

27. Chaudieu, *Au temps des charrues*, pp. 32–89 passim.

28. François-Paul Raynal, *Les artisans du village* (Paris: Editions de l'Institut d'Etudes Corporatives et Sociales, 1943), p. 9.

29. Gelly, *L'Artisanat rural*, pp. 10, 23. See also the stories relating the "situation tragique de l'artisanat rural" in *Information Artisanale. Organe officiel du CEAA et des Principales Confédérations Françaises de Métiers Artisanals*, 3 (March 1939), taken from *Front Economique*, 30 March 1939.

30. Cited in *Gazette* 13 (1 April 1927): 194–95.

31. Gordon Wright, *Rural Revolution in France: The Peasantry in the Twentieth Century* (Stanford: Stanford University Press, 1964), p. 41.

32. Hubert Ley once put the figure at around 70 percent (600,000 out of 850,000), and Gelly estimated that rural artisans made up about half (450,000 out of 900,000) of the artisanat, but these figures were surely inflated for effect: see *Gazette* 33 (17 August 1923): 530 and Ley's report to the twenty-second congress of the Crédit populaire, *Gazette* 27 (6 July 1928): 422. Also see Gelly, *L'Artisanat rural*, p. 62.

33. Barral, "Le monde agricole," p. 321.

34. Pierre de Felice, *L'artisanat rural* (Paris: Jouve, 1930), 54; Gelly, *L'artisanat rural*, p. 70.

35. Institut de Science Economique Appliquée (hereafter cited as ISEA), "Maréchal-Forgeron," *Enquête sur l'artisanat* (1946), p. 45.

36. Barral, "Le monde agricole," pp. 323–24; ISEA, "Maréchal-Forgeron," 22–23; La Société Savante d'Alsace, *Artisans et Ouvriers*, p. 342.

37. *Artisan Français* 101 (May 1931).

38. *Gazette* 37 (12 September 1930): 622.

39. Etienne, "L'Artisanat et l'Education," p. 187.

40. Jacqueline Constant, *Industrie à domicile salariée* (Paris: Librairie Technique et Economique, 1937), pp. 22–26; J. Klatzman, *Le travail à domicile dans l'industrie parisienne du vêtement* (Paris: A. Colin, 1957), pp. 120–21.

41. Sauvy, *Histoire économique*, 2: 116; J.-J. Carré, P. Dubois, and E. Malinvaud, *French Economic Growth*, trans. John P. Hatfield (Stanford: Stanford University

Press, 1975), pp. 162–63. See the artisans' discussion of the problem in APCMF, 26 November 1934, pp. 118–26.

42. Archives Nationales CE⁹, "Résumé de la question," 20 July 1937; and a report by the Fédération nationale du bâtiment et des travaux publics—both in the dossier labeled *Travail noir*.

43. On the question of *prisunics* see Archives Nationales F²² 679, The Annecy Chamber of Commerce's criticism of a report by Senator Callier; APCMF, 29 November 1933, pp. 141–42; *Gazette* 41 (13 October 1933): 785; 44 (3 November 1933): 835. For various plans to curb the expansion of big retailers see Archives Nationales CE⁸, report by Monsieur Maus, president of the Fédération des commerçants détaillants de France; Serge Berstein, "Le Parti Républicain Radical et Radical-Socialiste en France de 1919 à 1939," 3 vols. (thèse pour le doctorat d'état, Paris-Nanterre, 1976), p. 857.

44. Archives Nationales F⁷ 13696, "Commerçants, 1935–1936."

45. *Gazette* 30 (27 July 1934): 507.

46. Archives Nationales F¹² 8793, proceedings of the CNE meeting of 9 November 1932; Archives Nationales CE⁹, report by the Fédération nationale du bâtiment et des travaux publics; Gignoux, *L'économie française*, p. 88.

47. Archives Nationales F²² 669.

48. APCMF, 23 May 1938, p. 63; *Gazette* 22 (27 May 1932): 390–91.

49. *Artisan du Bois*. Journal mensuel et fiscal édité par le syndicat des artisans menuisiers du Havre et groupant toutes les professions similaires, 6 (July 1935).

50. Jackson, *Politics of Depression*, p. 4; Néré, *La Troisième République*, p. 126; Sauvy, *Histoire économique*, 2: 349.

51. Kuisel, *Capitalism and the State*, p. 97.

52. Sauvy, *Histoire économique*, 2: 356; Caron, *An Economic History*, p. 263; Stephen Cohen, *Modern Capitalist Planning: The French Model* (Cambridge, Mass.: Harvard University Press, 1969), pp. 84–85.

53. Sauvy, *Histoire économique*, 2: 357; Jackson, *Politics of Depression*, esp. Chapter 3, pp. 35–49; Peter J. Larmour, *The French Radical Party in the Thirties* (Stanford: Stanford University Press, 1964), pp. 74–75.

54. Sauvy, *Histoire économique*, 2: 361; see also Jackson, *Politics of Depression*, p. 47.

55. *Gazette* 51 (19 December 1930): 926.

56. *Artisan Français* 140 (30 June–15 July 1933); 170 (15 December 1934); *Cahiers* 14 (December 1935): 14; CEAA, 3e Cong. Nat., Toulouse, 1935, pp. 60–61. See also Daty, "L'Artisanat en Alsace," p. 74; Hector, *La législation*, pp. 253-60.

57. Debré, *L'Artisanat: Classe sociale*, p. 227.

58. See *Artisan Français* 119 (15 June 1932); 140 (30 June–15 July 1933), for the specific problems of the Seine department.

59. Léon Mabille, "Les modifications à la loi des assurances sociales concernant les artisans," *Cahiers* 9 (June 1935): 16. See also Hector, *La législation*, pp. 235–47; and the debate on artisanal *caisses de chômage* in APCMF, 15 May 1936, pp. 71–84.

60. Archives Nationales F²² 678.

61. Archives Nationales F²² 678. Cartons 676 to 683 in this series, "Voeux locaux rélatifs au chômage, 1934–1936," are full of the correspondence of the labor minister with the committees of the unemployed, municipal and departmental councils, chambers of trades, and chambers of commerce. See also Albert Paulin's interpellation of the government, in the *Journal Officiel*, Chamber of Deputies, 26 March 1935.

62. Archives Nationales F^{22} 683, letter of 12 June 1936.

63. Archives Nationales F^{22} 677–678.

64. See the report by Fernand Peter, "Why a CEAA?" in CEAA, 2e Cong. Nat., Lille, 1934, p. 103.

65. *Artisan Français* 155 (28 February 1934).

66. See, for example, François Goguel, *La politique des partis sous la Troisième République* (Paris: Editions du Seuil, 1948), pp. 547–50; Jacques Ollé-Laprune, *La stabilité des ministres sous la Troisième République* (Paris: Librairie Générale de Droit et de Jurisprudence, 1962), pp. 296–98.

67. François Caron and Jean Bouvier, "Guerre, crise, guerre, 1914–1939," *Histoire économique*, 4: 793.

68. Maier, *Recasting Bourgeois Europe*, pp. 583–93. Covering some of the same ground, though not always with the same insight, are Shepard B. Clough, *France: A History of National Economics, 1789–1939* (New York: C. Scribner's Sons, 1939), p. 298; Kuisel, *Capitalism and the State*; Jean-Philippe Parrot, *La représentation des intérêts dans le mouvement des idées politiques* (Paris: Presses Universitaires de France, 1974), pp. i–iii. Yves Ullmo writes in this regard: "Government was the main beneficiary [of the shift in concern to social and economic issues] through a gradual weakening of the parliament, without the government itself, for lack of a framework for ensuring consistent action, being able to appreciate all the practical implications of the day-to-day economic and social decisions which it took." Yves Ullmo, "France," *Planning, Politics and Public Policy: The British, French, and Italian Experience*, ed. Jack Hayward and Michael Watson (Cambridge: Cambridge University Press, 1975), p. 24.

69. Jackson, *Politics of Depression*, p. 114; Kuisel, *Capitalism and the State*, p. 105; Parrot, *La représentation des intérêts*, p. 155; Sauvy, *Histoire économique*, 2: 357.

70. Quoted in Georges Dubost, *Le Conseil National Economique: Ses origines, son institution et son organisation. Son oeuvre et son avenir* (Paris: Editions Domat-Montchrestien, 1936), p. 117. For a general discussion of these plans see Dubost, *Le Conseil National Economique*, pp. 353–60; and Kuisel, *Capitalism and the State*, pp. 98–118.

71. Alroy, "Radicalism and Modernization, p. 3; Berstein, "Le Parti Républicain Radical et Radical-Socialiste," pp. 58, 213; Larmour, *The French Radical Party*, pp. 18–19.

72. The quote is from Berstein, "Le Parti Républicain Radical et Radical-Socialiste," p. 683; on the radical Young Turks also see Jean-Thomas Nordmann, *Histoire des Radicaux, 1820–1973* (Paris: La Table Ronde, 1974), pp. 237–42; Kuisel, *Capitalism and the State*, p. 102.

73. On corporatism see Matthew Elbow, *French Corporative Theory: A Chapter in the History of Ideas* (New York: Columbia University Press, 1953); and Gaëtan Pirou, *Les doctrines économiques en France depuis 1870* (Paris: Librairie Armand Colin, 1925), pp. 172–82.

74. *Gazette* 39 (28 September 1934): 697.

75. On the Union des corporations françaises and the Institut Carrel see Yves Guichet, *Georges Valois. L'Action Française—le Faisceau—la République Syndicale* (Paris: Editions Albatros, 1975), p. 99; and Eugen Weber, *Action Française: Royalism and Reaction in Twentieth-Century France* (Stanford: Stanford University Press, 1962), pp. 205, 212. For the fascists' affinity for corporatist social theories see Klaus-Jürgen Müller, "French Fascism and Modernization," *Journal of Contemporary History* 11

(1976): passim; J. Plumyène and R. Lasierra, *Les fascismes français, 1923–1963* (Paris: Editions du Seuil, 1963); Zeev Sternhell, *Neither Right nor Left: Fascist Ideology in France*, trans. David Maisel (Berkeley: University of California Press, 1986), pp. 64, 92.

76. Parrot, *La représentation des intérêts*, pp. 3, 83.

77. For just a sample of the literature see "La lutte contre le communisme. L'ordre corporatif," Compte-rendu des journées d'études de la Fédération nationale catholique, Paris, 26–27 October 1936; Roger Bonnard, *Syndicalisme, corporatisme et Etat corporatif* (Paris: R. Pichon et R. Durand-Auzeas, 1937); Maurice Bouvier-Ajam, *La doctrine corporative* (Paris: Librairie du Recueil Sirey, 1937); Fernand Fillon, *Vers le corporatisme* (Paris: Berger-Leurault, 1938); Pierre Jolly, *La mystique du corporatisme* (Paris: Hachette, 1935); François Perroux, *Capitalisme et communauté du travail. Corporatisme et capitalisme. Corporatismes réalisés. Communauté du travail* (Paris: Librairie du Recueil Sirey, 1938); Gaëtan Pirou, *Le corporatisme: corporatisme et libéralisme; corporatisme et étatisme; corporatisme et syndicalisme* (Paris: Librairie du Recueil Sirey, 1935); *Essai sur le corporatisme* (Paris: Librairie du Recueil Sirey, 1938); *Néo-libéralisme, néo-corporatisme, néo-socialisme* (Paris: Gallimard, 1939); Louis Salleron, *Un régime corporatif pour l'agriculture* (Paris: Dunod, 1937); Georges Viance, *Démocratie, dictature et corporatisme* (Paris: Flammarion, 1938); *Restauration corporative de la nation française* (Paris: Flammarion, 1936).

78. Henry Laufenburger, *L'intervention de l'état en matière économique* (Paris: Librairie Générale de Droit et de Jurisprudence, 1939), p. 283.

79. Dubost, *Le Conseil National Economique*, pp. 59–63; Georges Lefranc, *Le mouvement syndical*, p. 287; Parrot, *La représentation des intérêts*, pp. 143, 148. See also the analysis of Leo Panitch, "Trade Unions and the Capitalist State," *New Left Review* 125 (January–February 1981): 26.

80. See Hubert Ley's "Rapport Moral," to the CEAA, 2e Cong. Nat., Lille, 1934, p. 20.

81. *Gazette* 16 (20 April 1934): 272.

82. For some of these plans see Fernand Peter, "Vers un corporatisme artisanal: le CEAA, champion de l'idée corporative dans l'artisanat," CEAA, 3e Cong. Nat., Toulouse, 1935, pp. 95–99; *Gazette* 39 (28 September 1934): 697; Ley, *L'Artisanat*, p. 175.

83. *Gazette* 45 (8 November 1935): 749.

84. *Gazette* 52 (29 December 1933): 940.

85. *Gazette* 16 (20 April 1934): 272.

86. *Artisan Français* 103 (July 1931); also see Robert Tailledet, "L'Artisanat et les doctrines économiques," *Cahiers* 31 (May 1937): 136.

87. *Artisan Français* 119 (June 1932).

88. The first quotation is from "Le CNE," *Cahiers* 18 (April 1936): 5; the second is from *Artisan Français* 242 (1 September 1937). See also "La création et le fonctionnement d'une représentation professionnelle et économique devant l'état," *Cahiers* 3 (December 1934): 137.

89. Armand Kopp, *Le rôle de groupements professionnels dans l'organisation de la profession* (Nancy: Bailly et Wettstein, 1937), p. 108.

90. *Artisan* (Le Puy) 11 (November 1931).

91. Arno Mayer, "The Lower Middle Class as Historical Problem," *Journal of Modern History* 47 (September 1975): 436. See also Henri Colliard, *Le corporatisme et la lutte des classes* (Rive-de-Gier: Imprimerie de Grataloup, 1940); Nicos Poulantzas, *Classes in Contemporary Capitalism*, trans. David Fernbach (London: Verso, 1978),

p. 295; Frank Bechhofer and Brian Elliot, quoted in Richard Scase, "The Petty Bourgeoisie and Modern Capitalism: A Consideration of Recent Theories," *Social Class and the Division of Labor. Essays in Honor of Ilya Neustadt*, ed. Anthony Giddens and Gavin Mackenzie (Cambridge: Cambridge University Press, 1982), p. 149. For a general consideration of the question see Pierre Ayçoberry, *The Nazi Question: An Essay on the Interpretations of National Socialism, 1922–1975*, trans. Robert Hurley (New York: Pantheon, 1981), esp. Chapter 9, pp. 149–79.

92. Seymour Martin Lipset, *Political Man: The Social Bases of Politics* (Garden City: Doubleday and Co., 1963), pp. 127–37; Wolfgang Sauer, "National Socialism: Totalitarianism or Fascism?" *American Historical Review* 73 (December 1967), passim. Even Robert Soucy writes that "French fascism was essentially part of a middle class backlash to Marxism and to the Third Republic that had allowed it to grow," in Soucy, *French Fascism*, p. xix.

93. See the pamphlets in the Bibliothèque Nationale, Paris: Jeunesses Patriotes, *Tractes Politiques, 1928–1935*; Parti Populaire Français, *Tractes Politiques, 1932–1938*; Croix de Feu, Parti Social Français, *Tractes Politiques, 1934–1939*.

94. On the decree-law of July 1934 see *Artisan* (Le Puy) 1 (January–February 1935); *Artisan Français* 163 (31 August 1934); Caro, "Le regime des artisans," pp. 100–101; Coulon, *L'artisanat devant l'impôt*, p. 11; *Journal Officiel*, Chamber of Deputies, 26 March 1935: Interpellation of the government.

95. *Gazette* 7 (15 February 1935): 103.

96. See the promises of the finance minister, Piétri, to Paulin in *Journal Officiel*, Chamber of Deputies, 26 March 1935; also *Gazette* 2 (10 January 1936): 28.

97. APCMF, 26 November 1934, pp. 123–26. See also Archives Nationales F²² 679, "Syndicat Français de la Couture," letter to the labor minister, Froissard, 5 January 1936.

98. *Gazette* 23 (7 June 1935): 371.

99. Archives Nationales CE8, "Report by the Chambre de Commerce de Lyon to the Commission chargée d'examiner la situation des magasins à commerce multiples," 7 November 1938. See also the census of artisans conducted by the Grenoble Chamber of Trades in 1939, which counted a large number of foreign-born artisans, especially among the mirrormakers and glaziers, 94 percent of whom were not French: *Artisan des Alpes*. Organe officiel de la Fédération des Artisans des Alpes et des Unions et Syndicats d'Artisans de la Région des Alpes (Grenoble), 119 (February 1939).

100. *Artisan du Loiret* 8 (October 1935); Hector, *La législation*, pp. 181–93; Sauvy, *Histoire économique*, 2: 374.

101. Hector, *La législation*, pp. 172, 205–09.

102. Archives Nationales F²² 679, "Prix Uniques: Fight Against Them!"; *Artisan* (Le Puy) 2 (February 1934); Berstein, "Le Parti Républicain Radical et Radical-Socialiste," p. 857; Caron and Bouvier, "Guerre, crise, guerre," p. 807; *Gazette* 10 (6 March 1936): 162; Titus Petringenar, *Le rôle des classes moyennes dans le société contemporaine* (thèse pour le doctorat, Faculté de Droit, Paris) (Paris: Maurice Lavergne, 1940), pp. 143–44.

103. "Essai d'un Plan de Redressement Artisanal (II)," *Cahiers* 49 (January 1939): 6. See also Dubost, "Conseil National Economique," pp. 106, 118–19.

104. See, for example, *Artisan Français* 175 (28 February 1935).

105. Demondion, *L'Artisanat dans l'état moderne*, p. 13; Mourier, "L'artisanat," p. 8.

106. On the supposed flaws of French capitalists see Tom Kemp, *The French*

Economy, 1919–1939: A History of National Decline (London: Longman, 1972), p. 84; Stanley Hoffmann, "Paradoxes of the French Political Community," *In Search of France: The Economy, Society, and Political System of the Twentieth Century*, ed. Hoffmann (New York: Harper and Row, 1965), p. 6; David Landes, "French Business and the Businessman," *Modern France: Problems of the Third and Fourth Republics*, ed. Edward Mead Earle (Princeton: Princeton University Press, 1951), p. 334.

107. On the contract between the republic and small property see R. D. Anderson, *France, 1870–1914: Politics and Society* (London: Routledge and Kegan Paul, 1977), p. 32; Sanford Elwitt, *The Making of the Third Republic: Class and Politics in France, 1868–1884* (Baton Rouge: Louisiana State University Press, 1975), p. 9; Herbert Lüthy, *France Against Herself: The Past, Politics and Crises of Modern France*, trans. Eric Mosbacher (New York: Meridion Books, 1957), esp. Part II, Chapter 4, pp. 158–69.

108. Sauvy, *Histoire économique*, 2: 376. For similar analyses see Jean Alexandre, *Le métier artisanal: souvenir, utopie, réalité?* (Paris: Casterman, 1947), pp. 68–71; Laufenburger, *L'intervention de l'état*, p. 309.

109. Archives Nationales CE[37], meeting of the tenth professional section (leather and skins), 8 February 1938: see the remarks of Hannotin.

110. Archives Nationales CE8, report by the Commission constituée pour examiner l'opportunité d'une prolongation des effects de la loi du 22 mars 1936, sur la protection de l'industrie et du commerce de la chaussure; François Caron and Jean Bouvier, "Structure des firmes, emprise de l'état," *Histoire économique*, tome 4, vol 2: 807; Kopp, *Le rôle de groupements professionnels*, p. 31; Kuisel, *Capitalism and the State*, p. 95; Laufenburger, *L'Intervention de l'état*, p. 178; Petringenar, *Le rôle des classes moyennes*, p. 145.

111. *L'Artisan* (Le Puy) 1 (January 1932); 9 (September 1932).

112. Sauvy, *Histoire économique*, 2: 372.

113. Archives Nationales CE[8], report by the Commission . . . de la loi du 22 mars 1936.

114. Archives Nationales CE[35], meeting of the tenth professional section, 7 April 1937.

115. Archives Nationales CE[37], meeting of the tenth professional section, 8 February 1938.

116. Archives Nationales CE[35], meeting of the tenth professional section, 7 April 1937.

117. Archives Nationales, CE[37], meeting of the tenth professional section, 29 October 1937.

118. *Artisan Français* 154 (15 February 1934). I have no doubt that among the rioters of February 6, 1934 were a number of master artisans, but I have found no evidence that any of the artisanal organizations were involved as such or that artisans were represented to any significant extent. On the *journée* of February 6, in general, see Serge Berstein, *Le 6 février 1934* (Paris: Editions Gallimard/Julliard, 1975).

Chapter 4

1. Berstein, "Le Parti Républicain Radical et Radical-Socialiste," p. 1146; Georges Lefranc, *Histoire du Front Populaire (1934–1938)*, 2nd ed. (Paris: Payot, 1974), p. 285.

2. Lefranc, *Histoire du Front Populaire*, p. 142; Jackson, *Politics of Depression*, p. 131.

3. *Artisan Français* 207 (10 June 1936).

4. Etienne, "L'Artisanat et l'Education," p. 68.

5. *Artisan de l'Ouest* 15 (July 1936). See also Archives Nationales CE[35], meeting of the ninth professional section (construction and public works), 8 January 1937; J.-C. Asselin, "La semaine de quarante heures," p. 191; "Les 40 heures et les artisans," *Cahiers* 31 (May 1937): 14–44; *Gazette* 32 (6 August 1937): 567, reference to an article by André Lavedan in the *Journée Industrielle*; Lefranc, *Histoire du Front Populaire*, p. 312; also the report of the Special Commission on the Artisanat, summarized in *Semaine de la Coiffure* 120 (4 November 1938).

6. Quoted in *Gazette* 26 (26 June 1936): 430.

7. *Artisan de l'Ouest* 15 (July 1936).

8. Quoted in *Gazette* 29 (17 July 1936): 487.

9. Quoted in *Gazette* 47 (20 November 1936): 820.

10. *Artisan Français* 206 (1 June 1936).

11. *Artisan Français* 209 (20 July–1 August 1936).

12. CEAA, 3e Cong. Nat., Toulouse, 1935, p. 70. See also APCMF, 24 May 1933, p. 146 on the forty-hour law. The *Artisan de l'Ouest* 24 (May 1937) thought the forty-hour law a good idea in theory but ruinous in practice.

13. *Artisan Français* 208 (10 July 1936).

14. *Artisan Français* 238 (10 June 1937).

15. Kopp, *Le rôle de groupements professionnels*, p. 2; Lefranc, *Histoire du Front Populaire*, p. 287.

16. Berstein, "Le Parti Républicain Radical et Radical-Socialiste," pp. 515–16; Dubost, *Le Conseil National Economique*, pp. 131–32; John Hackett and Anne-Marie Hackett, *Economic Planning in France* (London: George Allen and Unwin, 1963), p. 50.

17. See the article, "Conseil National Economique," in *Cahiers* 17 (April 1936): 1–9; also Parrot, *La représentation des intérêts*, pp. 146–48.

18. Kuisel, *Capitalism and the State*, p. 128.

19. In the summer of 1936 the APCMF voted to determine its four delegates and elected the president of the Assembly, Dupuis, Peter, Grandadam, and Rochette, the *eminence grise* of the APCMF and president of the Rhône Chamber of Trades. Forty-seven of the existing fifty-one chambers participated, and the election predictably broke along organizational lines. The chambers *confédérées* all voted for one set of candidates. Those associated with the CEAA cast their ballots for a different slate. The result was something of a standoff. See the archives of the Conseil Economique et Social, Paris, "Textes Officiels: Organisation du CNE, 1936."

20. *Gazette* 42 (16 October 1936): 711–12.

21. *Cahiers* 17 (April 1936): 8; Archives of the Conseil Economique et Social, Paris, "Liste des Sections Professionnelles."

22. Archives of the Conseil Economique et Social, Paris, "Séance du 18 Mai 1936." See also Archives Nationales F[12] 8973, "Séance du 25 Mai 1936."

23. Néron and Paul-Boncour were quoted in *Cahiers* 17 (April 1936): 8–9; see also the Archives of the Conseil Economique et Social, Paris, "CNE: Séance du 28 Avril 1936."

24. *Artisan Français* 263 (20 April 1938); Archives of the Conseil Economique et Social, Paris, "Textes Officiels: Organisation du CNE, 1936–1939;" and Archives Nationales F[12] 8792, "Composition du CNE."

25. Archives Nationales F[12] 8792; CE[1], "Section 25: 'Artisanal.' " See also *Artisan de France* 41 (December 1938).

26. Archives Nationales CE³⁸, first meeting of the twenty-fifth professional section (Artisanal), 13 January 1939.

27. Lefranc, *Histoire du Front Populaire*, p. 327.

28. Lefranc, *Histoire du Front Populaire*, p. 458; APCMF, 16 June 1937, p. 48.

29. *Artisan Français* 209 (20 July–1 August 1936).

30. Archives Nationales CE³⁶, meeting of the ninth professional section, 19 November 1937.

31. Archives Nationales CE³⁵, meeting of the ninth professional section, 29 January 1937. The *Artisan Français* contended that artisanal enterprises accounted for 73 percent of the construction industry in the Haute-Savoie.

32. Archives Nationales CE³⁶, meeting of the ninth professional section, 10 November 1937. Massé claimed to take his figures from an interpellation of Lebas in the *Journal Officiel*, Chamber of Deputies, 29 July 1937.

33. Archives Nationales CE³⁶, meeting of the ninth professional section, 19 November 1937.

34. Archives Nationales CE³⁴, meeting of the ninth professional section, 9 October 1936: A CGAF note to the CNE protesting its absence from discussions about the application of the forty-hour work week in the construction industry.

35. See the dispute over wages in the textile trades: Archives Nationales CE³⁷, meeting of the eleventh professional section (textiles), 4 July 1938. Also see Archives Nationales CE³⁷, meeting of the eleventh professional section, 21 January 1938; and the reports on artisans' involvement in a strike in the Lyon construction industry: *Artisan de France* 38 (September 1938); and 45 (April 1939).

36. See the report on CGAF activity, "Le 15e Congrès National devant les problèmes de l'heure," reprinted in *Cahiers* 44 (July 1938): 200–4.

37. APCMF, 27 November 1936, pp. 89, 92; *Artisan de France* 3–4 (January 1937); *Artisan de l'Ouest* 22 (March 1937).

38. *Cahiers* 37 (December 1937): 340.

39. *Artisan Français* 214 (1 October 1936); Lefranc, *Histoire du Front Populaire*, p. 312fn.

40. Archives Nationales CE³⁷, "Convention nationale collective du travail: Chaussure," signed 19 February 1937.

41. *Artisan de France* 29 (December 1936).

42. *Artisan de l'Ouest* 16–17 (August–September 1936).

43. *Gazette* 52 (25 December 1936): 909.

44. *Artisan de France* 24 (May 1937).

45. *Gazette* 10 (11 March 1938): 154.

46. *Gazette* 22 (28 May 1937): 329.

47. Mougin, "Un projet d'enquête," p. 329.

48. Archives Nationales F¹² 9505, report from the prefect of police to the minister of commerce and industry, 18 July 1938. Pugi was vice-president of the Beziers Chamber of Commerce and of the Ligue de défense des classes moyennes and president of the Groupement du petit et moyen commerce et artisans. See also the study by the Catholic cleric, (Père) André Desqueyrat, *Classes moyennes françaises: crise, programme, organisation* (Paris: Editions Spes, 1939), pp. 117–19, 183.

49. On the CGCM see Berstein, "Le Parti Républicain Radical et Radical-Socialiste," pp. 1162, 1197; Georges Izard (Deputy and general secretary of the Groupe parlementaire de défense des classes moyennes), *Les Classes Moyennes* (Paris: Editions Rieder, 1938), passim; Mougin, "Un projet d'enquête," pp. 336–39.

50. On the CGSCM see Desqueyrat, *Classes moyennes françaises*, pp. 197–98;

Mougin, "Un projet d'enquête," pp. 331–33. On Emile Roche see Zeev Sternhell, *Neither Right nor Left*, p. 117.

51. On the CGACM see Desqueyrat, *Classes moyennes françaises*, pp. 213–15; Mougin, "Un projet d'enquête," p. 330.

52. Gaston Lecordier, *Les classes moyennes en marche* (Paris: Bloud et Gay, 1950).

53. Michael Marrus and Robert Paxton, *Vichy France and the Jews* (New York: Basic Books, 1981), p. 38.

54. *Artisan de France* 43 (February 1939).

55. The record of artisanal participation in the movement of the "middle classes" is in *Artisan* (Le Puy) 3 (September–October 1938); *Information Artisanale* n.s. 4 (April 1939); Desqueyrat, *Classes moyennes françaises*, pp. 205, 247; *Gazette* 47 (19 November 1937): 811–12; 26 (1 July 1938): 464; and 36 (9 September 1938): 635.

56. CEAA, 2e Cong. Nat., Lille, 1934, pp. 113, 119.

57. *Artisan Français* 226 (1 February 1937).

58. *Artisan Français* 228 (20 February 1937).

59. *Gazette* 16 (19 April 1935): 246; 27 (5 July 1935): 426; 43 (25 October 1935): 716; 22 (29 May 1936): 353; and 42 (16 October 1936): 713.

60. *Artisan Français* 78 (June 1929); 140 (30 June–15 July 1933); 161 (30 June–15 July 1934); and 183 (31 July–15 August 1935). The CGAF in the 1930s became increasingly reluctant to give out figures on its membership. But the numbers for the CGAF were in any case more meaningful than those for the CEAA, because the CGAF was a more stable, cohesive organization.

61. Demondion, *L'artisanat dans l'état moderne*, pp. 180–83.

62. *Artisan de France* 46 (May 1939); also Mourier, "L'artisanat," p. 181.

63. *Artisan de France* 45 (April 1939).

64. *Artisan de France* 3–4 (January 1937).

65. The Ille-et-Vilaine and Maine-et-Loire figures are reported in *Artisan de France* 22 (March 1937); those from the Manche and Finistère are in 23 (April 1937).

66. Mourier, "L'artisanat," p. 176.

67. *Artisan de France* 25 (June 1937); also Abbé Ar. Vallée, "Réflexions sur l'artisanat—Quelle doit être l'attitude des catholiques en face du problème artisanal?" *Dossiers de l'Action Populaire* 381 (10 March 1937): 576–77; and Lecordier, *Classes Moyennes*, pp. 171–72. Lecordier reports, incidentally, that Vallée died at Mathausen, in March 1945.

68. *Artisan de France* 30 (January 1938); 43 (February 1939).

69. *Artisan de France* 25 (June 1937).

70. *Artisan de France* 32 (March 1938); Charles, *L'Artisanat*, p. 26; Vallée, "Réflexions sur l'artisanat," p. 555.

71. *Artisan de France* 48 (July 1939).

72. *Artisan de France* 33 (April 1938).

73. *Artisan de France* 2 (November 1936).

74. *Artisan de France* 47 (June 1939).

75. On the breakdown of the working population in *coiffure* see Marcel de Ville-Chabrol, "La concentration des entreprises en France avant et depuis la guerre," *Bulletin de la statistique générale de la France et du service d'observation des prix* 22 (April–June 1933): 439; and Statistique Générale de la France, *Résultats statistiques du recensement général de la population, effectué le 8 mars 1936*, tome 1; 3e partie, "Population active et établissements," p. 164; tomes 2 and 3: "Population présente, résultats par départements," (Paris: Imprimerie Nationale, 1943–1944).

76. Marcel de Ville-Chabrol, "La population active en France avant et depuis la

guerre," *Bulletin de la statistique générale de la France et du service d'observation des prix* 21 (October–December 1931): 133.

77. *Coiffeur-Parfumeur* 7 (15 July 1923).

78. *Artisan* (Le Puy) 2 (July 1939). See also Esther Picard and Vivianne Jacot-Descombes, *La coiffure à travers les siècles* (Paris: Editions de l'Artisanat Moderne, 1973), p. 50.

79. *Artisan Coiffeur* 42 (April 1936).

80. *Coiffeur Confédéré.* Organe mensuel de la fédération nationale des syndicats confédérés d'ouvriers coiffeurs de France et des colonies, 46 (December 1928). See also the article by A. Lemehaute, president of the Union des syndicats d'artisans des Côtes-du-Nord and secretary of the Syndicat des coiffeurs in *Artisan de France* 35 (June 1938).

81. See the article, "Histoire: misère, opulence, remiséré," in *Reveil des Coiffeurs* (Le seul journal professionnel expédié tous les jeudis à 15,000 coiffeurs) 121 (7 March 1935).

82. Archives Nationales F⁷ 13866, "Grèves en coiffure, 1919–1931."

83. *Coiffeur-Parfumeur* 8 (15 August 1923); 33 (15 September 1925).

84. *Coiffeur-Parfumeur* 1 (15 January 1923).

85. *Coiffeur-Parfumeur* 3 (15 March 1923).

86. Archives Nationales, F⁷ 13866.

87. *Coiffeur-Parfumeur* 2 (15 February 1923).

88. On the decrees of August 26, and October 30, 1921 see *Coiffeur-Parfumeur* 5 (15 May 1923).

89. *Coiffeur Confédéré* 2 (December 1923).

90. *Coiffeur Confédéré* 3 (January 1924).

91. *Coiffeur Confédéré* 20 (July 1925).

92. Complaints about violations and inspectors' reports to the labor minister can be found throughout the records in Archives Nationales F²² 421 and 422, "Huit heures en *coiffure*: 1920–1931; and 1931–1935."

93. *Coiffeur-Parfumeur* 2 (15 February 1923).

94. *Reveil des Coiffeurs* 121 (7 March 1935).

95. *Artisan Coiffeur*, 2 (November 1932).

96. *Artisan Coiffeur* 6 (March 1933). Another vice-president of the syndicate, Briland, disagreed with Lesourd's suggestion. What beauties could you work with short hair? he wondered; short hair would cost hairdressers their professional reputation. Besides, he said, *coiffeurs* accommodate fashion, they do not make it: *Artisan Coiffeur* 7 (April 1933). See also the proposal by a Monsieur A. Dumont, president of the federation of the Centre-Est in *Coiffeur du Sud-Ouest.* Organe officiel de la Fédération des patrons coiffeurs artisans de Guyenne-Gascogne-Languedoc-Quercy (Montauban), 66 (November 1937).

97. *Syndicalisme.* Organe mensuel de la Confédération française des travailleurs Chrétiens, 32 (September 1938).

98. *Semaine de la Coiffure* 94 (15 April 1938); see also *Reveil des Coiffeurs* 282 (14 April 1938).

99. *Coiffeur-Parfumeur* 171 (15 March 1937); *Coiffeur du Sud-Ouest* 27 (August 1934).

100. *Artisan Coiffeur* 6 (March 1933).

101. *Artisan Coiffeur* 5 (February 1934).

102. *Artisan Coiffeur* 6 (March 1933).

103. *Artisan Coiffeur* 61 (November 1937).

104. *Semaine de la Coiffure* 39 (19 March 1937).

105. *Coiffeur-Parfumeur* 137 (15 May 1934).

106. *Artisan Coiffeur* 35 (September 1935); *Coiffeur Confédéré* 44 (October 1928); *Coiffeur-Parfumeur* 154 (15 October 1935); *Semaine de la Coiffure* 2 (24 June 1936).

107. *Ouvrier Coiffeur*. De la région du Sud-Est et de la Côte-d'Azur. Organe de la Chambre syndicale des ouvriers coiffeurs et parties similaires de Marseille, 7 (July 1939).

108. *Reveil des Coiffeurs* 121 (7 March 1935).

109. *Coiffeur Confédéré* 89 (February 1933), article by Maurice Baugé, secretary of the Fédération des coiffeurs confédérés.

110. *Coiffeur du Sud-Ouest*, (July 1936).

111. Archives Nationales F^{22} 422, see the booklet on *The problem of working hours in coiffure*, put together by the hairdressers' syndicate attached to the CGTU; also CCIP I 8.21, "Syndicats Professionels-Patronaux, Régimes," in a folder headed, "Commerçants étrangers inscrits au registre du Commerce, 1939."

112. *Coiffeur Confédéré* 103 (July–August 1934); 106 (December 1934). Several instances of the application of the 10 percent rule can be found in Archives Nationales F^{22} 422.

113. *Coiffeur-Parfumeur* 135 (15 March 1934).

114. On the strike of May 21–30, 1926 in Paris see Archives Nationales F^7 13866; also Archives de la Préfecture de Police, Seine, 12.000-111.

115. *Coiffeur Confédéré* 82 (June 1932).

116. *Coiffeur Confédéré* 99 (January–February 1934). On the formation and membership of the new patrons' syndicate, see Préfecture de Police, Seine, Bureau des Affaires Réglementaires, Dossier des Syndicats 5368: Syndicat des coiffeurs de Paris.

117. *Reveil des Coiffeurs* 276 (3 March 1938).

118. *Semaine de la Coiffure* 89 (11 March 1938). On Bagnaud's career see the CCIP I 2.15, "Marcel Bagnaud, décédé, le 21 avril 1964"; and I 2.61, "Protestation de la Chambre de Commerce de Paris contre un article paru dans l'*Hebdo-Coiffure* (1938)." On the *Intransigeant*, see Claude Bellanger, et al., *Histoire générale de la presse française*, tome 3: *De 1871 à 1940* (Paris: Presses Universitaires de France, 1972), pp. 535–37.

119. *Artisan Coiffeur* 76 (February 1939).

120. *Coiffeur Confédéré* 100 (March 1934); *Coiffeur-Parfumeur* 183 (15 March 1938).

121. *Artisan Coiffeur* 76 (February 1939); *Coiffeur Confédéré* 100 (March 1934).

122. *Coiffeur Confédéré* 87 (December 1932).

123. *Semaine de la Coiffure* 11 (4 September 1936).

124. *Reveil des Coiffeurs* 265 (16 December 1937).

125. *Reveil des Coiffeurs* 271 (27 January 1937).

126. *Coiffeur Nantais* 17 (July 1936).

127. *Artisan Coiffeur* 46 (August 1936).

128. *Semaine de la Coiffure* 6 (24 July 1936); 7 (31 July 1936); and 49 (4 June 1937).

129. *Semaine de la Coiffure* 35 (19 February 1937).

130. *Semaine de la Coiffure* 38 (12 March 1937).

131. On Law 900 see *Coiffeur Populaire*. Organe mensuel du syndicat des coiffeurs permanteurs et mixtes de France, 1 (July 1937). (This was the journal's only number.) See also *Artisan Coiffeur* 65 (March 1938); *Coiffeur du Sud-Ouest* 54 (November 1934); *Ouvrier Coiffeur* 7 (July 1939); *Semaine de la Coiffure* 102 (10 June 1938).

132. On the February convention see *Semaine de la Coiffure* 30 (15 January 1937); 31 (22 January 1937); 34 (12 February 1938); and 37 (5 March 1937).

133. *Semaine de la Coiffure* 40 (26 March 1937); 41 (2 April 1937). On worker demands see *Figaro*, interview with Louis Tison, an officer of the CPC, 15 May 1937; and *Humanité*, 12 May 1937.

134. Information on the strike comes from the Paris daily newspapers (13–21 May 1937) and from the Archives de la Préfecture de Police, Seine, 12.000-111.

135. On the Martin ruling and subsequent application see *Semaine de la Coiffure* 57 (13 August 1937); 61 (27 August 1937); 62 (3 September 1937); and 64 (17 September 1937). On the continuing evasion of the convention and *arrêté* see *Semaine de la Coiffure* 108 (22 July 1938).

136. *Semaine de la Coiffure* 37 (5 March 1937); *Reveil des Coiffeurs* 290 (9 June 1938).

137. *Semaine de la Coiffure* 89 (11 March 1938).

138. *Semaine de la Coiffure* 44 (23 April 1937).

139. On the population of the Chambre syndicale see *Semaine de la Coiffure* 2 (June 1936); 32 (29 January 1937); on the population of the CPC in Paris, *Semaine de la Coiffure* 88 (4 March 1938).

140. *Coiffeur du Sud-Est* 70 (March 1938); 87 (August 1939); *Reveil des Coiffeurs* 317 (18 May 1939).

141. *Artisan Coiffeur* 79 (May 1939).

142. *Semaine de la Coiffure* 109 (29 July 1938).

143. I base this assertion on a mass of indirect evidence and on my interview with François Magnien on July 12, 1988, who dealt frequently with both men and who apparently knew Bagnaud quite well.

144. *Hebdo-Coiffure*. Journal d'informations et de propagande artisanale et économique, 125 (12 March 1938).

145. *Hebdo-Coiffure* 128 (2 April 1938). Tison's reply was reprinted in *Coiffeur-Parfumeur* 185 (15 May 1938).

146. The story of the SMAC decision to join the CPC can be found in the *Coiffeur-Parfumeur* for 1937 and 1938, passim.

147. See the *Coiffeur du Sud-Ouest* for 1937 and 1938.

148. *Coiffeur du Sud-Ouest* 37 (June 1935).

149. Lefranc, *Histoire du Front Populaire*, p. 321; Néré, *La Troisième République*, p. 161.

150. Néré, *La Troisième République*, pp. 147–51; Claude Nicolet, *Le Radicalisme* (Paris: Presses Universitaires de France, 1967), p. 89.

151. See the summary of Reynaud's decrees in Lefranc, *Histoire du Front Populaire*, pp. 279–80. For artisans' remarks see *Artisan Français* 275 (10 September 1938); 285 (20 December 1938–1 January 1939); *Cahiers* 48 (December 1938): 348–50; 55 (July–August 1939): 146; and *Gazette* 40 (1 October 1937): 698; 22 (3 June 1938): 397–98.

152. On the work of the commission see *Artisan de France* 35 (June 1938); *Artisan Français* 258 (20 February 1938); "Les travaux de la commission chargée d'enquêter sur la situation actuelle de l'artisanat français," *Cahiers* 46 (October 1938): 282–84; *Gazette* 24 (17 June 1938): 434.

153. For the details of the 1937 Artisanal Exposition in Paris see *Artisan Français* 247 (20 October 1937); APCMF, 15 May 1936, pp. 136–39; *Cahiers* 32 (June 1937): 162–69; *Gazette* 4 (22 January 1937): 62.

154. *Gazette* 32 (6 August 1937): 559.

155. *Gazette* 30 (29 July 1938): 532.

156. "Réforme fiscale," *Cahiers* 28 (February 1937): 33; *Gazette* 17 (23 April 1937): 306.

157. *Artisan de France* 41 (December 1938).

158. Zarca, "Survivance ou transformation," pp. 349–52.

159. APCMF, 16 November 1937, pp. 59–72. Also on the Walter-Paulin law see APCMF, "Etudes sur le droit rélatif à l'exercise des métiers," (Paris), 1963, pp. 1–3; "L'apprentissage," *Cahiers* 18 (May 1936): 1–5; Hector, *La législation actuelle*, pp. 326–27.

160. Azzano, *Mes joyeuse années*, p. 17.

161. Blasquez, *Gaston Lucas*, pp. 36–42.

162. Daniel Bertaux, "Stories as clues to sociological understanding: the bakers of Paris," *Our Common History: The Transformation of Europe*, ed. Paul Thompson (London: Pluto Press, 1982), p. 103.

163. Isabelle Bertaux-Wiame, *Transformations et permanence de l'artisanat boulanger en France*, vol. 2: *L'Apprentissage en boulangerie dans les années '20 et '30: Une enquête d'histoire orale* (Paris: Maison des Sciences de l'Homme, 1978).

164. Bertaux-Wiame, *Transformations et permanence*, pp. 33–35; the articles in the convention on apprenticeship are reproduced in the annex, pp. 1-7.

165. *Information Artisanale* 32 (March 1944). Also see Charles, *L'Artisanat*, p. 61.

166. Mourier, "Essai," p. 83; Zarca, "Survivance ou transformation," p. 382.

167. APCMF, "Etudes," pp. 1-3.

168. "Ce qu'il faut savoir," *Artisan Français* 311 (February 1940). On the moratorium see Gresle, "Indépendants et petits patrons," p. 94.

169. Laffaille, "L'artisanat et la défense nationale," p. 196.

170. Laffaille, "L'artisanat et la défense nationale," p. 182.

171. Ministère de l'Armament, *Circulaire de Monsieur Dautry, ministre de l'armament*, 21 November 1939. See also the comments on this circular in *Artisan Français* 310 (1 January 1940); and Laffaille, "L'artisanat et la défense nationale," pp. 177–78.

172. Laffaille, "L'artisanat et la défense nationale," p. 194.

173. *Artisan de France* 47 (June 1939); 50 (December 1939).

174. *Artisan Français* 315 (1 June 1940).

Chapter 5

1. *Artisan Français* 319 (November 1941).

2. Philippe Pétain, *Message adressé aux artisans, ouvriers, techniciens et patrons: ler Mai 1942* (Vichy: Imprimerie Jacques Haumont, 1942), p. 4.

3. André Demaison, Centre d'expansion française, *La Ronde des Métiers: recensement des forces économiques de la nation* (Clermont-Ferrand: Cahiers de France, 1943), p. 5. This was the transcript of a number of radio programs written by Demaison. Marius Coulon put it this way: "Artisans represent traditional France, with their taste for work, their sense of savings, and their love of family. For these reasons they have the right to protection from a government which, in contributing to their prosperity, will contribute to the renovation of the country." Coulon, *L'artisanat devant l'impôt*, p. 106; also Georges Chaudieu, *L'artisanat cet inconnu* (Paris: Paillard, 1942), pp. 45–46.

4. *Artisan des Alpes* 131 (September–October 1940).

5. Jean Dutouard, *Au bon beurre, ou dix ans de la vie d'un crémier* (Paris: Gallimard, 1952), p. 23.

6. Archives Nationales F^{12} 10152, "Rapport d'activité générale du groupement national d'ammeublement, du 15 Mai à 15 Juin 1941," records of the Comité d'organisation du bâtiment et des travaux publics.

7. Dutouard, *Au bon beurre*, pp. 26–27.

8. On the economy under the Occupation see Caron and Bouvier, "Guerre, crise, guerre, 1914–1919," Braudel and Labrousse, *Histoire économique*, tome 4, vol. 2, pp. 663–66; Caron, *An Economic History*, pp. 268–71; Carré, et al., *French Economic Growth*, p. 24; Alfred Sauvy, *La vie économique des français de 1939 à 1945* (Paris: Flammarion, 1978), passim. Ironically, the shortages could produce, what John F. Sweet calls "distributive socialism." For this idea and for the wartime economic situation in Clermont-Ferrand see John F. Sweet's, *Choices in Vichy France: The French Under Nazi Occupation* (New York and Oxford: Oxford University Press, 1986), especially Chapter 1, pp. 3–29.

9. In Caron, *An Economic History*, pp. 268–69, Caron estimates that payments to Germany represented half of public expenditure, and that the Nazis took 74 percent of France's iron ore production, 61 percent of iron and steel, 64 percent of motorcars and cycles, and 34 percent of chemicals. On German demands also see Lehideux's testimony in Hoover Institution, *France During the Occupation, 1940–1944*, trans. Philip Whitcomb (Stanford: Stanford University Press, 1957), 1: 26–29; Alan S. Milward, *The New Order and the French Economy* (Oxford: Oxford University Press, 1970), pp. 49–50; and Robert Paxton, *Vichy France: Old Guard and New Order, 1940–1944* (New York: Alfred A. Knopf, 1972), p. 220.

10. Quoted in Caron, *An Economic History*, p. 268.

11. On the organization committees see Claude Gruson, *Origine et espoirs de la planification française* (Paris: Dunod, 1968), p. 30; Kuisel, *Capitalism and the State*, p. 130; Jean-Guy Mérigot, *Essai sur les comités d'organisation professionnelle* (Paris: Librairie Générale de Droit et de Jurisprudence, 1943), pp. 85–100; Henri Russo, "L'organisation industrielle de Vichy," *Revue d'histoire de la deuxième guerre mondiale* 29 (October 1979): 27. On the issue of distribution see APCMF, 23 March 1941, pp. 82–83; Robert Catherine, *Economie de la répartition des produits industriels* (Paris: Presses Universitaires de France, 1943), passim; Joseph Jones, "Vichy France and Postwar Economic Modernization: The Case of Shopkeepers," *French Historical Studies* 12 (1982): 542; and Philippe Pétain, *L'oeuvre du Maréchal Pétain. Six mois de la Révolution Nationale. Documents* (Lyon: Imprimerie Commerciale du 'Nouvelliste', 1941), pp. 36–37.

12. Quoted in Jacques de Launay, ed., *Le dossier de Vichy* (Paris: Julliard, 1967), p. 279.

13. Quoted in Launay, *Le dossier de Vichy*, pp. 263–64; also see the testimony of François Lehideux, former director of Renault and another of Vichy's production ministers, in Hoover Institution, *France During the Occupation* 1: 37–38.

14. Kuisel, *Capitalism and the State*, pp. 132–33.

15. Quoted in *Artisan de France* (Cahors). Organe bi-mensuel d'information artisanale, n.s. 2 (September 1941).

16. CCIP I 2.55, "Marcel Bagnaud, décédé le 21 avril 1964." On the "aryanization" issue, see the letters exchanged between Bagnaud and the Ministry of Production in the winter of 1941.

17. See the article by André Jeannin in *Information Artisanale* n.s. 13 (August 1942). In 1942, when it began to publish again, the journal changed its masthead from

"Organe officiel du CEAA et des principales confédérations de métiers artisanaux" to "Publication mensuelle de l'Office Commercial et Technique de l'Artisanat (which used to be part of the CEAA).

18. APCMF, 22 March 1941, quote p. 22, figures p. 43.

19. *Artisan de France* (Paris) 52 (15 January 1941). This was the journal's first issue since December 1939.

20. Kuisel, *Capitalism and the State*, p. 132.

21. See the pamphlet which reproduces a Loyer speech, Pierre Loyer, *Les dessous maçonniques du Radicalisme*. Les affinités françaises. La maison des producteurs, 6 October 1936 (Paris: Société d'Editions et de Propagande, 1936).

22. Quoted in Zarca, "Survivance ou transformation," p. 412.

23. Mourier, "L'artisanat," p. 8. On the creation of the Artisanal Service see Archives Nationales F^{12} 10135, "Artisanat"; M. Grundler, "Le Service de l'Artisanat," in Institut d'Etudes Corporatives et Sociales. Ecole des Hautes Etudes Artisanales (hereafter cited as EHEA), Cours, 1941–1942, II: 43. For the personnel of the Service in 1944 see *Information Artisanale* 34 (May 1944):

Artisanal Service

Director: Pierre Loyer
Secretary: Grundler

Central Services:
Technical services: Cassard
Economic and Financial section: Mayet
Professional and Social organization: de la Chaise
Professional Training: Maurice Avril
Rural Artisans and Labor: Rousseau
Administrative and Legal services: François-Paul Raynal
Liaison service: Rousseau

24. Archives Nationales F^{12} 10227; F^{12} 10251^2, "Groupements Artisanaux Professionels": see the circular of 5 July 1941, "Creation of GAP." Also see circulars from the Artisanal Service on 29 January 1942 and 7 April 1942.

25. Mourier, "L'artisanat," p. 176.

26. For further information on the GAP see APCMF, "Rapport sur les Groupements Artisanaux Professionnels," 23 November 1941, pp. 48–49; Pierre Loyer, *Les incidences sociales du Statut de l'Artisanat: Conférence* (Vichy: Editions du Centre d'Information et de Documentation Artisanales, 1945), pp. 29–30; Edmond Verdun, "Les Groupes Artisanaux Professionnels" (an unpublished pamphlet by a member of the Ecole des Hautes Etudes Artisanales, available at the library of the Assemblée Permanente des Chambres de Métiers, Paris).

27. Archives Nationales F^{12} 10251^2; circular of 7 April 1942. On the BAM see André Jeannin, *L'artisanat à la croisée des chemins* (Paris: Institut d'Etudes Corporatives et Sociales, 1943), p. 69; G. Bozet, *L'artisanat devant le rationnement des matières primaires* (Lyon: Imprimerie Jacquier et Cie, 1941). On the *cartes d'acheteurs* see APCMF, "Report on Cooperatives and Buyers' Groups," 23 March 1941, pp. 43–50.

28. *Artisan de France* (Cahors) 2 (1 September 1941).

29. *Information Artisanale* 22 (March 1943); and 23 (June 1943).

30. Jacques Juillard, "La Charte du Travail," in Fondation Nationale des Sciences Politiques, travaux et recherches de science politique, *Le gouvernement de Vichy*,

1940–1942: institutions et politiques (Paris: Armand Colin, 1972), p. 161; Léon Liebmann, "Entre le mythe et la légende: l'anti-capitalisme de Vichy," *Revue de l'Institut de Sociologie* 37 (1964): 128–29.

31. Quoted in APCMF, 24 November 1941, p. 39; see also Launay, *Le dossier de Vichy*, p. 279.

32. Robert O. Paxton, *Vichy France*, p. 217; Sauvy, *Vie économique*, pp. 201–2.

33. APCMF, "Report on the Labor Charter," 24 November 1941, pp. 40–41. See also Demondion, *L'artisanat dans l'état moderne*, p. 260; and René Belin's understandably biased analysis in Hoover Institution, *France During the Occupation* 1: 176–89.

34. "La Charte du Travail," *Artisan de France* 65 (October 1941); Demondion, *L'artisanat dans l'état moderne*, pp. 267–68; Belin's testimony in Hoover Institution, *France During the Occupation*, pp. 182–83; Jeannin, *L'artisanat à la croisée des chemins*, p. 66.

35. Archives Nationales F^{12} 10135, letter from the Direction of textiles and leather to the general secretary for industrial production, 6 April 1944.

36. See the series of pamphlets covering various aspects of artisans' existence under the Charter: M. Boudeau, "Les coopératives et le crédit artisanal"; Marc-Edouard Morgaut, "Les Chambres de Métiers"; M. Murat, "Les groupements artisanaux professionnels"; and M. Pavot, "L'Apprentissage," in "Sessions artisanales de l'école des cadres civiques du Mayet-de-Montagne (Allier), available in manuscript at the Assemblée Permanente des Chambers de Métiers, Paris.

37. *Artisan de France* 61 (June 1941).

38. *Artisan Catalan*. Organe officiel de la chambre des maîtres-artisans des Pyrénées-Orientales (Perpignan), 4 (April 1942).

39. *Artisan de France* (Cahors) 11 (15 February 1942).

40. *Artisan de France* (Cahors) 6 (1 November 1941).

41. *Artisan de France* (Cahors) 3 (15 September 1941).

42. *Artisan de France* (Cahors) 7 (15 November 1941).

43. Caron and Bouvier, "Guerre, crise, guerre," pp. 665.

44. *Information Artisanale* 23 (June 1943).

45. *Artisan d'Aunis et de Saintonge*. Organe de la Fédération des groupements des maîtres-artisans d'Aunis et de Saintonge (La Rochelle), 9 (January 1943); *Artisan de France* (Cahors) 22 (December 1942).

46. *Information Artisanale* 31 (February 1944). Chasseigne was Commissaire général à la main-d'oeuvre et du travail.

47. *Artisan d'Aunis et Saintonge* 9 (January 1943).

48. Archives Nationales F^{11} 10135; "Artisan." See also the generally favorable *Compagnonnage* and *Information Artisanale*, passim, for the CEAA position and the *Artisan de France* (Cahors), passim, for that of the CAF.

49. For the problems caused by Vichy demographic policy see *Artisan Français* 318 (October 1941); also APCMF, "Report on Unemployment," 23 March 1941, pp. 53, 71, 99.

50. *Artisan Catalan* 4 (April 1942). Bourdet was Inspector general in the Ministry of Production.

51. *Artisan Rouergat*. Organe officiel de la Chambre de Métiers de l'Aveyron (Rodez), 6 (February 1944).

52. *Artisan de France* (Cahors) 12 (1 March 1942).

53. *Artisan des Alpes* 146 (February–March 1942); 156 (November 1942).

54. The cobbler's letter is reproduced in *Artisan de France* 59 (March–April 1941);

the blacksmith's comment is in *Artisan de France* (Cahors) 9 (1 January 1942). For an unsympathetic reading of the situation by a supporter of the National Revolution see Charles, *L'Artisanat*, pp. 102–4.

55. *Information Artisanale* 8 (March 1942).

56. From a presentation to the Ecole des Sciences Politiques, quoted in *Information Artisanale* 9–10 (April–May 1942).

57. On the confederations' dissolution see Demondion, *L'artisanat dans l'état moderne*, pp. 181–83; *Information Artisanale* 11 (June 1942); and 32 (March 1944); Mérigot, *Essai*, p. 93; Mourier, "L'artisanat," p. 176; Verdun, "Histoire du syndicalisme,"EHEA, (Cours), 1942–1934, p. 22.

58. Unfortunately, the minutes of this session have not survived. Brief synopses can be found in *Artisan Catalan* 4 (April 1942); *Artisan des Alpes* 13 (September–October 1940); and APCMF, 22 March 1941, pp. 14–17.

59. APCMF, 2 August 1941, p. 16.

60. See, for example, APCMF, 24 March 1941, pp. 123, 175; 4 August 1941, pp. 90–93; 4 June 1942, p. 123; and 5 June 1942, p. 193. For the particular situation in the department of the Vienne see Roger Picard and Gaston Rocault, "La vie économique dans la Vienne (1940–1944)," *Revue d'Histoire de la Deuxième Guerre Mondiale* 119 (July 1980): 32–33.

61. APCMF, 4 June 1942, p. 128.

62. APCMF, 3 August 1941, p. 32.

63. APCMF, 5 June 1942, p. 213.

64. APCMF, 3 August 1941, p. 33.

65. APCMF, 3 August 1941, p. 31. See also the remarks of Demondion, *L'artisanat dans l'état moderne*, p. 272; and Jeannin, *L'artisanat à la croisée des chemins*, p. 75.

66. APCMF, 5 June 1942, p. 162.

67. *Artisan de France* (CAF) 53 (25 February 1941).

68. *Artisan Français* 321 (1 January 1942).

69. Archives Nationales F^{12} 10251–10252, "Functions of artisanal delegates," 5 December 1941; APCMF, 25 November 1941, pp. 79–80.

70. For Lehideux's decree see *Journal Officiel de l'Etat Français* (lois et décrets), no. 341, 21 December 1941, p. 5493. The *arrêt* designating the Bardet executive is in *Bulletin Municipal Officiel de la Ville de Paris*, no. 76, 29 March 1942. Also see *Artisan de France* (CAF) 18 (August 1942); and *Information Artisanale* 11 (June 1942); 23 (June 1943); and 24 (July 1943).

71. APCMF, 5 June 1942, p. 167.

72. APCMF, 5 June 1942, p. 181. The confrontation that ensued is on pages 189–217.

73. *Information Artisanale* 19 (February 1943).

74. For a membership list of the consultative committee see Archives Nationales F^{12} 10135, "Procès-verbal des délibérations du comité consultatif de l'artisanat, 1–2 December 1942;" and a letter from Loyer to Norguet, of the Ministry of Industry and Commerce (3 September 1942). These were the members:

Presidents of Chambers of Trades

Coustenoble: baker (Nord)
Bardet: tailor (Seine)
Beaudet: carpenter (Seine-Inférieure)
Bossavy: mirrormaker (Corrèze)
Bourrières: baker (Lot)

Jeannin: plumber (Cher)
Pégeot: blacksmith (Calvados)
Seguinaud: (Gironde)
Crette: bookmaker, prof. at the Estienne school

Syndical representatives

Kergoat: electrician, general secretary of the mâitres-électriciens-en-bâtiment (Seine)

Mignot: blacksmith, president of the Confédération des maréchaux-ferrants et charrons de France

Ressicaud: weaver, general secretary of the Société coopérative des tisserands lyonnais (Rhone)

Tison: hairdresser, general secretary of the Confédération des coiffeurs de Paris

Vialatte: shoemaker, President of the Syndicat des mâitres-artisans cordonniers et bottiers de la Seine

Bissonnier: compagnon-jeweler, member of the Seine Chamber of Trades

Hebrard: compagnon-butcher, of the Seine Chamber of Trades

75. Jean Bichelonne, *Le Statut de l'Artisanat: extrait du Journal Officiel du 25 août 1943* (Clermont-Ferrand: Imprimeries Paul Vallier, 1943), pp. 1–2; Pierre Loyer, *Les incidences*, pp. 8–9; idem, *Le Statut de l'Artisanat* (Paris: Dunod, 1944), p. 1.

76. Bichelonne, *Le Statut*, p. 3; Loyer, *Le Statut*, pp. 66–70.

77. *Information Artisanale* 27 (October 1943).

78. Bichelonne, *Le Statut*, p. 4; Loyer, *Le Statut*, pp. 78–79. See also the critical observations in Pierre Demondion, *Le Nouveau Statut de l'Artisanat* (Paris: F. Lovitan, 1943), passim; and the comments on the authoritarian nature of the Statute in Jeannin, *L'artisanat à la croisée des chemins*, p. 70.

79. For an assessment from the artisans' perspective see *Artisan de France* (CAF) 31 (September 1943); also *Artisan Rouergat* 5 (November 1943).

80. Quoted in *Information Artisanale* 28 (September 1943). See also *Artisan de France* (CAF) 34 (November 1943).

81. *Information Artisanale* 31 (February 1944); 34 (May 1944). The deliberations of some of the *familles professionnelles* over the question of joining the Communities of Trades appear in the correspondence between Loyer and the Production Ministry from 1944 in Archives Nationales F^{12} 10135.

82. See the remarks of Didaret, secretary general of the Fédération ouvrière de l'alimentation et de l'industrie hôtellière, cafés et restaurants, and of Marcel Bonnet of the Fédération de l'habillement in *Information Artisanale* 26 (September 1943).

83. Archives Nationales F^{12} 10135, letter of 14 May 1943 from Lagardelle to Loyer.

84. The story of these various schemes is in Archives Nationales F^{12} 10135; see also *Information Artisanale* 35 (June 1944).

85. See the pamphlet by the Chambre de Commerce de Paris, *Définition de l'Artisan*, 4 July 1942.

86. APCMF, 28 November 1945, pp. 98–99.

87. Demondion, *L'artisanat dans l'état moderne*, p. 277; Loyer, *Le Statut*, pp. 6, 14. See also *Artisan Catalan* 9 (October 1942); *Artisan d'Aunis et Saintonge* 8 (Premier trimestre 1941); *Artisan de France* (CAF) 60 (May 1941) and 61 (June 1941); *Information Artisanale* 12 (July 1942). One area of the artisanal experience that the regime tried to revive was *compagnonnage*: Christian Faure, "Vichy et la renovation de l'artisanat: La réorganisation du compagnonnage," *Bulletin du Centre d'Histoire Economique et Sociale de la Région Lyonnaise* 3–4 (1984): 103–17.

88. Alain Rodet, *Commerçants et Artisans* (Paris: Centurian, 1976), p. 75.

89. Mourier, L'artisanat," p. 100; idem, "Essai," p. 80. The Production Ministry's survey no longer exists in its totality. Georges Chaudieu refers to a business census carried out by the chambers of trades and of commerce during the war; but I have found no other evidence of its existence: see Georges Chaudieu and Hélène London, *Les métiers d'appoint, leur utilité dans l'économie et la société* (Paris: La Nouvelle Edition, 1944).

90. Archives Nationales F¹² 9966, "Concentration: Petites et Moyennes Entreprises."

91. Archives Nationales F¹² 10226, "Artisanat Rural."

92. Herbert Lüthy, *France Against Herself*, p. 38. Pierre Nicolle, *Cinquante mois d'Armistice: Vichy, 2 juillet 1940–26 août 1944. Journal d'un témoin*, 2 vols. (Paris: Editions André Bonne, 1947) 1: 89.

93. Mourier, "L'artisanat," p. 180.

94. APCMF, 18 November 1947, p. 69.

95. Archives Nationales F¹² 10251², 29 January 1942, circular from the Production Ministry to the presidents and directors of the organization committees.

96. *Information Artisanale* 34 (May 1944); Archives Nationales F¹² 10251² contains numerous documents testifying to the ultimate failure of Vichy's attempts to organize aritsans. The issue of resistance is also discussed in Jeannin, *L'artisanat à la croisée des chemins*, p. 76; and Loyer, *Les incidences*, see especially the revealing questions by the artisanal representatives, Bernadot, Mayot, and Rivain, pp. 36–39. For the more widespread disenchantment among small businessmen see Jones, "Vichy France," pp. 553–54.

97. Quoted in Paxton, *Vichy France*, p. 194. David Thomson also referred to Vichy as the "revenge of the functionaries" against the Third Republic in *Democracy in France Since 1870* 4th ed. (New York: Oxford University Press, 1964), p. 64. Sauvy writes that "Never had a war produced such an accumulation of bureaucracy" in Sauvy, *La Vie Economique*, p. 9.

98. Richard Kuisel, "The Legend of the Vichy Synarchy," *French Historical Studies* 6 (1970): 365–98. Also on the Vichy Synarchy see Alexander Werth, *France, 1940–1955* (London: Robert Hale, Ltd., 1956), p. 83.

99. *Artisan de France* (Cahors) 11 (15 February 1942); and 25 (March 1943); *Information Artisanale* 11 (June 1942). A good deal of material from the EHEA is available at the library of the Assemblée Permanente des Chambres de Métiers, Paris, but most of this is more easily accessible in the published work of the authors involved.

100. Kuisel, *Capitalism and the State*, p. 149; Russo, "L'organisation industrielle," p. 28.

101. Paxton, *Vichy France*, p. 141.

102. Gruson, *Origine et espoirs*, p. 32. See also Ullmo, "France," p. 24.

103. *Artisan des Alpes* 46 (February–March 1942); see also the report of a Bichelonne speech at the Ecole des Sciences Politiques, *Information Artisanale* 9–10 (April–May 1942).

104. Kuisel, *Capitalism and the State*, p. 138; see also Adrian Jones, "Illusions of Sovereignty: business and the Organization of Committees in Vichy France," *Social History* 11 (June 1986): 1–31, passim.

105. Jean Bouvier, "Les grandes épreuves: Le capitalisme et l'état, 1914–1949," *Histoire économique* 4: 794.

106. Stanley Hoffman writes that, "Pétain's regime . . . despite its dream of corporations running the economy under a distant and discreet check from the state, was

unable to practice what it preached": in Stanley Hoffman, "Paradoxes of the French Political Community," *In Search of France*, p. 42.

107. Colliard, *Le corporatisme*, p. 186; Parrot, *La représentation des idées*, p. 73.

108. Paxton, *Vichy France*, p. 215.

109. Juillard, "La Charte du Travail," p. 194.

110. Loyer, *Le Statut*, p. 78. Bichelonne described it in similar terms in Archives Nationales F^{12} 10251^2.

Chapter 6

1. Laurence Wylie, "Social Changes at the Grass Roots," *In Search of France*, ed. Hoffmann, pp. 170–71.

2. Laurence Wylie, *Village in the Vaucluse* 3rd ed. (Cambridge, Mass: Harvard University Press, 1974), pp. 364, 373, 379.

3. Alexandre, *Le métier artisanal*, passim.

4. For the population growth of the postwar period see APCMF, 29 November 1948, p. 9; Paul Hunsinger, *Artisans et ouvriers d'Alsace*, p. 339; Mourier, "Essai," p. 80; idem, "L'artisanat," pp. 99–100; Rodet, *Commerçants et artisans*, p. 75.

5. Audibert, "Les Artisans," p. 19.

6. According to the Commission on the Artisanat for the Third Plan (1957), there were 899,866 people subject to the tax for the chambers of trades in 1955, some 20,000 higher than the APCMF figure. The Commission for the Fourth Plan (1961) found that this number actually increased slightly to 865,771 in 1956, before falling back to 821,855 in 1960. The commissions also found that there were enterprises on the registers not listed as paying taxes to the chambers of trades. INSEE, using the census, came up with yet another figure for the size of the artisanat: 737,000 artisans in 1954. See Commissariat général du plan de modernisation et d'équipement. Troisième Plan: "Rapport de la Commission de l'artisanat," 1956, p. 9; and Quatrième Plan: "Rapport de la Commission de l'artisanat," 1961, pp. 12–13; INSEE, *Mouvement économique*, p. 46.

7. Quatrième Plan, "Rapport," pp. 13–15.

8. Carré, et al., *French Economic Growth*, pp. 162-65. This does not contradict Table 6.1. Concentration, in the French case, meant that, while the number of establishments with less than ten employees decreased, France never developed the same degree of concentration of its largest businesses.

9. On the variation in prices see Carré, et al., *French Economic Growth*, pp. 345–48; for the indexes of gross domestic and industrial production, see pages 26–27.

10. Leborgne Lafont, "L'artisanat du bâtiment: un monde en transition," *Economie et Statistique* 56 (May 1974): 22. Also see Bachelard, *Industrialisation de la région Centre*, p. 125; and Zarca, "Barrières à l'entrée, turbulences et facteurs d'exclusion de l'artisan," *Consummation* 4 (October–December 1977): 59–60.

11. Zarca, "Survivance ou transformation," pp. 214, 239.

12. Troisième Plan, "Rapport," pp. 38–39, 121. Jean Malassigne provided these figures from the INSEE: 125,253 apprentices in 1954; 144,998 in 1958; and 205,000 in 1964: "L'artisanat," pp. 610–11.

13. Troisième Plan, "Rapport," p. 17; Hunsinger, "Métiers en voie de disparition," p. 460; ISEA, "Physionomie économique et sociale du Passementier-Forezein," *Enquête*, p. 85; and idem, "L'Artisan Radio-Electricien," *Enquête*, pp. 52–73.

14. Bernard, "L'artisanat en France," p. 80; Société Savante d'Alsace, *Artisans et ouvriers*, p. 281.

15. On the crisis among auto, bicycle, and motorcycle mechanics see Quatrième Plan, "Rapport," p. 16; Hunsinger, "Métiers en voie de disparition," pp. 339–40.

16. On the construction industry see Bernard, "L'artisanat en France," p. 78; Quatrième Plan, "Rapport," p. 16; Gérard Pelsonnier, *Renseignements statistiques sur l'artisanat rural en Bourgogne*, Institut d'Economie Régionale Bourgogne-Franche-Comté, (pamphlet, 1961), p. 2; Société Savante d'Alsace, *Artisans et ouvriers*, p. 276.

17. Wright, *Rural Revolution*, p. 41.

18. Carré, et al., *French Economic Growth*: on the concentration of agricultural holdings, p. 171; on the structure of the labor force, p. 91. Also Trotignon, *France au XXe siècle* 1: 19.

19. Caron, *An Economic History*, p. 222; Troisième Plan, "Rapport," p. 21; Quatrième Plan, "Rapport," p. 23.

20. Troisième Plan, "Rapport," p. 21; Quatrième Plan, "Rapport," pp. 22–23.

21. Wylie, "Social Changes," p. 170.

22. "Etude des moyens propres à retenir dans la vie rurale les artisans ruraux auxiliaire de l'agriculture," *Journal Officiel: Avis et Rapports du Conseil Economique*, 12 (10 July 1956): 454–64.

23. Pelsonnier, "Renseignements statistiques," pp. 3–5; Troisième Plan, "Rapport," p. 70.

24. David Schoenbaum, *Hitler's Social Revolution*: *Class and Status in Nazi Germany, 1933–1939* (Garden City: Doubleday and Co., 1967), p. 131.

25. INSEE, *Mouvement économique*, p. 155.

26. Cohen, *Modern Capitalist Planning*, p. 91; INSEE, *Mouvement économique*, p. 116; Kuisel, *Capitalism and the State*, 196–99, discusses the battle between Mendès-France and Pleven; Sauvy, *La vie économique*, p. 225.

27. Mourier, "L'artisanat," p. 30.

28. Joseph Jones finds the same kind of active dissatisfaction and refusal to co-operate with the administration among small shopkeepers in Jones, "Vichy France," pp. 553–54.

29. See the discussions about the distribution of materials and the presidents' comments in APCMF, 27 November 1945, pp. 10–19.

30. Kuisel, *Capitalism and the State*, p. 216.

31. APCMF, 2 June 1947, p. 20.

32. APCMF, 10 June 1948, pp. 27–29.

33. Mourier, "L'artisanat," p. 1.

34. On the population of the artisans' syndicates see Michel Drancourt, ed., *L'Artisanat Français* (Lille: Entreprise Moderne d'Edition, 1978), p. 31; Francillon, "Chambres de métiers," pp. 20–21; Mourier, "L'artisanat," p. 180.

35. Actually, Tailledet became chief of something called the Secrétariat Central d'Etudes artisanales as noted in Lecordier, *Classes Moyennes*, p. 265.

36. Lecordier, *Classes Moyennes*, pp. 152–54; Metton, *Brève histoire*, p. 11; Mourier, "L'artisanat," pp. 178–79.

37. On the CGPME see Gresle, "Indépendants et petits patrons," pp. 99–100; Jean-Daniel Reynaud, *Les syndicats en France* (Paris: Editions de Seuil, 1975), tome 1: 41; Peta Sheriff, "Industry and Commerce: Problems of Modernization," *Social Change in France*, ed. Michalina Vaughan, Martin Kolinsky, Peta Sheriff, (New York: St. Martin's Press, 1980), pp. 92–93.

38. For Jeanselme's report see APCMF, 7 May 1946, pp. 32–40; for the comment on "tendances" see President Chareille's (Cher) remarks, APCMF, 30 September 1946, p. 69.

39. Quoted in Robert Delille, "Classes moyennes en France," *Economie et Politique: Revue Marxiste d'Economie* 26 (August–September 1956): 56.

40. *Artisan Français* 178 (15 April 1935).

41. Lecordier, *Classes Moyennes*, p. 139.

42. For the record of these proceedings see "Comment sauver le petit commerce et l'artisanat," meeting at the Salle Wagram, 12 March 1945, sous la présidence d'André Marty (PCF), Bibliothèque Nationale, Paris.

43. CCIP II 5.413, "Apprentissage."

44. I have taken my information for the following section from the Assemblée générale, Chambre de Métiers de la Seine (Hereafter cited as A.G. Seine), *procès-verbal*. I would like to thank M. Jean Verrier, the Chambre de Métiers' general secretary, for allowing me access to these.

45. CCIP II 5.413, "Chambres de Métiers. Apprentissage Artisanal, 1950–1958"; and "Réorganisation de la Chambre de Métiers de la Seine, 1950."

46. See the minutes of this meeting, APCMF, 27–28 November 1945, passim.

47. APCMF, 26 November 1946, p. 16.

48. See the very similar resolution that the APCMF sent Pétain in APCMF, 24 March 1941, p. 161.

49. See the report by Pimpaud (Meuse) in APCMF, 28 November 1945, Annex 12, p. 149.

50. On the social security issue, see APCMF, 8 May 1946, p. 60; 27 November 1946, p. 76; and 2 June 1947, pp. 25–28. Also see Drancourt, *Artisanat français*, p. 23.

51. APCMF, 29 May 1956, pp. 75–77; also Serge Bernard, "L'Artisanat," p. 123.

52. The tax question, in one form or another, crops up at virtually every meeting of the APCMF. For other commentaries on the shape of artisanal fiscality see Caro, "Le régime des artisans," especially Chapter 4, pp. 88–105; Chambre de Métiers du Loiret, *Les charges fiscales et sociales de l'artisan et les avantages auxquels il peut prétendre*," 1954 (pamphlet available at the library of the Assemblée Permanente des Chambres de Métiers, Paris); Editions ouvrages commerciaux, économiques et fiscaux, *L'indicateur fiscal de l'artisanat*, preface by Emile Delanoë, president of the Chamber of Trades of the Seine (Paris: Emile Dessus, 1947); Institut de Droit Comparé de l'Université de Paris. Publications du Centre International d'Etudes de l'Artisanat I, *Le crédit artisanal en France et à l'étranger* (Paris: Sirey, 1958), especially the annexe, pp. 78–106; Stefanelly, "L'artisanat," p. 21.

53. Jean-Pierre Rioux, "La révolte de Pierre Poujade," *L'Histoire. Etudes sur la France de 1939 à nos jours* (Paris: Editions du Seuil, 1985), p. 258.

54. Maurice Lauré, *Traité de politique fiscale* (Paris: Presses Universitaires de France, 1956); quoted in Dominique Borne, *Petits bourgeois en révolte?* (Paris: Flammarion, 1977), p. 61.

55. Maurice Nicolas, *Avec Pierre Poujade sur les routes de France* (Sables d'O-lonnes [Vendée]: Les Editions de l'Equinox, 1955), p. 40.

56. Quoted in Borne, *Petits bourgeois*, p. 17; and Sean Fitzgerald, "The Anti-Modern Rhetoric of Le Mouvement Poujade," *The Review of Politics* 32 (April 1970): 174.

57. *L'Express* 22 January 1955, p. 5.

58. Stanley Hoffmann, ed., *Le Mouvement Poujade* (Paris: Armand Colin, 1956), p. 38.

59. For brief biographies of Poujade see Hoffmann, *Le Mouvement Poujade*, pp. 25–26; and Rioux, "La révolte de Pierre Poujade," p. 250. For Poujade's own account see *J'ai choisi le combat* (Saint-Céré: Société générale des éditions et publications, 1955); and *A l'heure de la cholère* (Paris: Albin Michel, 1977).

60. Werth, *France*, p. 726.

61. Roland Barthes, "Quelques paroles de M. Poujade," *Mythologies* (Paris: Editions du Seuil, 1957), p. 97.

62. André Desqueyrat, "De Colrat à Poujade," *Christianisme Social* 64 (May 1956), 549–61.

63. Gresle, "Indépendants et petits patrons," p. 801; Rioux, "La révolte de Pierre Poujade," p. 255.

64. *Fraternité Française* (17 August 1956): 4.

65. Quoted in Fitzgerald, "Anti-Modern Rhetoric," p. 181.

66. Borne, *Petits bourgeois*, p. 181. On the Poujadist program also see Jean Cluzel, *Les boutiques en cholère* (Paris: Plon, 1975), pp. 26–28.

67. *Fraternité Française* (12 May 1956): 4.

68. Rioux, "La révolte de Pierre Poujade," pp. 248–49.

69. Hoffmann, *Le Mouvement Poujade*, p. 38.

70. Hoffmann, *Le Mouvement Poujade*, pp. 315–18.

71. Christian Guy, *Le Cas Poujade* (Givors [Rhône]: Editions André Martel, 1955), p. 43.

72. See the minutes of the meetings of the A.G. Seine for 1954 and 1955, passim.

73. The new professional categories were *alimentation, bâtiment, bois et ammeublement, métaux-mécaniques-électricité, cuir-textiles-vêtements, hygiène* and others. Paris had a seventh category, *artisans d'art*: Magliulo, *Les Chambres de Métiers*, pp. 36–40. On the 1955 decree also see APCMF, 24 May 1955, pp. 34–38; Stefanelly, "L'Artisanat," p. 40.

74. Magliulo, *Les Chambres de Métiers*, pp. 57–58; Francillon, "Chambres de Métiers," p. 58. For Jeudon's figures see APCMF, circulaires SG/3272/JA, 22 August 1957.

75. *Le Monde*, 15 December 1956.

76. APCMF, session extraordinaire, 18 February 1957. President Denoue, from the Deux-Sèvres, claimed that the elections of 1956 produced thirty-six "amis UDCA": APCMF, circulaires 57/104/SG/256, 5 August 1957, open letter from Denoue to Jeudon.

77. Borne, *Petits bourgeois*, p. 226.

78. Cluzel, *Boutiques en cholère*, p. 28. See also the analysis of the Poujade Movement by Seymour Martin Lipset, who would set its strength "in the poorer, relatively underdeveloped and economically stagnant departments," in Lipset, *Political Man*, p. 160.

79. Rioux, "La révolte," p. 259.

80. See Laurence Wylie's assessment of the strong Poujadist vote in the town of Roussillon in Wylie, *Village in the Vaucluse*, pp. 329–30.

81. APCMF, 18 February 1957, p. 24.

82. APCMF, circulaires 57/104/SG/256, 5 August 1957, open letter from Denoue to Jeudon; and Jeudon's response in SG/3272/JA, 22 August 1957.

83. APCMF, 19 November 1957, pp. 28–31; APCMF, circulaires 57/153/SG/277, "Réunion des sages," 2 September 1957; and 57/157/SG/280, "Réunion des sages," 30 October 1957.

84. On the collèges syndicaux and the decree of 1959 see Assemblée des Présidents des Chambres de Métiers, "Etudes sur l'artisanat," 1963, annexe III: "Decret de 19 novembre 1959 rélatif à la composition des chambres de métiers et aux élections à ces chambres."

85. On the UDCA in the 1960 elections see APCMF, circulaires 60/83-SG/162

and 60/158-SG/207, brief accounts of the sessions extraordinaires of 21–22 June and 15–16 November 1960; Francillon, "Chambres de Métiers," pp. 60–61; Magliulo, *Les Chambres de Métiers*, pp. 58–63.

86. APCMF, 24 November 1954, p. 60. See also Jeudon's "moral report," to the session extraordinaire of the APCMF, circulaires 59//68-SG/45, 8–9 April 1959.

87. On Nicoud see Bernard, "L'artisanat," p. 181; and Gresle, "Indépendants et petits patrons," pp. 798–99. The CID-UNATI resulted from the fusion of Nicoud's Comité d'information et de défense with the Union nationale des travailleurs indépendants. For an interesting look at the bases of petty proprietors' anger see two articles by François Gresle: "Indépendance professionnelle et protection sociale: Practiques de classe et fluctuations idéologiques du petit patronat," *Revue Française de Sociologie*, 18 (1977): 577–99; and "Les travailleurs indépendants et la protection sociale," *Droit Social*, 4 (April 1983): 259–68. I would like to thank Professor Gresle for giving me copies of these articles.

88. Mourier, "L'artisanat," p. 178.

89. Francillon, "Chambres de Métiers," p. 21. See also Drancourt, *L'Artisanat Français*, p. 31.

90. Bernard, "L'Artisanat," p. 53; Durand and Frémont, *L'Artisanat en France*, p. 27.

91. Cohen, *Modern Capitalist Planning*, pp. 49–51.

92. On Monnet and the Monnet Plan (1945–1951) see Caron, *An Economic History*, p. 274; Jean Fourastié and Jean-Paul Courthéoux, *La planification économique en France* (Paris: Presses Universitaires de France, 1963), pp. 11–12; Kuisel, *Capitalism and the State*, esp. Chapter 8, pp. 219–47; Jean Lecerf, *La percée de l'économie française* (Paris: Artaud, 1963), pp. 26–28; Ullmo, "France," p. 33.

93. Kuisel, *Capitalism and the State*, p. 237.

94. Cohen, *Modern Capitalist Planning*, pp. 228–29; also Hackett and Hackett, *Economic Planning*, p. 27.

95. Cohen, *Modern Capitalist Planning*, pp. 193–94; also see Ullmo, "France," pp. 36–38. For the representation of artisans see Hackett and Hackett, *Economic Planning*, p. 170; and Quatrième Plan, "Rapport," list of members.

96. On the Economic Council see APCMF, 17 November 1947, p. 12; and 12 June 1948, pp. 44–53; Hackett and Hackett, *Economic Planning*, pp. 50–56; Jay Hayward, "Change and Choice: The Agenda of Planning," *Planning, Politics, and Public Policy*, p. 19; Kuisel, *Capitalism and the State*, p. 214; Ullmo, "France," p. 38.

97. APCMF, circulaires 59/45/SG/29, 5 March 1959.

98. On the 1956 decree-law see APCMF, circulaires, 59/45/SG/29, 5 March 1959, re: History of Attempts to Reorganize the Artisanat, 1946–56; APCMF, "Etudes," pp. 1–4; CCIP II 4.13, "Artisans, 1955–1960"; Conseil Economique et Social, "Les possibilités de création d'emplois dans le secteur artisanal," Etude présentée par la section du travail et des relations professionelles, 7 September 1977, p. 5.

99. APCMF, 19–20 November 1957, pp. 32, 58.

100. On the 1962 decree-law see APCMF, "Etudes," pp. 1–7; Bernard, "L'Artisanat," p. 29; Conseil Economique et Social, "Possibilités," p. 6; Durand and Frémont, *L'Artisanat*, p. 21; Zarca, "Survivance ou transformation," p. 63.

Conclusion

1. Marcelin, *Souvenirs*, p. 24. He adds that "the client was sometimes a friend, a protector, but most often a kind of master."

BIBLIOGRAPHY

Archives and Government Publications

National Archives, Paris

F⁷ Ministère de l'Intérieur
F¹² Ministère du Commerce et de l'Industrie
F²² Ministère du Travail
CE Conseil National Economique

Other Archives

Chambre de Commerce et d'Industrie de Paris
Conseil Economique et Social, Paris
Préfecture de Police, Seine
Préfecture de Police, Seine: Bureau des Affaires Réglementaires, Dossier des syndicats

Official Publications

Journal Officiel
Bulletin Municipal Officiel de la Ville de Paris

Journals

Artisan (Béziers)
Artisan (Le Puy)
Artisan (Lyon)
Artisan Catalan (Perpignan)
Artisan Coiffeur (Moulins)
Artisan Cordonnier (Paris)
Artisan d'Aunis et de Saintonge (La Rochelle)
Artisan de France (Cahors)

Artisan de France (Saint-Brieuc, Paris)
Artisan de l'Ouest (Saint-Brieuc)
Artisan des Alpes (Grenoble)
Artisan du Bois (Le Havre)
Artisan du Loiret (Orléans)
Artisan Français (Paris)
Artisan Rouergat (Rodez)
Cahiers de l'Artisanat (Paris)
Coiffeur-Confédéré (Paris)
Coiffeur du Sud-Ouest (Montauban)
Coiffeur Nantais (Nantes)
Coiffeur-Parfumeur (Bordeaux)
Coiffeur Populaire (Paris)
Compagnonnage (Paris)
Gazette des Métiers (Strasbourg)
Hebdo-Coiffure (Paris)
Information Artisanale (Strasbourg)
Information Artisanale nouvelle série (Paris)
Ouvrier Coiffeur (Marseille)
Reveil des Coiffeurs (Paris)
Semaine de la Coiffure (Paris)
Syndicalisme (Paris)

Books, Articles and Theses

Agulhon, Maurice. *La vie sociale en Provence intérieure au lendemain de la Révolution.* Paris: Société des études robespierristes, 1970.

Alexandre, Jean. *Le métier artisanal: souvenir, utopie, réalité?* Paris: Casterman, 1947.

Alroy, Gil. "Radicalism and Modernization: The French Problem." Dissertation, Princeton University, 1962.

Anderson, R. D. *France: 1870–1914: Politics and Society.* London: Routledge and Kegan Paul, 1977.

Aron, Raymond, ed. *Inventaires III: Classes Moyennes.* Publications du Centre de Documentation Sociale de l'Ecole Normale Supérieure. Paris: Librairie Félix Alcan, 1939.

"Artisans et Artisanat." *Les Cahiers Français: documents d'actualité* 30 (1958): 2–7.

Asselin, J.-C. "La semaine de quarante heures, le chômage et l'emploi." *Mouvement Social* 54 (January–March 1966): 183–204.

Assemblée des Présidents des Chambres de Métiers. "Etudes sur l'artisanat." Paris, 1963.

—"Etudes sur le droit rélatif à l'exercice des métiers." Paris, 1963.

—Procès-verbaux des séances, 1933–1959.

Audibert, P. "Les Artisans." *Informations Sociales* 12 (1977): 1–30.

Avril, Maurice. *La formation des prix dans l'artisanat.* Paris: Editions de l'Institut d'Etudes Corporatives et Sociales, 1943.

Ayçoberry, Pierre. *The Nazi Question: An Essay on the Interpretations of National Socialism, 1922–1975.* Translated by Robert Hurley. New York: Pantheon, 1981.

Azzano, Laurent. *Mes joyeuses années au faubourg: souvenirs du faubourg Saint-Antoine*. Paris: Editions France-Empire, 1985.

Bachelard, Paul. *Industrialisation de la région Centre: Transformations économiques et socio-politiques*. Tours: Gilbert-Clarty, 1978.

Barraud, Marcel. *Les chambres de métiers en France*. Paris: Librairie Générale de Droit et de Jurisprudence, 1925.

Barthes, Roland. *Mythologies*. Paris: Editions du Seuil, 1957.

Baudelot, Christien; Establet, Robert; and Malemort, Jacques. *La petite bourgeoisie en France*. Paris: F. Maspéro, 1974.

Beaumont, G. de. *Comment choisir une profession, un métier*. Paris: Etienne Chiron, 1937.

Bechhofer, Frank, and Elliot, Brian. "The Petite Bourgeoisie in Industrial Society." *Archives Européennes de Sociologie* 17 (1976): 74–99.

Bellanger, Claude; Godechot, Jacques; Guiral, Pierre; and Terrou, Fernand, directors. *Histoire générale de la presse française*. 3 vols. Paris: Presses Universitaires de France, 1972.

Bénard, Claude-François. *La notion d'artisan dans la loi et les faits*. Paris: Librairie Ernest Sagot, 1927.

Bennet, Jean. *La protection sociale des travailleurs indépendants remonté à plusieurs siècles*. Etampes: Société régionale d'imprimerie et de publicité, 1959.

Berlanstein, Leonard. *The Working People of Paris, 1871–1914*. Baltimore: Johns Hopkins University Press, 1984.

Bernard, Serge. "L'artisanat en France aujourd'hui: sa situation et attitudes politiques." Thèse, Université de Caen, 1977–1978.

Berry, François. *Le fascisme en France*. Paris: Librairie de l'Humanité, 1926.

Berstein, Serge. "Le Parti Républicain Radical et Radical-Socialiste en France de 1919 à 1939." 3 vols. Thèse pour le doctorat en état, Paris-Nanterre, 1976.

—*Le six février 1934*. Paris: Editions Gallimard/Julliard, 1975.

Bertaux-Wiame, Isabelle. *Transformations et permanence de l'artisanat boulanger en France*. 2 vols. Paris: Maison des Sciences de l'Homme, 1978.

Bichelonne, Jean. *Le Statut de l'Artisanat: extrait du Journal Officiel du 25 août 1943*. Clermont-Ferrand: Imprimeries Paul Vallier, 1943.

Blackbourne, David. "The *Mittelstand* in German Society and Politics, 1871–1914." *Social History* 4 (January 1977): 409-33.

Blasquez, Adelaïde. *Gaston Lucas, sérurrier: chronique de l'anti-héro*. Paris: Plon, 1976.

Bonnard, Roger. *Syndicalisme, corporatisme et Etat corporatif*. Paris: R. Pichon et R. Durand-Auzéas, 1937.

Borne, Dominique. *Petits bourgeois en révolte? Le mouvement poujade*. Paris: Flammarion, 1977.

Bottomore, Tom. *Political Sociology*. New York: Harper and Row, 1979.

Bouilloux-Lafont, Maurice. *Les chambres de métiers: comment nous les concevons*. Paris: Payot et Cie., 1919.

Bouvier-Ajam, Maurice. *La doctrine corporative*. Paris: Librairie du Recueil Sirey, 1937.

Boxer, Marilyn. "Women in Industrial Homework: The Flowermakers of Paris." *French Historical Studies* 12 (Spring 1982): 401-23.

Boyer, Abel. *Le Tour de France d'un Compagnon du Devoir*. Paris: Librairie du Compagnonnage, 1957.

Bozet, G. *L'artisanat devant le rationnement des matières primaires*. Lyon: Imprimerie Jacquier et Cie., 1941.

Braudel, Fernand, and Labrousse, Ernst, eds. *Histoire économique et sociale de la France*. 4 vols. Paris: Presses Universitaires de France, 1970–1982.

Bris, Marcel. *Le campagnonnnage: à la recherche de sa vocation, 1900–1946*. Paris: Librairie du Campagnonnage, 1984.

Cahen, Lucienne. "La concentration des établissements en France de 1896 à 1936," *Etudes et Conjoncture* 9 (1954): 840–81.

Caillard, C. *Chambres de métiers et conseils de métiers*. Paris: Librairie de l'Enseignement Technique, 1920.

Caro, Jean. "Le régime des artisans en matière d'impôts directs." Thèse de droit, Université de Rennes, 1953.

Caron, François. *An Economic History of Modern France*. Translated by Barbara Bray. New York: Columbia University Press, 1979.

Carré, J.-J.; Dubois, P.; and Malinvaud, E. *French Economic Growth*. Translated by John P. Hatfield. Stanford: Stanford University Press, 1975.

Carter, Edward C. III; Forster, Robert; and Moody, Joseph, eds. *Enterprise and Entrepreneurs in Nineteenth- and Twentieth-Century France*. Baltimore and London: Johns Hopkins University Press, 1976.

Catherine, Robert. *Economie de la répartition des produits industriels*. Paris: Presses Universitaires de France, 1943.

Chambre de Métiers de la Mayenne. *Force et faiblesse de l'artisanat français*. 1959 (pamphlet).

Chambre de Métiers de la Seine, Paris. Procès-verbaux des séances de l'Assemblée générale (unpublished manuscripts).

Chambre de Métiers du Loiret. *Les charges fiscales et sociales de l'artisan et les avantages auxquels il peut prétendre*. 1954 (pamphlet).

Charles, Jean-Jacques. *L'artisanat: Sa situation. Ses besoins*. Clermont-Ferrand: F. Sorlet, 1941.

—*Bibliographie artisanale*. Paris: Jean-Renard, 1942.

Chaudieu, Georges. *L'artisanat cet inconnu*. Paris: Paillard, 1942.

—*Artisans et Commerçants*. Paris: Editions C.I.E.M., 1982.

—*Au temps des charrues. Basse - Brie -Montois - Bassée Morvois - Sénonais nord - Gâtinais français*. Etrepilly: Presses du Village, 1983.

—*De la gigue d'ours au hamburger, ou la curieuse histoire de la viande*. Chennevières: La Corpo, 1980.

Chaudieu, Georges, and London, Hélène. *Les métiers d'appoint, leur utilité dans l'économie et la société*. Paris: La Nouvelle Edition, 1944.

Childers, Thomas. *The Nazi Voter: The Social Foundations of Fascism in Germany, 1919–1933*. Chapel Hill and London: University of North Carolina Press, 1983.

Chilly, Lucien de. "La classe moyenne en France après la guerre: 1918–1924. Sa crise: causes, conséquences et remèdes." Thèse en sciences politiques et économiques, Faculté de Droit de Paris, 1924.

Clough, Shepard B. *France: A History of National Economics, 1789–1939*. New York: Charles Scribner's Sons, 1939.

Cluzel, Jean. *Les boutiquiers en cholère*. Paris: Plon, 1975.

Cohen, Stephen. *Modern Capitalist Planning: The French Model*. Cambridge, Massachusetts: Harvard University Press, 1969.

Colliard, Henri. *Le corporatisme et la lutte des classes*. Rive-de-Gier: Imprimerie de Grataloup, 1940.

Comité d'entente et d'action artisanales. Comptes-rendus des Congrès Nationaux, 1934–1937.

Comment sauver le petit commerce et l'artisanat. Meeting à la Salle Wagram, 12 March 1945. André Marty, president (pamphlet).

Commissariat Général du Plan de Modernisation et d'Equipement. "Troisième Plan: Rapport de la Commission de l'Artisanat," 1956.

—"Quatrième Plan: Rapport de la Commission de l'Artisanat," 1961.

Conseil Economique et Social. "Les possibilités de création d'emplois dans le secteur artisanal." Etude présentée par la section du travail et des relations professionnelles, Paris. 7 September 1977.

Constant, Jacqueline. *Industrie à domicile salariée*. Paris: Librairie Technique et Economique, 1937.

Coornaert, Emile. *Le compagnonnage en France du moyen age à nos jours*. Paris: Editions Ouvrières, 1966.

Coulon, Marius. *L'artisanat devant l'impôt*. Lille: Douriez-Bataille, 1943.

Croix de Feu, Parti Social Français. *Tractes Politiques, 1934–1939* (pamphlet).

Crossick, Geoffrey, ed. *The Lower Middle Class in Britain, 1870–1914*. London: Croom Helm, 1977.

—"The Petite Bourgeoisie in Nineteenth-Century Europe: Problems and Research." *Arbeiter und Arbeiterbewegung im Vergleich: Berichte zur internationalen historischen Forschung*. Munich: R. Oldenbourg Verlag, 1986.

Crossick, Geoffrey and Haupt, Heinz-Gerhard. *Shopkeepers and Master Artisans in Nineteenth-Century Europe*. London: Methuen, 1984.

Daniel, Alphonse. *Les chambres de métiers en France*. Rennes: Presse de la Bretagne, 1922.

Darnton, Robert. *The Great Cat Massacre and Other Episodes in French Cultural History*. New York: Random House, 1985.

Daty, Gabriel. "L'Artisanat en Alsace." Thèse de droit, Paris, 1933.

Debré, Michel. *L'Artisanat: Classe sociale. La notion d'artisan. La législation artisane*. Paris: Librairie Dalloz, 1934.

De Gré, Gerard. "Ideology and Class Consciousness in the Middle Classes." *Social Forces* 29 (1951): 173–79.

Delille, Robert. "Classes moyennes en France." *Economie et Politique: Revue Marxiste d'Economie* 26 (August–September 1956): 56–72.

Demaison, André. *La ronde des métiers: recensement des forces économiques de la nation*. Centre d'expansion française. Clermont-Ferrand: Cahiers de la France, 1943.

Demondion, Pierre. *L'artisanat dans l'état moderne*. Paris: F. Lovitan, 1941.

—*L'artisanat selon la Charte*. Paris: Editions de l'Institut d'Etudes Corporatives et Sociales, 1942.

—*Le Nouveau Statut de l'Artisanat*. Paris: F. Lovitan, 1943.

Desqueyrat, (Père) André. *Classes moyennes françaises: crise, programme, organisation*. Paris: Editions Spes, 1939.

—"De Colrat à Poujade." *Christianisme Social* 64 (May 1956): 549–61.

DeTarr, Francis. *The French Radical Party: From Herriot to Mendès-France*. London: Oxford University Press, 1961.

Drancourt, Michel, ed. *L'Artisanat Français*. Lille: Entreprise Moderne d'Editon, 1978.

Dubost, Georges. *Le Conseil National Economique: Ses origines, son institution et son organisation. Son oeuvre et son avenir*. Paris: Editions Domat-Montchrestien, 1936.

Duby, George, and Wallon, Armand, ed. *Histoire de la France rurale*. 4 vols. Paris: Editions de Seuil, 1972–1976.

Dudit, Isabelle. *Marbréry: Maître-Artisan*. Paris: Editions de la Confédération Générale de l'Artisanat Français, 1930.

Dumontier, René. *Un apôtre de l'artisanat et de la famille: Albert Dupuis, artisan-maître, 1873–1937. Sa vie et son oeuvre*. Yvetot: Imprimerie Commerciale, 1946.

Durand, Marc, and Frémont, Jean-Paul. *L'Artisanat en France*. Paris: Presses Universitaires de France, 1979.

Duroy, Jean-Pierre. "Le compagnonnage: initiateur de l'économie sociale." Thèse en économie sociale, Université de Maine, Le Mans, 1982.

Dutouard, Jean. *Au bon beurre, ou dix ans de la vie d'un crémier*. Paris: Gallimard, 1952.

Earle, Edward Mead, ed. *Modern France: Problems of the Third and Fourth Republics*. Princeton: Princeton University Press, 1951.

Ecole des cadres civiques du Mayet-de-Montagne (Allier). "Sessions artisanales" (unpublished manuscripts, n.d.).

Editions ouvrages commerciaux, économiques et fiscaux. *L'indicateur fiscal de l'artisanat*. Paris: Emile Dessus, 1947.

Ehrmann, Henry W. *Organized Business in France*. Princeton: Princeton University Press, 1957.

Elbow, Matthew. *French Corporative Theory: A Chapter in the History of Ideas*. New York: Columbia University Press, 1953.

Elwitt, Sanford. *The Making of the Third Republic: Class and Politics in France, 1868–1884*. Baton Rouge: Louisiana State University Press, 1975.

Etienne, François. "L'Artisanat et l'Education, 1921–1970." Thèse en sociologie de l'éducation, Université de Paris, 1977.

Faure, Christian. "Vichy et la renovation de l'artisanat: La réorganisation du compagnonnage." *Bulletin du Centre d'Histoire Economique et Sociale de la Région Lyonnaise* 3–4 (1984): 103–117.

Fédération Nationale Catholique. *La lutte contre le communisme. L'ordre corporatif*. Comte-rendu des journées d'études. Paris, 1936 (pamphlet).

Felice, Pierre de. *L'artisanat rural*. Paris: Jouve, 1930.

Fillon, Fernand. *Vers le corporatisme*. Paris: Berger-Leurault, 1938.

Fitzgerald, Sean. "The Anti-Modern Rhetoric of Le Mouvement Poujade." *The Review of Politics* 32 (April 1970): 167–90.

Fondation Nationale des Sciences Politiques, travaux et recherches de science politique. *Le gouvernement de Vichy, 1940–1942: institutions et politiques*. Paris: Armand Colin, 1972.

Fourastié, Jean, and Courthéoux, Jean-Paul. *La planification économique en France*. Paris: Presses Universitaires de France, 1963.

Francillon, Jacques. *Chambres de métiers et syndicats d'artisans: les éléments d'une symbiose*. Chambre de Métier de la Haute-Savoie, 1962 (pamphlet).

Gaillard, Jeanne. "France: la petite entreprise au XIXe et au XXe siècles." 1978 (unpublished manuscript).

Gellately, Robert. *The Politics of Economic Despair: Shopkeepers and German Politics, 1890–1914*. London: Sage Publications, 1974.

Gelly, Lucien. *L'artisanat rural: ses problèmes actuels*. Institut d'Etudes Corporatives et Sociales. Joigny: Paillard, 1944.

Giddens, Anthony, and Mackenzie, Gavin, eds. *Social Class and the Division of Labor*.

Essays in Honor of Ilya Neustadt. Cambridge: Cambridge University Press, 1982.

Gignoux, C. G. *L'économie française entre les deux guerres, 1919–1939.* Paris: Société d'Editions Economiques et Sociales, 1942.

Gilet, M. A. *L'organisation interprofessionnelle dans le Statut de l'Artisanat.* Centre de Documentation Artisanale. Conférences Artisanales du Mayet-de-Montagne. Roanne: Imprimerie Sauzet, 1943.

Goetz-Girey, Robert. "Stumulants et propagation de la croissance dans le 'pays de Montbéliard'." *Revue Economique* 11 (January 1960): 1–16.

Goguel, François. *La politique des partis sous la Troisième République.* Paris: Editions du Seuil, 1948.

Gresle, François. "Indépendance professionnelle: Actualité et portée du concept dans le cas français." *Revue Française de Sociologie* 22 (1981): 483–501.

——"Indépendance professionnelle et protection sociale: Practiques de classe et fluctuations idéologiques du petit patronat." *Revue Française de Sociologie* 18 1977): 577–99.

——"Indépendants et petits patrons: perennité et transformation d'une classe sociale." 3 vols. Thèse en sociologie, Paris, 1980.

——"Les travailleurs indépendants et la protection sociale." *Droit Social* 4 (April 1983): 259–68.

Gruson, Claude. *Origine et espoirs de la planification française.* Paris: Dunod, 1968.

Guichet, Yves. *Georges Valois. L'Action Française—le Faisceau—la République Syndicale.* Paris: Editions Albatros, 1975.

Guillaume, M. *La place de l'artisanat dans l'organisation économico-sociale nouvelle de la France.* Orléans: Imprimerie Nouvelle, 1943.

Guy, Christian. *Le Cas Poujade.* Givers [Rhône]: Editions André Martel, 1955.

Hackett, John, and Hackett, Anne-Marie. *Economic Planning in France.* London: George Allen and Unwin, 1963.

Hamel, Joseph, and Buquet, Léon. *Le crédit artisanal en France et à l'étranger.* Paris: Sirey, 1958.

Hamel, Joseph, and Bye, M., eds. *Annals de droit économique. Aspects de l'artisanat en France et à l'étranger.* n.s. 4 (1953).

Hamilton, Richard F. *Who Voted for Hitler?* Princeton: Princeton University Press, 1982.

Hanagan, Michael. *The Logic of Solidarity: Artisans and Industrial Workers in Three French Towns, 1871–1914.* Urbana, Illinois: University of Illinois Press, 1980.

Haupt, Heinz-Gerhard, and Vigier, Philippe, directors. *L'atelier et la boutique: études sur la petite bourgeoisie au XXe siècle.* Special number of *Le Mouvement Social* 108 (July–September 1979).

Hayward, Jack, and Watson, Michael, eds. *Planning, Politics and Public Policy: The British, French, and Italian Experience.* Cambridge: Cambridge University Press, 1975.

Hector, Edgar. *La législation actuelle de l'artisanat: Commentaire et jurisprudence.* Paris: Librairie du Recueil Sirey, 1939.

Hobsbawm, Eric J. *Labouring Men: Studies in the History of Labor.* London: Weidenfeld & Nicholson, 1965.

Hoffmann, Stanley, ed. *In Search of France: The Economy, Society and Political System of the Twentieth Century.* New York: Harper and Row, 1963.

——ed. *Le Mouvement Poujade.* Paris: Armand Colin, 1965.

Hoover Institution. *France During the Occupation, 1940–1944*. Translated by Philip Whitcomb. 2 vols. Stanford: Stanford University Press, 1957.

Institut d'Etudes Corporatives et Sociales. Ecole des Hautes Etudes Artisanales. "Cours." 2 vols. Paris, 1941–1943 (unpublished manuscripts).

Institut de Droit Comparé de l'Université de Paris. *Le crédit artisanal en France et à l'étranger*. Publications du Centre International d'Etudes de l'Artisanat. Paris: Sirey, 1958.

Institut de Science Economique Appliquée. *Enquête sur l'artisanat*. Paris: ISEA, 1946.

Institut National de la Statistique et d'Etudes Economiques. *Mouvement économique en France de 1944 à 1957*. Paris: Presses Universitaires de France, 1958.

Irvine, William. *French Conservatism in Crisis*. Baton Rouge: Louisiana State University Press, 1979.

Izard, Georges. *Les classes moyennes*. Paris: Editions Rieder, 1938.

Jackson, Julian. *The Politics of Depression in France, 1932–1936*. Cambridge: Cambridge University Press, 1985.

Jaeger, Christine. *Artisanat et Capitalisme. l'envers de la roue de l'histoire*. Paris: Payot, 1982.

Jeannin, André. *L'artisanat à la croisée des chemins*. Paris: Institut d'Etudes Corporatives et Sociales, 1943.

Jeunesses Patriotes. *Tractes politiques, 1928–1935* (pamphlet).

Jobard, Jean-Pierre. *Les disparités régionales de croissance: Analyse économique des départements situés dans le Centre-Est de la France, 1801–1962*. Paris: Armand Colin, 1971.

Jolly, Pierre. *La mystique du corporatisme*. Paris: Hachettte, 1935.

Jones, Adrian. "Illusions of Sovereignty: business and the Organization of Committees in Vichy France." *Social History* 11 (January 1986): 1–31.

Jones, Joseph. "Vichy France and and the Postwar Economic Modernization: The Case of Shopkeepers." *French Historical Studies* 12 (1982): 541–63.

Judt, Tony. *La reconstruction du parti socialiste, 1921–1926*. Paris: Presses de la Fondation des Sciences Politiques, 1976.

—*Socialism in Provence, 1871–1914: A Study in the Origins of the Modern French Left*. Cambridge: Cambridge University Press, 1979.

Kemp, Tom. *The French Economy, 1919–1939: A History of National Decline*. London: Longman, 1972.

Kindleberger, Charles. *Economic Growth in France and Britain, 1851–1950*. Cambridge, Massachusetts: Harvard University Press, 1964.

Klatzman, J. *Le travail à domicile dans l'industrie parisienne du vêtement*. Paris: A. Colin, 1957.

Kocka, Jürgen. "The First World War and the *Mittelstand*: German Artisans and White-Collar Workers." *Journal of Contemporary History* 8 (1973): 101–24.

Kopp, Armand. *Le rôle de groupements professionnels dans l'organisation de la profession*. Nancy: Bailly et Wettstein, 1937.

Kriegel, Annie. "Histoire ouvrière aux XIXe et XXe siècles." *Revue Historique* 235 (April–June 1966): 455–90.

Kuisel, Richard F. *Capitalism and the State in Modern France: Renovation and Economic Management in the Twentieth Century*. Cambridge: Cambridge University Press, 1981.

—"The Legend of the Vichy Synarchy," *French Historical Studies* 6 (1970): 365–398.

Lacquer, Walter and Mosse George L., eds. *International Fascism, 1920–1945*. New York: Harper and Row, 1966.

Lafaille, Bernard. "L'artisanat et la défense nationale." *Politique* 3 (March 1940): 174-99.

Lafont, Leborgne. "L'artisanat du bâtiment: un monde en transition." *Economie et Statistique* 55 (April 1974): 3–24; 56 (May 1974): 17–27.

Larmour, Peter J. *The French Radical Party in the Thirties.* Stanford: Stanford University Press, 1964.

Laufenburger, Henry. *L'intervention de l'état en matière économique.* Paris: Librairie Générale de Droit et de Jurisprudence, 1939.

Launay, Jacques de. *Le Dossier de Vichy.* Paris: Julliard, 1967.

Lauré, Maurice. *Traité de politique fiscale.* Paris: Presses Universitaires de France, 1956.

Lecerf, Jean. *La percée de l'économie française.* Paris: Artaud, 1963.

Lecordier, Gaston. *Les classes moyennes en marche.* Paris: Bloud et Gay, 1950.

Lefebvre, Jacques. *L'évolution des localisations industrielles. L'exemple des Alpes françaises.* Paris: Librairie Dalloz, 1960.

Lefranc, Georges. *Histoire du Front Populaire (1934–1938).* 2d ed. Paris: Payot, 1974.

—*Le mouvement syndical sous la Troisième République.* Paris: Payot, 1967.

—*Les organisations patronales en France.* Paris: Payot, 1976.

Lenormand, Maurice H. *Vers le régime corporatif.* Paris: Les Editions de la Nouvelle France, 1943.

Ley, Hubert. *L'Artisanat: Entité Corporative.* Paris: Dunod, 1938.

Liebmann, Léon. "Entre le mythe et la légende: l'anti-capitalisme de Vichy." *Revue de l'Institut de Sociologie* 37 (1964): 109–48.

Lipset, Seymour Martin. *Political Man: The Social Bases of Politics.* Garden City: Doubleday and Co., 1963.

Loyer, Pierre. *Les dessous maçonniques du Radicalisme.* Paris: Société Française d'Editions et de Propagande, 1936.

—*Les incidences sociales du Statut de l'Artisanat: Conférence.* Vichy: Editions du Centre d'Information et de Documention Artisanales, 1945.

—*Le Statut de l'Artisanat.* Paris: Dunod, 1944.

Lüthy, Herbert. *France Against Herself: The Past, Politics and Crises of Modern France.* Translated by Eric Mosbacher. New York: Meridion Books, 1957.

Magliulo, Bruno. *Les Chambres de Métiers.* Paris: Presses Universitaires de France, 1985.

Maier, Charles S. *Recasting Bourgeois Europe: Stabilization in France, Germany, and Italy in the Decade after World War I.* Princeton: Princeton University Press, 1975.

Malassigne, Jean. "L'artisanat: vestige du passé? utilité économique? nécessité sociale?" *Droit Social* 12 (December 1966): 1–30.

Marcelin, Paul. *Souvenirs d'un passé artisanal.* Nîmes: Anciens Etablissements Chastenier Frères et Bertrand, 1967.

Mayer, Arno. "The Lower Middle Class as Historical Problem." *Journal of Modern History* 47 (September 1974): 409–36.

Mazgaj, Paul. *The Action Français and Revolutionary Syndicalism.* Chapel Hill, N.C.: University of North Carolina Press, 1979.

Mérigot, Jean-Guy. *Essai sur les comités d'organisation professionnelle.* Paris: Librairie Générale de Droit et de Jurisprudence, 1943.

Merkl, Peter. *Political Violence Under the Swastika: 581 Early Nazis.* Princeton: Princeton University Press, 1975.

Metton, Noël. *Brève histoire de l'artisanat en France, 1925–1963*. Lyon: L'Artisan de la Métallurgie du Rhône, 1964.

Milward, Alan S. *The New Order and the French Economy*. Oxford: Oxford University Press, 1970.

Ministère de l'Armament. *Circulaire de Monsieur Dautry, ministre de l'armament sur la collaboration de l'artisanat et de la petite industrie aux fabrications d'armament*. 21 November 1939 (pamphlet).

Moss, Bernard. *The Origins of the French Labor Movement, 1830–1914: The Socialism of Skilled Workers*. Berkeley, California: University of California Press, 1976.

Mourier, Henri. "L'artisanat, sa structure et son intégration dans l'économie moderne." Thèse en droit, Paris, 1952.

Müller, Klaus-Jürgen. "French Fascism and Modernization." *Journal of Contemporary History* 11 (1976): 75–108.

Néré, Jacques. *La Troisième République, 1914-1940*. Paris: Armand Colin, 1967.

Neret, Jean-Alexis. *Pour aller à la terre. Guide practique complet*. Paris: Plon, 1941.

Nicolas, Maurice. *Avec Pierre Poujade sur les routes de France*. Sables d'Olonnes [Vendée]: Les Editions de l'Equinox, 1955.

Nicolet, Claude. *Le Radicalisme*. Paris: Presses Universitaires de France, 1967.

Nicolle, Pierre. *Cinquante mois d'Armistice: Vichy, 2 juillet 1940–26 août 1944. Journal d'un témoin*. 2 vols. Paris: Editions André Bonne, 1947.

Nord, Philip. *Paris Shopkeepers and the Politics of Resentment*. Princeton: Princeton University Press, 1986.

Nordmann, Jean-Thomas. *Histoire des Radicaux, 1820–1973*. Paris: La Table Ronde, 1974.

Ollé-Laprune. Jacques *La stabilité des ministres sous la Troisième République*. Paris: Librairie Générale de Droit et de Jurisprudence, 1962.

Olphe-Galliard, G. *Les industries rurales à domicile dans la Normandie orientale*. Paris: Bureau de la Science Sociale, 1913.

Panitch, Leo. "Trade Unions and the Capitalist State." *New Left Review* 125 (January–February 1981): 21–44.

Parrot, Jean-Philippe. *La représentation des intérêts dans le mouvement des idées politiques*. Paris: Presses Universitaires de France, 1974.

Parti Populaire Français. *Tractes Politiques, 1932–1935* (pamphlet).

Paxton, Robert. *Vichy France: Old Guard and New Order, 1940–1944*. New York: Alfred A. Knopf, 1972.

Pelsonnier, Gérard. *Renseignements statistiques sur l'artisanat rural en Bourgogne*. Institut d'Economie Régionale Bourgogne-Franche-Comté, 1961 (pamphlet).

Perrin, Maxime. "La région industrielle de Saint-Etienne. Etude de géographie économique." Thèse pour le doctorat es-lettres, Paris, 1937.

Perroux, François. *L'artisanat dans le capitalisme moderne*. Paris: Jean Lesfauries, 1938.

—*Capitalisme et communauté du travail. Corporatisme et capitalisme. Corporatismes réalisés. Communauté du travail*. Paris: Librairie du Recueil Sirey, 1938.

Pétain, Philippe. *Message adressé aux artisans, ouvriers, techniciens et patrons: 1er mai 1942*. Vichy: Imprimerie Jacques Haumont, 1942.

—*L'oeuvre du Maréchal Pétain. Six mois de la Révolution Nationale. Documents*. Lyon: Imprimerie Commerciale du 'Nouvelliste', 1941.

Peter, Fernand. *La situation de l'artisanat en Europe*. Presented to the 4th National Congress of the Comité d'Entente et d'Action Artisanales, 1937 (pamphlet).

Petringenar, Titus. *Le rôle des classes moyennes dans la société contemporaine*. Paris: Maurice Lavergne, 1940.

Picard, Esther, and Jacot-Descombes, Vivianne. *La coiffure à travers les siècles*. Paris: Editions de l'Artisanat Moderne, 1973.

Picard, Roger. "Les chambres de métiers." *Les Documents du Travail* 61 (May 1922): 147–60.

Picard, Roger, and Rocault, Gaston. "La vie économique dans la Vienne (1940–1944)." *Revue d'Histoire de la Deuxième Guerre Mondiale* 119 (July 1980): 17–44.

Pirou, Gaëtan. *Le corporatisme: corporatisme et libéralisme; corporatisme et étatisme; corporatisme et syndicalisme*. Paris: Librairie du Recueil Sirey, 1938.

—*Les doctrines économiques en France depuis 1870*. Paris: Librairie Armand Colin, 1925.

—*Néo-libéralisme, néo-corporatisme, néo-socialisme*. Paris: Gallimard, 1939.

Plumyène, J., and Lasierra, R. *Les fascismes français, 1923–1963*. Paris: Editions du Seuil, 1963.

Poulantzas, Nicos. *Classes in Contemporary Capitalism*. Translated by David Fernbach. London: Verso, 1978.

Poulot, Denis. *Le sublime, ou le travailleur comme il est en 1870 et ce qu'il peut être*. Reprint. Paris: François Maspéro, 1980.

Priouret, Roger. *Origines du patronat français*. Paris: Editions Bernard Grasset, 1963.

Rabinovitch, Hermine. "L'évolution récente de l'artisanat et ses problèmes." *Revue International du Travail* 17 (1928): 868–89.

Rancière, Jacques. "The Myth of the Artisan: Critical Reflections on a Category of Social History." *International Labor and Working Class History* 24 (1983): 1–16.

Rapagnol, André. "Situation et organisation du métier artisanal." Thèse de droit, Université de Toulouse, 1941.

Raynal, François-Paul. *Les artisans du village*. Paris: Editions de l'Institut d'Etudes Corporatives et Sociales, 1943.

Reddy, William. *Money and Liberty in Modern Europe: A Critique of Historical Understanding*. Cambridge: Cambridge University Press, 1987.

Reid, Donald. *The Miners of Decazeville: A Geneology of Industrialization*. Cambridge, Massachusetts: Harvard University Press, 1982.

Rey, E. S. *L'artisanat, problème d'aujourd'hui*. Paris: Editions Fleurus, 1961.

Reynaud, Jean-Daniel. *Les syndicats en France*. 2 vols. Paris: Editions du Seuil, 1975.

Rioux, Jean-Pierre. "La révolte de Pierre Poujade." *L'histoire: Etudes sur la France de 1939 à nos jours*. Paris: Editions du Seuil, 1985.

Robert, Jean. *L'artisanat et le secteur des métiers dans la France contemporaine*. Paris: Armand Colin, 1966.

Rodet, Alain. *Commerçants et Artisans*. Paris: Centurian, 1976.

Rogger, Hans, and Weber, Eugen, eds. *The European Right: A Historical Profile*. Berkeley, California: University of California Press, 1965.

Roux, Paul. *Monographie d'une commune rurale de l'Auvergne*. Paris: Bureau de la Science Sociale, 1912.

—*Le Montagnard Auvernat*. Paris: Bureau de la Science Sociale, 1914.

Russo, Henri. "L'organisation industrielle de Vichy." *Revue d'histoire de la deuxième guerre mondiale* 29 (October 1979): 27–44.

Rutkoff, Peter. *Revanche and Revision: The Ligue des Patriotes and the Origins of the Radical Right in France, 1882–1900*. Athens, Ohio and London: Ohio University Press, 1981.

Salleron, Louis. *Un régime corporatif pour l'agriculture*. Paris: Dunod, 1937.

Sauer, Wolfgang. "National Socialism: Totalitarianism or Fascism?" *American Historical Review* 73 (December 1967):404–24.

Sauvy, Alfred. *Histoire économique de la France entre les deux guerres*. 3 vols. Paris: Fayard, 1965–1972.

—*La vie économique des français de 1939 à 1945*. Paris: Flammarion, 1978.

Schoenbaum, David. *Hitler's Social Revolution: Class and Status in Nazi Germany, 1933–1939*. Garden City: Doubleday and Co., 1967.

Scott, Joan. *The Glassworkers of Carmaux: French Craftsmen and Political Action in a Nineteenth-Century City*. Cambridge, Massachusetts: Harvard University Press, 1974.

Service de l'Artisanat. *Ce que les artisans doivent savoir des travaux réservés*. Paris: Imprimerie Nationale, 1942.

Sewell, William, Jr. *Work and Revolution in France: The Language of Labor from the Old Regime to 1848*. Cambridge: Cambridge University Press, 1980.

Shapiro, David, ed. *The Right in France, 1890–1919: Three Studies*. St. Antony's Papers, no. 13. Carbondale, Illinois: Southern Illinois University Press, 1970.

Siegfried, André. *Qu'est-ce que l'artisanat? Son rôle dans le passé, dans le présent, dans l'avenir*. Paris: Horizons de France, 1941.

Smith, J. Wallace. "The Socio-Economic Bases of the Poujade Movement." Ph.D. dissertation, University of Pennsylvania, 1959.

Soboul, Albert. *The Sans-Culottes: The Popular Movement and Revolutionary Government, 1793–1794*. Translated by Rémy Inglis Hall. Princeton: Princeton University Press, 1980.

La Société Savante d'Alsace et des Régions de l'Est. *Artisans et Ouvriers d'Alsace*. no. 9. Strasbourg: Librairie Istra, 1965.

Soucy, Robert. *Fascist Intellectual, Drieu la Rochelle*. Berkeley, California: University of California Press, 1979.

—"French Fascism as Class Conciliation and Moral Regeneration." *Societas: Review of Social History* 1 (1971): 287–97.

—*French Fascism: The First Wave, 1924–1933*. New Haven and London: Yale University Press, 1986.

Statistique générale de la France. *Résultats statistiques du recensement général de la population, effectué le 8 mars 1936*. Volumes 1–3. Paris: Imprimerie Nationale, 1943–1944.

Stefanelly, Jean-Jacques. *L'artisanat, a-t-il sa chance dans le monde moderne?* 1955 (pamphlet).

—*Essai sur l'artisanat*. Tarbres: A. Hunault et fils, 1949.

Stephenson, Jill. *Women in Nazi Society*. London: Croom Helm, 1975.

Sternhell, Zeev. *La droite revolutionnaire, 1885–1914: les origines françaises du fascisme*. Paris: Editions du Seuil, 1978.

—*Neither Right nor Left: Fascist Ideology in France*. Translated by David Maisel. Berkeley, California: University of California Press, 1986.

Sweets, John F. *Choices in Vichy France: The French Under the Nazi Occupation*. New York and Oxford: Oxford University Press, 1986.

Tailledet, Robert. *La doctrine de classe de l'artisanat moderne*. Paris: Institut National des Métiers, 1937.

Tannenbaum, Edward R. *The Action Française: Die-Hard Reactionaries in Twentieth-Century France*. New York: John Wiley and Sons, Inc., 1962.

Théallier, H.; Buchmann, J.-F.; Bardet, G.; d'Aubigné, Dr. Merle; Barrère, J.-B.; and Bernard, J. *Hommes et Métiers*. Paris: Editions 'Je Sers', 1941.

Thompson, Paul, ed. *Our Common History: The Transformation of Europe*. London: Pluto Press, 1982.

Thomson, David. *Democracy in France Since 1870*. 4th ed. New York: Oxford University Press, 1964.

Tisserand, A. "Les classes moyennes: sont-elles trop nombreuses en France?" *Revue de l'Action Populaire* 62 (1952): 618–28.

Trotignon, Yves. *La France au XXe Siècle*. 2 vols. Paris, Brussels, Montreal: Bordas, 1968.

Vallée, Abbé Ar. "Réflexions sur l'artisanat—Quelle doit être l'attitude des catholiques en face du problème artisanal? *Dossiers de l'Action Populaire* 381 (10 March 1937): 555–78.

Vaughan, Michalina; Kolinsky, Martin; and Shariff, Peta. *Social Change in France*. New York: St. Martin's Press, 1980.

Verdun, Edmond. "Les Groupes Artisanaux Professionnels" (unpublished manuscript, n.d.).

Viance, Georges. *Démocratie, dictature et corporatisme*. Paris: Flammarion, 1938.

—*Restauration corporative de la nation française*. Paris: Flammarion, 1936.

Ville-Chabrol, Marcel de. "La concentration des entreprises en France avant et depuis la guerre." *Bulletin de la statistique générale de la France et du service d'observation des prix* 22 (April–June 1933): 391-462.

—"La population active en France avant et depuis la guerre." *Bulletin de la statistique générale de la France et du service d'observation des prix* 21 (October–December 1931): 81–148.

Vincent, L.-A. "Population active, production, et productivité dans 21 branches de l'économie française (1896–1962). *Etudes et Conjoncture* 2 (February 1965): 73–108.

Volkov, Shulamit. *The Rise of Popular Anti-Modernism in Germany: The Urban Master Artisans, 1873–1896*. Princeton: Princeton University Press, 1978.

Walter, Paul. *La signification culturelle de l'artisanat*. Paris: Editions Centre International de l'Artisanat, 1938.

Weber, Eugen. *Action Française: Royalism and Reaction in Twentieth-Century France*. Stanford: Stanford University Press, 1962.

Weber, Max. *From Max Weber: Essays in Sociology*. Edited by H.H. Gerth and C. Wright Mills. New York: Oxford University Press, 1958.

Weissbach, Lee Shai. "Artisanal Responses to Artistic Decline: The Cabinetmakers of Paris in the Era of Industrialization." *Journal of Social History* 16 (1982): 67–81.

Werth, Alexander. *France, 1940–1955*. London: Robert Hale, Ltd., 1956.

Wiener, Jonathan M. "Marxism and the Lower Middle Classes: A Response to Arno Mayer." *Journal of Modern History* 48 (1976): 666–71.

Winkler, Heinrich August. "From Social Protectionism to National Socialism: The German Small Business Movement in Comparative Perspective." *Journal of Modern History* 48 (1976): 1–14.

Wright, Gordon. *Rural Revolution in France: The Peasantry in the Twentieth Century*. Stanford: Stanford University Press, 1964.

Wylie, Laurence. *Village in the Vaucluse*. 3d ed. Cambridge, Massachusetts: Harvard University Press, 1974.

Zarca, Bernard. "Barrières à l'entrée, turbulences et facteurs d'exclusion de l'artisan." *Consommation* 4 (October–December 1977): 59–94.

—"Survivance ou transformation de l'artisanat dans la France d'aujourd'hui." 3 vols. Thèse en sociologie, Institut d'études politiques de Paris, 1983.

Index